Contents

MOON OF WINTERTIME
Missionaries and the Indians of Canada
in Encounter since 1534

Not many years ago the missionaries who introduced Christianity to the Indians of Canada were almost universally regarded, at least by other white people, as selfless benefactors who offered improvement and salvation to Indians sometimes puzzlingly reluctant to accept them. Today, largely because Indians have succeeded in making their opinions more widely known, the missionaries are almost universally dismissed as unwitting destroyers of a culture they seldom took the trouble to understand.

In *Moon of Wintertime* John Webster Grant tells the story of the encounter between Christianity and the Indian peoples over a span of 450 years, from 1534, when Jacques Cartier first erected a cross before Indians of the Gaspé, to the present. Grant examines both the aims and activities of missionaries of all denominations and the varying responses of Indians at different times and under different circumstances. His intention is not to justify or to condemn either missionaries or Indians, but rather to bring into focus both the nobility and the ambiguity that have marked the encounter.

Grant describes the introduction of Christianity to the Indians of the various regions of Canada, from New France, including Acadia, to Upper Canada and then to the north and west. He outlines the typical pattern of missionary activity that emerged towards the end of the nineteenth century, traces the origins of outspoken discontent in the twentieth, and analyses the parts played by missionaries and Indians as well as by traders and governments. He argues that the Indians, almost all of whom became at least nominally Christian, were touched by Christianity during their 'moon of wintertime, when ancestral spirits had ceased to perform their expected functions satisfactorily and angel choirs promised to fill a spiritual vacuum.'

This study makes a major contribution to Canadian history and to our understanding of the consequences of contact between differing cultures. It will long remain the definitive work on the meeting of Christianity and Indians in Canada.

JOHN WEBSTER GRANT is professor of Church History at Emmanuel College of Victoria University and is associated with the Department and Centre of Religious Studies at the University of Toronto. He is the author of a number of studies of Canadian religious history, among them *The Church in the Canadian Era* (1972).

'Twas in the moon of winter time,

when all the birds had fled,

that mighty Gitchi Manitou

sent angel choirs instead ...

JOHN WEBSTER GRANT

Moon of Wintertime

Missionaries and the Indians of Canada in Encounter since 1534

UNIVERSITY OF TORONTO PRESS

Toronto Buffalo London

© University of Toronto Press 1984
Toronto   Buffalo   London

Printed in Canada

ISBN 0-8020-5643-1 (cloth)
ISBN 0-8020-6541-4 (paper)

Canadian Cataloguing in Publication Data

Grant, John Webster, 1919-
Moon of wintertime: missionaries and the Indians
of Canada in encounter since 1534

Includes bibliographical references and index.
ISBN 0-8020-5643-1 (bound). – ISBN 0-8020-6541-4 (pbk.)

1. Indians of North America – Canada – Missions –
History. 2. Indians of North America – Canada –
Religion and mythology. 3. Christianity – Missions –
Canada – History. 4. Missions – Canada – History.
I. Title

E78.C2G72 1984   266'.008997   C84-098084-1

Publication of this book was assisted by a generous gift
to the University of Toronto Press
from the Herbert Laurence Rous Estate,
and by a grant from the Canadian Federation for the Humanities,
using funds provided by the Social Sciences and
Humanities Research Council of Canada.

English words from
'"Twas in the moon of winter time' by J.E. Middleton
used by permission of
the Frederick Harris Music Co Limited

Preface

This is not quite the book I originally had in mind. My initial thought was to analyse the terms of Indian-Christian encounter in Canada while depending on others to supply the narrative thread of its story. I soon discovered that I should have to do much of the spadework myself. Excellent studies of individual missions and missionaries existed, but no one had attempted, or seemed about to attempt, a global study of the encounter in its various phases. Having now made the attempt I recognize my presumption, while hoping that an initial effort will stimulate further study and inevitable revision of my conclusions.

A project too large already could not be extended further. I have reluctantly excluded consideration of the Inuit, who were subject to the same missionary influences but responded as the distinct people they are. The Métis posed a different problem. In the twentieth century increasingly assimilated into the broad category of 'non-status Indians,' they constituted in the nineteenth a separate community with a distinctive relation to their church. I refer to them where their religious history intersected that of the Indians but have attempted no systematic account of the complex development of their church life.

The title *Moon of Wintertime* is intended to suggest an aspect of Indian-Christian encounter. J.E. Middleton's rendering of the carol attributed to Brébeuf is by no means literal, and 'Gitchi Manitou' figured in Algonquian rather than Huron theology. Nevertheless, the words call attention to the significant circumstance that when most Indians were introduced to Christianity, the bird and animal spirits to which they had looked for illumination were no longer readily found in their accustomed places or seemed already to have fled from them.

As a comparative newcomer I have been most generously helped by a number of people with longer experience in native studies. I am grateful to Professors John S. Moir, Donald B. Smith, John Badertscher, and Charles Hamori-Torok, who read the manuscript and made comments that were sometimes all the more helpful for their severity. I should also like to thank those who provided items of information or lent studies that would otherwise have been unavailable. I cannot be sure now of remembering all such favours, but I should like to mention at least Professors Douglas Leighton, Conrad E. Heidenreich, and Eugene V. Gallagher, Dr Martha McCarthy, Bennett McCardle, Louise Taylor, the Rev. Gerald Hutchinson, and Dennis Martel. Canon James P. Scanlon graciously consented to the use of an excerpt from *The Inlanders* on page 200. Bernice Andrews rendered invaluable help at one stage as a research assistant, especially in relation to the intervention of the Hon. S.H. Blake. I am also grateful to the students of several classes for their responses as I tried out ideas. Librarians and archivists were uniformly helpful. I owe a special debt to the Rev. Gaston Carrière, omi, of the Archives Deschâtelets, Ottawa, who not only read considerable portions of the manuscript but shared with me his valuable collection of file cards.

The book has been greatly improved by the comments of readers of the University of Toronto Press and the Canadian Federation for the Humanities, by the editorial advice and encouragement of Gerald Hallowell, and by the copy-editing of Susan Kent. For all such assistance, and for that of others who may inadvertently have been overlooked, I should like to express my thanks. Those who contributed so significantly to the writing of the book cannot, of course, be held responsible for any opinions expressed in it.

JOHN WEBSTER GRANT

The first Methodist service at Whitefish Lake, Alta,
conducted by the Ojibwa minister Henry B. Steinhauer

Jean-Baptiste Assiginack,
or 'the Blackbird,'
a leading Roman Catholic
chief among the Ottawas

Peter Jones, a pioneer
Methodist missionary
in Upper Canada,
of Welsh-Ojibwa parentage

Silas T. Rand, a Baptist clergyman who spent fifty years
among the Micmacs of the Maritimes

OPPOSITE

Teachers and pupils at the McDougall orphanage, Morley, Alta.
The Methodist missionary John McDougall appears prominently
in the foreground.

Ovide Charlebois, vicar apostolic of Keewatin, illustrating the
portable 'chapel' carried by Oblate missionaries

Salvation Army band, Port Simpson, BC

Blackfoot Home in southern Alberta,
sponsored by the Church Missionary Society

A scene from the first Indian passion play at Kamloops, BC

A Cree class at the Anglican residential school at Lac la Ronge, Sask

Potlatch on Songhees reserve, Victoria, Vancouver Island, 27 May 1895

OPPOSITE
Blackfoot Indians with tree branches for a sun-dance lodge
Spogan Garry, leader of a pre-missionary Christian movement
in the interior of British Columbia during the 1820s and 1830s,
in later life

An anonymous painting of the Blessed Kateri Tekakwitha
in the museum of the Roman Catholic Church at Caughnawaga

A procession during an Oblate mission at Betsiamites, PQ

The Cree syllabics of James Evans,
Methodist missionary at Norway House, Man

Cree syllabics as adapted for the Carriers of British Columbia
by the Oblate Adrien G. Morice

Early Oblate writing from the Mackenzie Valley

Micmac ideographs, originally invented by the
Récollet Chrestien Le Clercq and modified by Pierre Maillard
of the Society of Foreign Missions

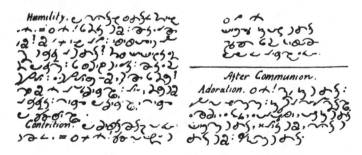

An adaptation of shorthand for British Columbia Indians
by the Oblate Jean-Marie Le Jeune

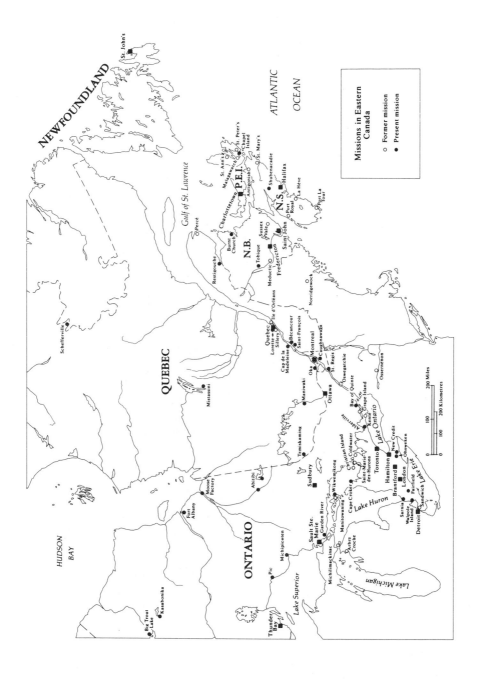

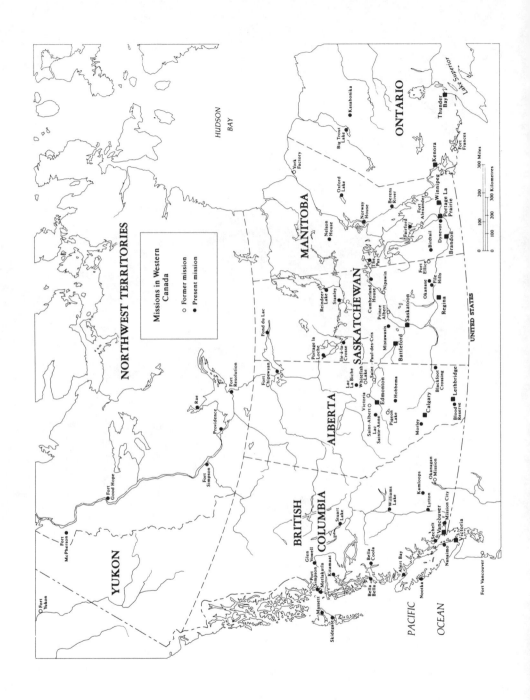

Missions in Western Canada

○ Former mission
● Present mission

NORTHWEST TERRITORIES

YUKON

BRITISH COLUMBIA

ALBERTA

SASKATCHEWAN

MANITOBA

ONTARIO

HUDSON BAY

PACIFIC OCEAN

UNITED STATES

Fort Yukon

Fort McPherson

Fort Good Hope

Fort Simpson

Providence

Rae

Fort Resolution

Fort Chipewyan

Fort Hope

Fond du Lac

Portage la Loche

Île-à-la-Crosse

Reindeer Lake

Stanley

Lac La Biche

Whitefish O Lake

Saint O Paul-des-Cris

Saint Albert

Lac Sainte-Anne

Victoria

Edmonton

Hobbema

Pigeon Lake

Morley

Calgary

Blackfoot Crossing

Lethbridge

Blood Reserve

Mistawasis

Battleford

Prince Albert

Saskatoon

Cumberland House

Nipawin

The Pas

Regina

File Hills

Okanase

Fort Ellice

Birdtail

Dynevor

Brandon

Fairford

Nelson House

Norway House

Berens River

Fort Alexander

Winnipeg

Portage La Prairie

Oxford Lake

York Factory

Big Trout Lake

Kasabonika

Kenora

Thunder Bay

Fort Frances

Lake Superior

Williams Lake

Stuart Lake

Kamloops

Lytton

Okanagan O Mission

Vancouver

Mission City

Victoria

Nanaimo

Sechelt

Nootka

Alert Bay

Bella Coola

Bella Bella

Kitamaat

Metlakatla

Fort Simpson

Glen Vowell

Massett

Skidegate

Fort Vancouver

300 Miles

300 Kilometres

Moon of Wintertime

Transatlantic Encounter

The first recorded presentation of Christian teaching to Indians within the present boundaries of Canada took place at Gaspé on 20 July 1534, when Jacques Cartier erected a cross and indicated as well as he could to visiting Iroquoians from Stadacona, now Quebec, that they should look to it for their redemption. In the following year his crew harangued the villagers of Stadacona on the folly of their beliefs and elicited in response what they interpreted as a mass request for baptism. On his departure Cartier took several Indians, including the chief Donnacona, to France, where at least three of them received baptism before their premature deaths.[1] After this beginning, which missiologists today would regard as less than exemplary, we hear of no further significant contacts for more than seventy years. Pierre du Gua de Monts's first colonizing parties to Acadia in 1604 included two priests and a Huguenot minister, but the Huguenot could not legally seek Indian converts and there is no evidence that either of the priests did so. The honour of being the first recognized missionary to the Indians thus fell to Jessé Fléché, a secular priest of the diocese of Langres, who was recruited for Acadia in 1610 simply because expediency dictated that the infant colony should be provided with a priest. De Monts had recently lost his charter for exclusive trade because King Henri IV was not satisfied that he was making serious efforts to christianize the local Micmacs. Jean de Biencourt de Poutrincourt, the grantee of Port Royal, was thus under considerable pressure to secure any priest who might be available. Fléché was the one he found.

Port Royal at the time of Fléché's arrival was not so much a colony as a gathering place for a score or so of adventurers eager to exploit the fur trade along the Atlantic coast. Fléché was expected to find his real work among the Micmacs, and despite his unfamiliarity with their language he did what he could. Membertou, a neighbouring Sagamo, was already on good terms with the French. With the help of considerable persuasion by Poutrincourt, Fléché was able to bring him and his band of twenty-one to Christian baptism. The occasion was an impressive one, and to crown it Membertou and his followers received French names. Membertou became Henri after the king, word of whose assassination had not yet reached Port Royal. After the pope and the rest of the royal family had been similarly honoured, members of the expedition and other French dignitaries had their turns. Two weeks later, Poutrincourt's son Biencourt sailed for France to carry the good news to the court. For this hasty act, performed after virtually no instruction, Fléché was censured in retrospect by his successors. He must have had an impressive presence, however, for the title 'patriarche' accorded him long remained the standard designation of a missionary among the Micmacs and even spread to the neighbouring Abenakis.

Poutrincourt's difficulty in finding a priest was not due to a lack of willing volunteers. The Jesuits had been projecting work in New France since 1605, and in 1608 Pierre Biard had travelled from Lyon to Bordeaux in expectation of a passage.[2] Poutrincourt was most reluctant to receive Jesuits, however, and even when his son Biencourt agreed for financial reasons to take them, his Huguenot outfitters refused to provide them with supplies.[3] Only through the intervention of the wealthy marquise de Guercheville, who by canvassing her friends succeeded in purchasing for the Jesuits a share in the expedition, were Biard and Enemond Massé enabled to reach Acadia in 1611.[4] Fléché welcomed them cordially and then departed for France, where according to some historians he died later in the year.

In France, as elsewhere, the Society of Jesus had a reputation that marked it off from all other orders. Founded in 1534 by St Ignatius Loyola, a Basque of military background, and given papal sanction in 1540, it grew with amazing rapidity and was soon active throughout Europe and in many missions abroad. Jesuits were universally respected for their ability to attract able and often well-born candidates, for the thoroughness of their training, for persistence in the pursuit of their objectives, and for willingness to undertake the most disagreeable and dangerous tasks. They were widely distrusted for their lack of the outward marks of austerity and

humility usually associated with the religious, for supposed laxity in applying the rules of the confessional, and for actual or suspected involvement
in secret financial transactions and diplomatic negotiations. In France they
were especially suspect to many patriots for their vow of unconditional
obedience to the pope, and their refusal on technical grounds to take the
oath of allegiance to Henri IV led in 1594 to eight years of exile from Paris.
Thus the very name of Jesuit was charged with an emotional resonance
that powerfully attracted some people and as strongly repelled others.

The real Jesuit was at once more complex and less subtle than the popular stereotype. Outwardly urbane, and often giving the appearance of
affluence, he might well be wearing a hair-shirt or a belt of sharpened
spikes. Despite his reputation for laxity he was a moral rigorist, flexible in
the confessional only because he was so confident in the power of the
sacraments that he was reluctant to deprive sinners of their benefit. If
French he was almost certainly a fervent patriot, striving to maintain a
correct balance between spiritual and temporal authorities and even more
deeply upset than his critics by some expressions of the Jesuit theologian
Cardinal Bellarmine that seemed to suggest a divided allegiance.[5] Utterly
sincere, he could seem devious only because he valued the truth so highly
that he was prepared to dissimulate occasionally on its behalf.

This combination of apparently contradictory qualities was inherent in
the original design of the order. Loyola's intention was to shape a body of
men who could serve as shock troops of the church against indifference,
Protestantism, and, above all, heathenism. His chief weapon for this purpose was a set of 'spiritual exercises,' a series of meditations designed not so
much to stimulate disinterested contemplation as to impress strongly on
the imagination the pains of hell, the joys of heaven, and the desperate
needs of the world.[6] An intended Jesuit was expected to take the exercises
under direction for a month and then to renew them in an eight-day
retreat each year. Having undergone this discipline, a Jesuit was assumed
to be inwardly formed and thus not to require many of the usual monastic
routines. He was also assumed to be capable of making decisions for himself when necessary; the famous Jesuit obedience was more a matter of
learning to think with the church than of depending on rules or orders
from above.

The two pioneers in Acadia, in line with the tradition of their order,
sought efficacious means of carrying out their assignment. Massé visited
Micmac camps, learning the language and ways of the people, while Biard

as leader spent more time at Port Royal. Unfortunately Biard had more zeal than tact, and Poutrincourt's early prejudice against the order proved to be indelible. Tension soon mounted to the point where the only solution for the Jesuits seemed to be a separate establishment free from interference by traders. Mme de Guercheville secured a site at Pentagoët, on the coast of what is now Maine, and there in 1613 a reinforced party of Jesuits founded the mission of St Sauveur. How well it might have succeeded will never be known, for in July Samuel Argall of Virginia seized the settlement on the claim that it lay within English territory. Gilbert du Thet, a lay brother who had been sent out as Mme de Guercheville's agent, was killed in the initial bombardment. The others made their way, after various adventures, back to France.[7]

Little remained in Acadia to show the effects of this abortive mission. Membertou proved a faithful and enthusiastic convert, but his death in 1611 left the little Christian community leaderless, and for some years no missionary appeared to follow up the initial sowing. Yet the mission left two important legacies. Massé had made a lifetime commitment to the Indians, which he would fulfil by propagandizing the cause at home and by returning to New France when opportunity offered on the St Lawrence. Biard's description of the mission for French readers inspired a long series of Jesuit *Relations* that helped to fix seventeenth-century conceptions of the Indians and still constitute our best source of information about the missions of the period.

Even before Fléché's arrival another centre of French influence had begun to take shape. Samuel de Champlain, one of the founders of Acadia, was not content to regard the new world merely as a source of quick profits. He conceived the vision of a new society, French in culture and Christian in religion, whose population would consist of converted Indians leavened with French colonists. Such a dream could not easily be realized in Acadia, with its limited population and extended coastline. Much more suitable was the St Lawrence, where furs were better and more abundant and where the river line offered greater possibilities of control. Champlain, acting as lieutenant to de Monts, accordingly established at Quebec in 1608 what would become a permanent settlement. Missionaries were clearly essential to his vision. He first attempted to persuade Mme de Guercheville to buy the habitation and presumably to sponsor Jesuits.[8] When she declined, he was able to secure the services of a branch of the Franciscan order known as Récollets.

Ever since its foundation by St Francis of Assisi in the thirteenth century, the Franciscan order has been racked by dissension over the extent to which it should be bound by his stringent directions. Believing absolute poverty essential to holiness, Francis forbade not only his individual followers but the order itself to possess property. Even within his lifetime his rule was relaxed, and ever since there have been repeated calls for a return to it. The Récollets, one of several 'observant' bodies emerging in the sixteenth century, were not a distinct religious order but were granted a separate constitution in 1595 and a measure of autonomy in 1601. The speciality that gave them their name was the provision of rustic 'houses of recollection' for spiritual renewal. Their particular qualification for work among Indians was a growing reputation for social service.

Arriving at Quebec in 1615 with one lay brother, three Récollet priests proceeded to carve up their vast mission field with heroic optimism. One would cover the St Lawrence from Trois-Rivières to a point somewhat below Quebec. One would go to Tadoussac to look after the Montagnais of the Saguenay region. The third, Joseph Le Caron, would make a thousand-kilometre journey to Georgian Bay to carry the message to the Hurons, middlemen in the fur trade with whom Champlain had begun commercial relations. This last venture was by far the most ambitious. It fitted well into Champlain's design, however, for as a sedentary, agricultural people the Hurons seemed the most likely prospects for speedy conversion into 'civilized' Christians. Le Caron set out in the very first year of the mission, reaching Huronia even before Champlain, and spent the winter investigating the possibility of a permanent mission. Despite his report of a cordial reception the Hurons must have had reservations, for not until 1623 could they be persuaded to receive him a second time. On this occasion he took along Father Nicolas Viel as well as a lay brother, Gabriel Sagard, who has left us a delightfully open-minded account of his experiences.[9] In the previous year another Récollet, Guillaume Poulain, had succeeded in reaching the country of the Nipissings after falling into the hands of the Iroquois and briefly suffering tortures at their hands. Back in Quebec, meanwhile, the order had established a convent and a seminary.

Despite this brave start the mission did not prosper. Popular as they were in France, the Récollets notably failed to endear themselves to the Company of Merchants, which controlled the colony, or to its successor, the Montmorency Company. Most of the traders, being Huguenots, regarded the conversion of the Indians to Roman Catholicism as the

replacement of one form of idolatry by another. The poverty-sworn
Récollets, in turn, could not pass over without occasional comment the
avarice of the fur traders or their lack of scruple in dealing with the Indians. Without Champlain's support they could scarcely have maintained
their position. An even greater difficulty was their lack of resources to cope
with the logistic problems of a transatlantic mission or to comply with
Indian patterns of mutual present-giving. Joseph de la Roche Dallion sadly
concluded, 'to think to live in these countries as mendicants is self-deceit.'
Meanwhile, several Récollets of the province of Aquitaine working on
the Baie des Chaleurs and along the Saint John River were having even
greater difficulties. In 1619 they had secured the sponsorship of a group of
Bordeaux merchants, but the company folded in 1624 and the missionaries
had to make their way to Quebec as best they could.

In these straits the Récollets sought the collaboration of the Jesuits.
The latter were not their first choice, and in many ways it was surprising
that they should approach them at all. Franciscans and Jesuits were already
at odds over missionary methods in China, and Champlain was lukewarm
to the proposal. On the other hand, the Jesuits had the financial resources
the Récollets lacked, including a ship of their own that would provide
some independence of the trading company.[10] On their arrival in Quebec
the Jesuits were universally snubbed, and the Récollets had to share their
meagre quarters with them. Nevertheless, the work went forward with
new vigour. In 1626 Dallion was accompanied to Huronia by the Jesuits
Jean de Brébeuf and Anne de Noüe, and over the winter of 1627–8
Brébeuf was there alone. The Jesuits also had the political clout to bring
about a change in the management of the colony. In 1627 Richelieu
revoked the charter of the Montmorency Company and entrusted direction to a new Company of One Hundred Associates, from which Huguenots were excluded. The chief purpose of the company was to be the
furtherance of the conversion of the aborigines.

What now seemed a promising missionary venture was almost immediately aborted. In 1629 Quebec surrendered to an English flotilla commanded by David Kirke, a London merchant with connections in Dieppe,
and its missionaries were sent back to France. To all appearances this brief
initial stage of Christian-Indian encounter had been without permanent
results, for the one convert on whom the missionaries had pinned high
hopes returned to his native ways during the English occupation.[11] Already,
however, in these first contacts a number of significant participants in the

encounter had been introduced. From Europe came missionaries, government officials, and traders. Permanently on the scene were Indians, who varied greatly in language and culture but shared a common attachment to the land. The backgrounds and attitudes of each group had and would continue to have important implications for the conduct and effects of the missions. They warrant fuller introduction at this early stage.

The missionary impulse is as old as Christianity itself, and indeed was prefigured by the Jewish quest for proselytes. It derived naturally from belief in one God who cares for all and has a claim on the allegiance of all. It took on a new urgency when the conviction spread that the coming of Jesus, culminating in his death and resurrection, opened up new possibilities of fulfilment. This compulsion to spread the faith was strengthened still further by belief in a culmination of history yet to come. Only in the eschaton would the meaning of the cosmos be fully revealed, and from early times it was widely believed that the millennial reign of Christ would come only when the gospel had been diffused throughout the world. Christianity thus offered salvation to everyone regardless of accidents of birth and culture, while by the same token it claimed acceptance from everyone. In the early centuries it was promoted in every region that its emissaries could reach. It achieved its greatest success in moving westward, but by the sixth century it had also reached China.[12]

During the Middle Ages the missionary flame was considerably dimmed. Acceptance by Rome awakened suspicion among Rome's eastern rivals, while the rise of Islam not only interposed an almost impenetrable barrier between Christendom and the rest of the world but thrust the balance of power within Christendom to the less exposed north. Christianity, which once had been impatient of ethnic limitations, became itself practically an ethnic religion that could worship only in Latin. Nevertheless, the missionary flame was never totally extinguished. There were still pagans to convert in northern Europe throughout the Middle Ages, and indeed the last Lapp had scarcely been baptized before the Indians of Canada were being approached. Even the crusades, in which Christendom attempted to escape its virtual encirclement by Islam, could be regarded as a perverse expression of the missionary spirit. Although Christendom was on the defensive in the late Middle Ages, popular movements such as those led by St Francis and St Dominic were already preparing the way for future expansion. Their greatest contribution, apart from the spark they kindled,

was the invention of a new kind of religious order that could readily be
turned to a missionary purpose. Fortified by a monastic discipline but also
worldly-wise through the experience of preaching to audiences of all
kinds, the friars were obvious candidates for the mission field. St Francis
set the example in 1219 by preaching before the sultan in Egypt, and by
the next century his order had a number of representatives in China.

The voyages of Columbus to America in 1492 and of Vasco da Gama to
India in 1498 opened the world to European initiative, and within a few
decades thousands of preaching friars were seeking converts abroad. Secular and religious expansion were connected by intimate but complex ties of
mutual influence. Secular imperialism was inspired by a European – or at
any rate Latin – sense of mission that had a distinctly religious component:
Columbus set off with the active backing of the primate of Spain and
many other prominent members of the clergy.[13] In turn, growing awareness of the outside world helped to stimulate a sense of mission on the part
of the church. One of St Ignatius's best-known exercises was simply a
stretching of the imagination to encompass the activities and needs of
different races in every part of the earth.

Both European and Christian expansion were made possible by a growing sense of confidence that marked the beginning of the modern era. In
the secular realm this expressed itself in the renewal of arts and letters,
along with the scientific advance, that is generally known as the Renaissance. In the church it led to the movement of Catholic reform, which was
in part a response to the Protestant Reformation but had roots in a deepen-
ing of popular piety and a determination to rid the church of inefficiency
and corruption that had begun some decades earlier. An important ingredient in the revival was simply a growing conviction that despite the scandalous behaviour of some popes and bishops, despite the Turks, and despite
Luther and Calvin, Catholicism could and would make it. The resulting
mood, on the part of zealots who made the missions possible, was one of
unquestioning loyalty to the church and its dogmas, of unbounded confidence in its future, and of dedication to the point of readiness for martyrdom. The missionary revival had little immediate effect on Protestants,
whose concern for 'justification' or a right relation with God expressed
itself more readily in a strict moralism and in devotion to the civic virtues.

For several reasons the effects of the Catholic Reformation were slow in
reaching France. Throughout the sixteenth century the country was distracted by controversy between Roman Catholics and Huguenots that

began with theology and culminated in civil war. There was also a long-standing tradition of national independence that insulated France some-what from the influence of Mediterranean movements; the disciplinary decrees of the Council of Trent, which embodied many of the emphases of Catholic reform, were never officially received in France. By the end of the sixteenth century, however, there were signs of a general resurgence of religious interest. Of particular concern was the cultivation of personal spirituality, for guidance in which one normally looked to a carefully chosen spiritual director. Soon there was a wide choice of methods of prayer, including the Ignatian, the Salesian, the Berullian, and others. Much spiritual fervour was centred in fashionable salons, where a heady atmosphere of religious exaltation was not uncommon. The movement also had its practical side, represented by the social-service work of St Vincent de Paul and others. Sanctity was, indeed, expected to issue in good works or at least in patronage of them. Among such good works the missions always ranked high. It may not be irrelevant to note that Massé was for a time Mme de Guercheville's spiritual director.

Fléché was not blazing a new trail when he reached Port Royal in 1610. The church, and especially the preaching orders, had already accumulated much missionary experience and established many precedents. Much of this experience was among Indians, for Latin America had been the scene of missionary labour for more than a century. In 1510 there had been established the first missionary *encomienda*, a regulated agricultural unit designed for the settlement and protection of the native inhabitants. This in turn was based on precedents already set in the Balearic and Canary Islands when they were colonized by the Spanish.[14] In Fléché's time the Jesuits had just begun an ambitious development of the same idea in a series of model villages known collectively as 'Paraguay.' As the very latest in missionary techniques, it may have helped to inspire the Jesuit settlement of St Sauveur in 1613.

There had also been time for the orders to become embroiled in controversies over missionary approach. In line with the general conservatism of the Catholic Reformation most missionaries were content to propagate Latin Catholicism with unswerving rigidity. The greater flexibility of the Jesuit order allowed some of its members to adapt Christian practice to the circumstances of other cultures. In China, Matteo Ricci sought to meet Confucian sensibilities by recognizing some tokens of respect for ancestors as merely secular customs and by using for 'God' a familiar Chinese term

that seemed to some other missionaries less than orthodox. In India,
Roberto de Nobili similarly accepted caste as a social convention and presented Christianity in the context of traditional Hindu concepts. The 'Chinese rites' especially gave rise to a stormy controversy and eventually to a
series of condemnations that proved ruinous both to the China mission
and to the reputation of the Jesuits in many quarters. This storm, just
brewing when the first Jesuits reached Acadia, would in later years do
much to sour relations among missionary agencies. Its chief long-term
effect was to make missionaries fearful of any hint of compromise with the
practices of other religions.

The state, the second main determinant of the terms of encounter, has
been concerned with religion from time immemorial. In ancient Rome
municipal officials doubled as priests of the official cult. Christianity, by
contrast, stood at first at such a distance from the state that the theologian
Tertullian asserted flatly, 'Christians could not be Caesars.' Under Constantine and his successors of the fourth century, however, Christianity
became successively a recognized, privileged, and established religion. In
return for this favour the state expected to regulate the temporal affairs of
the church, administer its endowments, and make use of the political and
diplomatic talents of its clerics. In time it was possible to speak of Christianity as part of the common law, so that anyone who did not profess it
had either to be excluded or to be treated virtually as a foreigner.[15] The rise
of strong monarchies in early modern times and the process of secularization that went with it had at first the effect of tightening the connection.
There was no room in an absolute state for a competing jurisdiction.

When European states began to extend their military and political
power, they inevitably expected to take Christianity with them. Spain and
Portugal, the two countries most directly involved, had struggled throughout the Middle Ages to wrest the Iberian peninsula back from Moorish
control. Each gain, including the final capture of Granada in 1492, was
accompanied by the expulsion or forcible conversion of Moors and Jews.
Political expansion was thus part of an unrelenting war against Islam that
was the particular Iberian contribution to the crusading idea. It was only
natural that the same logic should be applied to conquests beyond the
boundaries of Europe. Spain and Portugal were content for the most part to
leave the initiative in the conversion of infidels to the religious orders, but
they had no thought of allowing them a free hand. The Spanish monarchy
regarded the christianization of its share of Latin America as its particular

responsibility. Portugal went so far as to assert, on the basis of a papal division of responsibility for the non-Christian portion of the world, its exclusive jurisdiction over all Christians and Christian missions in the Orient. The papacy and the religious orders also had claims to jurisdiction, and when these collided with those of the state, the result could be bitter and sometimes protracted conflict.

Although the French never matched the messianism of the Spanish or the possessiveness of the Portuguese, they drew on a long tradition that identified the Franks as special protectors of the church and especially of the church abroad. The ninth-century emperor Charlemagne not only introduced Christianity into conquered areas such as Saxony and Denmark but proclaimed his patronage over the Holy Places and the pilgrim route to them. The crusades, ostensibly designed to restore the Holy Places to pilgrim use, were largely a French-Norman enterprise. Only with the emergence of the ugly American, indeed, has the term 'Frank' ceased to serve for any Western intruder in the Middle East. Within much more recent times the papacy has looked to the French, sometimes in vain, as guarantors of the papal states.

Whatever considerations of idealism or national honour may have entered, the king of France had practical motives for maintaining his status as protector of the church. The legitimacy of the French monarchy ultimately rested, in principle, on the coronation of Charlemagne as Roman emperor by Pope Leo III and even more on that of his grandfather Pepin II by Stephen II. Until this time the Carolingians had been mere mayors of the palace, albeit unusually powerful ones. In later times the title of 'most Christian king' was a potent weapon in advancing royal power over against that of feudal nobles. As such it was never more important than in the period immediately following the Reformation, when Protestantism became associated with decentralizing tendencies within the nobility.[16] No matter how strenuously a French monarch might insist on the autonomy of the French church in relation to Rome, he could never afford to throw away the internal advantages of his association with Catholicism. Henri IV, the Protestant king of Navarre who became king of France only when he decided that Paris was worth a mass, was a fitting sponsor of the first mission to the Indians of Canada.

Official patronage was in effect a two-way street. It carried the implication that French culture should include Christianity but also that Christianity abroad should promote French culture. Champlain's dream of

a christianized and francified Indian population was fully in accord with
official French policy, and a provision in the charter of the One Hundred
Associates that a christianized Indian should have all the privileges of
French citizenship clearly assumed that a christianized Indian would be
French in culture.[17] So long as missionaries endeavoured to further this
design they could count on a large measure of official support. When they
formulated plans of their own that threatened to interfere with it, they
were likely to incur the displeasure both of Versailles and of local authorities.

The motive that brought most Frenchmen to North America was not
zeal for either souls or honour but the hope of making money. For more
than a century before Fléché's arrival, traders had been frequenting the
Atlantic coast, and during much of that interval they were familiar with
the lower St Lawrence as well. Already they had begun to put their stamp
on the country, and they would continue to do so throughout both the
French and British regimes. Over a long period they were virtual rulers of
large parts of Canada, subject only to ineffective supervision from afar and
to the ultimate threat of the cancellation of their charters. Since the fur
trade especially could be carried on only with the co-operation of the Indians, the missionaries worked constantly under its shadow.

Relations between missionaries and traders, the third major factor in
Indian-Christian encounter, were seldom easy. Initially the difficulties
were compounded by a natural antipathy between Roman Catholic missionaries and predominantly Huguenot traders, but the example of the
Catholic Poutrincourt demonstrates that there were other reasons for them
as well. The basic problem, transcending individual likes and dislikes, was
a fundamental incompatibility of purpose. Traders valued Indians for their
native skills and dreaded any change in their manner of life that would
dull these. Missionaries wanted to transform the Indians and, most incon-
veniently from the standpoint of the traders, to settle them. Traders were
not above selling brandy or rum if this would induce the Indians to part
with more furs, and in a situation far removed from European conventions
most of them regarded relations with Indian women as a normal outlet for
sexual appetites. Missionaries wanted to protect the morals of the Indians
and, worse still, to reform those of the traders in order to prevent them
from corrupting the Indians. Each thus interfered with the plans of the
other. Most seriously of all, each threatened to spoil the Indians for the
other's purposes.

Despite constant friction, punctuated by occasional sharp complaints on either side, the relation between missionaries and traders was not one of unrelenting hostility. Merchants who were merely transients, without stake in the country beyond the hope of a quick profit, had no incentives to help the missionaries and often many to resent their presence. Those with exclusive charters took on, willy-nilly, some of the responsibilities of governments and were affected by some of the same motives. They needed a measure of law and order, along with the inculcation of habits of industry and responsibility compatible with Western concepts of trade, and these the missionaries could help to supply. On the other hand, traders did not wish to accept the burden of supporting Indians out of their own resources and were sometimes relieved when missionary settlements promised a measure of relief from it. In a surprising number of cases, therefore, it was through trading companies that missionaries secured a foothold and were provided with necessary transportation and supplies.

Fluctuations in the energy and effectiveness with which missions were prosecuted can be traced back in many cases to the interplay of these three factors: the missions themselves, the state, and commercial interests. When lust for gain and the glory of God conflicted, human nature being what it is, the former usually won out. They did not always appear to conflict, for Canada was never regarded only as a means to profit but also as an opportunity for the extension of French (and later British) prestige and honour. When profit was emphasized, there was likely to be friction and jealousy. When other motives came to the fore, there might be close collaboration. The Company of Merchants and that of the One Hundred Associates have already introduced both possibilities.

The Indians unwittingly caught in the path of Christian advance belonged to two widely distributed linguistic and cultural groups. Those first encountered in Acadia and on the St Lawrence were woodland peoples of Algonquian speech. Along the eastern seaboard as far as the Gaspé peninsula lived the Micmacs, while the Maliseets occupied the Saint John Valley. Both were closely related to the Abenakis and other tribes then resident in northern New England. Around Quebec and the Saguenay were the Montagnais, linguistically related to the Crees and Naskapis of the Canadian Shield. The Algonquins, who were encountered mainly in the Ottawa-Montreal area, shared a basically common language with the Ottawas and Ojibwas farther west. Le Caron, journeying to Huronia, made contact there with people of an Iroquoian tongue and a culture based primarily on agriculture. Possibly a coalition of previously independent tribes, the Hurons had close affinities with the Khionontateronons or Petuns immediately to the west, the Neutrals of southwestern Ontario, and the Five Nations Iroquois of northern New York. The missionaries thus made an early acquaintance with forms of speech current over much of the northern half of North America.

The ancestors of both groups, as of all Indians of the Americas, had made their way from Siberia during intervals between ice ages over a land bridge that existed from time to time in the vicinity of Bering Strait. Although estimates of the first human occupation of America are constantly being pushed back, the largest migration took place near the close of the last ice age, circa 11,000–10,000 BC. The chief migration route led southwards in the lee of the Rocky Mountains to the western American plains; only as the glaciers continued their retreat, although certainly not much later than 10,000 BC, were some groups able to make their way northwards into eastern Canada. Whether because they represented a late migration or simply because conditions of life remained more stable, the culture of the Algonquians retained more reminiscences of the Siberian past than did that of Iroquoians. The latter had closer cultural links with areas to the south. Despite such reminders of earlier migrations and despite inevitable shifts and dislocations in later times, it is generally agreed that both Algonquians and Iroquoians were residents of long standing in what is now eastern Canada.[18]

The economy of the woodland Algonquians was based on the harvesting of what nature provided, supplemented on the southern and western margins with a little agriculture. Through most of the year the staple food was fish, usually from rivers and lakes although in the case of the Micmacs including what would be today a very expensive amount of shellfish. Fish was supplemented in summer by wild fruits, especially blueberries gathered on numerous *brulés*. In winter it was necessary to hunt animals, which provided more interesting but less reliable fare. Garnering these scattered resources involved a great deal of moving about. In summer the lakes and rivers served as highways, and clusters of conical birch-bark wigwams dotted favoured sites along them. In winter snow trails made the woods more passable, and where necessary resort was had to river ice. The canoe, snowshoe, and wigwam, along with techniques of making fur clothing, were all part of a common inheritance known from Siberia to Acadia.

They made possible a way of life that was hard but viable and, in the absence of communicable diseases, a span of life and a measure of health that compared well with those of Europeans of the time. Europeans unfamiliar with the country were able to learn much from the Algonquians.

Such a diffuse economy called for flexible units of social organization. Since game animals were sparsely distributed through the forests, the winter group consisted of a few nuclear families who stayed together for mutual support and insurance against disaster. Summer conditions allowed larger and somewhat longer gatherings, often around fishing stations or near berry fields, of a number of such groups that composed a band. At such gatherings there was time for games and feasts, matchmaking, and a general cementing of social ties. Although the point has been much disputed, such properties as rights to hunting territories seem in pre-contact times to have been band possessions subject to an annual distribution.[19] The band was the largest significant social group, for the tribe had no existence beyond mutual recognition of kinship based on a common tongue.

Larger groups were essentially extensions of the family, and leadership was patriarchal in nature. Each band had a chief, who owed his position to common recognition of his fitness to lead. An appropriate family background helped, and indeed in some bands chiefships were virtually hereditary. Other important qualifications were prowess in hunting and generosity to others, both of which would make the chief a good provider, along with magnanimity and wisdom. The chief was expected, in short, to be a person of superior spiritual discernment and power. Since he lacked any power to command, his authority depended on his ability to retain respect. Those who could not accept him usually joined another band, although in extreme cases there might be a challenge to his leadership or a split in the band. This dependence on consensus required a good deal of consultation, which led in turn to the cultivation of rhetoric as a highly valued art. While there was neither formal education nor policing, there was considerable intentionality in maintaining and transmitting the traditions of tribal life. Education consisted mainly in the recital of the myths, legends, and moral aphorisms of the tribe, normally by a grandfather.[20] Discipline was maintained, usually with considerable effectiveness, by bringing the weight of community opinion to bear on those who departed from convention in ways that endangered the cohesion of the band.

Religion was not a segregated area of life but manifested itself in a variety of procedures associated with normal activities such as hunting, travel, and war. There were certain ritual requirements, things that had to be done. Crossing a river or venturing out into a lake might call for an offering of tobacco. Asking pardon of an animal about to be killed ensured that the victim would not be offended and warn off its fellows. War could not be undertaken without flights of rhetoric and the seeking of omens. There were also taboos, things that had not to be done. The bones of a slain animal could not be fed to dogs without offence, nor could one hope to be victorious in battle after sexual intercourse. As in most other societies, the reproductive process was surrounded with taboos of unusual number and severity; contact with a pubescent girl or menstruating woman was fraught with danger. Religion came closest to being a specialized activity in the treatment of illness. For minor ailments natural remedies were used, but for serious illness and especially for illness that seemed to involve a 'loss of spirit' it was necessary to make contact with the spirit world. The underlying assumption of Algonquian – as of all Indian – religion was that human life is essentially continuous with the rest of nature. The cosmos was conceived as a circle or 'sacred hoop' within which all parts must be in balance if the whole was to cohere.[21] In practice most spirits were animal spirits, and propitiating them was a means of maintaining or restoring harmony with fellow dwellers in the cosmos.

To note how integral religion was to life is, however, to tell only half the story. Familiar as the spirit world might be in many of its aspects, it far transcended the everyday. To describe it as 'supernatural' would be to import a European concept, but it was certainly extraordinary and awesome, a realm where things were not as they seemed. Powerful spirits might have the shape and form of beavers, but they were no more ordinary beavers than the leviathan of ancient mythology was an ordinary crocodile. Ultimately all myths pointed to a primordial time, all ritual practice to a power inherent in the cosmos, even if in both cases the relation was usually only implicit. Establishing contact with this power, while necessary to the continuation of life, was also arduous and dangerous. Making it available for human use ideally involved a trip to the centre of the spirit world and then a return to earth.[22] However much this might be routinized in practice, it demanded in principle a cycle of death and resurrection.

Although spiritual power was good inasmuch as it held the cosmos together, those able to draw on it could put it to either helpful or harmful uses. Indian religion thus contained what is likely to strike someone of European background as an element of moral ambiguity. This element was graphically represented in Algonquian mythology by the figure of a culture hero, Gluskap of the Micmacs or Nanabozho of the Ojibwas. In much North American mythology the culture hero took the form of a 'trickster' who was often himself subjected to humiliating tricks and took more than his share of pratfalls. Gluskap and Nanabozho were figures of much greater dignity, commonly described as working impressive wonders, but they had a streak of playfulness and were far from infallible.[23] The culture hero represented the ambivalence of nature as observed. He was a being about whom people liked to tell stories, seen like nature itself as somewhat disorderly but not sinister.

Hunting, upon which the Algonquians depended for survival in winter, is an occupation not quite like others. Game animals are notoriously elusive, and even the most experienced tracker cannot count on locating them at need. Success in the hunt has always been invested with a certain mysterious quality, requiring more than technical skill or even luck but above all a rapport with the animals themselves and, in an animistic society, with the spirits of the animals. The religion of hunters has, therefore, always had rather special characteristics. The spirits of animals could not be manipulated but always had to be cajoled. Making contact with the spirit world was the special function of the shaman or medicine man or woman, whose authority derived not from official appointment or even from socially transmitted lore but rather from direct vision. More often than not the shaman was a person who had suffered from serious psychic illness and then experienced remarkable healing through contact with the spirits. He was consequently of special importance in healing, which was brought about usually by exorcising the spirit responsible for the disease. In some Algonquian tribes the shaman periodically renewed his power by seeking a special encounter with the spirits in a tent that shook of its own accord, a practice that provided another link with the Siberian past.

Despite the crucial importance of the shaman, contact with the spirit world was not the monopoly of a class. Young people, both boys and girls, were expected to seek a personal vision, for which they were carefully groomed in advance and then sent into the wilds for a period of isolation. There they were to make contact with a *manido*, normally representing an animal, who would give them some symbol of the encounter as well as a special identity conveying power and meaning for life.[24] Contact was also

made in dreams, which were carefully interpreted and applied, sometimes
through a literal acting-out.

To pass from Algonquians to Iroquoians was to encounter a very different economy and way of life. Huronia consisted of a series of palisaded
villages, each of which was surrounded by fields of beans, squash, sun-
flowers, here and there tobacco, and everywhere corn in great abundance.
These villages, estimated by the first observers to contain a total of thirty
thousand people, were grouped in close proximity in the area between
Lake Simcoe and Georgian Bay. Although they had to be moved every ten
to twenty years on account of the exhaustion of the soil, they housed what
was an otherwise sedentary population. Strategically located at the edge of
the Canadian Shield, the Hurons like their Petun neighbours were able to
trade surplus food for furs, copper, and other commodities of the north.
Hunting was of marginal importance, providing furs for clothing as well as
variety in the diet. Fish was much more a staple than meat. Catching it
was mainly men's work, while women tilled the fields.

The agricultural basis of the economy had implications for every aspect
of life. Social organization, by contrast with that of woodland peoples, was
essentially municipal rather than patriarchal. Clans retained considerable
importance, but so they did in Renaissance Italy. Leaders were officials
although not quite bureaucrats, holders of honorific titles that were handed
down from generation to generation. Public service rather than prowess
was the most reliable route to prestige and status. Iroquoian tribes grouped
themselves in formal although loose leagues and alliances, of which that of
the Five (later Six) Nations was the most elaborate and best known. Inheritance was matrilineal, normally through collateral lines. Decisions of state
were made by men, in formal councils marked by rhetoric of a high order,
but women chose those who were to make them.

Sharing with the Algonquians a common Indian inheritance, mingling
with them frequently, and engaging occasionally in the hunt, the Hurons
and their Iroquoian neighbours resembled them more closely in religious
belief and practice than differences in their way of life might suggest.
Shamanism and the vision quest were common to both cultures, along
with many prescriptions and taboos, while the importance of dreams
among the Iroquoians was attested to by every early missionary. The rites
of Iroquoians, however, were distinctly more elaborate. Voluntary societies
played important roles both socially and religiously, and the passing of the
seasons was marked by traditional feasts and ceremonies. Among these

latter the most spectacular was the Huron Feast of the Dead, at which
every ten years or so the bones of those who had died in the interim were
carefully cleaned and reinterred. Exquisite tortures inflicted on selected
prisoners of war reflected not a particular streak of ferocity but rather a
link with the sun-worship widespread among neighbours to the south as
far as Mexico. The Iroquoian, like other agricultural peoples throughout
the world, conceived nature not simply as ambivalent but rather as a scene
of conflict between two opposing forces. Among the Iroquois these were
represented by twin brothers, Hawenneyu and Hanegoategeh. The former
bestowed all useful and pleasant things, the latter everything harmful,
from poison ivy to discord among friends.[25] This polarity was given ritual
expression in the division of the tribe for ritual purposes into two moieties
or halves.

Among both groups the presence of Europeans had long ceased to be a
novelty when Christian missionaries made contact with them. When Cartier visited the Baie des Chaleurs in 1534, the local Micmacs showed their
familiarity with French ways by welcoming the visitors enthusiastically to
trade while sending their young women to hide in the woods. At first,
contact seemed more beneficial to Indians than to Europeans. They soon
learned to bargain astutely for knives and kettles vastly superior to those
possible with stone-age methods, while many early French traders suffered
financial ruin. From the outset, however, the European presence proved
damaging to Indian societies. Contact brought disruption of sexual mores
and customs of hospitality, along with a commodity, alcohol, with which
few Indians were able to cope. Trade, which inevitably involved Indian
middlemen, had repercussions beyond the area of direct contact. Existing
trading patterns were disrupted, tribal boundaries dislocated, tribal identities sometimes destroyed. Animal resources, never more than adequate for
the existing population, were swiftly depleted. Communicable diseases,
largely unknown in the past, took an enormous toll as they swept the
continent well in advance of Europeans.[26] Most seriously of all, the Indians
must have suffered a severe psychic shock comparable to that which we
might feel if extraterrestrial beings set out to colonize the earth. All of
these things were already part of the experience of the first Indians
encountered by the missionaries.

Europeans and Indians were products of societies so different that the latter did not hesitate to refer to them as different worlds. Europeans were

accustomed to an urbanized, technological society that required for its functioning both religious and secular bureaucracies, with all the paperwork these entailed. Indians, even Iroquoians, lived close to nature and survived by reading and interpreting its signs. It was only natural that each party should be most acutely aware of what the other lacked. The French admired the physique, the bearing, and the rhetorical skill of the Indians. They saw them, however, essentially as people without cities, without roads or bridges, without governments or courts of law, without what they could recognize as a written language, and, most seriously, without civilized manners. The Indians, on their side, marvelled at some of the products of French ingenuity but missed the skills, the feeling for nature, and above all the gravity that were to them the signs of true manhood. Mutual misunderstanding was accentuated by difficulties in communication. Indian languages differed from those of Europe not only in vocabulary but in grammar and in analysis of the process of thinking. Early communication had to do largely with commodities, prices, and articles necessary for survival. The missionaries quickly concluded that Indian languages, while complex and expressive, were ill adapted to the conveyance of abstract ideas. The Indians, observing the missionaries' difficulties, may have concluded with equal legitimacy that the French language suffered from precisely this lack.[27]

The same absence of mutual comprehension applied to religion. The missionaries noted among the Indians no churches, no ordained priesthoods, no regular hours of worship, and no ceremonies that they could readily identify as religious. Their first impression was that the Indians had little if any religion, or at the most a few superstitions, and that their own task would be to fill a vacuum. The Indians in turn saw the French, including the missionaries, routinely breaking their most honoured taboos and failing to take the most elementary ritual precautions required for living off the country. They cannot have thought the French very religious either. Even when each came to recognize a spiritual component in the other's culture, the immediate effect was not always to engender mutual respect. Missionaries still missed in the Indians the reverence and zeal that seemed to Catholics indispensable aspects of religion. Indians observed that Catholic rites failed to give the French any great success in the hunt or, at first, in war. On one occasion they concluded from the length of a religious ceremony that the French were having little success in drawing a response from their deity.[28]

Points of contact began to emerge as initial barriers to communication were broken, and over the years the missionaries would make considerable use of them. The Algonquian *kitchi-manido* or 'Great Spirit,' interpreted by some anthropologists as an impersonal power but regularly described in seventeenth-century accounts as a personal being, needed little adaptation to become the Christian God. Familiarity with the ambiguously divine-human culture hero likewise made the concept of Jesus Christ as mediator between God and man relatively easy to assimilate. Heaven was easily accepted and identified with the happy land to the west or beyond the Milky Way where the dead continued the activities of this life. Hell was more difficult, but the mythology of the Ojibwas and many others made reference to the dangerous crossing at death of a log or other slender bridge from which the ill-prepared might fall to destruction.[29] The dualism native to the Iroquoians lent itself, in some ways, to even readier adaptation. The myth of the cosmic twins suggested parallels to both God and the Devil, and their eternal struggle lent credibility to Christian insistence on the necessity of choosing between the two.

Although some parallels may seem artificial or coincidental, Christianity and native religion were genuinely congenial in the high value they placed on the element of personal encounter. Tribal religion in some parts of the world consists mainly of magical incantation and manipulation of unseen powers. A different quality in both Christianity and Indian religion stems from a common tradition of migration and nomadism, derived in the one case from Israelite wanderings in the desert and in the other from a history in which hunting has bulked large. It led, in both forms of religion, to a quest for personal vision, to prayer conceived as genuine encounter with the unseen, and to periodic prophetic movements combining recall to origins with claims to direct personal inspiration.[30] These resemblances, while not always evident to either missionaries or Indians, nevertheless both aided communication and smoothed the transition from one religion to another.

Helpful as such parallels could be in the presentation of Christianity, they could also mask differences that ran very deep. Expressions of dualism in Indian mythology and Christianity constitute as good an example as any. Contrasts in later Algonquian belief between a good *kitchi-manido* and a bad *madji-manido* are probably regarded correctly as reflections of Christian teaching rather than as native to the culture. The Iroquoian polarity between Hawenneyu and Hanegoategeh, on the other hand, was undoubtedly original. One has to ask, however, how closely it really corresponded to the dualism implicit in Christianity. The Christian sees good and evil, personified in God and the Devil, as locked in a conflict that must ultimately end in the victory of good. In the Iroquoian myth it does not appear that the conflict is ever to be resolved, or even that it needs to be. It seems most realistic to interpret the Iroquoian twins as representing two aspects of nature, one favouring and the other opposing human desires but both ultimately necessary to the equilibrium of a universe in which humanity does not count for everything. In one strand of biblical thought, to be sure, Satan appears as an agent of God who performs the necessary role of man's accuser.[31] Even this is not quite the same as the Iroquoian concept, for it assumes an ultimate resolution that does not seem necessary on Indian presuppositions.

Underlying many differences in detail and undercutting apparent similarities was a profound difference in expectation between Christianity and Indian religion. To the Christian the world as we know it is provisional, preparatory to a new order that will fully reveal the ultimate meaning of history. Religious belief and practice point to this culmination, preparing the individual for life in a new order of existence and calling for the social changes indicated by its imminence. For the Indian the meaning of existence was already given, the purpose of religious practice and even of prophetic movements being to maintain or restore the equilibrium inherent in nature. Christianity calls for repentance from conformity to the present age and for commitment to participation in God's intended transformation of life. The Indian sought alignment with the cosmos so that it might remain in place, so that the moose would appear in due season, the fish bite, and the body be maintained in health. For the Indian the ultimate religious symbol was the circle, represented in the campfire or the circuit of the heavens. For the Christian it might well be an arrow running from the creation of the world through God's redeeming acts in history to the final apocalypse. Misunderstandings were bound to arise from the imposition of one world-view on another. Such terms as 'sin,' 'grace,' and 'faith,' which derived their meaning from one, were not easily comprehended by those accustomed to the other. What could sin be for the Indian, for example, other than the breaking of a taboo or the commission of an offence warranting ostracism from the band?

These differences were considerably complicated by the association of Christianity with a society relatively advanced in science and technology.

Europeans were accustomed to conceive time or space as a continuum that could be measured out at will into discrete portions. Indians were more inclined to associate time and space with experienced events: the time when blueberries ripen, the bend of the river where pickerel can be caught. The point must not be pressed too far, for practically everyone can both measure and experience time and space. The fact remains that often despite themselves, and despite Biard's confidence in the healing power of a bone of St Lawrence O'Toole, the missionaries unwittingly represented a society in process of secularization.[32] Even while they sought to propagate a new religion, their rationalistic assumptions tended to brush away a little of the mystery which the Indian saw inherent in nature.

During the first brief period of encounter these ambiguities were only dimly apparent. The missionaries thought of the Indian mind, so far as religion was concerned, as essentially a *tabula rasa* to be filled with the truths of revelation. The Indians saw the missionaries as shamans of a medicine that so far seemed to promise more benefits to the French than to them. Only with changed circumstances and the formation of Indian congregations would the ability of both missionaries and Indians to bridge some of these chasms of understanding be fully tested.

CHAPTER TWO

'Overthrowing the country'

The return of Canada and Acadia to France in 1632 signalled the beginning of what would be the most ambitious missionary projects of the French era. They were favoured by a royal policy, instituted in 1627 but put into full effect only after the English occupation, that sought to make trade subservient to settlement and the christianization of the native peoples. The trading monopoly of the One Hundred Associates was now to be paralleled by religious monopolies in each colony, and traders and missionaries were to work together for the glory of France and the advancement of the faith. The Canadian field was first offered to the Capuchins, a reforming segment of the Franciscans who took their name from their distinctive hoods and were accounted even more austere than the Récollets. Having accepted a special apostolate to England, they passed up the opportunity on the St Lawrence in favour of the more difficult Acadian field, which they hoped to use as a springboard to the English colonies to the south. Canada was then offered to the Jesuits and accepted by them with alacrity. The Récollets, who had no place in the plan, blamed the Jesuits for their unexpected exclusion. The culprit was more likely Joseph Tremblay, Richelieu's Capuchin adviser for whom the term *éminence grise* was invented, but the Récollet sense of grievance persisted for many years.[1]

On the St Lawrence the first care of the Jesuits was to reopen the work among Montagnais and Algonquins that had lapsed during the English occupation. The Quebec station was immediately reopened and a new one established at Trois-Rivières upon its foundation in 1634. During the winter of 1633–4 Paul Le Jeune, the superior, tried the experiment of wintering with a band of Montagnais hunters. He found the experience extremely trying and was able to learn little of the language. This disappointment reinforced the conviction of the Jesuits that stability of residence was a necessary condition of thorough christianization.

In 1637 the Jesuits commenced their most ambitious project for the Algonquians, a residence at Sillery near Quebec where Montagnais and Algonquins were invited to take up land for farming. Several factors suggested its desirability. Depletion of game resources and concentration on the hunting of fur-bearing animals had already made it necessary to import food from Europe for the small French colony, and the Indians were sometimes so close to starvation that the colonial authorities saw agriculture as their only hope. Many of the Indians agreed, and one eloquent Montagnais was reported as saying: 'We are like seeds which are sown in diverse places or rather like grains of dust scattered in the wind. The country is failing us; there is scarcely any more game in the neighbourhood of the French. Unless we reap something from the earth, we are going to ruin.'[2] Inspired by the 'reductions' or supervised missionary settlements of Paraguay that had been founded some years previously, Sillery also promised the stability Le Jeune desired. It absorbed much missionary energy for some years, and each year's *Relation* contained an enthusiastic report. A companion colony was later established at Cap-de-la-Madeleine.

The focus of Jesuit attention, however, was the Huron country, where both the difficulties and (it was thought) the opportunities were greater than anywhere else. The difficulties sprang from the remoteness and isolation of the mission. At first it was necessary for missionaries to row their share of the back-breaking canoe trip up-river, an ordeal especially hard on greenhorns. Once there, they depended for communication with Quebec and France on Huron traders who might be drowned or attacked by Iroquois on the way or might decide to winter in Quebec. The compensating opportunity was the presence of a people who were sedentary and therefore available for sustained instruction, along with a strategic location that offered the prospect of contact with other sedentary tribes. The Jesuits staked much on the mission.

Although he was unable to arrange transportation in 1633, Brébeuf succeeded in reopening the Huron field with two companions in 1634. Henceforth the order did not spare its resources to build up the mission. Its nucleus always consisted of priests, but in time the Jesuits were able to recruit a corps of *donnés* or lay volunteers whose contracts assured them lifetime support but no wages. In 1639 there were in the Huron country 27 Frenchmen, including 13 Jesuits, constituting a significant portion of the European population of New France. By 1647 there 42 Frenchmen, including 19 Jesuits, and in 1648 the mission was substantially reinforced. Those appointed to the mission generally stayed there, providing a laudable measure of continuity and experience. Over the years, however, there were several changes in organization. Under Brébeuf's direction the missionaries worked in selected Huron villages, eventually securing private accommodation for themselves but spending most of their time mingling with villagers. Jérôme Lalemant, appointed superior in 1638, introduced a new policy of centralization. Henceforth the missionaries lived together at the new residence of Sainte-Marie, where they could say their prayers more regularly and plan their mission more systematically.[3] In 1643, however, it was decided to reopen residences in outlying villages.

At first the Hurons welcomed the missionaries as pledges of French friendship, which as middlemen of the St Lawrence fur trade they naturally valued. The welcome was quickly worn thin by the spread of a disease resembling measles in the year of their arrival and by outbreaks of influenza in 1636 and 1637. Not unnaturally the disease was blamed on the visitors, especially since they were unaffected by the last and most serious epidemic. In 1637 the Huron council repeatedly discussed the death penalty for the missionaries. At one time the latter even gave a farewell feast of the dying in accordance with Huron custom, but no blow fell. In the same year, however, they baptized their first adult convert in good health. By 1639 they could report three hundred baptisms, including those of more than a hundred healthy adults, but a serious epidemic of smallpox that year reduced this flourishing congregation to 'three or four heads of families, and a few old women' in the following year. Recovery from this setback was slow, but by 1646 there were probably about four hundred professing Huron Christians.[4]

Meanwhile, despite difficulties and reverses, the missionaries had made Huronia a base for further outreach. In 1639 Lalemant opened a mission among the neighbouring Petuns. In 1640 Brébeuf led a small party to the country of the Neutrals to the south, although with little result beyond annoyance to Hurons who sensed a threat to their trade monopoly. The same year was marked by visits to the Nipissings, already familiar from their custom of wintering among the Hurons, and to the Ojibwas of Sault Ste Marie. Another short-lived mission resulted indirectly from the work among the Hurons. In 1642 a Huron flotilla homeward-bound from Trois-Rivières was intercepted by a party of Mohawks. Isaac Jogues and a *donné*, René Goupil, could have escaped but chose to offer spiritual succour to their companions. Goupil was killed after he had been seen making the sign of the cross over a child. Jogues, after preliminary torture, was adopted by a Mohawk woman and eventually helped to escape by the Dutch. In 1646, when the Mohawks showed some signs of friendship, he volunteered to return to them as an ambassador of peace. On the day after his arrival at Ossernenon he was struck down by a hatchet blow, apparently because of a suspicion that the contents of a small chest left behind on his first visit had tainted the corn crop. During the late 1640s, as the pace of conversion among the Hurons accelerated, the Jesuits concentrated their efforts on them and the Petuns. The *Relation* of 1648–9 reported more than 2700 baptisms in the previous thirteen months.[5]

The Capuchins, unlike the Jesuits, were never able to enforce their monopoly. Acadia during much of the seventeenth century consisted of fiefdoms of semi-independent traders who sought commissions from the crown as licences for personal profit. For a religious order to be in favour with one of these could be a distinct disadvantage in dealing with the others. In 1632, when they arrived at La Hève on the Atlantic coast with a colonizing expedition under Isaac de Razilly, the Capuchins found that two Récollets had already reached Acadia in 1630 with a crew sent to revictual the veteran trader Charles de Saint-Etienne de La Tour. The presence of the Récollets became a distinct embarrassment when the death of Razilly gave rise to a comic-opera war of succession between La Tour and Razilly's lieutenant, Charles de Menou d'Aulnay. Each order backed the claims of its sponsor with zest until 1645, when La Tour's attempts to recruit support in Protestant Boston led the Récollets to abandon him. The east coast of Acadia from Cape Breton to Gaspé was the domain of Nicolas Denys. Here in 1629 the Jesuits opened a mission at St Ann's on Cape Breton Island, and by 1646 they had established four missions. Oddly, their only recorded jurisdictional dispute with the Capuchins concerned the Kennebec area of Maine, which they reached overland in 1646 in consequence of contacts with Abenakis at Quebec.[6] Capuchin sensitivity to territorial encroachments clearly increased as one approached New England.

Despite its handicaps the Capuchin enterprise was serious and well supported, and at the height of Aulnay's power from 1645 to 1650 it achieved

a considerable measure of stability. At least thirty Capuchins served in
Acadia at one time or another. Some of them maintained a school at Port
Royal where French and Micmac children were educated together. Others
served stations at Saint John and Penobscot, while La Hève and St Peter's
on Cape Breton Island were among numerous places occasionally visited.
Probably the most adventurous friar was Father Balthazar of Paris, who
from his headquarters at Nipisiguit (now Bathurst) spent the years from
1648 to 1654 itinerating among the scattered Micmacs between the Baie
des Chaleurs and the Strait of Canso.[7] Aulnay, who has been treated
unsympathetically by most historians, appears in Capuchin annals as a
benevolent protector of his flock of settlers and an active supporter of
missionary work.

Both Huron and Acadian missions flourished briefly and came to sudden ends. At the moment of its greatest promise the days of the Huron
mission were already numbered. Each summer throughout the 1640s the
Iroquois pressed attacks upon the tribes allied with the French and occasionally even threatened the tiny French settlements. In 1648 the Iroquois
overran the outlying village of Saint Joseph, where Antoine Daniel died in
his church as he sought to baptize and absolve all whom he could. In 1649
they captured Saint Louis and Saint Ignace, where they killed Brébeuf
and his companion Gabriel Lalemant after the tortures which they customarily inflicted on distinguished prisoners. Many Hurons, both Christian
and other, shared their fate. The demoralized Hurons soon fled to nearby
Christian Island, where they were decimated by starvation over the succeeding winter despite all the relief that the missionaries could give. They
then decided to abandon their ravaged country, and the Huron mission
was over. That of the Capuchins lasted until 1654, when one of the New
England raids that punctuated Acadian history forced them to return to
France. Despite persistent efforts they would not regain a foothold in Acadia until 1894. Yet there was one exception. In 1656 Father Balthazar
succeeded in rejoining 'his dear disciples in Christ,' eventually to die
among them at a place and time unknown.[8]

After a period of preliminary probing that left little apparent residue of
Christianity in native societies, the return of Canada to the French in 1632
heralded the first systematic efforts to plant the faith. In the course of
these ambitious experiments many assumptions were made, approaches
tried, and problems encountered that have been repeated with variations

in many settings over three centuries. The period has a special interest, therefore, as establishing an initial pattern with which others may be compared. Although the Capuchin enterprise in Acadia may not have been much less ambitious than its Jesuit counterpart in Huronia, even its industrious chronicler Candide de Nant has been unable to unearth many details of its day-to-day functioning. We are thus left largely dependent for first-hand information upon the Jesuit *Relations*, supplemented by the Récollet accounts of Le Clercq and Sagard and by occasional references in government documents and the works of explorers. In reading the *Relations* one must always be aware that their primary function was to stimulate interest in the missions, above all among potential donors. For the most part, however, they maintain an admirable level of frankness and allow us to see the missions, if not with complete objectivity, at least much as the missionaries saw them.

The primary aim of the missionaries, one is constantly reminded in the *Relations*, was to save Indian souls. The contrast between the joys of heaven and the torments of a literally conceived hell, so alien to the twentieth-century mind-set, was drilled into the Jesuit imagination in a celebrated meditation during the first week of the spiritual exercises of St Ignatius. Whatever long-term or overarching goals may have been sought by the missionaries, there was none that would not take second place when opportunity offered to affect the eternal destiny of an individual Indian. The missionaries also saw themselves as agents of French civilization. During these early years all missionaries conceived of France and the Roman Catholic Church as twin pillars of an indivisible structure. When they appealed to Indians to accept their faith, they also urged them, almost as a matter of course, to accept military alliance and trading partnership with the French. They rejoiced when Indians preferred French culture to their own, seeing in a taste for things French a significant step towards Christian faith. They planned their seminaries as agents of assimilation and sent a few of their brightest prospects to France for finishing.[9]

Beyond the immediate objectives of missionary policy there loomed the vision of new provinces won for the faith and of reborn Indian nations provided with priesthoods, monasteries, and cathedrals reminiscent of Europe. Anticipating by more than two centuries Canada'a choice of a national motto, a Jesuit of the period predicted: 'he shall rule ... from the great river St. Lawrence, which is the chief of all rivers, to the remotest confines of the earth, even to the furthest boundaries of America and to the Islands of Japan ... and beyond.' For the most part this vision was merely implicit in Jesuit writings, however, betraying its presence chiefly in a providential sense that pervaded the operation. Celestial portents were linked with the baptism of a dying Indian, opposition attributed to the rage of demons who anticipated inevitable defeat. The same sense of divine direction steeled the missionaries to face the hardships of their work, for since the early centuries it had been a Christian commonplace that without a cross there could be no crown. Long before the need arose, Brébeuf had inscribed in his journal a vow 'never to fail, on my side, in the grace of martyrdom.'[10]

A major premise of the Jesuit missionary approach was the existence of considerable continuity between the natural endowments of humanity and the supernatural grace of God. All peoples, they believed, have apprehensions of divinity that require not denial but rather completion through the Christian revelation. All, likewise, have elements of natural goodness that become effective for salvation only when God imparts his supernatural aid, especially through the sacraments. Accordingly Jesuits in all mission fields systematically sought out elements of culture and thought that might provide soil in which the gospel could take root and grow. Copious references to Indian customs in early missionary literature were thus expressions not of idle curiosity but of an urgent theological compulsion. This relaxed approach to universal human nature was balanced by a militancy characteristic of the Catholic Reformation. One of the most crucial of the spiritual exercises was that of the Two Standards, in which the initiate was called upon to picture armies of Christ and Satan in mortal combat and to identify himself in imagination and will as one of those enrolled under Christ's banner.[11] French Jesuits who conducted parish missions in Huguenot areas of their homeland in order to win back heretics to the Catholic fold undertook their task as a holy war in the spirit of the Two Standards. They found it equally natural to apply military metaphors in the New World when opposition manifested itself.

These presuppositions had to be applied and tested in field experience. The Jesuits surpassed others in the flexibility of their approach, committing themselves as an order to no particular methodology of mission but allowing circumstances to dictate strategy. The first requirement was to learn the local languages, not only for preaching but for translating Scripture and liturgical texts, for interpreters were scarce and better acquainted with the lingo of trade than with the subtleties of theology. This was a major task in itself, for Indians were sometimes reluctant teachers, and mingling in the cabins was time-consuming. The languages themselves, although regular, were extremely complex and as yet unprovided with grammars or lexicons. Even when the missionaries had begun to learn them, they had difficulty in expressing the ideas they wished to convey, failing to find words not only for God and the Trinity but for such biblical figures as flocks and vineyards. The Jesuits, although making the inevitable mistake at the outset of trying to conform local Indian languages to Latin norms familiar from their own education, soon proved themselves through their mental discipline and pragmatic outlook much better linguists than the Récollets. Ability to communicate was a major factor in the effectiveness of individual missionaries, and the Jesuits soon had an invaluable stock of competent linguists.[12]

Learning the language was useful only if one could gain a hearing. The Jesuits proved themselves adept in making use of both European experience and native custom for this purpose. The first Jesuits in Acadia gathered an audience by making a bold appearance to the accompaniment of impressive ceremony and chanting. When they had become familiar with local customs, the Jesuits of Huronia made a formal approach with presents that requested the adherence of the community to Christianity; the favourable response demanded by politeness at least gave the missionaries some public standing. Another technique was to follow up such public assemblies with more select gatherings to which chiefs and elders were invited with gifts of tobacco. In 1638 Brébeuf was recognized as a chief, a status that gave him the privilege of summoning public meetings on his own authority.[13]

The precise nature of the appeal depended on the missionary appraisal of the religious capacity of the hearers. The search for bridges to the gospel turned up many positive qualities: the Indians were unacquisitive (Sagard, the Franciscan lay brother); possessed of a remarkable sense of justice (Biard); 'hardly barbarians, save in name' (Bressani, who had undergone Iroquois torture). Brébeuf, who proved the most persevering natural theologian, concluded cautiously that by the grace of God some of their superstitions might be turned into true religion 'like spoils carried off from the enemy.' The general view, however, was that Indian apprehensions of God were too vague to provide a useful point of contact. Despite their disappointment the missionaries concluded – mistakenly, as they soon learned – that at worst Indian religion would offer little resistance to the spread of Christianity. This view of the Indian mind as religiously a *tabula rasa* suggested indoctrination in Catholic belief and practice as the most promising approach. The necessity of choosing between a hell of fire and a blissful heaven prepared only for the baptized was a staple theme, hammered home in public addresses and illustrated by many lurid pictures. Indians were also taught pious practices and included in religious processions so that, in Biard's words, 'they become accustomed to act as Christians, to become so in reality in his time.'[14]

Later, when the Jesuits realized that Indian religious beliefs went much deeper than they had supposed, their militant aspect came to the fore. They met objections with a directness incompatible with Indian conceptions of courtesy, seeking to catch out questioners in contradictions and openly ridiculing traditional religious practices. They frequently enlisted the aid of European science and technology, impressing the Indians with mechanical gadgets and demythologizing their world by predicting eclipses. They quickly recognized the shamans as their most formidable opponents, vacillating between denouncing them as servants of Satan and attempting to convict them of simple chicanery. In such contests they sometimes failed to carry their audiences; when Le Jeune attempted to expose a Montagnais shaman in 1634, he merely exposed himself to public ridicule. Nor were the missionaries consistent in their appeal to the regularity of the natural order. While rejecting native miracles, they built up their own prestige in 1635 by successfully praying for rain.[15]

Since most arguments depended for their effectiveness on the acceptance of unfamiliar presuppositions, and since Catholicism was not only an intellectual message but a way of salvation, the missionaries placed as much reliance on images as on words. The Jesuit *Relations* abound in references to a remarkable assortment of non-verbal aids: pictures of holy subjects or of the sufferings of lost souls; rosaries, medals, and portable statues; coloured beads or pieces of fruit as prizes for successful memorization; mnemonic devices such as coloured sticks for tallying sins or following the church calendar; ceremonies, chants, and processions on holy days or on such personal occasions as baptisms, marriages, and funerals; the mission church itself, with its cross, bell, and candles.[16] Through such means the Indians were surrounded by a Catholic ambience that awakened their interest, stimulated their emotions, invited their participation, and could even accompany them on the hunt or at war.

The intended culmination of this process of persuasion and instruction was baptism, a means of salvation in itself and the gateway to an imposing structure of sacramental supports. So crucial was baptism that missionaries went to great lengths to ensure that no one died without it. They sometimes baptized children surreptitiously on various pretexts, but in the case of adults the rules of the church required consent and, unless there was immediate danger of death, a measure of Christian knowledge. Each deathbed was therefore the call to a constant vigil of persuasion, the arrival of each Iroquois captive destined for torture the signal for an intense spiritual assault that would continue until victory or until the victim's death. Such scenes were occasions of rejoicing by the Jesuits, who reasoned that if these children had survived or these Iroquois had escaped torture they would almost certainly have gone to perdition.[17]

Adults in good health posed a different problem. On them the future of native Christianity clearly depended, but experience showed that more often than not they would revert to their former ways. In this case they would profane the sacrament, discredit Christianity, and, if they committed mortal sin, leave themselves in a worse state than before. It was, therefore, necessary to test carefully the sincerity of each applicant. In principle the Jesuits were less rigorous than the Récollets, believing that baptism itself could have a converting effect. Actual practice varied with the circumstances. Hoping to convert entire communities rather than isolated individuals, the Jesuits were rather free with baptism at first in Huronia. When this practice led to some scandals, they restricted baptism to tested Christians of great age or of proven fidelity in marriage. In the last years of the mission, when a mass movement showed promise of embracing the entire confederacy, they eased their practice again somewhat.[18]

Whatever the degree of strictness, missionaries always had to be on the alert for ways of ensuring the stability of their converts. One method was education. In 1636 the Jesuits began to send Huron boys from prominent families to a recently established seminary at Quebec, well within the range of French and missionary influence. They soon found that young boys lacked status and therefore influence at home. Their next attempt was with a school for adult converts of which Brébeuf took charge in 1641, but little came of this experiment either. The formation of stable families was soon seen to depend on marriages within the community, and means for providing dowries for Christian girls were eagerly sought in

France. Another precaution was the removal of temptation in the form of promiscuous French traders. The Jesuits of the Huron mission replaced them quickly with their own employees and later with the reliable and dedicated *donnés*.[19] They also instituted some measures of segregation from non-Christian Indians, although they were restrained in these by their unwillingness to impede the progress of conversion.

Converts were submitted to a strict regime of disciplined living without precedent in Indian society. Everywhere the missionaries enforced the ecclesiastical system of penances, including public humiliations for scandalous sins. At Sillery, where the Jesuits were trustees for the sedentary Indians, discipline was publicly administered, with flogging for such offences as listening to a pagan suitor. Enforcing such a regime would have been impossible for the priests without assistance from native leaders: *dogiques* both male and female in Huronia to catechize and baptize in emergencies, captains for secular and ecclesiastical affairs at Sillery and Tadoussac. The missionaries were always in charge, however, maintaining a network of information and even personally watching over the cabins. At the other end of the scale, sodalities were organized for the growth and grace of the more devout. At least one Indian, the exemplary Huron convert Joseph Chihwatenha, was put through the spiritual exercises.[20]

In line with their assumption that colonization was essentially auxiliary to the missions, both Jesuits and Capuchins looked to secular authorities for support and received it at first in generous measure. Aulnay became patron of the Capuchin school at Port Royal. Jean de Lauson, director of the One Hundred Associates, proved a friend of the Jesuits from the beginning, and the appointment of the Jesuit-educated Charles Huault de Montmagny as governor in 1635 confirmed the alliance. The company was obligated by its charter to maintain three priests in each community it established. In addition the Jesuits received an annual government grant of five thousand livres along with certain fishing rights, and over the years they were assigned a number of properties that would figure in later Canadian history as the Jesuit Estates. Special privileges for Christian Indians, such as the right to carry firearms, served both as inducements to conversion and as means of cementing friendship. Jérôme Lalemant would have welcomed even more direct support, regretting the lack of 'that sharp sword that serves the Church in so holy a manner to give authority to her Decrees, to maintain Justice, and to curb the insistence of those who trample under feet the holiness of her Mysteries.'[21]

Equally important were the moral and spiritual resources of the colony. Under the twin patronage of the company and the Jesuits, Quebec took on during the 1630s such an atmosphere of piety that the missionaries exulted that the Christianity of early centuries was being reborn and that even those who had been careless about religion at home were transformed in New France.[22] This sense of being engaged in a sacred enterprise was intensified by the arrival in 1639 of two convents of nuns, Ursulines to teach Indian girls and hospitallers to win Indians by kindness. Although neither was conspicuously successful among the Indians, the Ursuline superior Marie de l'Incarnation and her lay friend Madame de La Peltrie were able to raise even higher the moral tone of Quebec society and to inspire it with something of Marie's mystical vision. The climax of this holy adventure, which was followed with great interest in France, was the foundation of Montreal in 1642 not as a mere trading post but as a Christian beacon far out in Indian country. Much reliance was placed on such influences to impress upon surrounding Indians the merits of Christianity, although at first the little community of devotees at Ville-Marie was too vulnerable to Iroquois raids to attract many Algonquins.

Among those who have sought to christianize the Indians of Canada, the early Jesuits stand out as models of self-dedication. Coming for the most part from well-to-do backgrounds, they were prepared to surrender not only their lives but also comforts and consolations that must have been in some ways even more difficult to part with. Their chief motive was the well-being of the Indians as they understood it, doubtless along with the salvation of their own souls, and the seeking of power and dealing in furs for which they have often been criticized had ultimately no purpose other than to facilitate the success of their missions. To this task the Jesuits also brought a training that has never been equalled by later Canadian missionary agencies, combining a fine-tuning of the mind with the cultivation of methodical habits. In planning their work they were always flexible with regard to proximate goals, clear and unwavering in the pursuit of ultimate ones. On a Jesuit mission all problems were thought through, nothing left to chance.

The less attractive qualities of the Jesuits constituted almost a mirror image of their virtues. In Europe the complaint was often made, doubtless to their bewilderment, that they were too clever for their own good. In Canada as well their plans often seemed to be so completely the result of calculation as to exclude the possibility of spontaneously human behaviour. They came with ready-made answers that seemed to them so incontrovertible that they showed little curiosity about the questions or concerns of their hearers. Objections to their teaching were mere obstacles to be overcome, not genuine difficulties to be wrestled with. Art, literature, and even charity never seemed to be valued for their own sake but rather utilized as bait for souls in need of salvation. This obsessive pursuit of a single goal could be self-defeating. Lack of concern for the societies in which they laboured, other than for what under Jesuit direction they might become, often prevented genuine understanding of them and resulted in psychological blunders of the first magnitude.

One result was a narrowness of outlook that prevented the Jesuits from envisaging a form of Christianity to which the Indians themselves could contribute significantly. They were, to be sure, far more open than the Récollets to the possibility of distinctively Indian Christian communities. A visitor to a Huron or Montagnais mission could not have missed such indigenous expressions of Christianity as chants in the native tongue, possible through a permission not accorded in Europe; the punctuation of services by informal questioning and commentary; the continuation of such burial customs as the placing of symbolic possessions in the grave; and concessions to Indian taste in ecclesiastical art. The Jesuits were not particularly troubled by such adaptations, admitting some relativity of cultural values.[23] While they were prepared to tolerate, adapt, and use elements of native practice, however, there is little indication that they expected any significant enrichment of Christianity from them. Like other expressions of the human spirit these were merely means to the greater end of salvation.

Indian response to the missionaries was determined, at first, almost entirely by the relation of the latter to the French trade goods upon which they were becoming increasingly dependent. The Hurons received the Jesuits into their villages and allowed them to proclaim their message simply because the French authorities made this a condition of trade. The arrangement was one they could readily understand, for in Indian societies commercial arrangements always involved a personal bond between the participants and often called for an exchange of guests who combined the roles of adoptive kinsmen and of hostages. This situation placed the missionaries in some danger, for, as they sometimes ruefully observed, an Indian with a sense of grievance against any Frenchman might wreak his

vengeance on them. On the other hand, concern to maintain trading relations with the French was the factor beyond all others that led the Hurons
to tolerate the presence of the Jesuits and even to admit them to their
councils at a time when they were still feared and distrusted.[24] Despite
many rumours and alarms, no missionary is known to have been struck
down by a trading partner of the French.

It did not take the Indians long to recognize that the missionaries maintained a traffic with the spirit world that distinguished them from other
Frenchmen. Like their own shamans the blackrobes handled sacred
objects, foretold the future, and performed rites in aid of the sick. At first
their procedures were of limited interest to the Indians, who had proven
ways of propitiating the spirits and were not greatly impressed by the spiritual potency of the French as demonstrated by success in coping with
nature. On the other hand, the remedies of the missionaries were generally
acceptable if they proved helpful. Why not? There was nothing in the
principles of native religion to limit access to spiritual power to a single
cult, and borrowing from the religious repertoire of other tribes was a
common practice. The early Récollets in Huronia had already established
some reputation for ability to deal with the spirit world, although after
successfully ending a rainy spell Sagard was hard put to explain why he
could not make the ears of the local dogs curl like those of the dogs introduced by the French. On the same understanding a Huron took a picture
of Christ to war for assistance against his enemies, and a woman reported
that baptism gave her such a sense of peace that she wanted it again.[25]
Even the teachings of the missionaries carried some supernatural sanction,
for it would naturally be assumed that like the shamans they had received
their messages directly from the spirits in dreams.

Unfortunately for the missionaries, increasing recognition of their spiritual powers could also give rise to apprehension and suspicion. Spiritual
power was fraught with ambiguity, for it could be used either to help or to
harm. Sorcery was the usual explanation in Indian societies for abnormal
or merely unexplained events, and since the line between shamans and
sorcerers was never very clearly drawn, there was always a certain amount
of suspicion in the air. The missionaries, combining such unfamiliar habits
as going about at night with pretensions to supernatural power, would in
the most favourable circumstances have awakened serious doubts. The
epidemics and defeats that invariably seemed to follow their arrival put a
hard edge on these suspicions. Sorcery was the charge on which Jogues was

killed by the Iroquois in the customary way by a sudden hatchet blow, and the crosses, bells, clocks, and other strange objects which the missionaries handled were sources of constant alarm. Charges of witchcraft may sometimes have been convenient expressions of a dislike that had other sources, but we cannot mistake the sincerity of a Huron youth who offered to return a stolen crucifix in return for assurance that pestilence would spare his village. The missionaries themselves admitted that the charges against them were plausible and especially that their practice of baptizing mainly the dying led inevitably to the conviction that baptism was fatal.[26] Perhaps, many Indians reasoned, the activities of the missionaries were merely devices by which the French treacherously planned to destroy them.

Gradually the Indians began to recognize that more was involved even than hexes individual or collective. The missionaries were not merely religious practitioners who offered additions to the existing stock of spiritual remedies but propagandists out to replace them with a totally different system. Realization was slow in dawning because the Christian concept of exclusive truth was beyond Indian experience or comprehension. As it became clear that the missionaries were in earnest, however, and as they began to make some progress towards their objectives, indifference gave way among traditionalists to alarm. The Indians could see, all too plainly, that the missionaries were threatening to subvert their value-structure and way of life. Being accustomed to individual decision on every question, they greatly disliked the authoritarianism evident in the missionary approach; in Le Jeune's words, they had 'great difficulty in abandoning the wicked liberty of the Savages and submitting to the yoke of God.' They particularly dreaded the social rift implied in the separation of Christian converts from others after death. They were also aware of more practical difficulties. Strict application of the rule of monogamy, for example, could condemn a deserted husband to a wandering life or expose an abandoned wife to starvation. Most seriously of all, the missionaries threatened to deprive the Indians of rituals and taboos which they regarded as essential to successful hunting, good health, and even survival. 'I believe that your proposition is impossible,' a Huron chief complained to Brébeuf; '... you are talking of overthrowing the country.'[27]

A closer look at Christianity had for most Indians the effect of hardening indifference into rejection, and the missionaries among the Hurons had to admit that the 'best minds' were not those most inclined towards Christianity. The most determined opponents of Christianity were the shamans. Often placed on the defensive by missionary propaganda, they had their innings when important feasts recalled tribal traditions or when illness stimulated a demand for proven remedies. In time, as Christianity began to threaten national cohesion, countermovements took more definite shape. In 1640, in the wake of a smallpox epidemic, a young Huron was warned in a vision by 'the one whom the French wrongly call Jesus' that only the expulsion of the blackrobes would save his village from new scourges. A young man of Tadoussac proposed a similar blend of old and new, combining a call to belief in Christ with the practice of polygamy and condemnation of Christian prayers. Perhaps the most effective form of resistance, however, was psychological. 'They will believe all you please, or at least will not contradict you,' Le Caron had observed long before, 'and they will let you, too, believe what you will.'[28]

That the spread of Christianity was resisted need occasion no surprise, given the conservatism of Indian societies and the incompatibility of European and Indian world-views. Rejection was not the only response to missionary preaching, however, and over the years sizeable Christian communities came into being. First came individual conversions, sometimes precipitated by personal crises but more often the result of gradual familiarization. Individuals often brought other members of their families, who clustered into congregations that might disintegrate in periods of conservative reaction but tended in time to become more stable. By the mid-1640s extended families, bands, and even tribes were beginning to move towards Christianity in what missionary literature calls 'mass movements.' This phenomenon could be observed not only in long-cultivated Huronia but on the Saguenay and beyond. It was not always the direct result of missionary activity. Bands of Attikamegues on the St Maurice who had never seen Europeans picked up fragments of Catholicism from their neighbours and rushed to accept baptism when it became available. If success is to be measured by the speed of conversion, few modern missions could compare with that of New France. The results surprised the missionaries themselves, for in 1640 Le Jeune wrote that he had hoped for two Christian families before his death.[29]

Early conversions reflected a variety of motives. To begin with, there were nonconformists in Indian society who seem almost to have been waiting for the missionaries to appear. Sagard noted that many Huron women were terrified of spirits, and Lescarbot's comment that among the Micmacs only Christians were able to go out boldly at night may explain some conversions.[30] Some individuals may have been looking for excuses not to participate in community rituals of sharing. Doubtless others were simply misfits. Some Indians, impressed by the potency of missionary *mana*, probably saw in conversion a means of sharing in its exercise or at least insuring themselves against its harmful effects.[31] Others may have been attracted by the colour of Catholic ritual or captured by its ambience of busy devotion.

Despite this variety, conversion to Christianity and some form of affiliation with the French usually went hand in hand. That Christian profession may sometimes have represented little more than a calculated effort to solidify commercial relations by securing the favour of the missionaries is suggested by a correlation between conversion and direct involvement in the fur trade to which Trigger has called attention. More reputable converts, such as Noël Negabamat of Sillery and Joseph Chihwatenha of Huronia, seem to have sensed that the French represented the wave of the future and to have concluded that only the French faith would enable the Indians to cope with French technology. Reminding his fellow Hurons that they had not rejected French implements when these had proven to be 'incomparably better and more convenient that our stone hatchets and our wooden and earthen vessels,' Chihwatenha suggested that it would be logical 'to believe what they believe, and to live compatibly to this belief.'[32]

Later mass movements had a somewhat different origin. Long before the destruction of Huronia the missionaries recognized that calamities, although occasions of temporary hostility to Christianity, were in the long run the most powerful incentives to its acceptance. Mass conversion followed social breakdown for reasons that were in part social and economic. Epidemics that carried away many elderly custodians of tradition created a serious vacuum of leadership which the missionaries were available to fill, while the disorganization caused by military defeats called for the acceptance of a pattern of imposed order that only the missionaries seemed able to provide. With accelerating conversion, too, the old rituals seemed to lose their effectiveness.[33] There may also have been a more specific reason. Death, both individual and corporate, became during this period a major preoccupation of Indian communities. Indians had always had methods of dealing with death, among the Hurons very elaborate ones. These had been intended to operate within the normal rhythm of life, however, and a strong reluctance to discuss the dead indicated that even in this context they were not totally satisfactory. The missionaries of the period, with two centuries of pestilence in their immediate historical background, were by contrast familiars of death. In turning to them Indians were enabled not merely to face death with resignation but even to derive from it a sense of spiritual exaltation. Christianity, for many, was essentially a way of dying well.[34]

By the middle of the seventeenth century most of the Indians of Acadia and the St Lawrence basin had some awareness of what they called 'the prayer' in distinction from the traditional invocation of spirits. From Sillery and Trois-Rivières the new religion was making its way to the Montagnais of the Saguenay, the Attikamegues of the St Maurice, and the Abenakis of the Kennebec and the Penobscot. There were Christian cells in most villages of the Hurons and Petuns, and Ossossané, where the Jesuits had worked almost from their arrival, was becoming known as a Christian village. The effects of Christianity varied greatly in degree from place to place and from person to person. A good many Indians postponed baptism until the approach of death, having come to regard it as insurance for the future life rather than as a means of a quick entry into it. Others were content to allow the priests to instruct their families while themselves maintaining the traditional ways. Even among actual converts there was a fair proportion of opportunists, and many whose adherence was genuine readily resorted to the old ways in illness or adversity, in the company of non-Christians, or simply under the impulsion of dreams.[35]

In view of their brief experience of the faith, however, most Indian converts displayed remarkable fervour and staunchness. They attended services regularly regardless of weather or distance, celebrated feast days with élan, observed fasts punctiliously even under conditions of extreme scarcity, and treasured rosaries and medals. Having accepted the difficult concept of sin, they engaged in the struggle against it with gusto. The Christians of Sillery showed a zeal for punishing delinquents that frightened unbelievers and struck even the priests as excessive. A Montagnais of Tadoussac created a stir by flagellating himself on the rocks within sight of French observers. At the same place, according to Lalemant, a little girl informed the priests of the faults of others 'with a zeal and childish sweetness wholly lovable.' Some of the new Christians were capable of considerable self-reliance. In Huronia they carried on services in the absence of priests, while bands in the north woods kept faithful track of fasts and holy days during the hunting season. Some Indians became zealous missionaries for their new faith. Membertou urged Biard and Massé to learn Micmac quickly so that they might impart the information he would need to become a teacher himself, while the Jesuits conceded that the Huron

Etienne Totiri had been a more effective evangelist among the Neutrals
than they had been.[36]

Fervent as they might be in their Catholicism, these converts carried
over many of the features of the old religion into the new. Priests performed the functions once expected of shamans, and for the most part
their miracles were not greatly different in kind. Crosses and holy medals
replaced amulets and medicine bags and were doubtless understood to have
much the same virtues. The regulations of the church, with their rhythm
of abstinence and feasting, corresponded to old taboos and ritual requirements and were kept in much the same spirit. Among the taboos of the
new religion was a prohibition on traditional ceremonies. Converts were
thoroughly aware of it and kept it as their strength allowed, but an attachment to guardian angels that pleased the Jesuits recalled the personal
manidos that had traditionally given direction to life. For the most part
Indian Christians did not cease to believe in the reality of the familiar spirit
world or in the potency of the rites associated with it. They could scarcely
have been expected to do so when the priests themselves had difficulty in
deciding whether shamans were mere charlatans or had some access to
demonic power.[37] Conversion itself represented not so much a rejection of
the old way as a conviction that Christianity offered more powerful *mana*
for a changed situation.

The Jesuits, confident that nature could provide a foundation on which
a superstructure of grace might be raised, were not unduly troubled by
these carry-overs. They were unimpressed by Tertullian's insistence that
conversion to Christianity should represent a clean break with the past,
preferring the advice of Pope Gregory the Great that churches should
deliberately be built on the sites of pagan shrines in order to retain the
adherence of those who had formerly worshipped at them. To them the
new converts were pilgrims on the road to the celestial city, and it would
matter little when they arrived that they carried with them some dust
picked up on the journey. Others have taken a less positive view, adducing
this continuity with traditional faith and practice as evidence of the imma-
turity and superficiality of Indian Christianity. The issue has remained
controversial, and we must return to it in due course.

The impact of Christianity on the total fabric of Indian society varied
greatly from one area to another. In readily accessible Acadia missionary
instruction was seldom able to compete with secular French example. The
Capuchins claimed some success in mixing Indian and Acadian pupils, but
this effort was limited to Port Royal. The Jesuits found that the results of

their teaching were repeatedly undone by the visits of promiscuous sailors and by the ready availability of alcohol. Among the Hurons Christianity had little effect on social and economic patterns, but in the final years a Christian majority at Ossossané was able to suppress traditional religious practices and to enforce a rigid code of sexual morality.[38] Changes in lifestyle were most far-reaching at Sillery, where the economic basis of society was considerably transformed and where Christianity as taught by the Jesuits was the accepted norm of behaviour. Even there the traditional pattern of the winter hunt was not broken, however, and the cultivation of corn by Indians in the St Lawrence Valley was not an innovation. Wherever Christianity was effectively planted, one could observe a tightening of communal family discipline and a strengthening of the bonds of authority. Although these ran counter to traditional Indian individualism, they may well have served a useful function in a period of rapid and sometimes chaotic change.

The centres from which Christian influence was beginning to radiate in the second quarter of the seventeenth century were not destined for permanence. The forced departure of the Capuchins from Acadia was followed by a hiatus in missionary work that compelled a practically new start there. The destruction of Huronia brought an end to the Jesuit dream of establishing a firm base in the heart of North America from which the gospel could be carried to tribes otherwise inaccessible. The same wave of Iroquois aggression forced the inhabitants of Sillery to take refuge in Quebec, where they were so demoralized by contact with the French that their brave experiment in tilling the soil was never resumed. By mid-century little remained of the missionary structures that had been constructed with such care and at such cost. Such a débâcle calls for explanation, and it is only natural to ask whether by disrupting the Indians' value-systems and undermining their military virtues the missionaries may not have contributed significantly to the material destruction of the peoples whose souls they sought to save. The question puts itself with particular urgency in the case of the Hurons. Was the complaint that Brébeuf was 'overthrowing the country' a prescient statement of future fact? Many Indians of the time made precisely this accusation, and it has been echoed many times since.[39]

Put in such stark terms, the question does not admit a positive answer. European intrusion disturbed the course of Indian history in so many ways that it is virtually impossible to isolate the missionary factor. In Acadia and at Sillery the missionaries could be accused, at worst, only of failing to solve problems that were of others' making. Even the destruction of the Hurons may have been due less to internal factors than to the waging by the Iroquois of an unfamiliar and more purposeful style of warfare while others were still thinking in terms of raids for revenge and glory. Such an interpretation is suggested, at any rate, by the almost simultaneous destruction of the Petuns, who had been much less affected by missionary contact, and of the Neutrals and Eries, who were virtually untouched by it. By a strange turn of events, indeed, some of the Senecas attributed their victory over the Eries to the intervention of the Christian God. It was singularly unfortunate for the Hurons that Christians and traditionalists among them were at odds when consensus was most needed and that many traditionalists preferred surrender to the Iroquois to the triumph of Christianity at home.[40] On the other hand, it was only after the traditional approach had proved inadequate to defend their homeland that a significant proportion of the Hurons embraced Christianity. We can never know whether a thoroughly christianized Huronia, mobilized for common action after the European manner and presumably better supplied with French guns, would have put up a better show of resistance.

Valid as such qualifications may be, however, they fail to extinguish a nagging doubt. Aboriginal societies, while often appearing proud and fierce to Europeans who encounter them, prove extraordinarily fragile when confronted by an advanced technology. No matter how adaptable they may have been to changes of circumstance over millennia, they are not geared to cope with radically new and aggressive approaches to nature. Changing such a society in one respect is bound to set in motion a train of unpredictable consequences. To such subtleties the missionaries were almost totally insensitive. The Récollets changed all they could, the Jesuits only what seemed necessary, but neither saw much need to gauge the effects of change on sensitive and long-protected cultures. The absence of a science of ethnology in their time gave them ample excuse for this neglect, but the unfortunate result was that little effort was made to preserve what was precious in the old or even to ease the transition to the new. The charge of 'overthrowing the country' in this sense would remain a crucial issue in the encounter between the emissaries of Christianity and the Indians of Canada.

CHAPTER THREE

After the Earthquake

The Jesuit *Relations*, like most other annual reports, tend to become repetitive when followed year by year. Missionary concerns remain the same, or undergo changes so gradual as to be almost imperceptible. Promising converts reappear in glowing accounts until they eventually apostasize or succumb to tuberculosis. Even new anecdotes are the old ones with merely the names changed. Now and then, however, the reader is startled by a sudden new direction or perhaps becomes aware after the event that significant change has taken place. The destruction of Huronia, inevitably, constituted one such dramatic turning-point. The work of almost two decades was in ruins, and Iroquois success cast a shadow over possibilities for the future. During succeeding years Iroquois warriors seemed to be everywhere, preventing new missions and disrupting old ones, bringing death to a Jesuit even on the Hudson Bay watershed, and threatening the very existence of the French colony. The affairs of the society were in similar disarray. Martyrdom had removed some of the most experienced missionaries, and temporary underemployment of those remaining along with heavy expenses for relief compelled a further exodus to France. A shortage of missionaries with linguistic skills and the aging of those who remained would trouble the Jesuits for many years.[1]

A reader who follows the *Relations* through these desperate years is likely to be struck most forcibly by the rapidity with which Jesuit morale revived. Three hundred of the surviving Hurons who resolved in 1650 to seek refuge at Quebec were inspired on their journey by the sight of 'a young man of rare beauty and majestic glory' who walked beside Charles Garnier and urged them to accept his instructions. This was probably

Antoine Daniel, whom Pierre Chaumonot had already reported as appearing in a vision 'to revive us all with his strong counsel and with the divine spirit which filled him.' Shaken confidence was further restored in 1653 when Wyandot canoes reopened the western route with a consignment of furs, and the arrival in 1656 of Médard Chouart des Groseilliers and a companion with news of distant peoples speaking tongues allied with Huron and Algonquin stirred missionary wanderlust again. By 1658 the author of the *Relations* was eagerly sending home long lists of nations to the west and north as yet unreached, noting also thirty others to the south, 'all stationary, all speaking the Abnaquiois tongue and all more populous than were the Hurons of old.' The way was still blocked, he admitted, but so it had often seemed 'in the first age of the Church.'[2] François de Laval, arriving in 1659 as the first bishop resident in New France, encouraged this expansive urge.

Even before the catastrophe one Jesuit had begun to establish a missionary pattern that would prove very useful after it. Ever since Le Caron and Le Jeune had tried with limited success the experiment of wintering with nomadic Indians, it had been conventional wisdom that christianization would work only among settled peoples or people who could be persuaded to settle. In 1643, however, Gabriel Druillettes spent a hunting season with the Montagnais in order to learn their language better. Despite a scarcity of game and a painful attack of snow-blindness he later spent several winters with the Abenakis of northern New England, inaugurating what would prove a long association. By 1704 the Jesuits had permanent missions among the Abenakis on the Kennebec and Penobscot rivers, as well as one at Meductic among the cognate Maliseets of the Saint John. Charles Albanel applied similar techniques of wintering among the Montagnais of the Saguenay.[3]

Around the upper Great Lakes various tribes that had been broken by the Iroquois incursions were attempting to regroup. They included Ojibwas, Ottawas, and others of Algonquian speech, along with Huron and Petun refugees who came to be known as Wyandots. Experiments in wintering had clear relevance to them, but at first it was difficult to find suitable candidates. After two unsuccessful attempts the arrival of Claude Allouez in 1665 set what came to be called the Ottawa mission on its feet. He was soon able to establish missions at Saint-Esprit on the south shore of Lake Superior, at Green Bay on Lake Michigan, and at Sault Ste Marie. St Ignace at Michilimackinac, founded by Jacques Marquette in 1671, became the chief base in the region and a centre from which Jesuits went out on missionary forays through a territory that included much of what is now northern Ontario. During the same period the Saguenay and the north shore of the Gulf of St Lawrence were served by the long ministries of François de Crespieul and Pierre Laure, and in 1672 Albanel accompanied the first European party to reach James Bay overland.

The first major new mission after the destruction of the Hurons was established, however, not in the west but among the Iroquois who had caused the disaster. In 1653, in an attempt to divide the French from their Indian allies, the Iroquois proposed peace on the condition that some Frenchmen should dwell in their country. The Jesuits volunteered, although many regarded them as 'so many victims destined to the fire and fury of the Iroquois.' After scouting trips in 1654 and 1655 four missionaries and fifty other Frenchmen set out in 1656 to establish a permanent residence among the Onondagas. Iroquois friendship did not last, and in 1658 the French withdrew hastily to Quebec.[4] The dream of a spiritual conquest of an earthly enemy was, however, not lightly to be given up. The Jesuits were able to re-enter Iroquoia in 1667 in the wake of a punitive expedition by the marquis de Tracy, eventually placing missionaries among all five nations. Evicted again in 1684, they were able to return only for a few troubled years between 1702 and 1709.

By the later years of the seventeenth century the Jesuits were no longer the only missionary agency in New France, although they continued to maintain the largest body of missionaries and the most consistent mission policy. Their first associates – or rivals – in the work were the Gentlemen of Saint-Sulpice, whose founder Jean-Jacques Olier had inspired through a mystical vision the initial settlement of Montreal. Interest in New France thus came naturally to the fledgling society, which took over the religious administration of Montreal from the Jesuits in 1657. Like their founder the Sulpicians were interested in Montreal chiefly as a base for outreach to the Indians. When war between the Iroquois and the Susquehannocks to the south drove many Cayugas to seek temporary refuge north of Lake Ontario, therefore, the Sulpicians sent Claude Trouvé and François de Salignac de la Motte-Fénélon to cover the area between the Bay of Quinte and the present Toronto.[5] The 'Kenté' mission was never very successful and came to an end in 1680 when the Cayugas found it possible to return home, but Sulpician involvement would eventually extend from Acadia to the Detroit border.

In 1670, thanks to the sponsorship of the intendant Jean Talon, the Récollets were able to return to New France. Laval, who saw no need for their services on the St Lawrence, directed them to Acadia as a needy and conveniently distant area. At least one of them, Chrestien Le Clercq, became an outstanding Indian missionary. Stationed at Percé on the Gaspé coast from 1675 to 1686, he not only ministered to the neighbouring Micmacs but studied their customs and developed a system of ideographs for recording their language. Laval opened up a further source of missionaries in 1663 by founding a seminary at Quebec, securing most of his candidates at the outset in France.[6] His model was the seminary of the Society of Foreign Missions at Paris, which began in the same year to train and sponsor secular priests for missionary work abroad. While most of Laval's graduates were required to meet the needs of the growing number of French settlers, priests of the society gradually replaced the Récollets among the Indians of Acadia. Among them was Antoine Gaulin, the first Canadian-born missionary to the Indians, who had a long apostolate among the Micmacs of peninsular Nova Scotia during the early part of the eighteenth century.

Missionary approaches during this period followed for the most part patterns already familiar. A constant attack on native religious practice was fortified with the familiar devices of ridicule, scientific prediction, and even – centuries before Freud – the rational explanation of dreams. Miracles continued to commend the faith, especially where Druillettes was present to work wonders 'by the efficacy of holy water and by the merits of saint Francis Xavier.' Surreptitious baptisms of infants and spiritual contests over condemned captives continued, and even in Iroquoia few seemed to die unbaptized. Always the appeal revolved around the awesome realities of heaven and hell, which were hammered home in sermons and conversations and illustrated in pictures or songs. Albanel used the fear of judgment to urge his guides to continue with him to James Bay, while Milet at Onondaga made up for the lack of a church bell by running through the village before service calling out 'Fire! fire! ever-burning hellfire.'[7]

The hardships often reported in earlier accounts, far from decreasing, were intensified by the new policy of following the Indians deep into the forests and often living permanently in their habitations. Some of the missionaries became connoisseurs of survival. Gaulin lived for long periods on

mussels, Jacques Bruyas at Oneida on dried frogs, Louis André at Manitoulin on acorns, lichens, and moose skins, of which he complained that
he was usually served the parts that had been least boiled. Druillettes
described how on one return trip from the Abenaki country, when after
the Lenten fast he and a companion had had to go for ten days without
food, 'they bethought themselves to boil their shoes, and afterward the
Father's undershirt, which was made of Elk-skin; and when the snow had
melted, they also cooked the cords or lacings of the snowshoes, which,
when it was deep, they used to keep themselves from sinking.' Of constant
dangers to life, especially in the Iroquois cantons, where a sudden change
in the political climate was an ever-threatening possibility, Jacques Bigot
wrote with breathtaking understatement, 'these things are distressing, and
apt to make life pass very heavily.'[8]

Rustic as the settings might be, missionaries of the period showed more
sophistication than their predecessors in the use of techniques, reflecting
the increasing European preoccupation with method. Although practically
all missionaries made use of visual aids, the most imaginative was Jean
Pierron. Applying among the Mohawks a technique developed by the Breton missioner Michel de Nobletz, he made a number of cards representing
the Christian mysteries that could be used by Indians to explain the faith
to others. Then, inspired to greater originality, he invented the game of
'Point to Point' – 'the point of birth to the point of Eternity' – by which
through emblems the Mohawks might 'learn by playing to effect their
salvation.' André, who always seemed to be on the verge of starvation,
nevertheless made use on Manitoulin of a sphere, a 'trigon' or triangle to
explain the Trinity, and various sacred pictures. His specialty, however,
was 'a sweet-toned flute' with which like a pied piper he was able to
instruct 'not only those who loved the faith, but also those who hated it;
for, in their wish to hear their children sing, they learned everything with
them, almost without intending to.' Missionaries relying on such methods
were apt, like Pierron, to lose interest in the teaching of literacy.[9]

These devices, although intended solely to win converts, represented
none the less a growing recognition of the necessity of catering to Indian
tastes. Assimilation into French society might be seen as the ultimate destiny of the Indians, but on the shores of Lake St John or Lake Superior it
seemed too remote to determine immediate strategy. Sometimes adaptation was the only means of gaining a hearing, as when Simon Le Moyne on
entering Onondaga in 1654 followed the Iroquois custom of approaching

the town with a continuous harangue complimenting all the local notables by name. Sometimes Christian and native customs coincided, as when Allouez discovered at Green Bay that those who did not practise fasting were regarded as wicked and hence 'deemed it a duty to sanctify their very superstitions, and to make of a Guilty fast a meritorious one.'[10] Perhaps the most significant single innovation among nomadic peoples was a pre-arranged annual season for renewing instruction, administering the sacraments, and often transacting tribal business. In its essentials this was imported from France, but it fitted the Indian sense of time much better than the regular weekly cycle.

Despite this readiness to adapt, missionaries sometimes took a much harder line towards opponents than their circumstances would seem to have warranted or than their predecessors would have dared to attempt. Pierron, considering himself offended by one of the Mohawk leaders, deliberately arranged a confrontation and let it be known that he would leave if he did not receive satisfaction. Milet at Onondaga almost simultaneously performed the same manoeuvre. Each initiative resulted in the calling of a council that renounced native religious practices and, in the case of the Mohawks, vainly promised allegiance to Christianity. This boldness reflected the missionaries' strong sense of representing French power and prestige, upon which, despite the loss of the earlier easy rapport with authority, they depended for their positions. Other confrontations followed a more classical pattern. Allouez on two occasions cast down images he found on his route, and the western superior Henri Nouvel compelled a Christian Algonquin to make reparation for the sin of having sacrificed a dog. Yet Crespieul observed astutely from the Saguenay, 'More is gained with All the Savages ... by patience than by anger, which makes them lose their esteem for the Missionary.'[11]

Indian responses followed patterns as familiar as those of missionary argument. Missionaries were confronted by the same indifference, sometimes masked by an outward politeness; the same resistance to change in traditional life-styles and more especially to the abandonment of trusted remedies; the same accusations of sorcery, reinforced among the Iroquois by an oft-repeated charge that missionaries took souls to heaven to burn them; the same association of baptism with misfortune and death. More positively, they reported the same curiosity about their services, which could lead to deeper involvement; the same awe of their persons, which Marquette hoped might some day become love; the same hope that Christianity might prove helpful in sickness or hunting.[12] As missionaries won personal acceptance, however, and perhaps above all as European power increased, Christian practices gradually gained in prestige even where Christian belief made little headway. If some Indians still associated baptism with death, we begin to hear of others who used it as a healing ritual. At Green Bay, André seemed to achieve most of his success by outdoing the local 'missipissi' or shamans in attracting sturgeon to the Indians' weirs. At Sault Ste Marie a chief even asked the missionary to pray to 'JESUS, the God of war,' adding, 'He alone can protect us.'[13]

From their arduous effort the missionaries reaped a mixed harvest. Well before the end of the seventeenth century some missionaries, especially in areas of long-continued contact, were already in pastoral situations where their task was that of attending to the spiritual and material needs of at least nominally Christian communities. Others in the north and west were still contending with initial indifference and hostility. Sometimes, as among the northern Montagnais, the favourable response overwhelmed the missionaries themselves. 'It is beyond belief,' Nouvel wrote, 'how easily they are won over when one speaks to their hearts from his own.'[14] Elsewhere the missionaries ran into stone-wall resistance, especially among tribes such as the Ojibwas where the system of native medicine was closely woven into the social fabric. Hazarding a broad generalization, one might say that the Iroquois showed some readiness to renounce elements of their traditional religious practice without becoming greatly interested in Christianity, whereas the more nomadic peoples were receptive to Christianity but reluctant to give up their shamanism.

The Jesuit *Relations* are generally marked by sobriety of judgment and by restraint in the expression of emotion. Even the grief and disappointment called forth by the Huron débâcle must be read to a considerable extent between the lines, although a remarkable conversion could inspire fairly rhapsodic prose. The lid is off in the *Relation* of 1662–3, however, and unrestrained excitement shows through. In that year New France was thrust into turmoil by a series of remarkable events. In the autumn of 1662 a coil of fiery serpents was seen in the sky, and shortly afterwards a great ball of fire passed over the colony to the northeast. On 7 January 1663, and again a week later, three suns were seen at once. On 3 February an earthquake shook the whole valley of the St Lawrence, bringing about remarkable changes in the terrain although fortunately causing no loss of life. Aftershocks continued for months, and in December an eclipse of the sun prolonged a sense that something most unusual was taking place.

Despite, or perhaps because of, a general panic the earthquake was more pleasing than otherwise to Jérôme Lalemant, the author of that year's *Relation*, for it led to a remarkable revival of piety. His words speak for themselves: 'It was a beautiful sight, I say, to see Jugglers break and demolish their Tabernacles; Apostates appeal for mercy, and beg with flowing tears to be admitted to the Church; little children uplift their voices in the brief Catechism and the prayers which they recited; and old men turn Disciples of their children in order to learn of them, and follow the Father whithersoever he went, without giving him any respite, night or day, that they might lose none of his teachings.'[15] One can appreciate Lalemant's satisfaction, but its intensity takes a constant reader by surprise. That the earthquake should cause shamans to reflect was natural enough, but the piety of the French inhabitants had been a constant theme of earlier *Relations*. What had happened to make revival necessary, and how had the colony come to be invaded by apostates? A glance back over preceding reports gives the answer; complimentary references to the colonists had indeed been thinning out during the immediately preceding years.

The worm that had entered the apple was the growing involvement of colonists in the fur trade. During the early part of the century the trade had not been particularly lucrative, and the One Hundred Associates had taken seriously the promotion of French civilization and Christianity that was the stated purpose of their monopoly. Gradually, however, financial stringency compelled the company to relinquish its exclusive rights, and by 1648 the citizens of Quebec were allowed to engage independently in trade. Conditions at that time did not favour expansion, but the peace with the Iroquois that lasted through much of the 1650s stimulated a fever for fur. In these circumstances the repentance that followed the earthquake was bound to be ephemeral, and indeed a series of events thereafter resulted in a continued escalation of temptation. In 1663, the year of the earthquake, the One Hundred Associates lost their American seigneury. In 1664 the crack Carignan-Salières regiment was demobilized in New France, bringing a sudden increase in population along with the moral attitudes of a military camp. In 1665 royal government was instituted, and Talon as intendant instituted a policy of pushing vigorously westwards for furs. In 1667 the marquis de Tracy forced a temporary peace upon the Iroquois, opening the Great Lakes to French navigation. Within a few

years, several hundred *coureurs de bois* were in the west country, and
after the arrival of Count Louis de Buade de Frontenac as governor in 1672
the prospect of making a fortune in the trade seemed to obsess everyone in
the colony right up to the highest officials.

The new policy was in many ways helpful to the missions. The military
presence that gave French traders a measure of security in the west performed the same service, wittingly or unwittingly, for Christian missionaries. The desire for French trade, as in Huron days, gave the Indians an
incentive to receive the missionaries and hear out their story. On the other
hand, some disadvantages of the connection soon became apparent. Contrary to earlier expectations that French example would be a powerful
factor in preparing the Indians to adopt Christian ways of living, free-
traders quickly proved to be the worst possible advertisements for missionary teaching. They cheated the Indians on every possible occasion, plied
them with brandy, and entered into promiscuous relations with their
women. Sometimes they deliberately undermined the influence of the
missionaries, encouraging the Indians to avoid them and ignore their
teaching. As early as 1660 traders at Tadoussac tried to prevent Druillettes
and Jacques Frémin from going there, and conflict remained typical of
that open port. Tension was also of long standing in Acadia, where a long
coastline encouraged competition. Bishop Jean-Baptiste de Saint-Vallier,
visiting the region in 1686, noted it as full of 'libertines.' In the largely
unregulated west, the situation was so unfavourable that the Jesuits joined
with Montreal merchants who were troubled by a glut of furs to persuade
the French government to dismantle its forts on the upper Great Lakes in
1697.[16]

The complex relations of missionaries and traders represented a pattern
of interaction that will be met again more than once in this study. One has
often prepared the way for the other, and it has seldom been possible for
either to operate successfully without collaborating with the other. Each
has also desired to secure a position of influence among the Indians in
order to pursue a particular set of aims, and since these aims have not
always been compatible, a fair amount of tension and mutual recrimina-
tion has resulted. The ideal of the French missionaries was to bring into
being stable communities living by strict moral standards, and they were
naturally indignant when traders introduced their own easy morals and
their readiness to use almost any means to induce Indians to part with
their furs at a favourable price. The traders, on their side, saw the mission-

aries as interfering busybodies who foisted unnatural life-styles on the Indians and encouraged them to devote to prayer hours they might more profitably have spent at the trapline. They also suspected the missionaries of competing with them on the side, and perhaps with some reason. Armand de La Richardie set up his own store at Detroit, and it is interesting to note liquor as an item traded in it.[17] Doubtless he hoped to discourage his customers from dealing with others who would have been more liberal with it.

Among the complaints made against traders, indeed, the most serious and persistent was that they debauched the Indians with brandy. The alcohol problem was not new, but only in the second half of the seventeenth century did it emerge as the great spoiler of missionary endeavour. Complaints poured in from every field. Nicolas Denys blamed liquor supplied by traders for the failure of Jesuit missions in Acadia; Louis-Pierre Thury of the Society for Foreign Missions was compelled to give up a mission on the Miramichi for the same reason, and Gaulin was still fighting a losing battle at Antigonish in the 1720s.[18] Already in 1648, according to Lalemant, drunkenness at Tadoussac was threatening 'to become as deeply rooted among the forests as it has ever been in the heart of Germany.' In the 1730s Jean-Pierre Aulneau found it equally entrenched among the Crees and Assiniboines of the Lake of the Woods, whose 'only topic of conversation was brandy.' Joseph-François Lafitau saw its results as marital breakup, debt, and desertion to the English, while Louis Davaugour foresaw 'not only the loss of religion, but the total overthrow of the French colony.' Bishop Laval used excommunication as a weapon against it, but neither this nor any other remedy proved effective. The authorities agreed that the brandy trade was evil but insisted that it was necessary to maintain relations with the Indians.[19]

Recent commentators have tended to play down the seriousness of the alcohol problem, attributing the shrill tone of contemporary criticism to missionaries inclined by temperament to abstinence. The priests in question were French, however, and kept wine on their own tables as a matter of course. Jacques Bigot was careful not to condemn as a sin 'the act of taking a few Drinks of brandy or of wine' and defended moderate drinkers from criticism by other Abenakis. The Hurons of Lorette were required only not to drink 'to excess,' although wine was later excluded from the reduction as a matter not of ecclesiastical discipline but of a special promise to Mary. The missionaries condemned the liquor trade out of experience rather than prejudice, and in this they were not alone. In 1668 the Mohawks petitioned Governor Francis Lovelace of New York to prohibit it.

If the brandy problem should not be minimized, neither does it admit of simplistic explanations. Although the fable that a single drink is fatal to an Indian's equilibrium was current even in the seventeenth century, Crespieul insisted that many Montagnais would not take more than a glass or two and were able to ration supplies over a long period. Indians who drank to excess did so, apparently, with the deliberate purpose of becoming intoxicated. According to Jean de Lamberville, the relatives of a Christian woman at Onondaga who had been beaten by her husband felt it necessary to get drunk in order to seek revenge. A Cayuga who made life intolerable for Carheil insisted that drink was to blame, while adding that he did not intend to give it up. Drunkenness was thus at once a weapon and an escape, a gesture of covert rebellion for which no responsibility had to be accepted because the fault was really in the white man's liquor,[20] while the value assigned in native tradition to abnormal mental states induced by dreams or fasting provided positive warrant for the use of a substance with similar effects. To a considerable extent, as André Vachon has suggested, liquor may be regarded as not so much a problem in itself as the symptom of a deeper malaise from which it promised a means of escape or the compensation of a new form of ecstasy.[21]

Meanwhile the concerted support that had been such an asset of the missions was steadily being eroded. An ebbing of official interest betrays itself in the wording of commissions of governors. That of 1663 enjoins the marquis de Tracy, the newly appointed lieutenant-general of America, to call the native peoples 'by the gentlest ways possible to the knowledge of God, the light of the faith, and the Catholic, apostolic, and Roman religion.' Similar references in later instructions become steadily more perfunctory and eventually disappear altogether. At times, indeed, relations between church and state became distinctly strained as missionaries expressed dissatisfaction with the failure of governors to curb the brandy trade and as governors resented what they regarded as missionary interference. Relations among missionary agencies were not always much better. The Récollets, still nursing their old grudge against the Jesuits, aligned themselves with Frontenac against them. Members of the Society of Foreign Missions, foremost in attacks on the Jesuits for their adaptations of Catholic practice in China and India, were quick to charge them with similar syncretism in New France.[22] Sulpicians and Jesuits, while respecting each other as 'gentlemen,' were more often rivals than collaborators.

In following the Jesuit *Relations* into the 1670s one becomes aware of still another transition, more gradual and subtle than those already described. Reports of hardships in the west and dangers in Iroquoia lost none of their poignancy, but almost imperceptibly they gave up pride of place to accounts of pastoral work in sedentary missions inspired by the 'reductions' of Latin America. In time, indeed, reports from outlying missions came to seem little more than supplements to their story.

The settlements on which this attention was lavished were never numerous. Sillery, the pioneer and model, has already been noted. In 1650 the Iroquois menace forced a temporary evacuation to Quebec, and the original Montagnais-Algonquin settlement did not survive this interruption. An influx of Abenakis from the troubled New England border gave it new life in 1676, however, and despite several reports of its abandonment there were still (or again) Abenakis there in 1742. Cap-de-la-Madeleine, a companion to Sillery, was destined for greater permanence. Lorette, named by Chaumonot (Calvonotti) after a well-known shrine in his native Italy and provided with a replica of its church, figures prominently in the *Relations* as the home of a remnant of Hurons who sought refuge in the Quebec area.[23] Saint François near Lac St Pierre was opened in 1700 for western Abenakis who had already begun to settle there, and a few years later most of those who had been at Sillery were removed to Bécancour on the south shore of the St Lawrence. Sault-Saint-Louis, which after a series of moves became the present Caughnawaga, had its origin in 1668 when Pierre Raffeix invited seven Oneida and Mohawk converts to join him on a Jesuit property across the river from Montreal. Kateri Gandacteua, an Erie who had been enslaved by the Oneidas and was now the wife of an adopted Huron, was chiefly instrumental in attracting further settlers.[24] Caughnawaga eventually derived the bulk of its settlers, along with its present name, from a Mohawk village that represented a relocation of Jogues's Ossernenon.

All of these communities were sponsored by the Jesuits, and they are the ones that figure prominently in the *Relations*. In 1676 the Sulpicians established for the Iroquois a settlement on the slopes of Mount Royal known as the Mountain, later providing another for the neighbouring Algonquins. Others further up the St Lawrence were added in the middle years of the eighteenth century, both for Iroquois: Oswegatchie at the present Ogdensburg by the Sulpicians in 1749, St Regis by the Jesuits in 1755.[25] With the exception of Sillery and Oswegatchie, these communities all exist today and contain the bulk of the Indian population of the lower St Lawrence Valley. At the time of their foundation most of them were close but not adjacent to centres of French population.

A notable feature of these missionary settlements was the close supervision to which residents were subjected. It began with restrictions on access. The Sulpicians were not strict in this respect, populating the Mountain at first chiefly with Iroquois prisoners ransomed from their captors and with children given up by their parents. At Sault-Saint-Louis, however, a probation of two or three years was required, and drunkenness was punishable by imprisonment and expulsion. At Lorette a drunkard forfeited not only his place but the lands that had been assigned to him. A strenuous regime within the community was enforced by native leaders, whose precise functions varied from one reduction to another. At Lorette secular and sacred affairs were each the responsibility of one man and one woman elected by the people. In addition to these *dogiques*, each settlement had both male and female catechists to instruct the people, and at Sault-Saint-Louis each hunting party was provided with a sort of religious commissar. Through this system of indirect rule all affairs ultimately came under the scrutiny of the priest.[26]

During the heyday of the missions this hothouse atmosphere generated a remarkable intensity of religious life. Each day closed with prayers said aloud. Sunday was marked by a constant round of services, processions, and instructions, and Easter at Lorette was described as an occasion of unforgettable feasting and celebration. At the Mountain the church was decorated with brilliant pictures, while chants were accompanied by a guitar. At Lorette an image of the infant Jesus made a weekly round of the cabins, with blessings reported whcrever it went. Sault-Saint-Louis provided pious associations, a sodality for beginners and the Confraternity of the Holy Family to which only the more devout were admitted. Oka was described as in intention 'a sort of perpetual mission.'[27]

Some, especially among the women, were not content with this generous provision of aids to holiness. Outstanding among these was Kateri Tekakwitha, who in a brief residence at Sault-Saint-Louis from 1677 until her death in 1680 established a remarkable reputation for sanctity. Born at Ossernenon in 1656 to a Mohawk father and an Algonquin mother, Kateri lost her parents in childhood through a smallpox epidemic that also left her disfigured and afflicted with poor eyesight. Converted to Christianity by Jesuit missionaries who visited her home, she showed such zeal and such determination to remain single that she was persuaded to take refuge from petty persecutions among the Christian Mohawks of Sault-Saint-Louis. There she not only excelled in the usual exercises of piety but punished herself in all the ways her ingenuity could devise, flagellating herself with willow rods, sleeping on a bed of thorns, and even holding brands between her toes when told that fire was the ultimate test of willingness to suffer. Other women soon began to imitate her, carrying self-torture to such an extreme after her death that Claude Chauchetière rather implausibly saw behind their excesses a desire to 'render Christianity hateful even at the start.' Morbid as such practices may seem from a twentieth-century perspective, Kateri's sanctity has inspired about fifty biographies in some ten languages, along with Leonard Cohen's *Beautiful Losers*, and the recently bestowed title 'Blessed' points to probable canonization in the future.[28]

The reductions were severely criticized in their own time both by civil authorities and by other missionary agencies, not for religious excess but for a tendency to produce merely nominal Christians. Frontenac began the attack, claiming that instead of implementing the royal policy of assimilation the Jesuits sought to isolate and control the Indians. The Récollets eagerly took up the charge. Le Clercq's *First Establishment of the Faith in New France* claimed of the Indians that 'none are seen living among French Europeans, but only in neighbouring villages, cut off from intercourse, living in the Indian way, incompatible with real Christianity, giving no signs of religion but the chants of hymns and prayers, or some exterior and very equivocal ceremonies,' whereas the plan of the Récollets had been to mingle them among the French. The Sulpician historian Pierre Rousseau argued that by cutting off the Indians from all commerce with whites the Jesuits had produced the form but not the substance of Christianity, adding that Sulpician missions had succeeded by following the methods recommended by the king and Colbert.[29] The contrast between segregationist Jesuits and assimilationist rivals has become something of a commonplace among historians.

Such criticisms stemmed more from professional jealousy than from objective analysis. In Canada as in the Far East, Jesuits were prepared to make concessions to native taste that shocked other missionaries, and in time they adopted a deliberate policy of trying to protect their converts from contact with Europeans. The segregation for which they were often condemned was, however, the product of field experience rather than of a pre-arranged plan. All missionaries of the first half-century, Jesuits as much as Récollets or Capuchins, dreamed of Indian societies remade according to the French model. When some Iroquois visitors to Quebec asked 'how long it took to frenchify a girl,' the Jesuits regarded the question as highly complimentary to the Ursulines. Later wariness about intercultural contact arose from the discovery that, as the colony became more commercialized, Indians were more devout when kept to themselves.[30]

The discovery was not peculiar to the Jesuits. The Sulpicians at first made a point in their schools at the Mountain of teaching boys and girls to dress and dine 'à la française.' Experience of the temptations of Montreal led them in time to shift their activities to Sault au Récollet and then to Oka. Gaulin of the Foreign Missions likewise attempted to settle the Micmacs of Nova Scotia in a village of their own, first at Windsor, then on the St Mary's River, and finally at Antigonish.[31] Even the Récollet Chrestien Le Clercq, the missionary if not the author, urged his Gaspesians to settle at St François.[32] The issue that agitated the missionaries themselves was that of choosing not between assimilation and segregation but between the reduction and the wandering mission, and it was debated within rather than among missionary agencies. The Jesuits found both approaches necessary in varying situations. The Sulpicians, after a controversy that bitterly divided the Montreal society, opted for the permanent settlement.

Although criticisms of the reductions were seldom disinterested, they were not entirely beside the mark. The original intention behind Indian settlement, that of ensuring stability through agriculture, was always frustrated by the insatiable demands of corn upon the fertility of limited acreages of land, for even in the seventeenth century private land tenure was preventing the frequent relocations essential to traditional Indian farming. Many Indians of the reductions abandoned agriculture to become nomads of a new kind, commuting to war or the fur trade. Within the settlements, faction and discontent were frequently reported. Disharmony between national groups gave rise to crises at both Caughnawaga and Oka, while 'horrible discord' reported at Caughnawaga in 1722 was but one instance of resentment caused by the removal of a favourite missionary. Native religious practices, many times declared defunct, had as many times a way of reappearing.[33] The life of a missionary on a reduction was not so idyllic as some optimistic reports suggested, and with time the graph of piety tended downwards.

Life in a missionary settlement can never have been entirely satisfactory to the Indians either. Jacques Bigot observed that the Abenakis of Sillery were frequently sad and therefore taught them a 'little spiritual Song' set to 'various joyful tunes.' His observation that they were much given to scruples suggests that one reason for their sadness may have been his earlier use of 'certain Mournful Songs and some spectacular representations' to impress the horrors of hell on their minds. Another was the chronic poverty of sedentary Indians, which compelled many to depend on relief from the missionaries. Its chief source, however, was probably the strain of living in a cultural half-world that cut Indians off from many aspects of their own culture without giving them the resources to cope with that of the French. At the school of Joseph Rontaganha, a zealous young man who had made the trip to France, pupils might be seen each day 'ranged in his Cabin, well-behaved and modest, like so many little statues, without daring to stir.' One readily recognizes the apathy of people imprisoned in an environment not their own and reads without surprise that desertions to the Iroquois country were a source of occasional concern.[34]

Despite disappointments and drawbacks, the reduction offered so many advantages to the missionaries that they eventually accepted it as the norm to which missions whenever possible should be conformed. By concentrating a substantial number of Indians in one place this model made possible an economical use of experienced personnel, which were always in short supply. By fostering continuity of residence it provided the stability necessary for thorough indoctrination and for the cultivation of habits of prayer. Its relative isolation from French settlements offered some hedge against the infiltration of the temptations of civilization without adding significantly to difficulties of communication. Above all, perhaps, its organization under missionary auspices ensured a measure of control; the usual system of indirect rule left ultimate authority squarely in the hands of the priests.

The reduction must also have met more satisfactorily than any other available option the needs of many Indians. Despite its severe discipline it was by no means a concentration camp, for its inhabitants continued to spend the winter season in traditional and sometimes distant hunting territories and were in any case free to leave at any time if they found the life irksome. Some of them became ardent propagandists for their settlements. A Mohawk woman, rusticated from the nobility for becoming a Christian, went so far as to direct a letter to her nation urging them to remove in a body to Lorette. In 1677 a delegation of three Christians from Sault-Saint-Louis toured the Iroquois cantons seeking recruits.[35] They had considerable success, and some individuals such as the celebrated Kryn exerted themselves over the years to extol the virtues of settled life under Jesuit auspices. At times, indeed, excluding undesirables was a greater problem than attracting newcomers.

Many, perhaps most, of those who sought out the reductions welcomed them as an alternative to grave evils. Algonquins were threatened by starvation, Abenakis by English attacks, Hurons by the prospect of annihilation. For the Iroquois the chief attraction seems to have been relief from the drunkenness and disorder that followed contact with the Dutch, and a sense that only heroic measures could prevent a relapse into old habits may go far towards explaining religious austerities that otherwise seem excessive. Yet there was also a more positive aspect. It has often been observed that societies undergoing rapid and painful change make fertile soil for millennial and enthusiastic movements. The atmosphere of the reduction was hospitable to zealots, supplementing an essentially Iroquois spirituality with the resources of Catholic mysticism and the discipline of Catholic order. Any analysis of its appeal that neglects this urge to a novel spiritual solution for an unprecedented social crisis will omit a vital factor.

For further turning-points we must look to sources other than the Jesuit *Relations*, which came to an end in 1673 and were only partly replaced later by occasional notices in a series of *Lettres édifiantes et curieuses* from various mission fields.[36] From correspondence and missionary reports after this time one receives a distinct impression that the peak of missionary achievement in New France had been passed. Signs of decline, already apparent before the turn of the eighteenth century, multiplied towards the close of the French regime.

This decline was due, in part, to a slackening of support at home. France was moving into the era of the Enlightenment, and scepticism and indifference were drying up the springs of missionary zeal. The seminary of the Society of Foreign Missions provided few recruits after the turn of the century, while the Récollets acquired a reputation for enjoying the amenities of military stations more than befitted observant friars. The Jesuits were one of the few orders to maintain their numbers in France, but recruits for Canada were difficult to secure and recourse was increasingly had to Belgium. The romantic appeal of martyrdoms in Huronia wore increasingly thin as rumours of meagre results circulated in France and as missionaries applied themselves increasingly to the routine duties of the reduction. In New France itself, as the white population grew and as the seminary increased in importance, Indian work came to be regarded as merely one specialty among several.[37] To make matters worse, the various agencies were less capable than ever of working harmoniously together. The Jesuits were also distinctly out of favour with Bishop Saint-Vallier, while the Récollets were disliked by almost all bishops.

Problems created by the fur trade, far from being solved, became steadily more acute. During the late seventeenth century, missionaries in Acadia traced many of their difficulties to a coterie of unscrupulous officials grouped around Antoine Laumet de La Mothe Cadillac. Upon his appointment as commandant of the west in 1694 many of these associates followed him, and his foundation of a trading fort at Detroit in 1701 gave that locality a long-standing reputation for wickedness. Taking his own religion lightly, Cadillac distrusted the Jesuits and confided the chaplaincy of Detroit to Récollets. Etienne de Carheil was scandalized that under Cadillac's regime the post commandants themselves were encouraging traders to debauch the Indians through brandy and prostitution, and saw no alternative but to abandon his mission at Michilimackinac unless the situation were remedied.[38] He was compelled to do so temporarily in 1704 when the Wyandots removed to Detroit, and during the rest of the French era a series of wars with the Fox tribe prevented consistent missionary work in the region. In time, alcohol invaded even the reductions. In 1673 it was reported to have ruined Sillery but not Sault-Saint-Louis, in 1710 the latter but not Lorette.[39] Defensive measures adopted by missionaries against the brandy trade sometimes involved them in controversies that interfered with their work among the Indians. Jean-Baptiste Tournois, who encouraged two sisters named Desauniers to set up a store at Caughnawaga to counteract the attractions of Montreal, was expelled from his post in 1750 by Governor Jonquière.[40]

From the outbreak of war in 1684 until the final conquest of Canada the missions were embroiled in the struggle between England and France for the control of North America, an important aspect of which was a feverish effort on the part of each nation to assert its sovereignty over the interior of the continent. In the western country it became accepted practice to take Jesuits along on exploring expeditions, not primarily as evangelists but as scribes and surveyors; Jacques Le Gardeur de Saint-Pierre, who led an expedition to what is now the Canadian west in 1750, complained that Jean-Baptiste de La Morinie was a useless missionary because he had brought no mathematical instruments.[41] Other missionaries, especially near the borders, were even more directly involved in the struggle as the reductions became important reserves of manpower. The primary task of the missionary was to keep his people loyal to the French, at the very least preventing them from going over to the English and preferably persuading them not to make peace with them. When war came, he accompanied his people as their chaplain and general booster of morale.

Mission work was most conspicuously affected in Acadia, where the frontier was in a state of constant unrest. An early favourite of the government was Louis-Pierre Thury of the Society of Foreign Missions, whose station was strategically located on the Penobscot. In 1693 the authorities congratulated him for helping to maintain the fidelity of the Indians and promised to confide in him a forthcoming distribution of presents; in 1695 they granted him 1500 livres for his services to the state. The allegiance of the Indians became even more important in 1713, when the Treaty of Utrecht led in effect to the division of the old Acadia into French and British zones. In 1725 the French government ordered Gaulin 'to foment the war of these savages with the English,'[42] and indeed no missionary could avoid involvement in the conflict. Missionaries always insisted that they encouraged the Indians to fight humanely, but inevitably raids on English settlements provoked intense resentment. Sébastien Rale, a Jesuit whose mission at Norridgewock was closest to New England, was set upon and killed in 1724 by a raiding party from Massachusetts. Jean-Louis Le Loutre, operating first out of Shubenacadie and then from Fort Beauséjour on the Chignecto isthmus, was blamed by the English for practically every atrocity in Nova Scotia and imprisoned for five years after his capture at sea while returning to France.

Competition for Indian souls between Roman Catholics and Protestants, while not entirely the product of national rivalry, was greatly stimulated by it and became inextricably interwoven with it. Johannes Megalopensis, who arrived in 1642 as pastor of the Dutch Reformed church at Fort Orange, the present Albany, may have been the first to make converts for Christianity among the Iroquois. Competition became more systematic in

1693 when the New England Company, a Puritan missionary society
founded in 1649 to support the work of John Eliot among the Natick
Indians near Boston, began to subsidize Godfreidus Dellius and other
clergymen among the Iroquois. Although this venture was never successful, a mission among the Mohawks begun in 1704 by the Anglican Society
for the Propagation of the Gospel (SPG) was to have more permanent
results.[43] Roman Catholic missionaries were excluded from the cantons
after the Peace of Utrecht, which recognized British suzerainty over the
Iroquois, but continued to make occasional visits and to press the Iroquois
to settle in their reductions. Their last major initiative in this area was
taken in 1749 by the Sulpician François Piquet, who attracted three thousand Iroquois, mainly Onondagas and Oneidas, to the mission-cum-fort of
La Présentation at Oswegatchie. Each contender credited its rival with
considerable success. From 1717 to 1720 the New England Company also
sponsored missionaries along the Acadian frontier, although with little success. According to Philippe de Rigaud de Vaudreuil, the governor-general
of New France, they offered to build churches for the Abenakis, and the
French were obliged to follow suit. The political implications of these
moves are evident from a remark of the intendant François Bigot in 1715:
'Religion is the most powerful motive to hold these savages for us.'[44]

Given the circumstances of the time, this military involvement was
inevitable. Most Christians have seen no incompatibility between religion
and patriotism, and in the eighteenth century close links between church
and state made the two seem inseparable. The first SPG missionary to the
Iroquois was advised 'to instruct them in the true Religion and confirm
them in their duty to Her Msty,' and the corresponding French directives
were similar. To missionaries on both sides, moreover, great spiritual issues
were at stake. Catholic missionaries were convinced that an English victory would mean 'naught but sacrilege and profanation: altars overturned;
images broken' – and ultimately the souls of the Indians damned. Protestants looked forward to the same culmination as a day of liberation from
the yoke of the scarlet woman. Despite such sentiments, not all missionaries were prepared to subordinate their work to national interests. Gaulin,
chiefly intent on promoting Indian settlement, was not the only Acadian
missionary who had to be needled into greater support for the war effort.
The Jesuits of Caughnawaga came under attack for encouraging traffic
with Albany in order to promote conversions, especially when this traffic

frustrated French plans for forming an Indian alliance against the English.[45]

The effects of the conflict on Christian missions were not all negative. Especially among the Micmacs, a situation of almost permanent crisis forged strong bonds of common interest between the missionaries and their flocks that made tribal identity and allegiance to Roman Catholicism seem virtually inseparable. After Gaulin's departure in 1732 the most prominent missionaries were Le Loutre, who arrived in 1737, and Pierre Maillard, who preceded him by two years. Both were emissaries of the Society of Foreign Missions; both were graduates of the Seminary of the Holy Spirit, which had been founded in 1703 to educate impecunious students and to make them available as 'a kind of military detachment of auxiliary troops wherever needed.' Although Le Loutre is chiefly remembered for his warlike activities, his primary interest was in promoting agricultural settlement after Gaulin's model.[46] Maillard, who worked out of Chapel Island in Bras d'Or Lake under the protection of Louisbourg, gave Micmac Catholicism a cohesion it had hitherto lacked. By adapting Le Clercq's ideographs he was also able to give them chants and prayers in their own language.[47]

During the Seven Years' War the French colony under whose protection and with whose support Roman Catholic missionaries had been able to carry Christianity across half a continent moved inexorably towards extinction. Beauséjour 1755, Louisbourg 1758, Quebec 1759, and Montreal 1760 marked steps along the road to a conquest that was formalized by the Treaty of Paris in 1763. Henceforth Christian work among the Indians of Canada would be carried out under vastly different conditions.

The British conquest did not prove so calamitous to the Roman Catholic Church as its missionaries had expected, although desecrated altars were not unknown. To the Jesuits the conquest even brought benefits, for neither a decree of the parlement of Paris in 1762 secularizing the order in France nor a writ of Pope Clement XIV in 1773 suppressing it altogether was considered valid in British dominions. Indian missions were condemned to slow attrition, however, by a provision of the settlement that allowed male religious orders to continue only on sufferance and forbade them to receive new members. Those of the Jesuits became extinct with the death in 1783 of Joseph Huguet at Caughnawaga. The Sulpicians of

Oka now represented the one remaining vital link with the past, and they were rapidly dwindling in numbers.

The turning of a crucial corner was signalled by the arrival at Montreal in 1794 of practically the entire faculty of the Sulpician seminary of Lyon, exiled by the French Revolution and suddenly welcome as a result of British hostility to it. In that same year the Sulpicians opened a mission among the Maliseets on the Tobique River in New Brunswick, while along the Detroit River they helped to maintain a continuous ministry. Elsewhere secular priests gave what attention they could to the Indians in their areas; notable among them was Joseph-Mathurin Bourg, an Acadian graduate of the Seminary of the Holy Spirit, who worked along the Baie des Chaleurs.[48] Otherwise the Indians had to maintain their faith as best they could. When Roman Catholics were later able to begin to rebuild their shattered missions, what remained from a century and a half of sacrificial effort?

In retrospect it can be seen that the basis of the present Roman Catholic Indian population of Quebec and the Maritime provinces had been firmly laid. The Micmacs, Maliseets, and Abenakis had developed an almost fanatical loyalty to their missionaries, the church, and France – categories among which they made few fine distinctions. The Montagnais of the Saguenay, although served only intermittently by missionaries after the end of the seventeenth century, readily identified themselves as Catholics. So did the Algonquins, many of whom were now located at Oka. The Mohawks were by now all nominal Christians, although divided between Roman Catholicism in the St Lawrence Valley and Anglicanism in the home territory. Progress among the other Iroquois tribes had been less satisfactory, but a fair number of converts were scattered among the various mission settlements. At Detroit La Richardie had gathered a group of Hurons that inclined somewhat to restiveness. Among other western tribes all that remained was a memory, although one that would have some consequences in later years. Virtually all Indians around the Great Lakes had some knowledge of Roman Catholicism, and many of them occasionally brushed up on it by dropping in at Oka on the way to Montreal. Some vaguely regarded themselves as Catholics, or at least as destined to be Catholics if the priests should renew their visits.

From the missionary point of view, the quality of Indian Christianity left much to be desired. The Micmacs and Maliseets, although loyal to the church, were as yet imperfectly instructed and inclined to confuse Catho-

lic with native belief and practice. In the St Lawrence settlements little
remained of the religious exaltation that had been so conspicuous in the
late seventeenth century, and one looked in vain for successors to the
Indian leaders who had inspired it – for a zealot to equal Kateri Gandacteua, an apostle to rival Kryn, a saint to approach Kateri Tekakwitha. Nor,
despite much careful cultivation, was there a flowering of native vocations. In time there were a few Indian nuns, notably under Sulpician sponsorship, but no native priests. Indian Christianity was suffering already
from a certain routinization, marked by passivity, sterility, and lack of
direction. Alcoholism was a serious problem everywhere, among the
Anglican Mohawks as much as among any of the Roman Catholic Indians. After many years of Christian preaching, too, reversion to old ways
seemed to be an ever-present danger.

From the converts' point of view, however, too negative an appraisal
would not be justified. Some of them had demonstrated that it was possible
to become a fervent Christian without ceasing to be an Indian. The early
Récollet thesis that christianization could come about only through
assimilation into European society had long since gone by the boards, even
among the Jesuits' former critics in government.[49] Its abandonment was in
part politically motivated but chiefly the result of a silent but determined
refusal on the part of the Indians themselves. Accepting Christianity but
declining enfranchisement, they gradually evolved a distinctive style of
Catholicism that combined their own traditional sensitivity to the spirit
world with the rich visual and audial imagery of the baroque. To some
their religious practice may seem overstrained and naïve. It may still have
something to tell us, however, about the terms on which the Indian is
prepared to accept Christianity.

A final legacy of the period was a reservoir of experience that would be
drawn on in later times. Basic to it was the development of skill in commu-
nicating in native languages. According to Victor Egon Hanzeli, linguistic
progress came to a halt in the eighteenth century, while the failure of the
Jesuits to secure a printing press caused much of their work to remain in
obscurity and some of it to be lost. Nevertheless, later Sulpician studies of
both Iroquois and Algonquian languages became a major resource for nineteenth-century Roman Catholic missionaries, few of whom proceeded to
their fields without a period of orientation at Oka. Such techniques of
approach as the concentrated summer mission with its combination of the
spectacular and the solemn would reappear later in many parts of the

north and west. Most significantly of all, the program of collecting Indians
in mission-sponsored settlements would continue to provide a norm. Later
Protestants would be under greater necessity of finding their own way, but
they were not without some legacy from the earlier period. Anglican
Mohawks would take with them to Canada translations of Scripture and
Common Prayer prepared by Lawrence Claessen and Joseph Brant for the
SPG,[50] while patterns set by the New England Company and other agencies
in the British colonies would be influential in Canada. A missionary tradi-
tion was already taking shape, blended of European precedents and North
American experience.

CHAPTER FOUR

Christianity and Civilization

The arrival of the British did little to stem the decline in missionary zeal that marked the later years of the French regime, for most Protestants of the time were even less interested than Roman Catholics in winning converts for their faith. Britishers were already developing the habit of organizing voluntary societies for particular objects, however, and among these the conversion of the heathen was beginning to find a place. Several such societies already at work in the older British American colonies were destined to affect Canada as well. The New England Company and the SPG mission among the Mohawks have already been noted. The German-speaking Moravian Brethren, a combination of dissident Lutherans and descendants of medieval Hussites whom Count Nicolaus von Zinzendorf brought together in 1727 under one rule of community life, were active among the Delawares along the river of that name. Eleazar Wheelock, a Congregationalist preacher of the revivalist 'new light' tradition, founded a school for Indian children that became in 1769 Dartmouth College. Located at Hanover, New Hampshire, in the old hunting grounds of the Abenakis, it drew most of its Indian students over the next eighty years from the reservation at Saint François.[1]

Protestant missions to the Indians of British North America began in the Maritime provinces shortly after the foundation of Halifax in 1749, which signalled British determination to maintain permanent occupation. Thomas Wood, who was already familiar with Delaware from previous service in New Jersey, visited various Indian encampments during his tenure as an SPG missionary from 1753 until his death in 1758 and was eventually able to conduct services in Micmac. He also cultivated the friendship of Pierre Maillard and stirred considerable controversy after the latter's death by claiming to have been designated by the veteran missionary as his authorized successor.[2]

The New England Company, a refugee of the American Revolution, resolved in 1786 that its charter to conduct missionary work 'in New England and the parts adjacent in America' could legitimately be extended to New Brunswick. Despite its Puritan and indeed predominantly Presbyterian background, the company selected chiefly Anglican agents after the revolution and in later years became associated exclusively with Anglican work. Its efforts in New Brunswick, under the patronage of leading officials of the province, were conspicuously unsuccessful. They consisted of a series of projects followed after some years by investigations into reasons for their failure: several schools, of which the most ambitious at Sussex Vale was authorized in 1794, a scheme for apprenticing young Micmacs to Protestant families, approved in 1806, a last desperate proposal in 1824 for a new establishment at Saint John.[3]

When the New England Company finally withdrew from the Atlantic region in 1826, the Micmacs were still without exception Roman Catholic. They had had to make do and would continue to have to make do with such services as could be provided by diocesan priests in time spared from regular parochial duties. Until mid-century or later the supply of priests was so limited and the Micmac pattern of life so nomadic that contacts with the church were sporadic at best. In these circumstances Micmac families depended for the preservation of their traditions of Catholic devotion on Maillard's pictographic books, which were reprinted for them by the Austrian government as late as 1866. Annual summer gatherings during Saint Anne's moon, instituted early in the seventeenth century, became occasions for concentrated religious instruction, the performance of rituals impossible at other times, and the renewal of social ties.[4] The Catholicism of the Micmacs, perhaps more than that of any other Canadian Indians, was primarily a tribal affair.

In Upper Canada the first Protestant Indian communities came into being not through missionary expansion but through the migration of groups already Christian. During the American Revolution most of the Iroquois fought on the British side, but there was some division among them that tended to follow sectarian lines. The Anglican Mohawks were unanimous in their allegiance to Britain, whereas Samuel Kirkland and other Congregationalist missionaries were able to persuade many Oneidas and Tuscaroras to remain neutral or even to take the colonial side. Among those who came to Upper Canada as United Empire Loyalists there were thus a number of Mohawks who adhered to the Church of England. John Stuart, their former missionary at Fort Hunter, New York, followed them to Montreal in 1782 and helped them to settle in Upper Canada. He never ceased, as rector of Kingston, to conduct occasional services for Captain John Deserontyou's band on the Bay of Quinte, and after 1812 his son George carried on the tradition. For those along the Grand River, where Joseph Brant was able to secure a larger tract of land, Governor Frederick Haldimand built in 1785 the first Protestant church in Ontario. Although for almost forty years these Mohawks had to be content with semi-annual visits of clergymen, their lay readers continued to conduct regular Sunday services.[5]

Other Protestant Indians arrived in Canada for reasons having to do more directly with religion. Since 1740 the Moravians had been interested in the Delawares of eastern Pennsylvania. David Zeisberger, who began his missionary career in 1744, was especially successful in inspiring converts with Moravian ideals of piety and pacifism. As white settlement expanded, these peace-loving Delawares made their way westwards in a succession of perilous moves through Pennsylvania and the Ohio country, forced out of each refuge in turn by the mistrust of traditionally minded Indians or the hostility of white settlers. Permanence seemed almost within grasp in the Muskingum valley of Ohio when the revolution broke out, resulting in harassment by British agents and massacre by rebel militiamen. A final move in 1792 brought Zeisberger's Delawares to Fairfield or Moraviantown on the Thames, a location not remote enough to prevent the burning of the settlement by American troops during the War of 1812.[6]

By the early years of the nineteenth century missionary effort was no longer a preserve of pious coteries but was beginning to command widespread public support. Heightened sympathy for missions was an aftereffect of a series of evangelical revivals that concurrently swept the British Isles and the American colonies during the eighteenth century. William Carey, chief founder of the Baptist Missionary Society in 1792, gave this interest a world-wide dimension and a firm institutional base. Within a few years the movement was undergirded by numerous societies both denominational and non-sectarian, first in Britain, then in the United States, and finally in Germany and other parts of the continent of Europe.

Roman Catholic commitment, which had sagged badly after the suppression of the Jesuits in 1773, revived more slowly as the church recovered from the effects of the French Revolution. The reconstitution of the Society of Jesus in 1814 and the formation of many new orders provided the necessary personnel.

A notable feature of nineteenth-century missions was the mobilization of massive support through the accumulation of small gifts from a large number of people. John Wesley established the practice among the Methodists of assigning the raising of money to local officials who would be responsible for collecting dues from eight to ten people, and soon the missionary mite box was a familiar sight in Protestant homes. At Lyon Pauline Jaricot, a laywoman, applied the same principle of farming out the collection of money for missions to a large number of volunteers. The Society for the Propagation of the Faith (l'Oeuvre pour la Propagation de la Foi), founded in 1822 partly as a result of her efforts, became a major source of income for Roman Catholic missions around the world. The same process of decentralization shifted the support of missions everywhere from governments and wealthy patrons to a network of less affluent sponsors.

Humanitarian concern kept pace with missionary zeal. Beginning in the late eighteenth century a succession of reformers in both Britain and the United States sought to remedy social ills, appealing at first chiefly to individual consciences but increasingly seeking to mould public policy. In Roads to Ruin E.S. Turner graphically portrays the utter dedication of some British zealots to the rescue of selected groups of unfortunates, whether poachers from spring guns set by landlords, emigrants from the overloading of their ships by unscrupulous owners, or children from being hired out as chimney-sweeps by desperate fathers.[7] The annexation of the Cape of Good Hope in 1806 and the involvement of representatives of the London Missionary Society in the South Seas placed the protection of aborigines from the baleful effects of contact with Europeans squarely on the same agenda. Missionary and humanitarian interest were closely although not always comfortably related. Many reformers were evangelicals or Quakers, while others were secularists or sceptics. Missionary societies, fearful of being excluded from regions where souls might be won, generally disclaimed any intentions that might be interpreted as political. Yet the most other-worldly missionaries could seldom dissociate their soul-winning from the promotion of social change, and leading supporters of foreign missions were prominent among those who agitated for the Factory Acts and the abolition of slavery.

During the early years of the nineteenth century, humanitarians reached a fair measure of consensus about the application of their ideals to aboriginal peoples. They agreed that a lower culture coming into contact with a higher one was doomed to extinction. Aborigines could hope to survive only by becoming like Europeans, therefore, and it was the responsibility of missionaries and administrators to give them all possible help. Becoming like Europeans involved learning to cope with European technology, to adapt to European economic patterns, and eventually to adopt European manners and dress. Such externals would be useless, however, apart from the frame of mind that made sense of them. It would also be necessary, therefore, to cultivate the European values of sobriety, frugality, industry, and enterprise.

This interest in world-wide betterment gradually extended to the Indians of Canada, although at first with relatively little effect. The London Missionary Society entered Canada in 1799 with the Indians chiefly in mind, but none of its representatives ever made significant contact with them. In 1819 the Trappists established themselves in Nova Scotia in order to persuade the Micmacs to settle, likewise with meagre results. One of the most intelligent efforts was that of Walter Bromley, a Methodist half-pay officer who settled in Halifax in 1813 and sought the co-operation of Micmac leaders in several projects of education and settlement. Some Indians took up their own cause. As early as 1806 John Norton, a Mohawk chief at the Grand River despite his mixed Scottish-Cherokee background, drafted an ambitious scheme for a society to promote the civilization of the Indians of British North America that reflected the influence of British Quakers and of the secretary of the British and Foreign Bible Society. Joseph Brant made more than one effort to attract teachers and missionaries to the Grand River, even attempting to secure a 'Romish priest' when other agencies proved unresponsive.[8] Such stillborn proposals, along with others that bordered on the bizarre, at least gave promise of support if some effective project were launched.

In May 1823 the Canadian Methodists staged at Ancaster, near Hamilton, one of those camp meetings with which colonists were already becoming familiar. Camp meetings had an element of unpredictability, and this one threatened to be a disappointment. As it drew near its close, however, there stepped forward as converts two young half-breeds named Mary and Peter Jones. The eventual result was to touch off, after several decades of unfulfilled hopes, a spontaneous movement that led many Indians to become zealous Christians. Peter Jones, whose conversion proved to be the catalyst, was the offspring of a bigamous marriage between a government surveyor named Augustus Jones and a Mississauga woman. He was given an Indian childhood when his father, pricked in conscience by Methodist preaching, returned him with his surplus wife to her own people. Recalled in adolescence to his father's home at the Grand River, Peter received baptism but soon became disillusioned with Christianity through observing the behaviour of the Anglican Mohawks among whom he lived. His conversion gave the Methodists an opening among the Mississaugas and, as time would prove, a very effective missionary.[9]

A knot of converts among the Mississaugas was greatly augmented in 1825 by another camp meeting at Mount Pleasant near the Grand River. After this event, Methodism spread among the Mississaugas and other Ojibwas with astonishing rapidity. Two tours of southwestern Ontario in 1825 ran into some resistance, especially from traditionalist chiefs, but progress was made. Then the movement swept eastwards to Belleville, whence a revival associated with a meeting of the Canada Conference in 1827 carried it to Rice Lake. Egerton Ryerson joined the most effective Indian preachers, Jones and John Sunday, in a highly successful mission at Newmarket that same year, and by 1828 Methodism was well established on Lake Simcoe. From the outset native preachers played a prominent role, and in 1829 Sunday led several of them to the north shore of Lake Huron. Soon they were making regular visits to Michigan and Wisconsin. They were carefully selected and given some coaching by William Case, the superintendent of the Canada Conference, who was acclaimed by American Methodists as their most successful recruiter of Indian leadership.[10]

Although sudden and unexpected, the revival represented the culmination of a long preparation on the part of both Mississaugas and Methodists. The Mississaugas were a branch of the Ojibwa or Chippewa nation, originally centred at Sault Ste Marie and spread along the north shore of Lake Huron, who gradually moved southwards after the destruction of Huronia. In 1661 the Ojibwas won their first battle against the Iroquois, and by 1701 they controlled most of southern Ontario. Until 1783 they were protected by a British policy that reserved western lands for Indian use, but within the next year or two many of their hunting grounds were overrun by an influx of United Empire Loyalists and their economy began to crumble. Most miserable of all were the Mississaugas of the Credit, who were compelled gradually to sell their lands until by 1820 they had only two hundred acres. Meanwhile they had been reduced in numbers from five to two hundred and greatly demoralized by alcohol. They were too close to whites to be unaware of Christianity, and a few of them had already adopted it. A chief was baptized by the Methodist preacher Joseph Sawyer in 1801 and given his name, while in 1810 J. Cameron was led to accept Christianity by being convinced that the earth is round.[11]

Case, who despite his success as a preacher had a streak of shyness, declared himself as early as 1808 more at home with Indians than whites and expressed a desire to devote his life to them. Although the time was not ripe, he continued to cultivate the friendship of Augustus Jones. Meanwhile, interest gradually developed among the American Methodists, with whom the Canadians were affiliated until 1828. It was quickened by the activities of a black missionary, John Stewart, among the Wyandots of Ohio, which incidentally led in 1823 to the formation of a society on the Canadian side of the Detroit River. In 1821 the Genesee Conference, to which the Canadians belonged, set up a committee on Indian work of which Case was a prominent member, and in the following year it sent an American preacher, Alvin Torry, to the Grand River. Most of his work was among white settlers, but he was able to secure some members among Delawares who recalled earlier associations with the Moravians. In the spring of 1823 Methodism made a very strategic convert, the Mohawk chief Thomas Davis. Thus the Methodists opened the decisive camp meeting at Ancaster with some expectations, and Case was quick to recognize the possible consequences of Peter Jones's conversion. Yet this careful strategy had been formulated with the Six Nations almost exclusively in mind and implied mainly an intention to steal Anglican sheep. The conversion of the hitherto unchristianized Mississaugas was serendipity. Even Ancaster, indeed, was a near thing. Organizers had hoped that many Indians would attend, but very few did.[12]

The Methodists pointed to their success as evidence that it is possible to make Christians of uncivilized people, although the contrary conviction had held sway since the time of the Puritan settlers of New England. Case had originally stood out in the Genesee Conference as the only one who believed that conversion could precede civilization, but in 1820 Bishop William McKendree made his position official by urging that only through the preaching of the gospel could the Indians be civilized. Given this starting-point, neither Methodists nor Mississaugas doubted that civilization could and should follow. The Mississauga village at the Credit was reorganized in 1826 as a model community, with church, school, and European-style houses. Grape Island in the Bay of Quinte, where the Belleville Indians were resettled in 1827, became an even more impressive showpiece. As at the Credit, village activities followed a rigid daily schedule,[13] and on at least one occasion Jones made a cabin-by-cabin inspection. Support from American Methodists, on which Grape Island largely relied, was maintained through periodic tours of northeastern cities led by Case but featuring Indian preachers. Methodist programs for Indian improvement were designed with some imagination. In 1829, for example, a travel grant was provided to make possible the introduction at Grape Island of the currently fashionable Pestalozzian system of education. Canadian Methodists neatly summed up their aims in expressing the hope that Indian youths trained in their schools would 'extend the knowledge of God, of learning, and of agriculture and Mechanism.'[14]

The movement shepherded by the Methodists was not the only example of spontaneous Indian response to Christianity. During the 1820s priests from Detroit were increasingly active in northern Michigan, while missionaries bound for Fort William or the Red River occasionally gave missions in the Sault area. About 1824 these attentions, combined with recollections of earlier Jesuit missions in the region, bore fruit in a spontaneous revival of Roman Catholicism among the Ottawas of Arbre Croche, now Harbor Springs, Michigan. Its leader, Andowish, was a band member who had returned from Montreal with some knowledge of that faith. In 1827 Jean-Baptiste Assiginack, another Ottawa of Arbre Croche who was commonly known as the Blackbird because of his ability to maintain a constant stream of oratory, resigned his post as interpreter of the British government's western depot on Drummond Island and returned home to assume leadership of this movement. Arbre Croche would later gain some repute as a model of successful acculturation.[15] More significantly in terms of this study, a number of these Ottawas would soon make their homes in Canada.

With the stage thus set, other agencies were soon in the field. In 1827 the New England Company decided to press the limits of its charter by moving into Upper Canada, agreeing to provide for material needs in the Rice Lake area while leaving religion and education to the Methodists. Since 1822 John Brant had been pressing the company to provide schools at the Grand River, and in 1829 it officially took over responsibility there from the SPG. By the late 1820s the Wesleyan Methodists of Britain were also becoming eager to enter the Canadian field. They distrusted the loyalty of Canadian Methodists, with whom they had no organizational ties, and with some reason doubted their ability to find the resources necessary for expanding the Indian work. A money-raising tour to England in 1831 by Jones and John Ryerson of the Canadian church elicited some reluctant aid but also strengthened the resolve of the Wesleyans to seize the initiative.[16] Meanwhile Charles Stewart, Anglican bishop of Quebec and a former travelling missionary, had given his church a local agency by founding in 1830 'the Society for Converting and Civilizing the Indians and Propagating the Gospel among Destitute Settlers in Upper Canada.' Through his efforts and those of his nephew by marriage, W.J.D. Waddilove, who from Hexham in northern England solicited funds energetically for a country he never saw, it supported for some time travelling missionaries who worked among both immigrants and Indians.[17] In 1835 Richard Flood voluntarily undertook work among the Ojibwas of Bear Creek and the Munceys of the Thames with help from a few friends in Ireland. In succeeding years various English societies sponsored local projects, of which the ministries of Andrew Jamieson at Walpole Island and of E.F. Wilson at Sault Ste Marie were best known.[18] Canadian Anglicans became seriously involved only with the formation of the Domestic and Foreign Missionary Society in 1883.

Other missions were of more indigenous origin. J.D. Cameron, a half-Ojibwa who pioneered Anglican work at Sault Ste Marie, embraced Baptist principles soon after his arrival there. He continued to work in the Lake Superior area for at least twenty-five years under the auspices of the American Baptist Missionary Society, gaining Indian adherents at both Fort William and Michipicoten. Baptists were also active in the Grand River area, securing a foothold among the Tuscaroras in 1842 through the defection of another Anglican catechist. Depending considerably on the initiative of independent native preachers, they were able to establish a strong and persistent presence. The Congregationalists entered the picture in 1850 by taking advantage of local dissatisfaction with the Methodist missionary at Colpoy's Bay. Several resulting missions around Georgian Bay were sponsored for some years by the undenominational Canada Indian Missionary Society of Owen Sound but were handed back to the Methodists during the 1880s. Even the tiny Universalists had for some time a small congregation on the Grand River, founded and cared for by an Indian pastor.[19]

The last major agency to undertake work in Upper Canada was the Society of Jesus. Secured for Canada in 1842 by Bishop Ignace Bourget of Montreal, Jesuits took over the Indian missions of the diocese of Toronto in 1843 in response to an invitation from Bishop Michael Power.[20] They were of the 'new' order, reconstituted by Pope Pius VII in 1814 more than forty years after the dissolution of the old. The new Jesuits had the old certainty about ends tempered with the old flexibility about means, the familiar preparedness to serve in a college or by a council fire. In at least one respect, however, they had learned from bitter experience. Although they continued to be alert for points of contact that might introduce converts gradually to Catholicism, they would indulge in no bold experiments in indigenization that might lead to a renewed condemnation. The new Jesuits were safe and conventional, although as ultramontane as their predecessors and no less suspect in French patriotic circles. Since about 1830 they had felt themselves strong enough to undertake missions abroad, and they had a natural desire to return to areas they had once occupied.

The Jesuits' first Indian assignment, in 1844, was at Walpole Island in Lake St Clair. They could scarcely have drawn a more difficult one. In 1831 the Ojibwas of the area had been given a choice of reservations, Sarnia for those who wished to be 'civilized' and Walpole Island for the others. Most of the Walpole Island Indians had come from the American side, partly for political reasons. Some had been companions of Tecumseh, and one was a grandson of Pontiac. Methodist and Anglican attempts to convert them had been equally futile, and the Anglican missionary John Carey reported in 1844 that the inhabitants were 'without one exception, in a state of Heathenism.' In this delicate situation the initial approach of the Jesuits was distinctly heavy-handed. Securing permission to build a church from the local Indian agent, Dominique du Ranquet appropriated a commanding height venerated as the site both of an early funeral mound and of a more recent burial ground and cut down a grove of century-old oaks to provide wood for the building. His superior Pierre Chazelle took a high line in response to complaints by the Indians that their permission should have been secured, insisting that government authorization was sufficient. Du Ranquet was ordered off the island in 1849, and shortly afterwards the church was burned. He doggedly returned and prepared to build another, but by this time his superiors recognized that their first attempt had failed and abandoned the mission.[21]

The Jesuits fared better in what is now northern Ontario. Taking over the mission of Wikwemikong on Manitoulin a few months after du Ranquet's arrival at Walpole Island, they soon made it the basis of an expanding enterprise among the northern Ojibwas. During the early years they were able to draw on the cultural and linguistic expertise of Frederic Baraga, a remarkable Slovene whose effective jurisdiction as bishop straddled the international boundary.[22] The location of several of their missions along a major canoe route to the northwest gave them further advantages. Roman Catholic missionaries had long been accustomed to give missions on their way to and from more distant posts, and many of the Indians were already inclined to favour French-Canadian voyageurs and their religion. At first, freed by relative isolation from the burden of a civilizing mission, the Jesuits were able to develop a Catholic ambience that would have been difficult to maintain in the presence of European settlement. Later, in order to meet Anglican competition, they set up a model farm and boarding schools that brought them more grief than satisfaction. They were eventually able to bring a substantial majority of the Ojibwas of northern Ontario into the Roman Catholic Church. Further south they had limited success, competing with the Methodists in the Muskoka and Saugeen areas but penetrating no further.

The British government, through the Indian Department of its Colonial Office, had its own reasons for keeping a close eye on the situation in Canada, and its policies had important consequences for the programs of the churches. In earlier years the British thought of the Indians almost exclusively in military terms, cultivating them as potential allies in war and seeking to keep them contented in case they should disturb the peace. Annual presents, recognizing past favours and subtly suggesting future ones, were given in the context of elaborate ceremonial that offered patronizing friendship while insisting on the incomparable might and generosity of the British monarchy. This policy of conciliation did not rule out support for missions so long as they avoided controversy and even encouraged such gestures as the building of churches and the subsidizing of missionaries when these were likely to please the Indians, but it did not favour activities that encouraged radical social change.

Especially after the War of 1812, government policies had to take account of new elements in the situation. The Indians, less and less able to

fend for themselves, were becoming a welfare problem and threatened to
become a very expensive one. The steady increase of the white population
put increased pressure on Indian lands, which from the colonists' point of
view were not being used efficiently. Moreover, the presence of people
who seemed by European standards mainly alcoholics and vagabonds was
both an embarrassment and a threat to a society seeking to achieve stability. Sir Peregrine Maitland, the lieutenant-governor of Canada, proposed
in 1820 and elaborated in 1821 a systematic application of humanitarian
principles as a solution to these problems. In selected Indian communities – he proposed to begin with the Grand and Credit rivers – there should
be schools to teach not only the basics of reading, writing, and arithmetic
but also necessary skills in agriculture and industry. The whole program
should be designed to inculcate a moral sense, and to ensure this a Christian missionary should be an integral part of each educational team.[23]

Despite its boldness this scheme appealed to many contemporaries as a
reasonable solution to otherwise intractable problems. Although initially
expensive, it promised an ultimate saving by helping the Indians towards
self-sufficiency. It would also open Indian hunting grounds to white settlement while actually benefiting the Indians, for it would fit them for a
manner of life that offered greater economic rewards. Despite natural suspicions today of a proposal that undertook at once to save money and
to alienate Indian land, there is no need to impute cynical motives to
Maitland. He was at one time a vice-president of the Church Missionary
Society (CMS), an agency that had been founded in 1799 by Anglican evangelicals for propagating Christianity abroad. On a later posting as com-
mander-in-chief of the Madras Army he would demonstrate the strength
of his convictions, if not the breadth of his sympathy, by resigning his
command rather than punish two Christian privates for failing to fire their
muskets in honour of a Hindu procession.[24] That Christian conviction and
colonial self-interest should so neatly coincide must have seemed to him
only what one might expect of a wise providence.

Similarities between the program enunciated by Maitland and that
implemented by the Canadian Methodists only a few years later will not
have escaped the reader. There was the same emphasis on settlement and
practical education, the same centrality of the Christian mission. In the
case of the Credit, even the locale was one that Maitland had already
selected. This last resemblance, at least, did not come about by accident. It
was John Strachan, rector of York and confidant of Maitland, who in July

1825 suggested that the Mississaugas should set up a model village on the Credit. Maitland subsequently offered twenty houses and a school and asked his Indian agent, Colonel James Givins, to make the necessary arrangements for the village. Givins was impressed by what he saw and highly commended the Methodist preachers.[25] The authorities had good reason to co-operate with them, for they were in effect proving that Maitland's proposals could be implemented successfully.

Harmonious relations between the Methodists and the government were destined not to last long. In January 1828 Strachan informed Jones that the government would continue its aid only if the mission were placed under the established church, and in the next two years attempts were made to block Jones's election as chief and then to woo him from the Methodists with the offer of a superintendency. This souring of relations may have been due in part to resentment of Methodist interference with the Mohawks of the Grand River and of the Bay of Quinte, whom Anglicans regarded as their preserve, but this was scarcely a new grievance. Objections to American connections were scarcely credible when the authorities must have known that Canadian Methodists were in process of breaking them, although we must not underestimate the emphasis still laid on military security in dealings with the Indians. A sense that government funds should be reserved to established churches carried weight with Anglicans if not necessarily with officials. The chief objection to the Methodists, however, was that they had become involved in opposition politics. Unfavourable comments on preachers of American origin in Strachan's memorial sermon for Bishop Jacob Mountain of Quebec in 1825 had called forth a defence by Egerton Ryerson, a Methodist probationer stationed on the Yonge Street circuit, who compounded his offence by publishing his article in William Lyon Mackenzie's *Colonial Advocate*.[26] The goodwill built up by Methodist success among the Indians must have been further eroded by the circumstance that Ryerson continued his agitation while stationed at the Credit village.

In 1828 Sir John Colborne replaced Maitland as lieutenant-governor of Upper Canada, while Sir James Kempt became governor-general. They were able to persuade the home government, mainly with fiscal arguments, to authorize the implementation of Maitland's proposals and even to extend them to other tribes. There still remained the problem that the Methodists, by now more active politically than ever, seemed at once indispensable and unacceptable. In 1827 Strachan had already made an unsuccessful request to the CMS for missionaries to replace them. In 1829 Kempt, having noted expressions of interest on the part of the British Wesleyans, urged the home government to secure their involvement. Presumably they would have the same evangelizing and organizing skills as the Canadians while maintaining a properly deferential attitude to authority. By 1832, banking on Colborne's promise of an annual grant of £1000, they were operating in Canada independently of the local conference. Thomas Turner, their first missionary to the Indians, set off for Sarnia with a letter of recommendation from Strachan in his pocket.[27] In the following year the Canadian Methodists, unable to finance their Indian work properly and despairing of competing successfully with British preachers in the larger towns, accepted union on unequal terms with the British Conference. The immediate result was to restrain the Canadian Methodists from political agitation, although not to disarm their suspicion of official intentions.

The first serious attempt to apply the new government policy was in the Coldwater area between Georgian Bay and Lake Simcoe, where in 1829 Colborne authorized an ambitious program for settling and 'civilizing' Indians. This experiment provided a setting in which several parties seeking to convert the Indians met and, in the event, collided. The local bands had already been evangelized by the Canadian Methodists, and Colborne had little choice but to co-operate up to a point with their representatives. A number of Roman Catholic Ottawas and Ojibwas from the upper lakes had also been attracted to the vicinity by the handing-over of Drummond Island to the Americans in 1828 and the transfer of the British western headquarters to Penetanguishene. Assiginack moved to Coldwater in 1832 and was soon vying for the leadership of the Catholic Indians.[28] Colborne's chief agent on the spot, Captain Thomas G. Anderson, was a strong Anglican with long experience in the Indian service who saw his own role as that of chief missionary.

This bringing together of divergent interests brought to a head a growing religious ferment among the northern Indians. Annual distributions of presents at Penetanguishene became occasions for religious debate, often followed by decisions for a particular form of Christianity. Leading speakers included Anderson, Assiginack, Jones, and later Adam Elliot, agent for the Home District of the Society for Converting and Civilizing the Indians. Assiginack's major prize was John Aisance, Methodist chief of the Coldwater band, while the Methodists rejoiced over chiefs who suddenly turned in their medicine bundles. Although the debates were conducted with customary Indian politeness, Anderson's obvious support of Anglican claims provoked discord. Early in 1830 Colborne promised Jones not to compete with Methodist teachers, but Bishop Stewart exerted enough pressure to secure the appointment of an Anglican teacher, George Archbold, in June. His school proved acceptable to neither Methodists nor Roman Catholics,[29] and the accessibility of white whisky-sellers at Orillia combined with various grievances to doom the experiment.

Eager to extend European ways among the Indians but disillusioned by the effects of close proximity to whites, Anderson persuaded Colborne in 1835 to invite the Indians of Coldwater and Lake Huron to settle on Manitoulin Island. In 1836 Anderson and Elliot arrived with a schoolmaster to establish a mission in which church and state would collaborate to promote Christianity and civilization. Their project received a severe check later in that year when Sir Francis Bond Head succeeded Colborne as lieutenant-governor. Head had an appreciation of native culture that was rare at the time but also believed that the Indians were doomed to extinction and would be happiest if allowed to spend their last days free of white interference. He therefore strongly approved of the policy of segregation on Manitoulin but sought to people the island not by attracting northern Indians but by inducing the more settled southern bands to surrender their lands. Having no use for missionary establishments, he abruptly ordered Anderson and Elliot off Manitoulin.[30]

In 1838 Head was replaced by Sir George Arthur, his native policy discredited in both Canada and England. All Protestant missionaries had opposed it, although Roman Catholics were pleased by the prospect of removing the Indians from contamination by Europeans. In England the policy of civilization was urged upon the government by Robert Alder, a Wesleyan official who detested the politics of Canadian Methodists but thoroughly approved of their methods with the Indians. He was vigorously supported by the Aborigines' Protection Society, formed in 1836 to cement an alliance of 'friends' of the aborigines who had worked together on a parliamentary select committee. Their success ensured that henceforth Christianity and civilization would be pressed by the state not as mere expedients but as part of the moral responsibility of the British people.[31] One of the first effects of the new policy was to revive the Manitoulin project, and in the fall of 1838 a party representing varying skills and headed by Anderson and the Anglican clergyman Charles Brough established itself at Manitowaning.[32] The delay of two years, however, was fatal to the success of the mission. A number of Roman Catholic Indians had already settled on the island, including some Ottawas from Arbre Croche among whom was Assiginack.[33] A priest, Jean-Baptiste Proulx, established residence there in 1838. This head start was never overtaken, and upon the removal of imperial support in 1859 Brough's successor, F.A. O'Meara, withdrew to Sault Ste Marie.

Despite this initial setback the policy of civilization was firmly in place and would determine the policies of both Protestant and Roman Catholic missionaries during the years to come. All that remained was to determine the most effective method of encouraging the Indians to adopt European ways. Education found increasing favour, and the 'manual-labour school' emerged as the preferred model. As developed in 1804 by Gideon Black-burn, a Presbyterian missionary among the Cherokees, its most distinctive feature was a schedule that allotted equal time to study and to work in the fields, shops, or kitchen of the institution. Several young Canadian Indians from Methodist missions had attended such a school at Jacksonville, Illinois, and seem to have brought back enthusiastic reports. Missionary response was favourable, for the system seemed to offer both practical education and financial self-sufficiency. Case adopted it at Alderville, opened in 1844 chiefly for female students, and the enthusiastic advocacy of the earl of Elgin as governor-general led to the establishment in 1849 of a more ambitious Methodist school at Muncey named, appropriately, the Mount Elgin Institute.[34] These developments inaugurated a new era in Indian missions, marked by the centrality of residential schools to which young people would be removed from parental influence in the hope that they would become effective emissaries of Christian civilization among their people.

In Upper Canada as elsewhere, Indians varied in their response to Christianity. Many offered objections, often ones that had been recorded by missionaries of the French era. Such were the claim of a visitor to the camp on Lake Huron of Methodist missionary James Evans that God had given white and red men different forms of worship and the hoary tale reported by O'Meara from Manitoulin of an Indian who accepted Christianity and found himself shut out of two heavens.[35] Objections based on the obnoxious behaviour of Europeans were more common than ever. 'The whites are Christians, and yet they are no better than we. They lie, cheat, get drunk, swear. They have injured the poor Indians,' stated some Muncey chiefs in declining an invitation to join the Methodists. Sometimes Indian answers were ambiguous. Snake, another chief of the Munceys, told Jones that his people would worship God in both 'your way and our way,' whereas the St Clair Indians insisted that both religions were equally good but that in fact they observed neither. Among the Six Nations, exposed longer than any others to British influence, many found their own alternative to Christianity. In 1799 a New York Seneca, Ganiodaio or Handsome Lake, had the first of a series of visions that offered a solution to his own alcoholism and to his people's lack of a sense of purpose. His 'Good Message' recalled the Iroquois to selected traditional practices while leaving room for accommodation to the European presence. Before his death in 1815 it had spread to the Grand River, where except among the Mohawks it retained the allegiance of a majority until the latter years of the century. Despite Handsome Lake's own openness to borrowing from whites, it became among the Canadian Iroquois a rallying point for opponents of innovation.[36]

Most striking to contemporary observers, however, was the ready welcome extended to Christianity. One Methodist, reflecting on the progress of Christianity among the Indians, could only compare it with the speed of the 'Apocalyptic angel flying through the midst of heaven.' Indian choices were sometimes made suddenly, as in the hothouse atmosphere of the Penetang debates; more often bands made up their minds only after conference and deliberation. Often the initiative was taken by the Indians themselves, so that Evans could write to his wife from Michipicoten, 'no missionary can seek these people more faithfully than they seek him.' Nathan Bangs, a preacher who later became a leading figure in American Methodism, described how this frequently happened: 'The fragments of tribes who are settled over the country hear of what is going on, send messengers to see what it means. These return and report. They then send and invite the missionary to come among them.' Benjamin Slight similarly wrote of Methodism as making its way westwards preceded by gifts of wampum that passed from one tribe to another.[37]

The openness to Christianity manifested in Upper Canada especially by the Ojibwas was the more remarkable when compared with the unwillingness of their fellow tribesmen west of Lake Superior, where organized shamanism prevented any significant Christian penetration for many years. Peter Jacobs, himself an Ojibwa and the first convert of the Belleville mission, struggled against constant discouragement there during the

1840s, while in 1870 E.F. Wilson reported that mention of Christianity still provoked anger.[38] Only at Walpole Island was there comparable resistance in Upper Canada.

The missions brought forward a roster of native leaders scarcely equalled in Canada at any other time or place. They belonged to two main categories, although with considerable overlapping of personnel between the two. On the one hand there were important contact persons whose conversion helped to pave the way for that of their people. Jones and Assiginack were prime examples. In a number of cases it was the influence of local chiefs that tipped the scales towards Christianity. One thinks of Snake of the Muncey Delawares, a war veteran who, after sitting on the fence for a few years, became an Anglican church warden and marched his people to church in military fashion each Sunday, or of Wawanosh of Sarnia, a wily leader whose support placed Methodist and Anglican missions in turn on a sound footing.[39] In the other category we might place those who went out to share their new faith with distant tribal members or even strange peoples. These had the great advantage of knowing the land and being able to live off it on their journeys without more than accustomed hardship. Henry M. Schoolcraft observed that at Sault Ste Marie they made an impression which no white speakers could have matched.[40] We have already noted missionaries who penetrated Michigan and Wisconsin. We could add to the roll William Doxtater among the Oneidas of New York, some of whom he later helped to bring to Ontario, and Henry B. Steinhauer among the Crees of northern Alberta. In this second category the Methodists notably excelled.

For the most part the Indians of Upper Canada accepted Christianity because rather than in spite of its association with European culture. Christian Indians lived in settled localities and often in European-style houses, farmed or worked at other steady jobs, increasingly dressed in European clothes, and sent their children to school. They exceeded many whites in moral strictness and delighted in such anecdotes as that of a group of Mississaugas who knocked over the whisky barrels of a trader who was trying to tempt them. Doubtless over-optimistic missionaries exaggerated the transformation, but even such a detached observer as the artist Paul Kane was impressed by some conversions. Few doubted that these steps towards assimilation were inevitable concomitants of Christianity; at the Penetang assembly of 1834 Elliot observed 'the Pagans quietly smoking tobacco, but the professors of Christianity behaving like civilized people.' Among tokens of Christian civilization that came in for special praise were the wearing of hats and the alignment of houses along a straight street. Later, partly at Jones's urging, the Indians in council agreed to the use of a quarter of the annuities from the sale of their land in support of manual-labour schools.[41]

The motives that impelled Indians to adopt Christianity with such alacrity were, from one point of view, as varied as the Indians themselves. Sometimes they involved very tangible expectations. At the Mount Pleasant camp meeting Thomas Davis assured his fellow Indians that, so long as they were faithful, 'when their moccasins were worn out, God would send them more; that if their corn was poor, He would provide; and that, after toil and hunting were over, He would take them to heaven.' For some benefits Indians looked not to supernatural aid but directly to the mission. When Davis and two other chiefs pitched their tents by a newly erected school, two hundred Mississauga families joined them. At Sault Ste Marie it was an offer of government houses that prompted the local band to opt for Anglicanism. Many missionaries regarded such inducements as legitimate aids to evangelization, helping to raise the Indians from what Conrad Van Dusen described as 'a pagan indifference to the comforts, pleasures, riches and honours of the world.' In other cases the attraction could be the possibility of personal transformation. In a testimony to his Christian faith James Thomas remarked simply: 'I was then poor and dirty. The Great Spirit has done much for me.' At St Clair one man joined the Methodists because they were able to cure a 'sickness of heart that had baffled the medicine men.'[42]

Greatly as these testimonies vary in detail, they yield a consistent pattern. The Indians of Upper Canada were in a desperate situation from which conventional remedies offered no escape. Alcohol and tuberculosis had brought the Mississaugas to the verge of extinction and were wreaking havoc everywhere. The land was exhausted or was rapidly being alienated. As it went, the spirits that had hovered over it lost their functions, their power, and eventually their credibility. In many areas traditional practices scarcely needed to be renounced, for they were vanishing with the way of life to which they had given meaning. Whites, by contrast, were prospering and occupying the land. Indians might resent their procedures but could see that they worked. Already dependent on white agencies for material support, they could see nowhere else to turn for the reconstruction of their society. Shinguacouse of Sault Ste Marie spoke for many similarly placed: 'Why should we not hear and receive your teacher, and your other kind offers towards our civilization? ... at present we are like as many wild animals in the woods, we have no place to shelter us from the bad storms, but where night finds us, there we are compelled to remain.' Often, Peter Jacobs noted, the great difficulty was simply to convince Indians that God could do for them what he had done for the whites.[43] Once assured that conversion was possible, they often needed little argument to persuade them that it was desirable.

In Upper Canada most Indians were offered a choice of at least two Christian denominations, and some were actively wooed by three or more.[44] Often the winner was simply the denomination that had made effective contact first. A surprising number of bands, however, carefully weighed the respective merits of rival claimants before making their decisions. The options were not radically different, for each denomination offered the common values of Christian Europe along with its particular brand of Christianity. Among the major contenders, however, there was enough difference that each choice reflected a somewhat different analysis of local needs.

The Methodist road was in many ways the most demanding, calling for a sudden and definite conversion in which the past was put behind, followed by a process of sanctification in which by degrees every vestige of the old nature was to be rooted out. This radical change was almost always interpreted as a transition from Indian to European ways; there was no place in Methodism for Indians who wished to remain as they were.[45] On the other hand, Methodist insistence that everyone regardless of race required this radical transformation helped Indians to make the transition with dignity. Essentially they were treated as sinners rather than as inferiors. They might backslide, as many whites also did, but if they persevered they needed only to demonstrate piety and rhetorical ability to attain positions of leadership. Methodism appealed most strongly to groups in desperate straits, especially in areas where farming offered a viable alternative to traditional means of support.

Roman Catholic missionaries also promoted civilization along with Christianity and were sensitive to occasional Protestant charges that they did not do so effectively. With their insistence on the continuity of nature and grace and their more sophisticated distinctions between the sacred and the secular, however, they were inclined to put less pressure on the Indians to conform to any one set of cultural norms. Their minority status as francophones and their links with the early history of the region helped them to give Catholic Indians a badge of differentiation that fortified their sense of identity as Indian.[46] Roman Catholics were also able to create an environment of mystery and miracle in which Indians whose culture was still somewhat intact could feel more at home than in the desacralized atmosphere of Protestantism.

The official connections of Anglicans led them to rely more than either Methodists or Roman Catholics on the total apparatus of a Christian society and correspondingly less on the specific operation of either sacraments or appeals to individual decision. To many Indians the Church of England seemed an integral part of the Indian Department, and its representatives unabashedly urged them to belong to the king's religion. They offered a middle road between Methodism and Roman Catholicism, equally remote, according to O'Meara, from 'wild fanaticism' and 'that dumb, lifeless parade ... which is only calculated to captivate the senses.' Methodists and Roman Catholics agreed that Anglicans were their least formidable rivals, thereby underestimating them. In the long run it proved an advantage to Anglicanism that it promised to lead to the heart of British civilization rather than into a sectarian corner. Anglicans had unusual success, perhaps through their respect for legitimate authority, in attracting and holding chiefs of the stature of Snake and Shinguacouse and even in winning a few from the Methodists.[47]

Never in Canadian history has conversion to Christianity been of such evident benefit to Indians as in Upper Canada during the second quarter of the nineteenth century. Where the situation was especially desperate, and commitment to Christianity correspondingly intense, the effect was to ensure the survival of peoples who were assumed to be destined to extinction. An inquiry by T.J. Baxter, MP, in 1836 brought replies from one missionary after another that Christianity had dramatically reduced the death rate, and the St Clair chiefs contrasted forty-seven deaths of adults and at least as many among children in the four years preceding conversion with three adults and eight children in the next four. Even where the threat was less immediate and conversion reluctant or half-hearted, the effect was at least to set in place the scaffolding of a new system of belief and practice to replace one that was palpably about to collapse. These benefits were partly the direct result of missionary programs of education and welfare. More basically, they were the products of a theology that

made sense for the Indians of the universe as the white man had transformed it and also left room for them in it. George Henry, an Ojibwa
preacher who exulted that from resembling 'the animals you call Ourang
Outangs' his people had reached a point where one of their chiefs had now
'got a good feather bed,' had in mind not only material benefits but also a
new respect the Ojibwas commanded both from themselves and from
others. Best of all, these benefits came about not merely with the consent
and co-operation of the Indians but to a considerable extent through their
initiative and leadership.

By mid-century the enterprise had lost much of its glamour. Most
Indian missions in Ontario had become rather routine affairs, with few
signs of excitement and even less of the native initiative that had marked
the earlier period. The first generation of Indian leaders had largely died
off, and few had arisen to replace them. Some of the most prominent had
fallen into disgrace. Peter Jacobs was dropped from the Methodist ministry
for financial irregularities and fell victim to alcohol. George Copway, celebrated for a time as both minister and author, was dismissed for embezzle-
ment and died a Roman Catholic. George Henry found a more colourful
way to scandalize his fellow Methodists, taking a troupe of 'wild-west'
Indian performers to England. If the falling-away was most conspicuous
among the ecstatically inclined Methodists, it also affected charismatic
leaders of other denominations. Assiginack proved a thorn in the flesh to
successive missionaries at Wikwemikong and ultimately died without the
last rites of the church.[48] What had happened to the first careless rapture?

Undoubtedly what happened was in part a natural descent from the
heights that characterizes almost every religious movement. Methodism
had performed the vital function of seeing the Mississaugas through a
crisis, and once the crisis was past, the normal means of sustaining life
came once more to the fore. Indeed, not only the Mississaugas but the Six
Nations and the Moravian Delawares were able in a measure to enter the
mainstream of provincial life, where they did not conspicuously exhibit
more or less piety than their neighbours. If other missions manifested no
greater excitement, they nevertheless made fairly steady progress throughout the latter half of the nineteenth century. Disappointment was to a
considerable extent the result of unrealistic expectations.

Conversion was, nevertheless, attended by problems. Some of these were
only ones that might have been expected. When some Indians from the
model community at Grape Island were seen drunk on the streets of King-

ston, for example, they were only behaving as immature converts of every age have sometimes behaved.[49] More serious were difficulties inherent in the very circumstances of christianization. One of the great attractions of Christianity was the hope that it would open to Indians opportunities hitherto available only to whites. Some of these opportunities, constantly held out as inducements by the missionaries themselves, were tangible and material. In seeking them the Indians ran an obvious risk of preferring the proximate to the ultimate rewards of Christianity. This temptation applied particularly to the conception of leadership roles. Christianity offered new means of attaining status within societies where such traditional avenues as prowess in hunting or war were no longer available. But how were such roles to be evaluated? Preaching and staging wild-west shows called for many of the same skills of organization and showmanship. To the Methodist mind one was an acceptable use of them for Christians, while the other was not. Was it altogether reasonable, however, to expect a relatively new convert to see any great difference between the two? Even more recent evangelists have been known to 'preach a little gospel, sell a few bottles of Dr Good.' Such confusion may have been a significant factor in the 'downfall' of some early Indian Christian leaders.

Even when they coincided with those of the missionaries, Indian expectations of Christianity were not always fulfilled, and disappointment could give rise to disillusionment and apathy. Some aspirations, such as that of turning hunters into efficient farmers almost overnight, were patently unrealistic, but failure to achieve them was none the less damaging to morale. Even when Indians performed what was asked of them, they found no great willingness in the white community to accept them as either economic or social partners. Among such frustrations the Indians complained most of their inability to secure clear title to their land. Jones sponsored repeated petitions of the Mississaugas, taking one of them to England, but the Mississaugas never obtained satisfaction and finally accepted an invitation from the Mohawks to resettle at the Grand River. Head's policies were repudiated but his land purchases were not annulled, and a large reserve embracing most of the Bruce peninsula eventually shrank like other proposed refuges into a few small parcels of land. As a Methodist missionary Van Dusen had his own agenda, preference for individual over communal ownership, but otherwise there can be little dispute with his judgment on Indian agriculture: 'The great mystery is, that many of them have succeeded in this, in the midst of all the opposition they have had to encounter, having so often been driven from their possessions, and not permitted to hold a foot of their own land, except by tribal tenure.'[50]

In the end, however, it may have been the missionaries and other civilizers themselves who did more than anyone else to stultify the movement they had begun with such promise. At the outset they had worked with Indian leaders in a relation of mutual dependence, and both had been highly gratified by the results. As time passed and the novelty of Indian self-improvement wore off, however, it began to be observed that progress in the arts of civilization was slow and that setbacks were frequent. New habits were difficult to acquire, old ones even more difficult to break. Alcoholism continued to be a problem; children were regularly withdrawn from school at berry-picking time, and even Mississaugas began to disappear during the hunting season. In 1844 the government-appointed Bagot Commission painted a depressing picture of Indian life in Canada West.

The obvious answer, already familiar from other contexts, was to let the older generation remain as it was and to raise up a new one that would be shaped in a different mould. In 1841 the Methodist missionary Sylvester Hurlburt saw hope for the Indians only in schools 'where the rising generation can be brought up entirely away from the instruction of their parents,' and during succeeding years an increasing proportion of missionary resources would be devoted to the foundation of such schools. The problem to which Hurlburt referred was a genuine one. Many of the Indians themselves recognized it, and in 1854 it was reported that prominent chiefs and other Indians wished literary classes to be taught entirely in English.[51] Their thinking reflected no discredit on Indian languages, resembling rather that of contemporary anglophone parents who enrol their children in immersion classes as the most efficient method of learning French.

During this period, however, a subtle but significant shift was taking place in the missionaries' conception of their task. Instead of seeking to help Indian converts to make a voluntary adjustment to a new situation, they attempted increasingly to impose Western values whether the Indians were willing or not. Other civilizers, including the Aborigines' Protection Society, were moving in the same direction. These views were embodied in the Civilization Act of 1857, which contrary to the desire of tribal leaders provided for the voluntary transfer of individual Indians to white status. J.S. Milloy suggests that this abandonment of the earlier policy of conciliation 'condemned civilizing efforts to founder on the rock of tribal nationalism.'[52] Certainly the very act of turning to children rather than their parents as the chief agents of acculturation left the Indians a marginal place in the missionary enterprise and discouraged the emergence of indigenous leadership. Never again would there be such a favourable opportunity for the inclusion of Indians as active partners in their own evangelization.

CHAPTER FIVE

The Race to the Northern Sea

When Christian missionaries began to arrive, northern Canada from the Saguenay to the Yukon was essentially Indian country and seemed destined to remain so for a long time. European hunger for land, so fateful elsewhere, was not yet a factor there. From the Arctic watershed to the Saskatchewan country in the west and from the Hudson Bay lowlands to the interior of Labrador in the east lived mainly Crees, an Algonquian people whose language was cognate with that of the Montagnais whom early French explorers had met at Quebec. Bordering them on the east were the closely related Naskapis. To the northwest were tribes of the Dene or Athapaskan linguistic family: Chipewyans around Lake Athabasca and Great Slave Lake; Beavers along the Peace River; Slaveys, Hareskins, and Loucheux along the Mackenzie; Dogribs between Great Slave and Great Bear lakes; and Tukudhs in the Yukon.

Despite inevitable variations in economy over such a vast area, these people resembled one another in depending largely on the natural products of the land. Migrating herds of caribou had a special importance to almost all of the Dene peoples, while the Crees had to forage for a greater variety of game animals and berries. Fish, in the well-watered Canadian Shield, was a stand-by everywhere; survival through the winter depended on securing a good supply in the autumn. Religion had many of the features noted elsewhere, prescribing rituals to propitiate the spirits that ensured good hunting and good health and promising personal contact with the unseen in visions, dreams, and shamanic inspiration. The Dene took particular care to seclude girls at puberty and women at times of menstruation and childbirth, while the Crees had a reputation for being especially devoted to the dance. Neither had the leisure or the affluence for the staging of elaborate communal rituals or for the formation of voluntary religious societies, so that missionaries could regard the northern peoples as virtually without religion.[1]

Although as yet he posed no threat to Indian occupation of the land, the white man had long been a familiar presence. Since the foundation of the Hudson's Bay Company in 1670 'home-guard' Crees near the coast had lived on intimate terms with traders, given them their daughters in marriages, and shared the privileges and obligations of in-laws. During the eighteenth century French explorers and traders were sufficiently numerous that by 1775 the resulting Métis were already being referred to as good hunters and warriors. In 1774 the Hudson's Bay Company set up its first inland post on Cumberland Lake, forty years before the first permanent Christian mission, and four years later Peter Pond opened the Athabasca country for one of the precursors of the North West Company. Even in the Yukon, first entered by whites in 1847, the trader was twenty years in advance of the missionary, and the Tukudhs there had long known European trade goods brought by Tlingit middlemen from the Alaskan coast.

The European presence had already had profound effects upon the Indian way of life. Tribal economies, which had formerly been designed to provide simple subsistence, were now integrated into the capitalistic trading system of the West with its emphasis upon profit. The Indians as usual proved themselves canny traders, accepting only goods that would bring tangible benefits, and in most of the north the difficulties and risks of transport limited trade to articles that could be received without great social dislocation. Along with improved technology, however, European contact brought problems with which the Indian was unable or unprepared to cope. One of several epidemics of smallpox decimated the Crees, Assiniboines, and Ojibwas in 1781 and swept on to wipe out an estimated 90 per cent of the Chipewyans. Alcohol, one of the few European goods that would induce Indians to make long journeys, was officially discouraged by the Hudson's Bay Company (HBC) but seemed indispensable when competition threatened. The depletion of resources already noted in the east was aggravated by the effects of systematic exploitation on the sensitive ecology of the Canadian Shield and the tundra, and starvation became a more imminent threat as precious time was diverted from food-gathering to trapping for export. Nor did traders scruple, when profit demanded it, to employ physical violence against the Indians or to set tribes against their neighbours.[2]

Over the century and a half that intervened between the inception of European trade and the institution of the first permanent Christian mission, virtually no effort was made to change the religious beliefs and practices of the northern Indians. Such prolonged contact, however, could scarcely have left no residue. French Jesuits sojourned briefly at James Bay in the late seventeenth century and on the prairies in the early eighteenth. They left behind no Christian communities, but presumably some memory. The rules of the HBC called for regular prayers at all posts. They seem to have been largely disregarded in the pre-missionary period, but the exceptions must have given a fair number of Indians a passing acquaintance with Anglican forms of worship. The progeny of interracial unions, especially those with French fathers, habitually mingled elements of Christian belief and ritual with traditional practice. Some of them, we know, taught their neighbours the sign of the cross and a few simple prayers. On the other side, native religion was so integral a part of a way of life that changes in the economy and knowledge of new possibilities must have impaired its efficacy, if as yet only to a tolerable degree. Some Indians began to incorporate Christian ideas of a good and an evil spirit and of eternal rewards and punishments into their own system of beliefs.[3] In all of these ways there was growing a certain receptivity to Christianity, and in some quarters an expectation that in due time Christian missionaries would arrive.

The Red River proved to be the gateway by which missionaries penetrated to the northwest and, in the case of Protestants, to the northeast as well. It was not on the main route of the North West Company and not even close to that of the Hudson's Bay Company. Its importance lay rather in its accessibility to the buffalo that provided the voyageurs' pemmican supply, which in time attracted a significant Métis population. Then in 1811 the Scottish philanthropist Lord Selkirk began to introduce Scottish and Irish settlers, promising them the services of a Presbyterian minister and a Roman Catholic priest. The minister failed to appear. Bishop Joseph-Octave Plessis of Quebec responded with alacrity, however, and in 1818 Joseph-Norbert Provencher, Joseph-Sévère-Nicolas Dumoulin, and a seminarian opened the first permanent mission in the region. They were followed by John West, who arrived in 1820 as company chaplain and as a special representative of the Anglican Church Missionary Society (CMS). This agency had been designed specifically for work in 'Africa and the East' and agreed to sponsor West only because his salary was already assured.[4]

First among the duties listed in Plessis's instructions to his missionaries was 'to draw from barbarism and the disorders that follow it the savage nations scattered in this vast country,' while Benjamin Harrison of the HBC committee persuaded the CMS to adopt the field officially by presenting to it an elaborate plan for the extension of schools throughout the northwest. Despite this show of interest in the Indians, the needs of existing settlers and of redundant employees who greatly swelled their numbers after the union of the Hudson's Bay and North West companies in 1821 absorbed most of the energies of the first missionaries. West opened a school that would train a generation of Indian leaders. His tactless comments on the foibles of Red River society led to his dismissal in 1823, however, and his successor David Jones concentrated on the local population. Dumoulin became an enthusiast for outreach to the Indians, but Provencher thought that his services might have been more usefully employed. In 1830 Provencher wrote of the evangelization of the neighbouring Indians as still a hope for the future.[5]

That the Indians began to receive more attention in the next decade was due almost entirely to the enthusiasm and initiative of two men: William Cockran, a rough-hewn north-country Anglican of practical bent; and George-Antoine Bellecourt, a charismatic French-Canadian with expansive dreams. In 1832 Cockran secured permission to farm Indian land down-river from Fort Garry and within five or six years was credited with 'civilizing' fifty families, mainly Cree. George Simpson, the HBC governor, at first welcomed a scheme that promised to divert the Red River Indians from trapping that only aided the company's American rivals, but was chagrined when most settlers proved to be its own trappers from the north. In 1832 Bellecourt laid out along the Assiniboine the townsite of Saint-Paul-des-Sauteux, where he encouraged agriculture among the local Ojibwas or Saulteaux. Objection in this case came from Provencher, now a bishop, who wished that Bellecourt would make converts instead of projecting ambitious plans. Bellecourt's settlement was destined not long to outlast his recall to Quebec in 1847, while later Anglicans would never duplicate Cockran's success in persuading Indians to farm. Meanwhile missionaries of both denominations became impatient to reach out and were greatly irked in 1838 when the company placed a ban on extension beyond the Red River.[6]

An uneasy equilibrium was shattered in 1838 by the news that two French-Canadian priests, Norbert Blanchet and Modeste Demers, were on their way to the distant Columbia, thus forestalling a keen Anglican desire to reach that region. The impatience of the Anglicans was further whetted by reports from the French-Canadian pair of a good reception on their journey from the Crees of the Saskatchewan. They responded in 1840 by opening a mission at Cumberland House on the Saskatchewan, soon moved to The Pas, and within two years had others at Lac la Ronge to the north and Fairford on Lake Manitoba. A contest was on that would eventually be extended to the Arctic and Pacific as well as into every corner of the plains. Of immediate concern here are developments that led northwards.

The race to the northern sea appeared to have been decided, almost before it began, by the entry of a new agency with many advantages. On 4 March 1840 the governor and committee of the Hudson's Bay Company informed their factors that they had accepted an offer from the Wesleyan Missionary Society to establish several missions in its territory. The society was to be responsible for salaries, but contrary to precedent the company would furnish free transportation and extend to the missionaries the provisions for accommodation and supplies it made for its own officers. The Wesleyan Methodists resembled the CMS in their adherence to an evangelical version of Protestantism, but pressed their evangelism with an intensity and sometimes a sensationalism that reflected its recognition of some place for the human will in the process of salvation. Preaching among blacks in the West Indies had made them sympathetic to the sufferings of colonized peoples, but they also had a tradition of deference to constituted authority. Technically the company merely granted them permission to enter its territory. The fields assigned them covered the entire area from James Bay to the Rocky Mountains, however, and the conviction of the company that the resources of the country further north would not sustain missionary establishments was well known. Anglican suspicions of an intended monopoly were heightened by a proposal that Evans should replace the ailing Cockran at the Red River.[7]

This newly formed alliance, although surprising on the surface, was not without some logic on both sides. Canadian Methodists, confident of their ability to handle missions in their own province, directed the attention of their English colleagues to Rupert's Land as early as 1831. Meanwhile they pushed their own missions westwards to Fort William by 1838, and in 1839 the Ojibwa minister Peter Jacobs was at the future Fort Frances. Company officials on their side had come to regard the CMS missionaries as a carping opposition. They were also alarmed by the exodus of able-bodied Cree trappers to the Red River, and in 1835 Donald Ross of Norway House had proposed a mission at his post as a means of stemming it. In 1839 James Evans, a Canadian missionary of English birth, had a congenial meeting with Simpson. Already convinced by a short stay on Lake Superior that agriculture would never be practical on the Canadian Shield, Evans apparently satisfied Simpson that the Methodists would not engage in dangerous social experiments.[8]

With Evans as superintendent and missionary at Norway House, the main HBC transfer point, the Methodists were soon energetically at work. Three of them were English Wesleyans, while Jacobs and Henry B. Steinhauer represented the Upper Canadian corps of Ojibwa evangelists. In the winter of 1841–2, after a visit to Fort Edmonton, Evans made a circuit that took him as far north as the junction of the Peace and Slave rivers and home by way of Ile-à-la-Crosse. He made a notable impression and baptized many Indians, but he was not to remain unchallenged. In 1844 Jean-Baptiste Thibault, a dogged priest who had already reconverted many of Evans's converts around Edmonton, passed through Norway House with the stated intention of visiting many of these same posts. This was too much for Evans, who hastily set out in a specially constructed tin canoe. This journey, which might have altered the shape of northern missions, was aborted when Evans accidentally shot and killed his capable interpreter Thomas Hassell. There would be no further attempt to press Methodism northwards, and in 1845 Thibault baptized 218 persons at Ile-à-la-Crosse.[9]

The decline of the Wesleyan mission was as spectacular as its inception had been. No further appointments were made, no new stations opened except Oxford House under Steinhauer. In 1846 Evans was summoned to London as the result of a bitter dispute with Simpson, and within a few months he was dead. Others withdrew until by 1850 only Evans's colleague William Mason and Steinhauer were left, and in 1853 Mason joined the CMS in despair of receiving reinforcement. Almost from the beginning, relations between the mission and the company had deteriorated. Simpson was displeased with the cost of missionary freight, with Evans's ban on Sunday travel by Methodist Indians, and perhaps most of all by Evans's insistence on acting as his own master. A suspicion that Evans was setting up a cottage industry at Norway House with contraband fur was the final straw that led to his recall. He also became involved in a charge of sexual misconduct on which he was acquitted both by his colleagues and by the missionary society, although this came too late to affect the outcome. One should not, however, discount other factors in the Wesleyan withdrawal, including a controversy in England that precipitated a financial crisis and even an unfavourable exchange rate. A break between Canadian and English Methodists that occurred in 1840 was healed in 1847, and in 1854 the remnants of the mission were handed over to the Canadians.[10]

Opportunities in the north were now available to the Roman Catholics, but even the persistent Thibault was in no position to exploit them alone. In 1845, however, Provencher was able to enlist the assistance of the Oblates of Mary Immaculate, a French order that Bourget had succeeded in attracting to Canada on the same trip on which he secured the Jesuits. Since 1841 they had been at work in eastern Canada, and in 1844 – at Provencher's suggestion – they had taken over the Indian missions of the diocese of Quebec. Like many similar orders they had come into existence in the wake of the restoration of the Bourbons, and like most of the others they professed the ultramontane ideals of fidelity to the papacy and opposition to liberalism. Most of their recruits were of peasant background, although favoured with a classical training that would lead W.F. Butler to single them out on his western travels as gentlemen of rare culture. Under the aristocratic Eugène de Mazenod, their founder and since 1832 bishop of Marseille, they had become missioners to the villagers of Provence, whom they addressed with homely appeals in their own language.[11] They had some difficulty at first in adjusting to the harsh climatic and cultural conditions of Rupert's Land.

Much to Bellecourt's disgust, the Oblates quickly decided that his Saulteaux had imbibed little Catholicism and showed such resistance to it as to make further work among them unprofitable. The order was more successful in the northern area that Thibault had pioneered. In 1846 Provencher sent Louis-François Laflèche, a secular priest, and Alexandre-

Antonin Taché, a newly vowed Oblate, to open a permanent mission at Ile-à-la-Crosse. These young French Canadians, both later to become prelates, proved to be effective missionaries. Taché, the younger and healthier of the two, was soon making forays to Athabasca and Reindeer lakes. In 1849 the missionaries received instructions to leave on account of the financial difficulties of the order but resolved to remain by living off the land so long as they could be provided with communion wine. The threat was lifted in the following year by Taché's election as Provencher's coadjutor, which persuaded de Mazenod that the field could not be abandoned. Expansion continued, despite the difficulty of breaking in newly arrived Frenchmen with no knowledge of Cree or Chipewyan, and during the early 1850s the Oblates ranged as far as Great Slave Lake.[12]

The Oblates were not the first religious order in the west, for in 1844 the Sisters of Charity of Montreal, commonly known as the Grey Nuns, had opened a house at St Boniface on Provencher's invitation. Founded at Montreal in 1738 by Marguerite d'Youville, they had been exempt at the conquest from the ban on recruiting imposed on male orders and were by the nineteenth century one of the most prestigious French-Canadian religious orders. In 1857 they entered into a permanent association with the Oblates of the west and eventually conducted schools, dispensaries, and charitable enterprises in all major centres where the latter were at work. As a result well-born and delicate women of this community were thrown into situations of great difficulty and sometimes danger, even being conducted over rapids on the Athabasca which fur traders had taken a great detour to avoid.[13] Less publicized because less dramatic than the daring journeys of missionary priests, their quiet work brought a distinctively Canadian component into what otherwise long remained largely a European enterprise.

The Anglicans, although outnumbered and outdistanced, were not out of contention. During the early part of the century the CMS had been handicapped by a scarcity of candidates and forced to rely on graduates of seminaries at Berlin and Basel who would not have been welcome in a British possession. The foundation in 1823 of a school at Islington in London for the training of young men without the qualifications for university entrance provided a supply of tough if uncultivated graduates who were considered suitable for Rupert's Land although not for more sophisticated fields in Asia. They made possible the continuation of the mission, although in 1838 Cockran held it alone and in 1841 a financial crisis threatened to

close it down altogether. The tide turned with the appointment as honor-
ary secretary in that year of Henry Venn, who gave the society a vigour
and a vision it had lacked. By the 1850s it was able to reinforce the mission
substantially. Meanwhile in 1849 a bequest from a Hudson's Bay factor
had made possible the appointment of a bishop, David Anderson, whose
presence gave the enterprise added visibility and authority. He immediately set himself to his task with a vigour that convinced William Mason
that there was no future for any other Protestant society in the region.[14]

Thought of expansion was now possible, and a new generation of CMS
missionaries began to plan a strategy for it. James Hunter at The Pas called
for an advance up the Saskatchewan towards Edmonton and the Rockies,
while Robert Hunt saw his station at Stanley on the Churchill River as
crucial for reaching the Dene and ultimately the Inuit. Both counted on a
liberal use of Indian auxiliaries to reach new areas.[15] Despite these ambitious plans, however, the Oblates were better placed for a thrust to the
Arctic. Their stations offered direct access to the Mackenzie basin, while
the Anglicans were blocked to the north by the Oblate mission at Reindeer
Lake and to the northwest by that at Ile-à-la-Crosse.

In 1858 Hunter was an unexpected passenger on the HBC brigade to the
Mackenzie. The Oblates were soon aware of his presence, for three priests
and two lay brothers embarked with him. Bishop Anderson's declared
intention in authorizing his journey was not to interfere with Roman
Catholic work but to press forward to unreached tribes. To the Oblates,
however, Hunter's presence was an intolerable affront. Henri Grollier,
their representative on the Mackenzie, did not let him out of his sight once
he had reached Resolution. In the following year Hunter's place was taken
by W.W. Kirkby, a dogged Englishman with few social graces whom the
Oblates resented but grudgingly admired as 'le petit Kirby.' His success on
the Mackenzie was limited. In 1861 Bishop Vital J. Grandin established
the Oblate mission of Providence below Great Slave Lake, and it soon
became a base for rapid expansion.[16]

Hunter's mission had its fruits, but they were reaped mainly in the
Yukon. Kirkby reached this territory in 1861 and found a ready response
among the Tukudhs. He was succeeded in the following year by Robert
McDonald, a Scottish-Ojibwa half-breed who had been ordained in 1852.
The Roman Catholics were quickly on his heels but were no more successful in winning Indians from their first-given allegiance than the Anglicans
had been on the Mackenzie. The most vividly remembered CMS mission-

ary associated with the Yukon was William C. Bompas, who arrived at Fort Simpson on Christmas morning in 1865 in response to an unfounded report that McDonald was on his deathbed. Named bishop of Athabasca in 1874, he chose the more remote portion in each of two divisions of this diocese and was ultimately left in 1891 with only the Yukon. His eccentricities made him the butt of much Roman Catholic mockery but did little to damage his effectiveness.[17]

Two thousand kilometres to the east a similar scenario was played out. George Barnley, the Wesleyan missionary appointed in 1840 to Moose Factory, was also responsible for Abitibi and gave it as much attention as he could spare. Meanwhile Roman Catholics were approaching James Bay from the south. From 1836 priests, notably Sulpicians, held summer missions on Lake Timiskaming and the upper Ottawa. In 1844 J.-N. Laverlochère, an Oblate associated with the diocese of Montreal, held missions at Timiskaming and Abitibi, and in 1847 he reached the bay. The Oblates made little impression at Moose, where the company refused them permission to establish a permanent mission, but were able to secure a foothold at Albany to the west. When Barnley left Moose in 1847 and the Methodists failed to replace him, the outlook for Protestantism in the area seemed bleak. With encouragement from the company, however, the CMS appointed John Horden to the post in 1851. He proved to be one of their most effective agents, becoming the first bishop of Moosonee in 1872. The most notable missionary who served under him was Thomas Vincent, a half-breed who established a strong Anglican presence east of James Bay. Many people today are surprised to learn that the Indians of northern Quebec are solidly Protestant, whereas a large proportion of those on the Ontario side are Roman Catholic.

North of the Gulf of St Lawrence, among the Montagnais and Naskapis, Roman Catholics faced little competition. Although the former may have retained some folk memories of the early Jesuits and received some attention in the early nineteenth century from neighbouring parish priests, it was once again the Oblates who effectively brought Christianity to these peoples. Many of these Indians lived well inland, and others joined them as settlers gradually occupied the coast. Under these circumstances it was often necessary to arrange summer missions at distant rendezvous where a year's instruction had to be concentrated within a week or two. Sometimes there were disappointments. In 1866 Louis Babel ventured into the interior of Labrador, along a route broken by frequent rapids and hazardous

portages across rain-soaked rocks, only to learn upon arrival at his destination that the expected Naskapis had already dispersed for the season.[18] Due
to the irregular terrain of the Labrador peninsula this region was accounted
the most difficult of all, but a series of determined missionaries was eventually able to establish a chain of missions.

The Hudson's Bay Company was the unquestioned master of the north,
and any account of missionary work that left it out of the picture would be
like *Hamlet* without some reference to the state of Denmark. Anyone
who entered the region was immediately made aware of its overarching
presence, and any agency that sought to affect the Indians had to reckon
with its power. Missionaries depended on it for transportation of themselves and their supplies, for its brigades were the only scheduled services.
They counted on its hospitality, for its posts were the only convenient and
comfortable hostels. They had to look to it for a multitude of services, for
carpenters and other tradesmen were almost all in its employ. They could
do little business without it, for it possessed a monopoly of trade. At times
they could scarcely survive without it, for its posts contained the only
reliable caches of supplies. Since both employees and Indian suppliers
depended on it for their livelihood, it could make life very uncomfortable
for a recalcitrant missionary by starting a train of gossip or even by institut-
ing an effective boycott.

Fortunately for the missions, the company did more to help than to
hinder. The company rather than an eager missionary agency took the
initiative that led to the appointment of the first Protestant clergyman.
Thereafter it usually went out of its way to provide for the needs of missionaries of all denominations. It furnished them travel and accommodation, often gratuitously, and customarily accorded them the privileges of
company officers at its posts. It carried their freight, which was considerable. It made its forts available for their services as a matter of course and
expected its officers to attend them. For these favours its motives were
partly altruistic, partly selfish. Several members of the London committee
were ardent evangelicals for whom the propagation of Christianity was
even more important than profit. All of them were aware that the company's Licence for Exclusive Trade, which periodically came up for renewal, called for the moral and religious improvement of the natives and that
such humanitarian agencies as the Aborigines' Protection Society were
alert to ensure that it was fulfilled. The 'wintering partners,' less easily

convinced, were reminded that it 'would be extremely impolitic in the present temper and disposition of the public in this country to show any unwillingness to assist in the conversion of the Indians.'[19]

Despite this show of goodwill, missionaries and traders regarded each other with more suspicion than affection. Missionaries complained of favouritism to other denominations, of the poor moral example set by some company officers, and of specific grievances such as the requirement of Sunday travel. Company officials chafed under missionary criticisms – 'intolerable meddlers and idiots,' Eden Colvile called the Anglicans – and resented the multiplication of establishments that involved an outlay 'greater than the Fur Trade can be expected to bear.' For the most part a multitude of complaints can be reduced to a fundamental one on each side. Cockran succinctly put the one case: 'Should the Directors of the Hudson's Bay Company be stiff, ask them if they can prove that they have ameliorated the condition of one Indian family through the whole traffic of 150 years.' Donald Ross of Norway House summed up the other in the charge that settled Indians did not produce equal returns.[20] Missionaries, by the nature of their calling, were agents of change. Company officers knew that their jobs depended on persuading the Indians to preserve their traditional skills.

Faced with the apparently inevitable presence of the missions, the company gradually developed a policy for coping with it. Simpson set forth the essentials of it in his journal by 1825, and further details were added as the result of experience. Missionaries should refrain from imposing their moral scruples, especially on such issues as company marriages. They should be closely related to the company establishment, preferably as company employees. They should make their headquarters at company posts, teaching company servants and such Indians as they could interest the rudiments of Christianity and English and promoting agriculture in depleted areas, but not spending much time in Indian encampments, where they might disturb Indians in their way of life or lead them to abandon it. They should avoid areas where missions would be financially burdensome or ecologically threatening, or where they might attract competition. Above all, they should not meddle with the company's trade. The agreement with the Wesleyans in 1840 was essentially an attempt to apply this policy. When it backfired, the company was not yet quite ready to abandon its policy of seeking a special relation with a favoured agency. The arrival in 1849 of a bishop of the established church combined with the 'papal-aggression' scare of the following year to suggest a rapprochement with the CMS. In 1851 the committee, in rebuffing a collective appeal from the Roman Catholic bishops of Canada, stated 'their intention to give all the support in their power' to the Church of England and their confidence that they would not 'either suffer in public opinion or endanger their charter by preferring Protestant to Roman Catholic missionaries as instructors for the native population.'[21]

In practice, however, a rather different policy was already beginning to take shape. As early as 1846 Simpson stated that the company stood for liberty of conscience so long as missionaries did not interfere with one another's converts. This ever afterwards remained its public policy, one that did not prevent it from showing a measure of favouritism on occasion but upon which it could always retreat when challenged. Increasingly the company adopted an attitude of laissez-faire, fostering goodwill by assisting some projects and discouraging others that threatened its interests, but for the most part leaving missions to their own devices. Difficulties with the Wesleyans were not the only or even the most important reason for this gradual disengagement. With the entry of a Roman Catholic religious order and then the appointment of an Anglican bishop, the company was confronted with external sources of power it could not hope to control. Even more significantly, its position in the territories was changing. A show of force by the Métis of the Red River in 1849 demonstrated its weakness, and it thereupon virtually gave up any attempt to enforce its monopoly. In 1859, when the company had failed to secure the renewal of its Licence for Exclusive Trade, Simpson announced that it no longer considered itself responsible for the enforcement of law and order or for missionary transport.[22]

The company and the missions could never ignore each other, however, and in the final analysis they complemented each other. The company, dependent for the success of its operations on the inculcation of regular work habits and on recognition of the sanctity of contracts, increasingly counted on the missions to instil into the Indians the necessary attitudes of mind. Missionaries, whose work required stability and order, came to see in the company's monopoly the surest guarantee of these. Jaye Goossen has documented a complex web of relations that bound mission and post at Stanley on the Churchill River. CMS missionary Robert Hunt and HBC factor Samuel McKenzie, the only white authority-figures within a broad area, could scarcely ignore each other's presence. In some respects they were rivals, for each required a measure of authority in order to persuade the Indians to further the ends he had in view. In others, as lonely representatives of European society, they found it desirable to collaborate. McKenzie helped the missionary with the Christian instruction of the Indians, to whom he had already taught some Protestant doctrines before Hunt's arrival. Hunt encouraged them to deal exclusively with the company in order to avoid the alcoholism and disorder that would result from competition.[23] As company and mission discovered the advantages of this symbiosis and as each came to recognize that the other was in the country to stay, their relations gradually mellowed. Tensions did not disappear, but crises became rare.

That the aboriginal peoples of the world could hope to survive contact with the European colonizers only by adopting their religion and civilization was a precept so deeply engraved on the British mind in the early nineteenth century that no missionary, of Protestant faith at any rate, could begin his work with any other expectation. West did not need to learn from experience in the country that Indians needed education but began to recruit boys for his school even before he reached the Red River. Cockran and Bellecourt in the next decade both made agriculture central to their approach to the Indians, not because they compared notes but because everyone knew that agriculture was necessary to the future of the Indians. The rhetoric of the civilizing program was carried readily into the north, and occasional attempts were made to apply it. In the 1840s Evans attempted to introduce farm animals at Norway House, and E.R. Young repeated the experiment about fifteen years later. The same conviction that agricultural settlement was essential to the survival of the Indian was expressed by the Oblates of Abitibi, and the diary of Henry Budd, a native Anglican clergyman, reveals that much of his time at The Pas was spent encouraging agriculture and a systematic fishery.[24]

It soon became evident, however, that the forests and tundra of the north did not provide hospitable environments for the church's civilizing mission. The first concern of missionaries, many of whom had to perform almost impossible feats of travel, was to ensure their own survival. The gardens often cited as evidence of an obsessive interest in agriculture were in fact essential sources of sustenance for people unaccustomed to a constant diet of fish. Even the sheep and pigs of Norway House, which proved in the end as ill adapted as camels in British Columbia and elephants in

Nova Scotia, were introduced as desperate expedients to keep the population alive and healthy during the meagre winter months. The missionaries
did try to introduce some of the appurtenances of European civilization.
The wearing of Western clothing was everywhere accepted as a mark of
genuine conversion, and at a Norway House the Youngs carefully demonstrated the proper setting of a European table. Most significantly, perhaps,
the missions encouraged the formation of the larger settlements feared by
the company.[25] For the most part, however, the missionaries soon recognized that they could do little to change economic realities beyond encouraging co-operative efforts for community betterment. Little was heard in
the north of the ambitious plans for transforming Indian society that had
bulked so large in Upper Canada. Instead the missionaries, often despite
themselves, learned to adapt in a measure to native ways of life.

On some matters, indeed, the missionaries could not compromise. Christianity as they understood it required extensive changes in moral if not in
economic behaviour. Early missionaries sought to root out infanticide and
the killing of orphan children, many of those rescued becoming wards of
the nuns. They also condemned the harsh treatment of women, bringing
about a change for the better although sometimes making the mistake of
imposing Victorian ideas of what was ladylike. The most troublesome
moral issue was polygamy, which performed a significant economic function in a nomadic society where an unattached woman could not easily
survive. 'Paganism,' which meant participation in shamanic rites, was also
regarded as a moral transgression and indeed a very serious one, although
missionaries were inclined to dismiss many traditional practices as harmless 'superstitions' that would inevitably die out as converts matured in the
faith.[26] Alcohol, which all churches forbade in excess and some churches
forbade altogether, was a less serious problem than in the south. Specific
religious requirements such as Roman Catholic rules of abstinence and
Protestant observance of the Lord's day, which were regarded as essentially
moral obligations, fitted well enough with Indian recognition of taboos that
they proved relatively easy to enforce. For the rest the missionaries were
content to leave Indian ways of life largely intact, although prohibitions of
polygamy and 'conjuring' had disruptive implications of which they were
not always aware.

In order to bring about religious and moral change, missionaries found
themselves from the outset drawn into teaching. Literacy had a centrality
for Protestants, with their reliance on the authority of the written word,

that it could never attain among Roman Catholics, who inclined more to the view that 'images are the best books of the savages.' One even senses a note of defensiveness in the hope of a nun of Providence that a school for Indian and Métis children might not only enable them to 'spread the knowledge of our holy religion among their relations and friends' but 'also give us Catholics a higher place in the esteem of our separated brethren.'[27] In practice, however, all agencies soon had ambitious educational programs.

Determining the language of instruction in Indian schools proved to be one of the most contentious issues to face the missions. The first Anglican missionaries at the Red River, with the exception of West, did not try to learn any native languages because they believed that the best way to christianize the Indians would be to teach them English as quickly as possible. Hunter made wide use at The Pas of Cree translations prepared by his second wife, who was Ross's country-born daughter, but these were in roman script to facilitate a later transition to English. Evans dealt a double blow to these hopes when he not only published material in Cree but devised for it a syllabic script that could be learned within a few days by speakers of the language. Hunter and the Anglicans at the Red River were unimpressed, and Bishop Anderson on his arrival sided with them.[28]

When Horden occupied Moose for the CMS after Barnley's departure, however, he found the syllabics immensely useful and soon convinced Anderson. Mason, after transferring to the CMS, was commissioned to complete Evans's translation of the Bible into syllabics, and henceforth practically every Protestant missionary in the north used or adapted them. Roman Catholic missionaries, few of whom spoke English as their mother tongue, had even less hesitation about the use of native languages. Provencher was sceptical of Bellecourt's attempts to give instruction in Ojibwa, pointing to what he regarded as the greater success of the English-oriented Red River Academy. Frederic Baraga, on the other hand, not only strongly encouraged the use of native languages around Lake Superior but provided valuable grammars and dictionaries. The Oblates encouraged thorough language study, adopted the syllabics without hesitation, and adapted them to other languages.[29]

The triumph of syllabics represented a dramatic admission that the traditional formula of Christianity and civilization could not be applied without modification in the north. Teaching in syllabics has never been without its critics. The complaint most commonly made in the past,

usually by whites, was that by making the learning of English less urgent
it kept Indians isolated from white society and failed to give them opportunities to advance in it. For this reason even William Mason thought of
syllabics as a temporary expedient.[30] More recently it has been con-
tended, on the other side, that by using syllabics entirely for the propagation of religious literature the missionaries damaged the oral tradition
and discouraged the emergence of native languages as instruments of
secular culture. Syllabics have, nevertheless, provided an incentive to the
preservation of native languages as literary vehicles and have served at
times as the only means of written communication among distant bands.
Both applications have facilitated the recent revival of Indian consciousness.

If the missions eventually agreed on a single orthography, in other
respects they offered remarkably variant versions of Christianity. An
Oblate mission, whatever it might offer by way of education and good
works, existed chiefly for indoctrination into the Roman Catholic faith
and the cultivation of piety. Frequent communion was encouraged, and
extraliturgical devotions that had gained immense popularity during the
nineteenth century in French ultramontane circles were successfully
transplanted to the Mackenzie. The cult of Saint Joseph was especially
popular and received fresh encouragement when a novena to him averted
almost certain famine by attracting a large herd of caribou at an unaccustomed season. The Methodists at first emphasized even headier forms of
devotion. Although English Wesleyans were considered less emotional
than their Canadian counterparts, Evans carried coals of fire from eastern
camp meetings. Letitia Hargrave, the wife of the local Hudson's Bay
factor, noted in her diary after he had visited York Factory: 'The Indians
here are all labouring under a religious frenzy. They preach   perform
miracles   speak unknown tongues, die & come to life again, won't hunt,
& it is extraordinary how many performances they have.' The pressure
was maintained, even after Evans's departure from Rupert's Land, in
class meetings where converts were expected to testify to their progress
on the road to perfection. Anglicans, like O'Meara in the east, eschewed
both 'wild fanaticism' and 'dumb, lifeless parade' in favour of a sober
liturgy and sedate prayer-meetings.[31] More than either Roman Catholics
or Methodists they insisted on the primacy of the written word, attaching scarcely less importance to schoolmasters than to preachers. Basic to
all their teaching was the Bible as the inspired word of God, interpreted

by Calvin and spelled out Sunday by Sunday in the Book of Common Prayer.

Although mutual fault-finding among rival agencies was basically a reflection of a highly competitive situation, some complaints were suggestive of genuine differences in approach. Protestants accused Roman Catholics of taking a light view of pagan practice, while Roman Catholics accused Protestants of condoning polygamy. These charges, for which there is little solid evidence, probably reflected an a priori Protestant identification of Roman Catholicism with idolatry and an equally a priori Roman Catholic conviction that heresy could offer no firm grounding for morality. Roman Catholics and Methodists were accused of administering baptism indiscriminately. There may have been some truth in this suggestion, for both Wesleyans and Roman Catholics attributed more efficacy to the sacraments than most evangelical Anglicans of the time were willing to concede. The most persistent charge against the Anglicans was that of making 'tobacco Christians' by offering material inducements. It was difficult for a relatively well-endowed mission to refuse help in time of need, especially to people who were accustomed to sharing their own meagre resources, and missionaries who attempted to stop indiscriminate giving only acquired a reputation for meanness. Gifts were deliberately used, however, to persuade Indians to give up conjuring and to send their children to school.[32] The line between commendable generosity and deliberate bribery was inevitably a fine one, and few missionaries of any denomination were able to trace it without ambiguity.

Apart from occasional pockets of resistance, Christianity received a remarkable welcome from the northern Indians. After receiving an initial rebuff from the Saulteaux the missionaries were delighted by the response of the Crees and even more by that of the various Dene peoples. Babel, venturing alone into the interior of Labrador, had only to establish a rendezvous in order to assemble a tribal gathering. Evans arrived at Norway House in July 1840 to find that Robert Rundle, who had preceded him by less than two months on his way to Fort Edmonton, had already gathered a group of penitents and baptized some of them. Sometimes the Indians did not wait for the missionaries. John Smithurst of the CMS reported that some of them made journeys of eight hundred to a thousand miles to receive the Lord's Supper at Cumberland. Others learned prayers from earlier hearers, who often became enthusiastic proselytizers. Emile Petitot, when an Oblate

missionary at Fort Rae, was startled in 1864 by the arrival at his cabin for
instruction of a band known as Takwil-Ottinés, who had never seen a
white person before. Nor was the excitement merely of a moment. When
Barnley left Moose in 1847, after a pastorate of only seven years, some of
his converts moved hundreds of kilometres to Norway House or the
American side of the Sault[33] so that they would not be deprived of Methodist services. This receptivity was responsible for much of the intensity of
denominational rivalry in the north, for it was rightly suspected that the
first missionary to arrive might gain an insuperable advantage.

Thomas Crosby, the best-known pioneer of Methodism among the
Indians of British Columbia, found evidence of a great spiritual awakening
that swept through the Indians of much of North America in the years
around 1840. He attributed to it the early welcome given to Methodism at
Norway House and to Roman Catholicism on the Columbia, saw signs of
it in what is now British Columbia, and observed that where missionaries
were not present to take advantage of it, the shamans led not the old
dances but new prayers to the sun god, the stars, or the storm.[34] Whatever
credence we attach to his analysis, it is difficult to escape the impression
that during this period an unusual sense of excitement and expectancy
pervaded the northwest. Originally stimulated by Métis memories of
paternal religion, perhaps, it was fanned by reports of missions at the Red
River, by propaganda for Cockran's agricultural settlement, and by the
return home of graduates of the CMS school. The Franklin expedition of
1845 and the free-trade agitation at the Red River may also have aroused a
suspicion that whites had plans for the region that would disrupt its life in
ways that could not be foreseen.

Although the religious allegiance of most Indians was determined by
accidents of geography, there was some indication of conscious selection.
Protestant missionaries were easier to assimilate, being similar to HBC factors in appearance and manners. Although their message and morals set
them apart, they were patently part of the advancing British culture and
promised readier access to the white man's secret of power. Even Taché
admitted that they could offer greater opportunities for education. Many
Crees visited Norway House from localities as distant as Churchill, Lac la
Ronge, and Berens River, and we are told in several cases that their chief
purpose was to learn syllabics. There was a widespread feeling, however,
that in most situations the Roman Catholics had the edge. They usually
lived closer to the Indians than the more palisade-bound Protestants. They

were more recognizably religious, and despite their uncompromising opposition to shamanism had about them a familiar aura of spiritual authority. Ross, observing Thibault briefly during his passage through Norway House, commented that 'the appearance of his long robes, careworn and cadavorous visage,' along with his fluency in the language, gave him advantages that Evans was unlikely to match.[35] In the end, however, each mission was able to find a substantial constituency to which its approach was most congenial. The favourites of the Roman Catholics were the Dene, described by Henri Faraud as 'mild in disposition, trusting in what one tells them, desirous to live well.' The Anglicans preferred the Tukudhs of the Yukon, 'rather more sharp-featured, more lively and intelligent, as well as more cordial and affectionate than the Tenni.'[36]

In at least one respect, that of finding a significant place for native leaders, the Anglicans were most successful. West laid the foundations of an Indian ministry with his school, which contributed several outstanding graduates. The CMS was committed internationally to the use of 'native helpers under European supervision.' Its intention that these helpers should take charge of old posts so that veteran missionaries might press on to found new ones was not fulfilled in the northwest, where instead Indian catechists and schoolmasters did much of the pioneering. Over the years the CMS employed a steady and growing number both as catechists and as ordained ministers, many of them Crees from the James Bay region or from the country north of the Saskatchewan. The Methodists, although securing a few able workers such as Benjamin Sinclair, were unable to duplicate the impressive missionary force they had recruited in Upper Canada. Indeed, the Indian clergy of both denominations in the northwest were largely of a different type, originally selected as promising youths for training rather than emerging as charismatic leaders during the course of revival. Sometimes there were problems. Several early catechists were accused of moral lapses, and in 1846 there were concerted complaints of unequal treatment by the CMS.[37]

The Oblates wrote slightingly of Anglican native agents, whom A.G. Morice described as 'third-rate, but fortified with goods.' They would have liked nothing better than to have had native priests of their own, however, and unsuccessful attempts to educate them had already been made in Provencher's time. Despite the lower priority they assigned to Europeanization, they had a harder task. Protestants, trusting in the power of the Word, could send out emissaries without asking them to make great changes in their style of life so long as they could give elementary teaching. Roman Catholics, exacting conformity to a precise and unfamiliar view of priestly character, ran into difficulties at every stage. The long process of formation at a seminary proved confining, and for many years no Indian candidate could forbear at some point to escape to the freedom of the forest. Celibacy was another trial, for there was no native tradition of it. These were difficulties enough, and priests bound to a monastic rule shaped in distant Provence were not always inclined to make allowance for them. Only in 1890 was the first Métis, Edward Cunningham, ordained to the priesthood.[38] The wait for a status Indian would be considerably longer.

By the early twentieth century the Indians of the northwest, regardless of denomination, had reached a state of equilibrium in which the company, the missions, and the people had equally recognized if not equal roles to play. Many older Indians today recall this period as an almost primordial time when they had come to terms with the consequences of European trade and when the dislocation brought about by modern technology had not yet intervened. To missionaries this situation had become normative, one that might be less than perfect but which they were more concerned to preserve than to change.

There may be a clue to the positive response of most northern Indians to Christianity in a remark almost casually dropped by Pierre Duchaussois in explanation of their failure to contribute to its support: 'The fact is that the Indian looks upon Priests and Nuns as rich. He says they only have to send a little bit of paper into the "Great Countries," and it will bring them back a cargo.'[39] The reference to 'cargo,' startlingly reminiscent of South Sea revitalization cults, points to an Indian perception of European wealth that was doubtless inspired in the first place by the affluence of company posts with their annually renewed supplies from abroad but also associated with the missions through the freight of which Simpson so bitterly complained. The reference to 'a little bit of paper' is also suggestive, highlighting the importance of literacy in making the cargo available. Arduous trips to Norway House to learn syllabics take on a new significance in this context, and Christianity can be understood as the quest for a grail with some very distinctly material aspects. The view of northern Indians as essentially 'tobacco Christians,' whether crudely brought with bales of clothing or more subtly enchanted by the promise of unimaginable wealth somewhere out there, acquires a good deal of credibility. It repeats a theme already noted in Upper Canada and corresponds with the observations of more than one HBC factor.

An examination of several dissident movements that flourished among the Indians of the northwest around the middle of the nineteenth century suggests, however, that the transition to Christianity was neither as easy nor as thorough as this account might imply and that the motives for its acceptance may have been more complex.[40] In 1843 Abishabis, a Cree who had thrust himself forward as a leader during Evans's revival at York Factory, received a revelation of his own after being rebuffed by the authorities. He and a companion, taking their cue from key words in two of Evans's syllabic hymns, applied to themselves the names of 'Jesus' and 'Wasetek' (light). They also drew up a chart that warned against the ways of the white man while pointing true believers to a paradise of game and all delights. The movement swept eastwards to Albany and Moose, where it carried everything before it until it was suppressed by the local factor, George Barnston. Abishabis was put to death on suspicion of murder in 1843, but one of his followers was still arguing with Mason at Norway House in 1848.[41] In 1859 a young Chipewyan, identified in the records only as the son of a chief named Bear Foot, called on the people of Ile-à-la-Crosse to abandon Roman Catholic practices and accept the authenticity of his visions. He beat up Grandin, the Oblate missionary there, and threatened violence on a visit to Stanley later that spring. Although his ideas were less well articulated or perhaps merely less fully reported, he could offer at least the kernel of a theology: 'Eternal life is from the earth and sun.' Somewhat parallel movements were reported from Portage la Loche, Fond du Lac, Fort Rae, Fort Norman, Good Hope, and Peel River.[42] Although I have elsewhere referred to these visionaries as 'messiahs,' there is no reason to suppose that they intended to make the exclusive claim implied by this term.

Several features of these movements call for particular comment. All of them, while rejecting missionary leadership and indeed hostile to the white man's presence, arose out of contact with Christianity in one form or another and drew a good deal of their inspiration from it. Abishabis and his companion were credited with introducing sabbath observance around James Bay, while fragments of Catholic doctrine and practice were important ingredients of prophetic messages among the Chipewyans. In their own way these movements were calls for an indigenous Christianity and were remembered as such almost a century later.[43] What is even more notable, perhaps, is that they unanimously called on the Indians to decline the white man's cargo. On the contrary they demanded the destruction of possessions, notably dogs, that were in any way associated with European commerce. A cargo was indeed promised, but it would be one of game that harmonized with the traditional way of life rather than one fetched from Europe. Its coming would coincide with the inception of a new age combining the Christian millennium with the renewal of Indian society on its former base. The appeal of these movements by no means disproves the importance of European success in attracting northern Indians to Christianity. It does suggest, however, that typical Indian communities, when confronted with a choice between the spiritual benefits of Christianity and the material enticements of Europe, were prepared at least in the heat of religious excitement to choose the pearl of greater price.

One way or another, Indians confronted with the breakdown of their traditional social order were seeking a new kind of cohesion. Although many of their problems manifested themselves in material terms, they sought a religious solution as they had always been accustomed to do. Budd furnished a clue to what was going on by observing that shamans around The Pas in his time were not merely carrying on the old ways but inventing new ceremonies such as the scalp dance.[44] Crosby, it will be recalled, noted precisely the same phenomenon. What Indians got, in the end, was Christianity according to the missionaries and under missionary leadership. This was probably inevitable, for only the missionaries could give a coherent account of the Christian message, and in any case, from the Indian point of view, they had the same proprietary right to it as shamans to their particular formulas and songs. For the most part northern Indians demonstrated their satisfaction in later years by the fervour with which they remained attached to one or another denomination and its beliefs, but signs of restiveness have occasionally manifested themselves. To this day there are prophets in the north, calling themselves Christians but attached to no church, who receive an attentive hearing wherever they go.

CHAPTER SIX

Taming the Thunderbird

To those responsible for christianizing the Indians of Canada, British Columbia long seemed remote and exotic. Approach from the east was time-consuming and arduous, especially since several of the easier mountain passes were useless because they did not lead to significant waterways. The coastal region was readily accessible by sea, but from a direction that linked it with China and the South Seas more readily than with British North America. The Russians made contact by the 1760s, and James Cook visited the coast in 1778 during his last voyage. In 1785 the first trading vessel arrived, and in 1789 the Spanish founded a settlement at Nootka. A profitable trade in the pelts of sea otters, encouraged by the discovery that furs could be bought cheaply from the coastal tribes and sold at exorbitant prices in China, soon attracted a large number of vessels of which the majority were American. The trade reached a peak in the early years of the nineteenth century and then declined rapidly as the Chinese market became glutted and as the Indians learned to exact higher prices. Already in 1793, however, Alexander Mackenzie of the North West Company had established the practicability of a land approach by reaching salt water at Bella Coola. His company established a post at McLeod Lake in 1805 and added several others in the interior in the next few years. Posts in what is now the coastal region of British Columbia were established later, dating from the era of the amalgamated Hudson's Bay Company.

In contrast with commerce in sparsely populated Rupert's Land, where of necessity much mingling of traders and natives took place, coastal trade by both sea and land was conducted mainly at arm's length. Sea captains dealt as a matter of policy with village or clan chiefs, while land-based

factors carried on their business from palisaded forts. The result was to
initiate an era of what Robin Fisher calls 'non-directed cultural change,'[1]
bringing Indians together in considerable numbers around the forts but not
otherwise disturbing the Indian way of life greatly. Having few opportunities for intimate observation, traders emphasized in their reports not the
advanced culture of the coastal tribes but such exotic customs as the flat-
tening of infants' heads and the insertion of labrets into women's lips. It
became evident, however, that the coast abounded in settled villages suitable for permanent missions.

Among the sea traders only the Spanish showed any interest in the
conversion of the native peoples. Priests accompanying their expedition of
1774 bought several enslaved children ostensibly to save them from canni-
bal feasts, and on departing for California took about twenty Indians with
them. Forty-five years then passed before some members of the North
West Company issued the next recorded appeal for missionaries west of
the Rockies, and the CMS considered the area briefly before deciding on the
Red River. In 1829 the American Board of Commissioners for Foreign
Missions, an undenominational Protestant agency that already had work
in Hawaii, sent Jonathan Green to reconnoitre the coast after a tour of the
islands, and a few years later the Society for Converting and Civilizing the
Indians placed the Columbia on its list of possible fields.[2] None of these
projects came to fruition.

During this period of stillborn proposals and unfulfilled aspirations,
Christian ideas and practices made their way to British Columbia without
direct assistance from professional missionaries. Various travellers in the
interior during the 1830s noted observance of the sabbath, Catholic feast
days, and regular hours of prayer, as well as the use of baptism and the sign
of the cross, all in the context of a religious practice that also contained
many indigenous features such as ceremonial dancing.[3] Most of these
reports referred to tribes south of the border, especially the Flatheads of
Montana, but Hudson's Bay factor John McLean noted at Stuart Lake in
1835 that 'a sort of religion whose groundwork seemed to be Christianity, accompanied with some of the heathen ceremonies of the natives,'
had spread northwards to Fort Alexandria in the Cariboo and was now
embraced by all of the local Carriers. As Leslie Spier points out, no Christian elements had been noted prior to 1830.[4]

The area between the Coast and Rocky mountains is one in which
several cultural traditions met and blended. The tribes of the central and

northern interior were mainly of Athapaskan stock and shared many traits with their Dene relatives to the north. Further south, influences from the prairies were stronger; at one time, indeed, the Kootenais had lived east of the Rockies. Coastal patterns persisted for some distance up the rivers, and in southern British Columbia Salishan languages were common to the coast and much of the interior. Ideas and practices made their way readily throughout the region, especially along the easy route from south to north that is now followed by Highway 97. The presence of the Hudson's Bay Company provided further outside contacts. Patterns of social organization were relatively tenuous, lacking either the strict hierarchical arrangement typical of the coastal tribes or the military discipline so evident east of the Rockies. The equilibrium of the region was under strain, and new movements found a ready welcome.

Two possible sources of the quasi Christian 'sort of religion' of the 1830s have been identified. About 1820 a group of Catholic Iroquois from Caughnawaga, presumably employed by the Montreal-based North West Company, settled among the Flatheads. Two of them, Ignace La Mousse father and son, later attained some celebrity by making several trips to St Louis in order to persuade missionaries to settle among them. They were also credited with teaching their neighbours the Lord's Prayer along with various other Christian practices. In 1825 Alexander Ross, a trader on the Columbia whom Simpson chose as a teacher at the Red River because of his lack of commercial success, set another train of events in motion by taking along two boys from the region as students. Named Spogan Garry and Kootenai Pelly after prominent company officials, they returned in 1829 to recruit new students. During their stay, Chief Factor Duncan Finlayson noted, they gathered and taught the people on Sundays as well as introducing such practices as grace before meals and such beliefs as eternal punishment for sin. He also observed that their teaching was by no means orthodox. McLean's ascription of the movement further north to the influence of two boys who had studied at the Red River points to an origin during this visit, for by 1830 Pelly and most of the other students had died at the Red River. Garry returned to his people, however, carrying on his preaching for some time before falling victim to alcohol. One may fairly infer from the evidence that the La Mousse family was responsible for the specifically Roman Catholic elements of native belief and practice, whereas Garry was more influential in spreading the movement and giving it an indigenous character. Information that the senior La Mousse was assisted by a transvestite active in other prophetic movements suggests, however, that there may have been an unorthodox side to his religiosity as well.

In later years, as word of these movements spread, they were widely hailed as evidence of the capacity of Christianity for spontaneous expansion. Spier was much more cautious in his appraisal, pointing out that at least half of the elements described by contemporary observers were of native origin and arguing that 'so far as the natives were concerned ... the new religion from the east was confirmation and stimulus to existing beliefs.' He adduced evidence for a 'prophet dance' tradition in the west, affecting tribes as far north as the Babines and Carriers of central British Columbia, that could have originated no later than circa 1790 when an eruption of Mount St Helens deposited a heavy fall of volcanic ash in the southern Okanagan. This tradition was marked by the appearance of occasional prophets, usually not of shamanic background, who advocated a strict morality, propagated their ideas with a zeal unusual in native societies, and – most conspicuously of all – called on entire communities to dance in order to avert calamity and to bring to realization the hope of a new life beyond death.[5] To Spier the movements unleashed by La Mousse and Garry were essentially forms of the prophet dance enriched with Christian elements. Most anthropologists would agree with his basic analysis, although some regard the prophet dance as itself a response to European contact and therefore less traditional than Spier suggested.

Where does a christianized traditionalism end and an indigenous Christianity begin? Such a question would probably have made no sense to the northwestern Indians of the 1830s, for there is no reason to think that they were aware of any fundamental incompatibility between Christianity and their traditional ways. They sensed a need for the renewal of their society and accepted possibilities of revitalization as these were presented. Undoubtedly the La Mousse family identified their teaching as Roman Catholic, Garry and his fellow students theirs as Protestant. Many of their followers, especially those who heard of their reputations at a distance, would scarcely have seen a need of labelling themselves although they were aware that Christianity provided what was new in these movements.

The era of the missionary was about to begin, and with its dawning the movements that had prepared the way for it faded into obscurity. As has frequently happened elsewhere, however, they left a residue that did not easily coalesce with missionary Christianity. In the 1850s, after the first missionaries to the interior had come and gone, a Babine named Beni or Peni set himself up as a priest, appointing watchmen, hearing confessions and assigning penances, and assuring his followers that they would become rich white men and 'speak a new language.' We might suppose his movement merely an expedient to fill a pastoral vacancy were it not that his songs reached the Haidas of the Queen Charlotte Islands and even left a memory at Cowichan in 1875. Spier also identified the christianized prophet dance of the 1830s as the ultimate source of the later Smohalla cult, which disclaimed any Christian connections, and perhaps of the still-extant Shaker cult whose Christian connections are obvious.[6]

The main fur-trade route to the Pacific reached its western terminus at Fort Vancouver on the Columbia River, and some of the richest and most accessible agricultural land in the region was not far away. As a result the first missions in the Pacific northwest were located a considerable distance south of what later became the international boundary. In 1831 Ignace La Mousse led a delegation of Flathead and Nez Percé chiefs to St Louis. To their disappointment the first missionaries to respond were Protestants, who passed over their territory in favour of the lower Columbia. Jason Lee, a Methodist, settled in the Willamette Valley of Oregon in 1834, while Samuel Parker of the American Board of Commissioners introduced Presbyterianism to what is now southern Washington. In 1836, after long delay, the HBC finally appointed an Anglican chaplain, Herbert Beaver, to Fort Vancouver. Possessing John West's tactlessness without his energy, Beaver was recalled after two years. American missions soon attracted westbound settlers, and the company sensed the urgency of counteracting their influence. With some reluctance, therefore, it agreed to the dispatch of the Roman Catholic missionaries Norbert Blanchet and Modeste Demers in 1838, and despite unfavourable reports of their work it continued to co-operate with them for the same reason.[7] There was some logic in their selection, for trading on the Pacific slope had been a venture of the North West Company and involved a high proportion of French-Canadian voyageurs.

Demers, although somewhat overshadowed in Oregon by Blanchet, was the first to explore the northern part of their vast mission territory. In 1841 he conducted a successful mission at Fort Langley on the lower Fraser, and in the following year he traversed 'New Caledonia' as far as Stuart Lake in the northern interior. On both occasions he was able to bring into play a

new audio-visual aid that Blanchet had devised in 1840. This was the
'Catholic ladder,' a pictorial chart of biblical and doctrinal history reminiscent in its direct appeal of Pierron's game of 'Point to Point.' A byway
representing the Protestant Reformation that led to a vividly portrayed hell
was a feature that seemed especially strategic at Fort Langley in view of a
rumour that the Presbyterians of Walla Walla intended to extend their
operations into the Fraser Valley. Later adapted by Albert Lacombe for use
on the prairies, it would draw the ire of Protestant missionaries throughout
the west. Meanwhile the last of four Flathead expeditions to St Louis, led
by the younger La Mousse after the death of his father on the previous trip,
had finally evoked a response from Bishop Joseph Rosati. In 1841 five
Jesuits under the leadership of Jean-Pierre de Smet, a Belgian who had
spent some years in Missouri, established themselves in their country.
From 1845 John Nobili, residing on Okanagan Lake, made annual trips
through the region previously visited by Demers until ill health forced his
recall in 1848.[8]

To all appearance the conversion of the interior tribes was accomplished
with astonishing rapidity. Although Demers's expedition of 1841 was the
first recorded visit of an authorized missionary of any denomination to the
interior of British Columbia, he was able to arrange for the erection of
what he described as a large church at Alexandria before his departure. In
1858 he noted that few natives in this region died without baptism,
although the area had been without a resident missionary for ten years. In
an area with a very diffuse political structure, a major incentive to the
rapid acceptance of Christianity may have been the desire of chiefs to
bolster their authority and especially to secure places in the fur trade hierarchy; observers reported that chiefs commonly led religious services during the revivals of the 1830s, while an early chronicler of the CMS mission
was careful to point out that Spogan Garry and his associates were chiefs'
sons.[9] It will not have escaped notice, moreover, that the region of speedy
conversion was precisely that which had been most deeply affected by
earlier indigenous movements.

Progress was less spectacular in the vicinity of Victoria, whither Jean-
Baptiste Bolduc followed the HBC in 1843 when it established its western
headquarters there. In 1847, as part of an over-ambitious scheme that
Blanchet had concocted for erecting more dioceses within his territory
than he then had available priests, Demers was consecrated bishop of Vancouver Island. He was not able to take up residence at Victoria until 1852.

Meanwhile a priest named Lempfrit, arriving in 1849, had established a successful school but had then been accused of fathering the child of an Indian woman and unceremoniously ordered out of the colony by Governor James Douglas. Demers was not much more successful with the priests whom he was able to recruit for the mission in its early years. In 1857 he complained that they had all left for California, and they were equally full of complaints about his constant fault-finding.[10]

Meanwhile in 1847 the Oblates had reached the Pacific northwest, taking up residence at Walla Walla, where Blanchet was now installed as bishop. The arrangement proved unhappy, and in 1858 the Oblates removed to Esquimalt. Two years later Demers confided the larger part of his diocese to them. Moving from the jurisdiction of Blanchet to that of Demers proved, however, to be at best a leap from the fire into the frying-pan. In 1866 the Oblate superior L.-J. D'herbomez, who had become vicar apostolic of New Westminster, withdrew all of his missionaries to the mainland. Although missions on Vancouver Island never recovered their momentum, Roman Catholics had remarkable success among the coast Salish who inhabited its southern extremity and the lower mainland of British Columbia. This people, although related linguistically to many of the tribes of the southern interior, inhabited a well-endowed section of the coast where some of their villages had been occupied continually for at least two millennia. Their Catholicism made much of spectacle and occasion. Churches, notably at Sechelt and Capilano, were conceived in the grand manner and lavishly decorated. Annual eucharistic gatherings that brought together Indians from a wide area for intensive instruction and religious services were enlivened by processions, rival brass bands, and extravagant fireworks. Most impressive of all was a passion play, thoroughly prepared for over a year both dramatically and spiritually, that drew large audiences from both sides of the international border.[11]

The most celebrated fashioner of the Oblate missionary approach was Paul Durieu, who became D'herbomez's coadjutor in 1875 and assumed major responsibility for Indian missions shortly thereafter. Noting a tendency for converted Indians to revert to their traditional practices, he set out to devise a system that would inculcate Catholicism so thoroughly into their minds as to obviate this possibility. When perfected, it involved the use of methods so carefully chosen as practically to guarantee the desired results. The first part of the process, involving negative sanctions, was designed to discourage vice. A set of rules, mostly relating to sexual behaviour and beginning 'Boys ... even small ones, will not play with girls,' was to be solemnly published. Breaches of this code called for public punishment, which could be as severe as flogging, on the principle that shame was an effective teacher. Negative measures were to be balanced by positive instruction. Periodic short-term missions were to be marked by more than the usual emphasis on the dedication of the will and the cultivation of a vigilant spirit. They should include daily catechism and frequent confession, but absolution should be given only at the end of the mission. Since Indians had no natural fear of the Eucharist, every effort should be made, through such methods as the cult of the Blessed Sacrament, to inculcate a spirit of reverence. A notable feature of the system was the part played in it by the Indians themselves. Regulations were to be enforced and punishments administered not by the priest directly but by the chiefs and specially appointed 'watchmen.' Ultimate obedience was due not to them but to the priest, however, who should have his own informers in the village to watch over the watchmen. The ultimate sanction was an interdict on religious observances including the Mass.[12]

The Durieu system, with its striking anticipation of the behaviouristic methods of B.F. Skinner, was not a utopian scheme but a program put into operation for many years by practically all Oblate missionaries in British Columbia. A Roman Catholic Indian village was a thoroughly controlled community from which all disturbing influences such as liquor vendors were rigidly excluded and within which processes of worship, education, and discipline ensured constant indoctrination. Its stringent regime was intended, however, not to impose police rule but to avoid it by moulding the characters of the Indians so that temptations would no longer tempt and vice would be overcome from within. The plan, for which Durieu received much praise, was original only in the thoroughness of its structuring. Through contact with Jesuits in Oregon the Oblates had been captivated by accounts of the Paraguay 'reductions' or model villages, and from the time of their arrival in British Columbia they set out to reproduce them as closely as they could.[13] In a situation where priests were scarce and most villages had to be content with periodic missionary visits, some such method of internal formation seemed especially desirable.

The best known Oblate missionary in British Columbia, so far as the general public was concerned, was not Durieu but Adrien G. Morice. Arriving from France in 1880, Morice spent three unhappy years teaching school at Williams Lake and then a brief period evangelizing the Chilcotins of the western Cariboo before beginning an eighteen-year stint at Stuart Lake that proved to be his last and most significant assignment. The local Carriers belonged to the Dene linguistic group, which he had already learned to admire through the ethnographic writings of his fellow Oblate Emile Petitot. Morice soon gained great influence over them as a guide on both spiritual and material matters. By learning the language – the only white in the area so qualified – he made himself indispensable to the local factor of the HBC, especially since he had no qualms about directing Indian trade elsewhere if better terms were offered. To the Indians he became an essential middleman in dealings with God as well as with the company and the government. Morice achieved renown not only as a missionary but as a historian, linguist, and naturalist. In most respects he faithfully reflected the value structure of the Oblates, advocating and applying the Durieu system and denouncing Protestantism and potlatch with equal vigour. Unlike most Oblates, however, he was not in favour of encouraging the Indians to adopt European ways or of giving them the European education that would facilitate this transformation. Admiring the Indians' simplicity and lack of artificiality, he preferred to restrict change to the sphere of religion.

Attractive as some of Morice's ideas appear today, a closer examination raises disquieting questions. His desire for 'pure' Indians arose less from respect for their culture, which in the case of the Carriers was already considerably eroded by European contact, than from a romantic view of them as overgrown children to whom he could be a necessary father-figure. Much of the difficulty stemmed from his egotism. Morice did not take readily to the community life of a religious order, and priests sent to assist him were tyrannized almost out of their wits. The same craving for power manifested itself in relation to the Indians, who were expected to carry him without charge through mountainous terrain on journeys that were designed, more often than not, to further his scientific interests. It is difficult to disagree with the judgment of Jacqueline Kennedy Gresko that Morice, while praising the Durieu system, departed from it in failing to seek the total inward transformation for which it was designed.[14] One could even say that he made of it precisely the police activity that Durieu had sought to avoid.

Oblate methods of control, whether Durieu's official one or Morice's highly individualistic version of it, depended on protecting Indians from contact with Europeans and were relatively successful so long as such isolation could be maintained. The conviction of Father Eugène Chirouse in 1892 for assault as the result of applying Durieu's methods led to a considerable relaxation, however, and the system fell into disuse as young people made more contacts off the reserves.[15] Even in its heyday its magnification of the authority of the missionaries made it difficult for chiefs and watchmen to exercise effective supervision in their absence. A present-day observer would be most likely to miss any recognition of an inherent right of the Indians to determine their own community life or even any provision for them to take control of it once they had been spiritually formed.

From early Roman Catholic reports we hear of intractable peoples farther north along the coast who, unlike the docile Salish and Carriers, went to war to enslave their neighbours and carried on unspeakable rites all winter.[16] Among these more northerly peoples one missionary after another admitted disappointment and defeat, although a foothold was eventually secured among the Nootkas of Vancouver Island. It was in this forbidding region, the very heart of darkness to early priests, that Protestantism found its strongholds among the Indians of British Columbia.

The Roman Catholic pioneers were not mistaken in reckoning that the coastal Indians to the north would be retentive of their traditions and resistant to European leadership. Representing a confusing variety of linguistic stocks – Haida, Tsimshian, Kwagiutl, Nootka, and Salish – they enjoyed an affluence unusual in Canadian Indian societies. Although the coastal Indians were essentially hunters and gatherers, the profusion of fish and the mildness of the climate made possible a complexity of culture unmatched elsewhere in Canada. Social organization was strongly hierarchical, with a finely articulated gradation of status from what Europeans called royalty to a numerous class of slaves over whom their owners held an absolute power of life and death. Commerce was more important and more sophisticated than elsewhere, and war to maintain an adequate supply of slaves more intrinsic to the economy. But perhaps the most striking feature of coastal life was the dedication of the winter season to a round of feasts and ceremonies in which art was blended with religion. Here alone surplus wealth elevated the cultivation of social and individual talent into activities that rivalled in importance and seriousness the more mundane tasks of earning a living. Ultimates became matters not of fleeting concern but of continual pondering by shamans and prolonged celebration by the community.

The Society for the Propagation of the Gospel, which had passed up an earlier opportunity to undertake the christianization of Rupert's Land, was the first organization apart from the Roman Catholics to make a commitment to work among the Indians of British Columbia. Robert Dowson, who arrived in Victoria as its emissary in 1858, had a commission that included the whole coastline. He made an exploratory trip as far north as Fort Simpson but departed within a year and left no discernible legacy. Already, however, events in the north had taken a different turning. According to a pious story, at least, Captain (later Admiral) James Prevost, an evangelically minded naval officer who later taught at an Anglican school at Kitkatla, was profoundly shocked during a northern cruise in 1854 by the sight of bodies floating in the sea after a battle between Haidas and Tsimshians. Being highly impressed by the achievements and potential of these peoples, however, he urged missionary authorities to send a Christian teacher and suggested that the Tsimshians would be especially suitable for instruction.[17] The CMS, which had hitherto resisted involvement in British Columbia, found his plea impossible to refuse. In view of experience in New Zealand, Henry Venn suggested sending a schoolmaster instead of the usual clergyman.

William Duncan, when selected for the assignment, was studying at a CMS training school at Highbury in preparation for a teaching post in Africa.[18] A former tanner's apprentice, he was a young man who combined conventional evangelical piety with a remarkable determination to succeed on his own merits. At Fort Simpson he found the usual society of a Hudson's Bay post surrounded by a variegated Indian population that had been attracted by its opportunities. He proceeded at first cautiously but shrewdly, opening a school at the fort and visiting the Indian settlement but suggesting few radical changes and not even venturing to hold church services for nine months. Gradually he secured a following mostly among younger people, whom he admitted to baptism only on the assurance that they would make no compromises with traditional Indian ways. Despite this measure of success, Duncan was soon convinced that Fort Simpson offered no long-term possibility for a stable and self-supporting Christian community. The population lacked cohesion, and after the gold rush the coastal Indians increasingly took their furs to Victoria for sale. As the post lost its importance, the various groups around it were increasingly at odds with one another and the company. Duncan began to talk up the idea of a move elsewhere, leaving the choice of a location to Indians who would volunteer. In 1862 a group of about fifty Tsimshians left the fort for a former village site at Metlakatla, across the harbour from where Prince Rupert now stands.

Metlakatla provided the opportunity for a community where the church would be at the centre and where liquor and potlatch would not be tolerated. Here, despite his initial deference to Indian decision-making, Duncan was from the outset the unquestioned leader. Even the influential trading chief, Legaic, who was at first his chief opponent, eventually became his strongest supporter. In time Duncan was able to set up the model of a Victorian village, with regular streets and improved sanitation. To prevent backsliding he promulgated a set of stringent rules, which he enforced indirectly through an ingenious system of companies and classes in which chiefs were allowed a prominent place. He also provided economically for the village by setting up his own store and introducing various industries. Although displaying an unusual tolerance of Indian customs that he judged harmless, he ruled with an absolutism that was based partly on his own moral authority and partly on his appointment as a justice of the peace. No aspect of Duncan's regime contributed more to his public image than his custom of getting rid of an unwelcome visitor by hoisting a black flag on the community flagstaff, trusting to public opinion to make the warning effective.[19]

Jean Usher has applied a valuable corrective to the Duncan legend by reminding us that Metlakatla 'was not the product of a brilliant original mind, but was the application to a particular aboriginal group of the ideas and the theories inherent in much of Victorian reform and particularly in the policies of the Church Missionary Society.' Many individual items of his program were, indeed, far from new in Canadian practice. The necessity of promoting Western-style civilization in conjunction with Christianity was a missionary commonplace, and Duncan's decision that he must 'wait ... for the Indians to gain some knowledge of civilization' before pressing the gospel[20] was in line with much Anglican thought. His rules for behaviour were not radically different from those promulgated by the Moravians at Fairfield, while their strict enforcement was reminiscent of Peter Jones's visits of inspection to the homes of Grape Island. The concept of a segregated Christian village recalled a long line of precedents from Sillery through the Credit to Cockran's Dynevor and Bellecourt's Saint-Paul-des-Sauteux. Parallels with Oblate practice in British Columbia are even more obvious, and like Durieu's system Duncan's Metlakatla was almost universally hailed within sympathetic circles as a model for imitation by other missionaries.

When all of these qualifications have been made, an irreducible core of stubborn individuality remains. Apart from other eccentricities, a community in which segments of Scripture were held back from the people and in which the sacrament of Holy Communion was not allowed to be celebrated was far from the missionary norm. Duncan could find some support in Henry Venn's admonition that missionaries were to seek to create not Anglican but ultimately native churches,[21] but Anglican evangelicals as a party were dedicated to the openness of the Word and, as much as Tractarians, recognized the sacraments as essential elements of Christian worship. Strikingly similar to Durieu's system in many details, Duncan's approach differed in one important respect. Durieu relied on a full-strength dose of ultramontane Catholicism to effect the spiritual transformation of the Indians. Duncan, while equally unwilling to compromise with traditional religious practice, was content to accept at least for the foreseeable future a considerably thinned-down evangelical Protestantism.

Despite general admiration for Duncan there was a limit to what the CMS would or could tolerate, especially since Duncan proved so overbearing that five clergymen successively sent to Metlakatla were unable to remain there long. George Hills, who became bishop of British Columbia in 1859, offered to pay a visit in 1877 but was refused entry. He then took the unusual step of asking W.C. Bompas, the bishop of Athabasca, to make a rare sally out of his northern fastness in order to bring Duncan around. The choice of one well-known eccentric to persuade another was fated either for brilliant success or for dismal failure. Unhappily, the two eccentricities failed to blend. The next step, taken in 1879, was the appointment of a bishop with specific responsibility for the northern area. Almost inevitably William Ridley chose Metlakatla as his episcopal see, and from the beginning there was friction. The community quickly divided itself into two factions, and at first Ridley's followers were so badly outnumbered that he and his family found themselves virtually under siege. In 1882, however, Ridley handed Duncan a letter of dismissal from the CMS, and five years later Duncan removed with a majority of his flock to Alaska. The crowning irony was Duncan's desertion by most of the hereditary chiefs, who had seen much of their power slip away to the native church elders – and to Duncan.

Such was Duncan's fame that other Anglican missionaries have received relatively little attention. Among the Tsimshians and Haidas, indeed, most extension was inspired and inevitably affected by his pioneer enterprise. Even those who left Metlakatla disillusioned, such as W.H. Collison, who opened a mission among the Haidas of the Queen Charlotte Islands in 1876, carried with them many of the lessons they had learned there. Duncan's methods without Duncan did not prove to be very unconventional, however, and especially after 1879 there was little incentive to depart from tried-and-true CMS methods. An exception was Robert Tomlinson, who withdrew from the church in sympathy with Duncan and established an independent Christian village. Missions dating from 1877 among the southern Kwagiutls around the northern tip of Vancouver Island were well outside the range of Duncan's influence. Elsewhere in the province most Anglican work among Indians was relatively late and on a small scale, often arising out of the interest of local clergymen in neighbouring bands. In the southern interior, however, Lytton on the Fraser River became an important centre. In 1867 John B. Good opened a boys' school there in response to a request from a group of Indians who were disaffected with their priests. Other institutions followed, crowned by the establishment of a boarding school in 1901 with the aid of the New England Company. In southern British Columbia, unlike areas where the CMS predominated, more than one Anglican sisterhood became involved in Indian education.[22]

In 1859, responding to news of the Fraser gold rush of the previous year, the Canadian Methodists sent four of their most experienced ministers to open work in British Columbia. The needs of miners and other settlers were chiefly in their minds, and the ministers selected had travelled mainly on white circuits. Methodists had a long tradition of including Indians in their ministrations, however, and practically all of the pioneer preachers went out of their way to look them up. Victoria, Nanaimo, and Chilliwack became centres of vigorous proselytizing, and inevitably there was keen competition with the recently arrived Oblates for Salish souls. Methods of mass evangelism already past their peak in Canada took on new life among miners and Indians, and indeed would persist in the province for several decades. Stirring camp meetings, held on Vancouver Island and in the lower mainland, drew crowds in which white and Indian hearers mingled.

A lay preacher who proved particularly effective on the sawdust trail was Thomas Crosby, a young man from Woodstock, Canada West, who had emigrated to the region in 1862 in response to a dramatic conversion experience that convinced him of a call to missionary service there. At first he could find only labouring jobs, but he made such an impression on local Methodists that by the following year he was in charge of an Indian school at Nanaimo. The Upper Canadian tradition of indigenous preaching was also renewed in British Columbia. Amos Cushan was regarded as the outstanding Indian preacher, although David Sallosalton showed such promise before his premature death from tuberculosis that Crosby wrote a little book about him. As the white population increased, however, correspondingly less attention was paid to the Indians. By 1884, an official historian admitted, work among the Indians of southern British Columbia was in ruins.[23] Several missions survived, however, and the building of the Coquileetsa Institute at Chilliwack in 1886 gave the enterprise a measure of stability.

Meanwhile fruits of the revival had appeared in an unexpected part of the province. The ultimate source of contagion seems to have been a barroom in Victoria rented in 1870 by a Prince Edward Islander named William McKay for a Sunday school. Indians from the north customarily spent long periods in Victoria, much to Duncan's chagrin, and McKay's quarters became one of their frequent haunts. Fervent preaching went on there, with Crosby and Sallosalton as frequent guests, and several northern Indians were converted. Another important milestone was a revival at Port Ludlow, Washington, led by W.H. Pierce, a Tsimshian who had been converted by Duncan early in life. Further fuel was added to the fire by a camp meeting at Chilliwack in 1873. From such beginnings northern converts carried the message back to their home villages. Charlie Amos became the apostle of Kitamaat, and Clah, alias Philip McKay, of Wrangell, Alaska. Bella Bella Jack took home a Bible from Victoria and predicted that a missionary would follow, while Bella Bella Jim built a church in anticipation of such an event. A scene of early action was Fort (now renamed Port) Simpson, where by early 1874 it was reported that every family had renounced paganism. Here the leaders of the movement were a woman chief named Diex and her son Alfred Dudoward, both of whom had been converted at Victoria. The northward progress of this indigenous movement was marked by signs and wonders and by spiritual contests reminiscent of the earlier conversion of Europe. At Kitamaat many Christians died mysteriously in the first days of the church, but the tide turned when Christians were rewarded for not fishing on Sunday by seeing the pagans' net broken by an unexpected shoal of black fish and then having a great catch of their own on Monday. At Bella Bella the drowning of a stubborn chief was the event that made the difference.[24]

Despite this impressive record of native initiative, converts recognized that they had little knowledge of Christianity or experience in applying it. Accordingly they appealed for help to the Methodists, who sent a young layman named C.M. Tate to Port Simpson for a few months in 1874. Later in the year Crosby, who had been ordained in 1871 without a college education and rather against his will, arrived as the first full-time Methodist missionary among the Indians of British Columbia. Remaining there for the rest of his career, he became the chief architect of Methodist expansion among the northern tribes. A vigorous program of travel along the coast and up the Skeena and Nass, in the early years entirely by canoe, led to the formation of additional missions: Kitamaat in 1876, others along the coast and up the rivers at various times. Missionaries appointed to them, notably George H. Raley at Kitamaat, achieved lasting local reputations. Crosby's range was greatly increased in 1884 by the acquisition of a steam vessel; the name of William Oliver, a Scottish layman who built and maintained the *Glad Tidings* and several successors, has become almost legendary along the coast. By 1892 Methodist influence had been carried south as far as Cape Mudge near the northern end of the Gulf of Georgia.

His own faith having been the product of revival, Crosby was admirably fitted in many ways to take charge of a movement that had begun so spontaneously. Rather than attempting the conversion of a region single-handed he helped the Tsimshians to organize evangelistic teams that carried Methodism from village to village. Far from flagging, the first impulse seemed to reproduce itself several times over. Being of a practical bent, Crosby was also able to turn the local tradition of ceremonial giving to account by encouraging the Indians to undertake the expense of building churches and mission houses. He put the same sense of occasion to good use in arousing enthusiasm for such events as agricultural fairs. Crosby was probably not the equal of either Durieu or Duncan in coherence of vision, but he made up for the lack in dedication and energy. Very much caught up in the moral crusades then fashionable in Canada, he saw the cleaning up of the coast as such a major part of his task that the Methodist mission secretary, Alexander Sutherland, once described him as 'the best-hated man in British Columbia.'

Anglicans were less than pleased by this invasion of their territory. Duncan's distrust of emotion[25] and his conviction that a measure of civilization would have to precede conversion were enough in themselves to arouse his suspicions, and even Ridley complained of a Methodist tendency to administer the Lord's Supper without discrimination. The Methodists, on their side, admired Duncan and sought to build on the foundation he had laid. In the course of time the two denominations spread over much the same territory, communities that gave the cold shoulder to one often responding positively to the other, so that even today Anglican and United Church areas form a kind of jigsaw puzzle without much apparent logic. Mutual relations were always ambiguous, compounded of sympathy and suspicion. On several occasions the Methodists handed over missions voluntarily to the CMS, but it is not altogether clear that they did so gladly.

The manner in which Methodism reached the northern tribes seems in some respects almost ideal. Recollection of the part they had played in their own conversion gave the Indians a healthy sense of proprietorship in their churches. They formed organizations in which the missionary played little part, arranged evangelistic tours on their own, and in some communities kept services going over many years in the absence of a regular missionary. Eventually, however, the process of conversion exacted a price. The Christianity first introduced by Indians returning from Victoria had many of the features of a revitalization cult, reminiscent in some ways of the earlier pre-missionary Christianity in British Columbia. Methodism, despite a similar origin, had been infused from the beginning by John Wesley with a strong sense of order and respect for constituted authority. Crosby, especially in his later years, regretted that the missionaries had not been able to establish firmer control over the young people's bands, which often displayed more enthusiasm for spectacular forays than for the regular support of local institutions. Mutual relations were not softened, either, by the increasing arbitrariness of Crosby's temper.[26]

Meanwhile the religious rivalries of the region had made Indians aware that the shifting of denominational allegiance could be an effective way of expressing discontent. In the spring of 1896, Crosby reported, a representative of the Salvation Army toured the coast in search of possible openings. Crosby showed him around and pointed out various places where no missionaries were serving. Instead the Army settled on Port Simpson, where local faction assured it a ready hearing. Soon brass bands of the two denominations were engaged in noisy rivalry along the main street. Such at any rate was the Methodist story; the Army historian's account of the same events suggests some remarkable parallels between its invasion of Methodist territory and earlier Methodist trespassing on Anglican ground. Once again, in this version, a spontaneous movement had its origins at

Victoria where, in 1887, several Tsimshians dropped in at meetings of the
then-infant Army. Attracted by its lively services, they set up their own
versions of it at Port Essington, Port Simpson, and Metlakatla as early as
1890. The official entry of the Salvation Army in 1898 was thus designed
not to intrude on established work but to regularize a growing but chaotic
movement. The Salvation Army proved itself more hospitable to native
practice than had either Methodists or Anglicans, although one notes with
interest that by 1903 the ensign in charge of Glen Vowell was not only
teaching school but promoting agriculture.[27]

Among the Nootkas of the west coast of Vancouver Island Roman
Catholics were at work, although only with moderate success. The Canadian Presbyterians, eager by the last years of the nineteenth century to
extend their Indian missions into British Columbia but unwilling to enter
into competition with other Protestant bodies, saw here their opportunity.
In 1891 they opened a day school at Alberni, gradually adding other stations in the vicinity.[28] The Presbyterian field was more circumscribed than
others but also more intensely cultivated. Its best-known early missionary
was Melvin Swartout, who was drowned in the course of duty in 1904.
Records of the mission leave the impression of a rather stern paternalism,
with little evidence of Nootka initiative or of much hospitality towards it.

Confrontation between Christianity and the traditional values of native
society, although a universal and inevitable result of proselytizing activity,
was more prominent and persistent in coastal British Columbia than
almost anywhere else in Canada. Everywhere the records tell of contests
with shamans and of resistance from elders and traditionally minded
chiefs, but elsewhere they usually go on fairly quickly to describe at least
the appearance of a Christian victory. On the west coast, by contrast, the
struggle was unrelenting and prolonged, and even into the twentieth century reports from many mission stations alternated between cautious
optimism and near-despair. At Nanaimo in the 1860s missionaries drama-
tized the contest by drawing a vivid contrast between 'Christian Street,'
where young Indians built European-style houses and provided themselves
with cattle and horses, and 'Pagan Street' with traditional communal
houses and few modern ideas. Pagan Street did not disappear in line with
missionary hopes, and even where conversion was nominally complete,
conservatives refused to fall in with the plans of the progressive element.[29]

For an explanation of these deep-seated tensions we must look primarily to the nature of coastal societies. These were highly structured and well fortified with social conventions. A winter of comparative leisure, made possible by the abundance of nature and an equitable climate, was given over to a series of feasts, dances, and mimes that recalled the past and legitimized the present of the village or clan. There was considerable variety from region to region. Among the Salish of the south the vision quest was highly esteemed, and ceremonial was less important to social cohesion. In the north – closer to Siberia, we might be tempted to say – shamans imparted a larger element of unpredictability to social events. In between, among the Nootkas and the southern Kwagiutls, was the heartland of ritual and ceremony. Everywhere, however, religion gave a necessary sacredness to the events that bound the clan together. It was an essential ingredient of artistic inspiration, social order, and even cultural survival. Missionaries soon became aware of this close linkage. Chiefs, shamans, and other guardians of tradition had no doubt of it. Such a well-articulated social order was bound to put up a stiff resistance to forces seeking to undermine it.

Other influential factors encouraged openness to change. Coastal Indians, being accustomed to affluence, were quick to recognize and to seek for themselves the advantages of European technology. They were also aware that the European presence was subjecting their society to almost intolerable strains and that their traditions failed to provide an effective antidote. Their interest in religion, which Werner Müller has described as virtually an obsession,[30] naturally led many of them to seek this antidote in the religious sphere. That confrontation was not merely between aggressive missionaries and reluctant Indians but had roots in native societies themselves is demonstrated by the spiritual contests at Kitamaat and Bella Bella that preceded the missionaries' arrival.

On the missionary side there was a hardening of attitude to traditional practice, attributable in part to the timing of missionary activity in British Columbia. In earlier times, especially when working among migratory peoples, the missionaries had had to take the Indians much as they found them. By the late nineteenth century they could expect the backing of well-organized and omnipresent governments with coercive powers. By this time, too, they were becoming accustomed to look to governments for the enforcement of elements of their moral code, such as the observance of the Lord's day and restrictions on the use of alcoholic beverages, for which they had previously depended on their own internal discipline. Missionaries, like most other white Canadians of the time, saw no reason why such moral regulations should not apply to Indians as much as to anyone else. They readily extended this logic to the outlawing of traditional religious practices, some of which seemed to them as disorderly and antisocial as any of the practices they were seeking to eradicate from white society.

Controversy in British Columbia came to centre on a ceremonial feast known as the potlatch. Similar to many other feasts in its accompaniments of music and ritual movement, the potlatch had as its most conspicuous feature the bestowal of gifts on a large number of invited guests. Its basic purpose was to legitimize the taking up of a title, the acceptance of gifts implying recognition by the community of the validity of the title claimed. Like most pivotal social conventions it could also mean many other things: the putting-down of a rival clan or village, an occasion for co-operative effort and community-building, an enjoyable outing, even an excuse for good-natured spoofing.[31] Since one was eventually expected to repay this generosity at another potlatch, it was also a means at once of discharging a debt and laying up a credit. In a highly graded society it gave ritual sanction to continuity of status while also providing for the limited measure of social mobility that was necessary to prevent fossilization and thwarted ambition. Scholars agree that the potlatch had existed on the coast for a long time.

The institution as most outsiders knew it had already undergone considerable changes as the result of European contact. Potlatches became more frequent as epidemics hastened the transfer of titles and as the suppression of intertribal war encouraged the use of other means to work off hostility. The greater availability of trade goods made possible not only more but larger potlatches; the founding of Fort Rupert in 1849 was largely responsible for their enhanced popularity among the Kwagiutls.[32] Further, as tribal mingling gave rise to new uncertainties about relative ranking, the potlatch could be used not only to sustain but to create status. Naturally the enhancement of prestige consequent on a successful potlatch put intense pressure on others not merely to equal but to excel the achievement, although a common assumption that gifts had to be doubled in return represents a late and probably never universal development. Inevitably, too, alcohol as a valuable trade item had to be present in good supply to maintain the obligation of hospitality, and drunkenness and disorder became common. It goes almost without saying that white traders capitalized on the popularity of the potlatch and encouraged its abuse.

One can readily understand the hostility of nineteenth-century missionaries to the potlatch. Most obviously, the drunkenness and promiscuity that frequently accompanied it were deeply offensive to their moralistic outlook. 'The picture is more like hell upon earth than anything of which we have heard,' Crosby wrote of it, and although his judgment was scarcely unbiased he was close enough to the Indians to recognize that the loosening of old moral sanctions was threatening their health and even survival. More basically, the missionaries saw in an institution that encouraged the dissipation rather than accumulation of capital a fatal obstacle to their program of progress. They were also aware that the staging of a potlatch was regularly followed by a slump in attendance at their services. J.F. Ross, principal of a Presbyterian boarding school, in asking for 'some restriction in regard to these pernicious heathen customs' offered as one justification that they were 'in direct opposition to Christian teaching and the work of the Holy Spirit.'[33] Generally these various arguments were not carefully distinguished. Potlatch represented the old backward way of life, and Christian Indians eager for change joined the missionaries in protesting against it.

With equal readiness one can appreciate the determination of many Indians not to let the institution go. Status in their society was of questionable validity without it, so that a title-holder who had not given a potlatch was rather like an uncrowned king or an adult Jew who had never been given a bar mitzvah. The cessation of potlatch would also leave many debts unpaid, offending honour on the one hand and damaging prudential interest on the other. The common plea of many Indians who claimed sincerely to desire the abolition of potlatch was, 'Let us first pay off our debts.' This was no mere excuse but the statement of a genuine problem, although of course Methodist missionary A.E. Green was correct in his contention that conceding the point would mean that 'this potlaching must go on forever.' More generally, potlatching was so integral to native culture that, like contemporary unbelievers who continue to celebrate Christmas, many for whom it lacked its former religious significance would have found the year empty without it. A leading missionary, eager to demonstrate that legislation against potlatch would not discriminate against non-Christian Indians, called attention to the prominence of Christians among its promoters.

In 1883 a church group that included several Indian chiefs petitioned the British Columbian Indian superintendent for the outlawing of pot-latch, and in 1884 the Canadian parliament prohibited the practice. For many years, as the result of an adverse decision by the celebrated Chief Justice Begbie and the reluctance of provincial administrators to undertake what seemed to them an impossible task, little attempt was made to enforce this legislation. In 1921, however, William Halliday, Indian agent at Alert Bay, succeeded in securing convictions against several Kwagiutls.[34] These resulted in the incarceration of several Indians in Oakalla Peniten-tiary and – what troubled the Indians even more – the surrender under pressure of the 'paraphernalia' used in the potlatch to the National Museum in Ottawa. A notable feature of the controversies of the 1920s was the support given to the potlatchers by Franz Boas, who was generally con-sidered one of the least political of anthropologists. Throughout the strug-gle the missionaries, practically without exception, were on the side of suppression.

Today potlatching has ceased to be controversial. The ban on it was removed from the statute books, rather quietly, in 1931. Many items of the surrendered paraphernalia have been returned to the bands to which they belong and are now attractively displayed in museums at Cape Mudge and Alert Bay.[35] In many communities it would be unthinkable for promoters of a potlatch not to invite the local minister and equally unthinkable for him or her not to attend. What remains is the unhappy memory of a time when missionaries aggressively sought the destruction of an institution that is now regarded as a key badge of Indian identity. No issue has raised more clearly the difficulty of seeking to improve a society without becoming in effect its destroyer.

Happily, some controversies pitted the missionaries not against Indian traditionalists but against white despoilers on their behalf. The situation in British Columbia presented many occasions for such intervention. The Hudson's Bay Company, so long as it ruled, had at least a vested interest in maintaining the Indians as viable trading partners. To the early settlers they were merely economic liabilities and competitors for scarce valley land, and some miners who had learned their attitudes to non-white peoples in California urged that they 'ought to be rooted out like tree stumps.' Sir James Douglas, the first civil governor, brought a Hudson's Bay background that led him to assume that lands could be secured from the Indians only by purchase. His successors adamantly refused to recog-

nize any aboriginal rights and assigned lands for reservations as if they
were conferring favours. The terms of confederation provided that tracts
for the Indians should be provided by the province to the federal government in accordance with 'a policy as liberal as that hitherto pursued by the
British Columbia Government,' with the result that the same grudging
provision continued to be made. A commission appointed on Duncan's
suggestion in 1876 proposed a greater measure of justice, but the province
paid no attention to its recommendations.[36] Discontent festered among the
Indians for generations, with the land issue as the crux of disagreement.

Missionaries were practically unanimous in calling for fair treatment of
the Indians. In the 1860s two Anglican clergymen appealed to Britain for
redress of injustice to the Indians, W.S. Green to the Aborigines' Protection Society and Bishop George Hills to the colonial secretary. In 1889 the
British Columbia Conference of the Methodist Church passed a strong
resolution in favour of Indian land claims and appointed a committee to
'watch the interests of the Indians,' in defiance of the report of a legislative
committee in the previous year that had assigned a large share of blame for
Indian discontent to the activities of Methodist missionaries. On several
occasions Morice intervened to secure fair trials for Indians who seemed
likely to be railroaded to prison, and Swartout was noted in a memorial
tribute as having offended some whites by his 'defence of the Indians
against the cruelty and injustice of whitemen.' That Indians could usually
count on missionary support for their claims was generally recognized in
the province. Already by 1860 the *Victoria Gazette*, which advocated the
extinguishing of Indian title, urged: 'Do it now, for it can be done at small
cost. But let priests and missionaries once gain the ear of the Indian then
farewell to so easy and inexpensive an arrangement.'[37]

Missionary complaints of discrimination were not always disinterested.
Some missionaries seem to have been less troubled by injustice to the Indians as such than by apparent favouritism to other denominations or even
to pagan Indians. The Methodist protest of 1889, for example, takes on a
somewhat different colouring when read in the light of resolutions passed
in the previous year that had placed more emphasis on injustice to Methodists than on injustice to Indians. Sometimes, too, missionary opposition to
government policy arose in part from a desire to further such favourite
projects as the promotion of individual enterprise and the elimination of
nomadism. Duncan achieved a considerable reputation as an advocate of
Indian rights mainly through his late opposition, on behalf of his own

party of Christian Indians, to CMS land claims at Metlakatla. At other times he had been more interested in promoting allotments to individual Indians, the creation of consolidated tribal reservations that would facilitate missionary supervision, or a collection of self-help communities near Victoria,[38] aims that did not necessarily coincide with Indian desires.

Few would deny, however, that the missionaries contributed significantly to the native cause, most effectively perhaps by encouraging Indians to press their own case. Durieu acted as consultant to a group of chiefs on the lower Fraser who presented a petition in 1868, and in 1874 he again supported their action.[39] Duncan and Crosby trained elders and class leaders who became in after years prominent advocates on behalf of their people. If resistance to missionary and governmental pressure on potlatch was one source of later Indian militant leadership, missionary encouragement of native land claims was another of major importance. Indian organizations that emerged in the twentieth century were led by persons such as Peter Kelly and Andrew Paull who had gained in the church much of their ability to speak effectively to white officials. The lawyer to whom they first turned for advice was a grandson of the O'Meara who had struggled for so many years to establish an Anglican cause on Manitoulin.

CHAPTER SEVEN

Range to Reservation

Tracing the progress of Christianity among the Indians of the plains only after following it to the Arctic and the Pacific is a procedure that calls for some explanation. Missions in western Canada began at the Red River, just within the eastern rim of the prairies. The country to the west was well known there, for most of the local French-speaking Métis depended for their livelihood on an annual buffalo hunt that ranged widely through it. Missionaries were prompt to show interest in its possibilities. Provencher and West each travelled as far as the Qu'Appelle country within a year or so of their arrival, and in 1845 Bellecourt initiated the practice of having a priest accompany the hunt.[1] One of the first missions beyond the Red River was at Fort Edmonton, near the far end of the prairies. Effective missionary occupation of the plains was, however, a much slower process. As late as the 1870s, when few Indians in British Columbia or the north remained unreached, there still intervened only a handful of missions along the fringes of the prairie grasslands or in well-watered river valleys.

This comparatively late penetration was, in part, a result of the communication system of the era. The main line of the fur trade, on which missionaries depended heavily for transport, ran from York Factory by the Hayes and Saskatchewan rivers and thence along connecting waterways across Portage la Loche to the Athabasca and Mackenzie. Next in importance was the route that led by the Saskatchewan and later the Athabasca Pass through the Rockies to the Columbia system. Natives along these routes were constantly exposed to influences from the Red River, Norway House, and ultimately Europe. They were also in contact with the Métis, who made their appearance wherever the fur trade penetrated, people who considered themselves Christian by birthright if not always consistent in their practice of it. The Indians of the open plains, who depended on the horse rather than the canoe for transport, were much less affected by the trade. They were important for supplies of pemmican, but the contacts arising from such provisioning were fleeting and superficial. The pattern of western transport later established by the Canadian Pacific Railway and confirmed by the Trans-Canada Highway and Air Canada was still far in the future.

The nature of plains culture posed an even more serious obstacle to missionary expansion. The economy of the region was based on the buffalo, which provided both food and clothing. Its importance to the tribes of the region varied. For the so-called Plains Crees and the Assiniboines, a Siouan tribe that had broken with the Dakotas to the south in early historic times, its exploitation formed part of an annual cycle. Most at home in the belt of parkland or savannah that forms a crescent on the north side of the Canadian prairies, these Indians customarily ventured into the open plains in summer and withdrew to the woodlands for other game in the winter.[2] By the time of the missionaries they had been joined by Ojibwas from the east, who became the Saulteaux of the west. The Blackfeet, whose range extended from the North Saskatchewan to the Missouri and from the foothills of the Rockies into western Saskatchewan, depended almost exclusively on the buffalo and were the true plains Indians of Canada. Constituting a confederacy of three tribes – Bloods, Piegans, and Blackfeet proper – they also had associated with them the Sarcees of Athapaskan origin.

The horse, which had been introduced into New Mexico by Don Juan de Oñote in 1598 and reached the Blackfeet before the middle of the eighteenth century, was a cultural determinant of almost equal significance. It proved useful in the buffalo hunt, as the gun would later. More important, since the Indians had long known effective techniques of herding buffalo into pounds, was the increased mobility that enabled them for the first time to venture far from ready sources of water. Competition for the control of a region that had hitherto been little exploited produced what was in many respects a new society, a wild-west frontier even before the white man. The ready wealth available through the buffalo encouraged a flowering of leisure activities, and the scale of the country encouraged large military aggregations similar to those of eastern Europe. Endemic warfare, waged less for economic advantage than for prestige symbolized by the capture of horses, inspired elaborate codes of chivalry. Newly synthesized religious rites, such as the sacred lodge or sun dance, helped to cement tribal identities and provided opportunities for individual self-realization. This high-spirited society felt little need for European intruders, who normally ventured into the region only under heavy escort and then at considerable risk. The obstacles it posed to missionary work were apparent as early as 1834, when a raid of Gros Ventres forced Belle-court to move his first agricultural settlement closer to the safety of the Red River.[3]

Robert Rundle, who arrived at Fort Edmonton in 1840 as its first Wesleyan missionary, was followed in 1842 by Jean-Baptiste Thibault. They were competitors from the outset. Rundle had a nineteenth-century Englishman's horror of popery, while Thibault did everything in his power to combat heresy. The two were in some ways strangely matched. Rundle, a Cornishman who arrived in his late twenties, was a romantic who went out of his way to catch glimpses of the Rockies, a hypochondriac who regularly noted in his journal a great variety of ailments, and a Methodist who kept equally careful track of fluctuations in his spiritual condition. Although he struck Hudson's Bay Company officials as unequal to his task,[4] he showed himself capable of enduring unlimited hardship and of making fast friendships with Europeans and Indians alike. Thibault, a down-to-earth French-Canadian, seldom allowed his imagination to divert him from his primary aim of saving souls.

Thibault had the advantage of a ready-made constituency, for many employees of the company were French-Canadians or francophone Métis. Although Rundle and his superintendent James Evans persuaded some of the latter to embrace Protestantism at first, these returned to Catholicism practically without exception on Thibault's arrival. During his first year Thibault paid a visit to the Blackfeet, with such success that in 1847 Rundle reported, 'Peagan chief showed picture and thing about popery, also papers.' His chief success, however, was among the more northerly Crees. John E. Harriott, the Protestant chief trader at Rocky Mountain House, admitted that not more than a dozen of them had escaped his influence. Rundle was not so well placed. There were few English at Fort Edmonton, and the ultra-Protestant Orkneymen there scorned the prayer-book services traditional among English Wesleyans. He soon saw that, despite the reluctance of the company, his only promising field of labour was in Indian camps. Harriott gave him invaluable help, both by preparing translations and by persuading the Indians to receive him, and Rocky Mountain House became his most reliable base of operation. At first Rundle thought that the Blackfeet would be the '1st to bow to sceptre of Immanuel,' but he was more successful among mountain Assiniboines or Stoneys. These had already heard of Christian teaching from Kootenais west of the Rockies and were thus predisposed to accept his message.

In traditional missionary fashion both pioneers promoted settlements away from the fort where Indians might learn to farm. Rundle spent considerable time surveying possible sites at Battle River and Pigeon Lakes, both southwest of Edmonton and thus readily accessible to Rocky Mountain House. He reported some Indian desire for a settlement, although one senses some ambiguity in his notation that 'indians helped as reward had been promised.'[5] As a company chaplain he had to wait for official permission, however, and by the time this was granted he was preparing to return to England to attend to a broken wrist that had not healed properly. Meanwhile Thibault had been able to proceed with greater freedom. In 1844, after an abortive attempt at Frog Lake, he succeeded in establishing a settlement at Lac-Sainte-Anne to the northwest of Edmonton. The site proved to be less than ideal, but the mission attracted an increasing number of Métis settlers.

After Rundle's departure in 1848 Methodist interests were cared for by Benjamin Sinclair, a native catechist from Norway House. Continuing Rundle's practice of itinerating, Sinclair was able to retain many of his converts. Some, such as the Cree chief Maskepetoon, would be pillars of Methodism in later years. Reinforcements arrived after 1854, when Canadian Methodists assumed responsibility for western missions. Among these none was more significant than Henry B. Steinhauer, an Upper Canadian Ojibwa who had served for some years in northern Manitoba before arriving in Alberta in 1855. Setting up a solitary farm at Whitefish Lake, fifty kilometres south of Lac la Biche, he gradually attracted enough Crees to form a self-reliant indigenous community. During these years, however, the Roman Catholics were moving ahead more quickly, and Steinhauer admitted that even many Stoneys had taken to wearing crosses when they decided that the Methodists had given them up.[6] The Oblates gradually took over the Roman Catholic work and were joined in 1859 by a convent of Grey Nuns at Lac-Sainte-Anne. In 1861 the Oblates began a new settlement at Saint Albert, near Fort Edmonton, and the Grey Nuns soon moved there also. Saint Albert, which was erected into an episcopal see in 1871, became an important centre both for the diffusion of Roman Catholicism and for the preservation of French-Canadian and Métis culture in the west. It also became the first major centre of agriculture in Alberta, although Rundle had done the first planting.

The most flamboyant figure associated with Roman Catholic work in this period, and probably the best-known prairie missionary of any denomination, was Albert Lacombe. Brought up on a farm in Lower Canada, he cherished a remote Indian strain in his ancestry. After serving a brief apprenticeship with Bellecourt in North Dakota, he was persuaded by Bishop Bourget of Montreal that he could work most effectively as a member of a religious order. He arrived at Lac-Sainte-Anne in 1852 and was soon a professed Oblate. He had a major role in the foundation of Saint Albert, which Taché is commonly said to have named in his honour. Apart from its superior soil, the site appealed to him on account of its greater accessibility to the Blackfeet of the plains. The plains Indians became his major preoccupation, indeed, and in 1865 he was set free from local responsibilities to devote his entire time to travel.[7] His ministry over the next seven years was exercised mainly in the saddle, and his biographers describe many hair-raising adventures. Lacombe was remarkably successful in gaining the friendship and confidence of the Blackfeet, while making most of his converts among the Crees.

Methodist fortunes took a turn for the better with the appointment of George McDougall as western superintendent in 1862. Raised on a pioneer farm near Barrie, he was a practical Canadian who had commanded two lake schooners in the Indian trade before entering the Methodist ministry and training for Indian missions under Case. It was typical of McDougall that, appointed by the church to Norway House, he quickly sensed the strategic significance of the prairies and transferred his energies there. Once on the scene he directed operations as a not always benevolent autocrat. Overruling the local missionary, Thomas Woolsey, who had chosen a more northerly site, he fixed the location of a new agricultural mission at Victoria (now Pakan) on the North Saskatchewan River below Edmonton. Like its rival Saint Albert, it attracted mainly settlers of mixed ancestry, although in this case English in speech. In 1868, in the afterglow of confederation, he persuaded the Methodist conference to spare him four new ministers and two missionary teachers. The race was still on, however, for in the same year Bishop Vital J. Grandin brought four new Oblate priests and several lay brothers from France.[8]

In 1866 the Canada Presbyterian Church, which was the product of a union in 1861 between the local branch of the Free Church of Scotland and the United Presbyterians or Seceders, inaugurated the first Indian mission ever to be sponsored by Canadian Presbyterians. The train of events that led to this decision began in 1851, when the Free Church at last satisfied the desire of Red River Scots by appointing John Black as their minister. In 1861 James Nisbet was named as his assistant. Black and Nisbet were acutely embarrassed by the failure of their church, alone among those represented in the west, to make any provision for the Indians around them. In 1864 Black sent an impassioned appeal to the synod that at last roused his church to action, and with an ecumenicity rare for the times the Presbyterians consulted both Methodists and Anglicans before deciding upon a site near Fort Carlton. Nisbet reluctantly accepted the appointment despite fairly advanced years and a confessed lack of linguistic skill. Arriving in 1866 with his brother-in-law John MacKay and several workmen, he bestowed on his mission the name 'Prince Albert' in honour of Victoria's consort. Although his instructions were to itinerate on the plains, he soon decided like others before him that settlement would provide the best opportunity for systematic instruction, especially since many Indians sought out the mission. Despite repeated admonitions, therefore, he placed much more emphasis on a school and model farm than on trips to Indian encampments.[9] A late entrant into the Indian field, the Presbyterians became a significant factor on the prairies where missionaries were still few.

The Anglicans, so active elsewhere, were slow to establish a significant presence on the prairies. From 1842 to 1859 the CMS maintained a mission at Fort Qu'Appelle. In 1852 Henry Budd opened a mission at Nipawewin (now Nipawin) east of the future Prince Albert that was seen at the time as 'one step in advance towards our approach to the Rocky Mountains,' and in 1857 the Palliser expedition encountered the native catechist Charles Pratt at Fort Ellice. Further developments awaited the erection of the dioceses of Saskatchewan and Athabasca in 1874. The few missionaries of Athabasca at the time of its formation were in the Arctic portion of the diocese, while the Indian work of Saskatchewan was almost entirely among the Wood Crees north of that river.[10]

Pioneer prairie missions had at least three important features in common. First, they all dealt with Indians in their accustomed habitat and therefore depended for success on satisfying Indian desires and aspirations.

That they were able to do so with considerable effectiveness is indicated by crowds that sought out the missionaries as arbiters and medical practitioners as well as spiritual guides.[11] Secondly, the missionary prescription for this situation was once again settlement, preferably agricultural. Even Lacombe, with his bent for wandering, set himself as one of his first tasks as a roving missionary the foundation of the village of Saint-Paul-des-Cris at what is now Brosseau, Alberta. Missionaries might admire 'wild' Indians, but they could only implement their programs by taming them. Thirdly, practically all early missions were within the parkland belt that rimmed the northern edge of the open plains. Both Methodists and Roman Catholics attempted to reach the Blackfeet, but the Crees and the Assiniboines, who had long acted as middlemen in the Hudson's Bay trade, provided their only converts. Some conditioning to European ways apparently helped.

Although the old ways still prevailed on the plains, no one who was well informed expected them to maintain their hold for very long. Despite Simpson's care to play down the agricultural possibilities of the region, there was already talk by mid-century of almost unlimited room for settlers. By the late 1850s, through the energetic propagandizing of George Brown of the *Globe* and others, Canadians were beginning to take for granted that the west would in time be theirs and that they would have the opportunity to people it – assuming, of course, that the Americans did not get there first. Signs of change were least visible on the plains themselves, but they could not be hidden altogether from the Indians. When the Hudson's Bay Company declined in 1859 to take further responsibility for missionary freight, other agencies were compelled to make their own arrangements. The result was the appearance of trails across the prairies, fit only for Red River carts and scarcely fit for them, but nevertheless the beginning of a transportation system that anyone was free to use. The sense of impending change, which for the Indians could bode no good, deepened with each successive exploring expedition or incipient settlement.

If change was inevitable, the missionaries reasoned, a large part of their task was to prepare the Indians to cope with it. They had seen their responsibility in these terms from the outset, indeed, and the chief purpose of their settlements was to provide an alternative way of life against the day when the old nomadic one would become impossible. With the passing of

time the work of preparation seemed ever more urgent. In 1858 the editor
of the *Church Missionary Intelligencer*, convinced that an influx of white
settlers was both inevitable and imminent, urged that by 'the invigorating
action of Christianity' the Indians must be enabled to 'hold their ground.'[12]
All missionaries regarded education as a vital element in preparation.
Nisbet, who was caught up in the nineteenth-century enthusiasm for religious education, made it central to his program at Prince Albert. Protestants were most deeply committed to some aspects of acculturation, but
Grandin was equally convinced that education and agricultural settlement
were likely to be the most effective means of ensuring Indian survival.[13]
With the stakes so high and the prospect of change so imminent, missionaries were willing to use fairly strong measures to force the pace of adaptation.

Instead of coming with the smoothness that Canadians tend to take for
granted, the transition was laced with problems, tensions, and ominous
incidents. The end of Hudson's Bay Company rule meant a breakdown of
any semblance of law and order. Inevitably during the transitional years a
good deal of missionary effort was absorbed in dealing with crisis situations
as they arose. The most immediate problem was the prevalence of intertribal war, especially on the open plains. Missionaries naturally regretted
the bad feelings and loss of life involved. They also found that fighting
seriously hindered their work, diverting Indians from a potential interest
in Christian teaching, confirming them in traditional practices, and prohi-
biting ready access to encampments. In 1845 the Jesuit de Smet crossed the
Rockies in an endeavour to make peace between the Kootenais and the
Blackfeet. The mission failed, according to Rundle because of the unsuit-
ability of an interpreter, although de Smet struck up a rare ecumenical
friendship with the young Methodist. Practically every missionary could
tell of similar attempts to persuade tribes to keep or restore the peace.
Woolsey was able to induce Maskepetoon to shake hands with the mur-
derer of his son, while Lacombe had his hat shot off on one occasion while
flying a white flag from a Blackfoot camp to attract the attention of attack-
ing Crees.[14]

Despite all that the missionaries could do, raids continued to increase
throughout the late 1860s. In the spring of 1869, Maskepetoon, the model
Methodist convert who had latterly been an assistant to the missionaries,
was killed while on a mission of peace to the Blackfeet. In an effort to
prevent catastrophe, George McDougall and his missionary son John

organized a monster gathering on the plains to promote peace and civilization. Crees and Blackfeet had separate camps, and Constantine Scollen, a lay brother from Saint Albert who had considerable experience among the Crees, was there to help.[15] John McDougall believed that the rally did some good, but tribal warfare continued to mount, and the Crees even raided the Victoria mission to secure supplies.

While the escalation of intertribal war was primarily the result of earlier legacies of European contact, notably the horse, the gun, and the trade in buffalo hides and tongues, the presence of an increasing number of whites on the prairies added a new complication. In 1867 a party of American miners passed through Alberta on the way to the Cariboo. Their arrogant attitude led to Blackfoot retaliation against a group of German immigrants in the following year. Then in 1869 American traders opened a post in the Blackfoot country, the first of eight such stores within the next five years. These whisky traders, operating out of forts with such colourful names as 'Whoop-Up' and 'Slide-Off,' sowed both disorder and distrust of whites on the plains. The Blackfeet in particular were goaded into frequent clashes with their neighbours and with Americans in the vicinity. In the resulting demoralization the missionaries naturally prescribed the gospel as a prime remedy. In 1873 George McDougall opened a mission at Morleyville (now Morley) in the foothills, mainly to evangelize the neighbouring Stoneys but in part to provide a nucleus of order for the region.

To complicate further an already complicated situation, trouble broke out at the Red River in 1869. The Canadian government, which had arranged to purchase Rupert's Land from the Hudson's Bay Company in that year, made the great mistake of assuming authority there prematurely. It ordered a survey without taking account of local traditions of land tenure and appointed a lieutenant-governor without prior assurances to the inhabitants. The result was to undermine the remaining local authority of the company and thus to prepare the way for a provisional government headed by Louis Riel and dominated by the French-speaking Métis. Although few English-speaking residents approved of Riel's procedures, old-timers of all ethnic backgrounds resented the assumption of recently arrived Canadian settlers that they represented the wave of the future. The local clergy, apart from the Methodist George Young, who had brought his attitudes with him from Toronto, sympathized with the grievances of the long-established residents and did what they could to restore peace and amity. The Indians of the area were only marginally involved in the whole episode, on one occasion ironically on the side of the Canadian settlers.[16]

Farther west the shock occasioned by the wholesale transfer of Indian land without Indian consent, along with the precedent of resistance set at the Red River, stimulated talk of a general rising. Of the attitudes of Protestant missionaries in this crisis there was never any doubt. George McDougall, who hastened to the Red River to secure supplies and military protection, offered to be one of a group of twenty men to take Riel's force by surprise but left for home when there was no immediate response. At the behest of the Canadian authorities John spent the winter of 1869–70 seeking to secure the loyalty of the Crees. The Oblates were in a more difficult position, for their sympathies were with the Métis and they regarded Riel's government as legitimate. George McDougall complained that the French priests 'had a hatred for everything that bears the name of English,' while John reported that Scollen's supportive attitude of the previous summer had turned to opposition. When a meeting of missionaries and Hudson's Bay factors was called at Edmonton, however, George McDougall reported to the Canadian-appointed governor William McDougall: 'For the sake of the Indians, the priests agreed to join us in securing ammunition and a guard of one hundred men for Edmonton.' Before this excitement could die down, the plains were swept by an epidemic of smallpox. The scourge was not new, having preceded even the fur trade to the west, and on this occasion the successful use of vaccine at Prince Albert and The Pas presaged early relief. Nevertheless, it was scarcely surprising that some Indians became 'sullen and insolent' or that in revenge infected articles were slipped into the McDougalls' missionary village.[17]

The Canadian government, in taking possession of Rupert's Land in 1870, assumed responsibility for administering the region. The most urgent problem was that of law enforcement, on the necessity of which all whites on the scene including the missionaries were agreed.[18] In 1873 the North-West Mounted Police were authorized as a paramilitary body, and in the following year a first contingent was dispatched to the west. Beyond mere peacekeeping, however, the authorities were soon aware of the need for a settlement of the land issue. They believed, with some reason, that only security of tenure would save the Indians from annihilation. They also recognized that the possibility of peaceful white occupation depended on coming to terms with the Indians, for without a settlement of some kind the Indians were certain to resist any attempt to encroach on their territory.[19]

To a greater extent than they can have realized, the missionaries were not only watchdogs for their Indian charges but harbingers of the new order. Nowhere was this clearer than at Prince Albert. Nisbet was well connected at the Red River, where many Presbyterians belonged to the 'country-born' or part-Indian majority of the English-speaking population, and arrived at his assigned post with the nucleus of a small settlement. These connections gave the mission an indigenous character it would otherwise have lacked but also ensured that the fertility of the soil around Prince Albert would be well known at Winnipeg. The Presbyterian Foreign Mission Committee kept urging Nisbet to restrict his farming and itinerate on the plains. They were afraid that Indians would congregate around the mission in expectation of hand-outs; in fact, as white settlers multiplied, the Indians moved away. By the time of Nisbet's death in 1874 Prince Albert was no longer a significant Indian mission, and Indian work there was totally abandoned in 1881 when John MacKay, Nisbet's brother-in-law, who had become an ordained minister, accepted an invitation from chief Mis-ta-wah-sis to open a mission on his reserve farther west.[20]

Other missionaries played equally important parts in 'opening the great west.' John McDougall published a book with this title, while his father left no doubt as to where his sympathies lay: 'For many years the Wesleyan Missionary has labored to direct public attention to the vast and fertile plains of British Central America. Now, men of the world will corroborate their statements and consummate the work.' Like a number of others, George McDougall was not only a missionary but a settler and the founder of a prominent western family. John became a minister, David a trader, and Eliza married a prominent HBC officer.[21] The family never became a dynasty to compare with the missionary offspring of Michener's *Hawaii*, but John Snow has called attention to its large holdings near Morley. Roman Catholic missionaries, most of whom were French and counted many French-speaking Métis among their parishioners, were naturally less enthusiastic about developments that could only bring alien and heretical ways. Yet when Lacombe was called away to Manitoba in 1872, he devoted much of his energy to the encouragement of francophone immigration. W.F. Butler observed after touring the prairies in 1871 that he had learned of only six incipient settlements and that all had been founded by missionaries.[22]

Sharing many attitudes and concerns, the missionaries were drawn with seeming inevitability into close collaboration with the government. They were alarmed for the future that awaited the Indians unless some settlement was made with them, and some of them were as eager as any that immigrants should have a place in the country as well. It was not surprising, therefore, that when Treaty Number 6 with the Crees was proposed, Lieutenant-Governor Alexander Morris should ask George McDougall in 1875 to take to the camps once again in order to prepare the way for it. It was to be his last such trip, for during the next winter he died in a prairie snowstorm. In view of the success of Roman Catholic missionaries in gaining the confidence of the Blackfeet, Scollen was persuaded despite his previous reluctance to perform a similar task in the following year in preparation for Treaty Number 7. The actual negotiations were conducted by government representatives and Indian chiefs, with the missionaries playing a modest role as interpreters and witnesses. Nevertheless, the presence of Anglican, Methodist, Presbyterian, and Roman Catholic representatives at the signing of Treaty Number 6 in 1876 lent dignity to the proceedings, and Bishop Grandin made a special trip to Fort Pitt to assure the commissioners of his good will. Scollen and John McDougall, the latter of whom attended the signing of Treaty Number 7 at the request of the Stoneys, were likewise reported to have 'rendered the Commissioners all the assistance in their power.'[23] No one doubted that the activity of the missionaries in explaining and promoting the treaties was an influential factor in facilitating the process.

As the missionaries saw it, their part in treaty-making was simply a necessary job well done. Some of them had regrets for the way of life that was passing, and John McDougall expressed his with some eloquence, but they had no doubt that they were acting in the best interests of the Indians whom they served. They knew that immigration was bound to come, that if unregulated it would issue in violence, and that the Indians would be the ultimate losers in any clashes that occurred. They reasoned that the signing of formal agreements was the only way to prevent such a catastrophe. They believed, indeed, that the Canadian people owed it to the Indians to negotiate treaties with them. In the circumstances they regarded themselves as natural advocates for the Indians and did their best to represent Indian desires. If they used a little rhetoric to persuade the Indians to sign, this was only because they were confident of having a clearer understanding of the possible consequences of delay. The Crees, at least, took a sufficiently favourable view of their activities that at the treaty-making they asked the government to provide them with missionaries.[24]

Ambiguities in the role of the missionaries became apparent only as the Indians began to realize the full import of the treaties. Probably the missionaries were almost as wide-eyed in their confidence that the government would somehow find a way to provide the Indians with a new and viable way of life. They can scarcely have been taken in by treaty assurances that Indians would have 'the right to preserve their avocations of hunting and fishing' except in lands required for other purposes, however, and their explanations were undoubtedly coloured considerably by their own sense of what was necessary and right. Their credibility as representatives of the Indians was even more seriously compromised by some mixture of motives on their part. Quite apart from the Canadian boosterism that some displayed, they were affected by their own interests as missionaries. Like most of their predecessors, they saw no possibility of inculcating their beliefs, practices, and moral precepts so long as the Indians were migratory and uncontrolled. Even Roman Catholics were anxious to see them settled, and the Presbyterians found the situation so frustrating that in 1874 they decided to send no more missionaries until reserves should have been set up.[25]

In justice to the missionaries we should not assess their behaviour as if they were working in a vacuum or had unlimited options at their disposal. They made what seemed to them the only possible choice in a difficult situation, and second-guessing today is at best hazardous. Even at the time, however, others saw treaties in a different light. George Monro Grant believed that in agreeing to them the Indians were signing their own death warrants, while John Semmens, a Methodist of conservative temper, suggested that the mission at Norway House had taught the Indians to be too trusting. Although they acted in good faith, missionaries who promised that the government would respect treaties expected by the Indians to 'last as long as the sun shines and the rivers run' were accepting a moral responsibility that would not be forgotten.[26]

The treaties constituted a charter of missionary advance, one for which the various agencies had long waited. Under the new order the missionaries could expect to have a greater influence than ever before. No longer would the Indians disappear for months into the trackless plains or be distracted from their catechisms by a sudden exchange of raids with a neighbouring tribe. Instead a centrally located mission would ensure a conspicuous presence on the reserve and enable the missionary to keep a close watch on behaviour and religious observance. This new opportunity coincided with a renewed stirring of missionary zeal within the churches. The CMS, after a rather dry period in the 1860s, rejoiced by 1871 in a 'sudden upturn of candidates.' In 1874 the Oblates received a contingent of four priests, two scholastics, and three lay brothers.[27] Canadian Protestants, especially Protestant women, were beginning to organize national societies that would in time constitute formidable support systems for missions. In 1874 a partial union of Methodist splinter groups, and in the following year a general union of Presbyterians, brought into being churches capable of operating from sea to sea.

During the 1870s all agencies were able to increase their mission staffs on the prairies. While Roman Catholics and Methodists consolidated their positions, others became more active. Among Sioux who sought refuge in British territory on account of various troubles in the United States was a group at Bird-Tail Creek (now Birtle) in southern Manitoba that had come under Presbyterian influence in the U.S. In response to their appeal the American Presbyterians in 1875 sent Solomon Tunkansuiciye, an ordained Sioux minister, to conduct services, and in 1877 the Canadian church gave him a permanent appointment. Lucy Baker, who joined the Prince Albert staff as a teacher in 1874, later became interested in a band of Sioux in that area. Devoting the rest of her life to them, she did much to interest Presbyterian women in the Indians of the west. The 1870s also saw the beginning of significant Anglican work among the Indians of the prairies. John McLean, an academic who was named bishop of Saskatchewan in 1874 with the needs of expected white settlers chiefly in mind, took an unexpectedly keen interest in the Indians. In 1879 he opened Emmanuel College at Prince Albert, the seed from which the University of Saskatchewan eventually sprouted, as a training school for Indian catechists and teachers. The Presbyterians, not altogether pleased to have a resident Anglican bishop in a community where they had been first comers, complained in 1879 that Anglican missionaries were increasingly taking over their Indian converts.[28]

Despite these initiatives, significant change on the prairies did not immediately follow the treaties. White settlers were still few and far between. The Indians, assured of their right to continue hunting and fishing in unoccupied areas, for the most part kept up their old migratory life. Several dramatic events would have to intervene before the situation would be greatly altered. Meanwhile missionary agencies sought to pre-empt strategic sites and impatiently awaited developments.

The first major change was the disappearance of the buffalo from the Canadian plains. Like death, this had long been anticipated as inevitable but never accepted as imminent. Although over the years the Métis had had to range farther and farther from the Red River to find buffalo, immense herds were still reported in the western prairies in the early 1870s. By the middle of the decade there was a definite waning, however, and in 1877 the buffalo were worrisomely scarce. In 1878 the American government intercepted the annual migration in order to starve out Sitting Bull and his Sioux, who had taken refuge in Canada after defeating Custer, and by the following year virtually no buffalo were to be seen in Canada. Over-hunting, stimulated in later years by the practice of killing animals for their hides and tongues alone, seems to have been almost totally responsible for the depletion of a resource that had once seemed limitless. The advance of settlement, which would eventually have doomed the herds in any case, came too late to be a significant factor in Canada.

The destruction of the buffalo was not entirely unwelcome to the missionaries. In assessing prospects on his first visit to Edmonton, Thibault had written, 'When the last buffalo is dead, it will be possible to attempt something on the prairies.' Many years later the tenderfoot Methodist missionary John Maclean, travelling with John McDougall to his assigned post, was shaken when his veteran companion justified the wanton slaying of a buffalo as necessary to settlement.[29] To the Indians the loss of their leading staple was an unmitigated disaster, accentuated by its unexpected suddenness at the end. All tribes with dealings on the plains suffered hunger as a result of it. The proud Blackfoot confederacy, whose economy was totally geared to the buffalo supply, was reduced to penury and help-lessness. To the churches, inevitably, the catastrophe represented a call to greater involvement. Most immediately the obligations of Christian char-ity demanded relief for Indians left destitute, and women's societies rushed to pack bales of clothing. Over the longer term the only prospect of recov-ery seemed to lie in acculturation, which as always was seen to include christianization as an indispensable component. Now at last permanent missions began to appear among the Blackfeet and their allies, the true plains Indians, who reluctantly recognized that the disappearance of the buffalo meant the end of their old way of life.

Even more significant than these local efforts for the future of the missions was a report presented to the Canadian government in 1879. The federal authorities, roused to an unaccustomed sense of urgency as they saw the old Indian way of life crumble, commissioned a well-known journalist, Nicholas Flood Davin, to examine and evaluate the experience of the United States in Indian education. Davin took his assignment seriously, talking at length with American administrators and suggesting a path that might be followed in the Canadian west. His report, in some ways impressive, was in others glaringly self-contradictory. He noted that the American government, after depending for many years on contracts with missionary agencies, had found the system unsatisfactory and was increasingly taking over direct responsibility for Indian schooling. For Canada he proposed a system of industrial schools, with funds supplied and standards set by the state, but then recommended for them practically the same system of contracting with the missions that had been found wanting in the United States.[30] Although he made no attempt to explain this inconsistency, the reasons for it were fairly obvious. The situation on the plains called for immediate action, and the churches had a reservoir of experience in Indian education that could not quickly be duplicated. Besides, any other approach would have called for a greater expenditure of money than the government was prepared to make. Acceptance of the basic recommendations of the Davin report ensured a major place for the churches in the vital area of education and – no less significantly – encouraged them to concentrate their efforts in this enterprise.

When these plans were being made, the Indians, despite their destitution, were still the principal occupants of the plains. They would not remain so much longer. The coming of a new era was most dramatically signalled by the construction of the Canadian Pacific Railway, a project made possible by the signing of the treaties. The resulting dislocation of Indian society was compounded by the decision to lay its tracks not along the familiar Hudson's Bay Company route but through the territory of more southerly tribes who were less accustomed to dealing with Europeans. By May 1883 these reached the Blackfoot country, and surveyors drew the line directly across the reserve. The Blackfeet, horrified by the betrayal of what they had believed to be a final settlement, refused to let the line through. Track-laying crews, unaccustomed to such a display of independence, were not disposed to take the protest seriously. At this juncture Lacombe, who had returned from Manitoba to Fort Macleod in the previous year, warned those in charge of construction of the dangers of the situation and was in turn asked to secure the co-operation of the Blackfeet. He had served for two years as chaplain to CPR construction crews and was thus well known to the company, but since his previous interviews with officials had largely been in support of unpopular causes, this request reflected unusual confidence and perhaps a measure of desperation. Through Crowfoot, a leading chief and a friend of long standing, he was able to persuade the Blackfeet to let the line go through. He had to promise that the governor himself would treat with them, and Lieutenant-Governor Dewdney made the promise good on 18 June 1883.[31]

Transition to the later west of grain-growers and ranchers was not to take place without one last convulsion. Towards the middle of the 1880s the pioneer settlers of Prince Albert began to vent some of the grievances that have become staple ingredients of western discontent. Caught in a world-wide depression, they grumbled vocally about high tariffs, excessive railway rates, and the general failure of the Canadian government to take account of the needs of those whom its rosy-hued propaganda had lured to the prairies. The Conservatives then being in power, some local Liberals were especially noisy in their agitation. They readily found support in nearby Métis communities that had recently been established along the South Saskatchewan, for with some reason most of the Métis believed themselves entitled to scrip for the purchase of land in compensation for the extinguishing of their ancestral rights to the soil. Such compensation had been given in Manitoba, but the government seemed to be in no hurry to extend the practice to the Saskatchewan. Lacking local leaders of stature the Métis, with encouragement from Prince Albert, invited Louis Riel to return from exile in Montana. Soon they were in touch with the Indians of the area, who also had good reason to complain of their treatment. The government, committed to financial retrenchment in any case, had persuaded itself that the Indians would take to farming only if compelled by hunger, and accordingly restricted rations to a bare minimum.[32] It not only made grossly insufficient allowance for the time that would be required for such an adjustment but failed to provide the instruction in agriculture that would have made even an effective beginning possible.

What began as an attempt to secure redress for specific grievances became, under Riel's increasingly impassioned leadership, a serious call to take up arms against the government. The basis of his appeal was essentially religious rather than political. Riel propounded the thesis, worked out in part years before, that God had a special mission for the Métis and that in fulfilling it he was in process of moving the seat of his authority from Rome via Bourget's Montreal to Taché's St Boniface. Although he derived his mythology from European ultramontanism rather than from Indian religion, his call for revitalization through a return to roots was similar to that of native prophets of resistance. As Riel's ideas became more radical, the anglophone settlers who had begun the agitation predictably bowed out, leaving armed resistance to the Métis and Indians. Although the rising achieved some initial successes on its home ground, the outcome was predetermined by the disparity of resources between the contenders and sealed by the availability of the CPR for speedy transport of troops. There could be no doubt, however, that the Indians of the prairies were disillusioned with the initial performance of the Canadian authorities.[33]

Since the missionaries were in most intimate contact with the Indians, their response to the rebellion was inevitably of considerable consequence. As in 1870 the attitude of Protestant missionaries was never in doubt. Although they recognized the existence of serious grievances, they saw the rebellion as a defiance of queen and empire and as a threat to the security of Ontario settlers. Once again they offered their services without hesitation to the government. The attitude of Roman Catholics was not so predictable. The prime movers in the rising were their parishioners, and they must have had difficulty in conceiving the struggle as other than a continuation of that of 1870. On the other hand, they were theologically committed to the support of legitimate authority and increasingly alienated by Riel's heterodoxy. In the event, they were called upon to exert themselves more than were Protestants in the cause of loyalty to Canada. Lacombe used his arts of persuasion on the Blackfeet, who must also have been aware of their location on the main line of the CPR. Scollen succeeded in the more difficult task of pacifying the Crees of Hobbema near Edmonton, while Grandin was able to prevent trouble at Saint Albert.[34] If the Roman Catholic missionaries could not say like the Protestants that they had kept all their people loyal, they could point out that two priests were the insurgents' only clerical victims.

Although the rebellion itself was a small affair, its repercussions were many and varied. The polarization of Canadians along ethnic lines that followed – and to some extent preceded – the execution of Riel has inevitably attracted the most sustained attention. Other consequences, although more localized, were as significant to those affected by them. The failure of the rebellion brought an end to the Métis's dream of composing a separate nation, compelling them to move towards the Indian style of life and in some cases to attach themselves to Indian bands. It hastened Indian settlement on reserves, demonstrating that the days of the wandering life were numbered. To the churches the rebellion was yet another stimulant to action. It brought the west to the forefront of eastern attention, leading the Presbyterian foreign-mission committee to resolve that same year that 'the mission work in the North-West be extended as rapidly as possible consistently with economy and efficiency.' Indian settlement also opened up new opportunities. Even the Roman Catholics, who complained that Protestant missionaries were rushing in to capitalize on the work they had begun, had been compelled to hold expansion in abeyance while the location of reserves was still in doubt.[35]

During the last quarter of the nineteenth century, as the open range gave way to a neat checkerboard of townships among which Indian reserves filled scattered spaces or formed irregular interruptions of the pattern, the work of the missions underwent dramatic changes. As late as the 1870s the situation outside the few missionary settlements was still much what it had been in the time of Rundle and Thibault, when missionaries could hope to reach the Indians only by sharing the hardships of their camps and presenting their message in terms that made sense in this context. By the 1890s the four leading denominations had missions wherever reserves provided concentrations of population sufficient to justify the presence of resident missionaries. They were largely sedentary affairs, with activities concentrated in mission buildings that now increasingly included institutions such as schools, orphanages, and hospitals. Some of the most important activities now took place away from Indian land altogether, in industrial schools that were normally located in cities or towns. Such older settlements as Victoria and Saint-Paul-des-Cris had lost their importance or disappeared, rendered obsolete by the reserve system. A pattern was taking shape that will be discussed in greater detail in the next chapter.

An explosion of new opportunities that would not recur gave rise inevitably to a good deal of jockeying for position. Missionary reports made frequent reference to unseemly competition, always on the part of rival agencies. Nowhere was it more evident than in the Blackfoot country, where opportunities were only beginning to open up. In 1880 the Methodists sent John Maclean to work among the Bloods, but, unable to secure

accommodation immediately on the reserve, he established his headquarters at the nearby fort. Samuel Trivett, appointed by the CMS to the
same Blood reserve, arrived only in 1881 but was able to take up residence
before Maclean. The circumstances were calculated to encourage each
missionary to persist in his claim to priority, and an unseemly and occasionally unpleasant rivalry between Maclean and Trivett ended only with
the withdrawal of the Methodists in 1890.[36] Lacombe, who became principal of an industrial school at nearby Midnapore in 1884, also exerted a
powerful influence among the Blackfeet. He too was resented, but this was
only to be expected in view of the state of Protestant–Roman Catholic
relations in this era.

Since government policy favoured the allotment of each reserve to a
single agency, however, the fragmentation of tribes through denominational rivalry was on the whole a more serious problem than local competition. Before the end of the nineteenth century most of the larger reserves
had been occupied, although in a somewhat piecemeal fashion that makes
the delimitation of fields of activity difficult. Anglicans and Roman
Catholics had missions in all three of the present prairie provinces. Presbyterian work was concentrated in the Qu'Appelle country and in the adjacent part of Manitoba, but by 1901 extended as far east as the Kenora area.
Apart from their long-established work in northern Manitoba, Methodists
were concentrated within several areas of the present Alberta.

As it assumed a new character, work among Indians began to attract a
new type of missionary. No longer was there the same call for pioneering
skills and the spirit of reckless adventure. Instead the demand was for
steady pastors and diplomatic administrators capable of working closely
with government agents and farm instructors. No longer having to live on
Indian terms, missionaries had less incentive to learn Indian ways and
therefore less opportunity to appreciate them. Learning Indian languages
also came to seem less urgent, especially among Protestants, although even
George McDougall had never attempted to preach without an interpreter.
Maclean, who not only respected the Indians with whom he worked but
became an authority of some repute on Indian languages and customs, was
judged by Methodist officials to be an ineffective missionary and eventually asked to move to another field of labour. Since the adoption of European patterns was believed to be the Indians' only hope for the future,
interest in their traditions was suspect as a kind of looking back towards
Sodom. Later, as immigrants began to flood into western Canada, mission-

ary attitudes underwent a further shift. The Indians now came to be
regarded as yet another minority, to be assimilated into the mainstream of
Canadian life on the same terms as Ukrainians or Italians.[37] Ironically
there were some advantages in this new outlook, which sought to ensure
that Indians would have at least equal opportunities with newcomers.

A conspicuous feature of the period was the emergence of Protestant
women as an important factor in Indian missions. Nuns had long been a
familiar presence in Roman Catholic centres, and a government official
was one of the first to suggest that Protestants might find a comparable
place for dedicated women. The women were ready for the challenge,
having already begun to organize missionary societies and to send representatives to the foreign field. The participation of Presbyterian women was
especially notable. The Woman's Foreign Missionary Society of the Presbyterian Church in Canada, formed in 1876, resolved in 1883 to undertake
work among Indian women and children and well before the end of the
century was contributing approximately two-thirds of their church's Indian budget.[38] At first the women were content with a modest supporting
role, disclaiming either the intention or the capacity to suggest to the completely male foreign-mission committee how their money should be spent.
By the early years of the twentieth century their president, Cecilia Jeffrey,
was making regular tours of western Canada and unblushingly calling
attention to deficiencies in administration. Methodist and Anglican
women were similarly diligent. The Methodists concentrated their efforts
in British Columbia, although Elizabeth Barrett did pioneering work in
Alberta. Anglican women tended to scatter their efforts among many local
enterprises, but those of Toronto took a particularly keen interest in the
Blackfoot mission.

Some veteran missionaries found it difficult to adjust to the changing
situation. Lacombe, returning to southern Alberta in 1882 after ten years
in a Winnipeg parish, was never entirely at home in surroundings that had
changed almost beyond recognition. John McDougall was another interesting transitional figure. Distinctly of a settler mentality, he was accused
with some exaggeration of 'ending each sermon with an invitation to the
Indians to pass into the trading room where his brother would care for
their needs.' He thought of his task in traditional terms of christianization
and civilization, and in later life frequently extolled the attractions of the
west in addresses to Canadian Clubs. On the other hand, a childhood spent
on Indian missions and a lifetime devoted to the Indians had given him a

distinct taste for native life-styles. When he was a delegate to a session of the Methodist general conference at Winnipeg, he startled his fellow ministers by spending his nights under canvas outside the city rather than accepting the cramped comfort of a billet. Later he displeased them by persuading a group of Indians to appear in traditional costume at the first Calgary stampede.[39]

Missionaries continued to be received with a measure of hospitality, without which indeed their situation on many reserves would have been intolerable. The Indians could not afford to decline some of the benefits they offered, while others coincided up to a point with their own desires. Many bands were in desperate need of the boxes of clothing that were assiduously packed by women's auxiliaries. They had no compunction about accepting them, for they were in the habit of sharing with others in times of scarcity. Indians recognized the value of education and asked repeatedly for schools, although in the event they would find European schooling little to their taste. They also recognized the practical utility of agriculture, especially in areas where game provided no sustenance. Although older Indians did not readily take to farming, finding the reversal of sex roles and the routinization of time it implied extremely difficult to accept, some of the younger people were more responsive to missionary promotion of agriculture. There were also more positive motives for accepting the missionaries. In contrast with government officials, who generally owed their positions to political patronage, the missionaries had an obvious interest in Indian welfare. They were also more accessible, showing their willingness to live in the reserves rather than commuting from homes in town. The fact that they spoke of spiritual matters was enough in itself to assure them a hearing from many Indians.

On the other hand, the circumstances of the missionary occupation could not fail to give rise to deep-seated resentments. For the most part the missionaries came unasked, or were received because destitute bands were in no position to refuse them. Despite their unique motivation, the missionaries were part of a white invasion that was destroying the bases of Indian society and claimed an authority that further damaged its already weakened status-structures. The Blackfeet showed great initial hostility to Christianity. Maclean's property was sometimes destroyed; fires broke out at the Anglican girls' home, and on one occasion the future Archdeacon Tims was shot at. Crowfoot ruefully suggested that since one Church had been built, all the old men and women and children had died; if another

Church was built, all would die. Such complaints were not limited to the Blackfoot country. An epidemic, as at Rolling River, might set off a wave of anti-missionary feeling. At Prince Albert the Presbyterian Church's right to its mission property, originally based on the Cree descent of missionary George Flett, was challenged by the Indians in 1884, and the issue eventually occupied more of the time of the foreign-mission committee than any single mission was able to claim.[40] The explosive possibilities inherent in Indian resentment of the missionaries were strikingly demonstrated by anticlericalism that surfaced during the North West Rebellion and cost the lives of two priests.

Missionary success varied considerably from one area to another. In some communities there was an enthusiastic response, so that Presbyterian Okanase could be described by the turn of the century as being 'as Christian as an ordinary Christian community.' At the other extreme were the Blackfoot reserves, where the Methodists reported virtually no progress, the Anglicans performed no adult baptisms within their first decade, and the Roman Catholics secured more goodwill than conversions until the deathbed baptism of Crowfoot, a latter-day Constantine, in 1890. In other sections the response usually fell between these two extremes. The Crees, long accustomed to European contact through the fur trade, were capable of eager acceptance or bitter refusal; if converts most readily appeared among them, so did supporters of the Métis's appeal to arms in 1885. The Ojibwas, as earlier at Fort Frances, were extraordinarily retentive of their traditional medicine. The Sioux closely followed developments in the United States, and rumours of the ghost dance followed them into Canada.[41]

In the end most of the Indians of the plains became Christian, or at least so reported themselves to census enumerators. At Whitefish Lake, where Steinhauer's long regime eventually provoked discontent among both conservative older men and impatient young people, a series of revivals in the early 1880s restored the mission to a healthy condition. Taché claimed that Indians involved in the 1885 rising were penitent afterwards, accepted their punishments, and gladly received baptism. At File Hills, the Presbyterians reported with pleasure in 1907, the young people had built and paid for a new church with the aid of a small loan from the committee. During the same decade Sioux Christians of various churches organized their own branch of the YMCA and held annual evangelistic conventions. After the baptism of Crowfoot, Christianity began to take hold even on the Blackfoot reserves. By 1899 the Anglicans could report a 'remarkable change coming over the Blackfeet and kindred tribes in Calgary Diocese, in their attitude towards the Gospel,'[42] and Roman Catholics made even more rapid strides.

Despite these optimistic reports, one misses both the fervour and the native initiative conspicuous in other parts of Canada and even in the days of the first missionaries of the plains. Instead there was open-eyed, unemotional, sometimes calculating acknowledgment that old ways were not well adapted to new circumstances and that Christianity was an inescapable part of the new order. Indian congregations, except occasionally among Crees and Assiniboines, were not so much self-propagating Christian communities as clienteles of the missions. On many reserves, and within many individuals, traditional and Christian ways coexisted without coalescing into a new outlook. Underneath the surface old resentments persisted, and indigenous rites such as the sun dance took on a harder edge in defiance of white and Christian ways than their counterparts elsewhere in Canada. Unquestionably Christianity affected the belief-structures and behaviour of the prairie Indians. It was less successful in winning their hearts.[43]

CHAPTER EIGHT

The Classical Pattern of Indian Missions

A source of both frustration and fascination in this investigation has been the repeated experience of hearing references, often in casual conversation, to missionary work among the Indians conducted by individuals and small societies of whose very existence one had been unaware. The greater part of the story of Indian-Christian encounter can be told in terms of a few major agencies whose work has spanned large areas and sometimes several centuries. A number of factors, however, also encouraged the undertaking of projects on a more limited scale. One of these factors was the relative accessibility of some Indian bands, which obviated the serious logistic problems involved in dispatching missionaries to Asia or Africa. Others included the romantic appeal of the noble savage and the sense of responsibility felt by Canadians, and sometimes by Americans and Europeans, for the welfare of people who were seen to have been harmed by the presence of whites. To attempt to do justice to these small-scale efforts, or even to make a complete catalogue of them, would be neither profitable nor practicable. A few examples, however, may give some indication of the variety of missionary approaches that persisted even into the later years of the nineteenth century.

The diary of Emma Baylis, a member of a prominent Montreal family who served the Canada Indian Missionary Society for some years at Spanish to the north of Lake Huron, has survived to record the hopes and tribulations associated with a small pioneer mission.[1] It runs from 1872 to 1885, with a hint that she was already at work when she began it. Emma Baylis was evidently a woman of intense dedication, for she had worked among the fishermen of Labrador before taking on her Indian assignment.

Attempting to secure a foothold in an area that had been worked by Jesuit
missionaries for some years, she regarded Roman Catholicism and traditional Indian religion as almost indistinguishable enemies of the pure gospel. She seems to have lived in a state of perpetual anxiety, appalled by the
improvidence and drunkenness of 'poor deluded people,' shocked when a
white photographer appeared to take pictures on the sabbath, and dis-
tressed by the 'ignorant' Indian practice of isolating the sick. On one occasion, when she saw an old priest following her, she was convinced that he
had designs on her life. In the midst of such discouragement her main
weapons were prizes for good behaviour and attainment at school, special
days to attract the parents, and the formation of a temperance association.
The diary as a whole oscillates between moods of despair and exaltation: 'I
do not think that I am doing any good here ... I feel isolated and alone, and
trials to bear'; 'Oh I would like to be one of the greatest missionaries that
ever lived, devoting my life and talents to the Saviour.' While marvelling at
her apparent lack of preparation for her task, one can only admire the
courage that led her to endure a thoroughly distasteful situation for almost
fifteen years out of sheer devotion to a cause in which she believed.

A few missions owed their origin to Indians who brought back to their
own bands forms of Christianity with which they had come into contact
elsewhere. The correspondence of Peter Paul Osunhirine suggests the
complex web of relations that could result when such a self-motivated
missionary sought outside support. Osunhirine, an Abenaki of the St
François reserve near Pierreville, Lower Canada, studied like others from
this locality at Dartmouth College in New Hampshire. At some time,
presumably during his stay there, he became a Protestant. In 1830 he
returned to St François as a teacher in government employ, preaching and
holding prayers on the side. He was opposed by the local priest, but more
seriously by two Dartmouth graduates who had reverted to Roman Catholicism, and after several years was deprived of his government appointment. He was able to carry on with aid from the undenominational
American Board of Commissioners for Foreign Missions. In 1836 he
received Presbyterian ordination, but when he was able to organize a
church in 1838 he affiliated it with the Congregationalists. Meanwhile the
Anglican rector of Trois-Rivières had been supplying him with Bibles. A
small Protestant group continued but, as Osunhirine repeatedly lamented,
ceased to grow after the first few years. It was not even all of one mind, for
in 1849 several parishioners formally charged Osunhirine with 'irreligion.'

In 1866 the mission was taken over for the Anglicans by the Colonial and Continental Church Society, although the formation of an Adventist congregation in 1884 suggests that seeds of discord remained.[2]

The best-known independent ministry of the nineteenth century was the lonely fifty-year itinerancy of Silas Tertius Rand among the Micmacs of the Maritime provinces. After preparing himself linguistically in the course of several Baptist pastorates, Rand persuaded his denomination in 1849 to sponsor him as a full-time missionary to the Indians. In the following year he exchanged its backing for that of an undenominational Micmac Missionary Society, and in 1864 he resolved to accept only such support as came in direct answer to prayer. He made virtually no proselytes among the Roman Catholic Micmacs, and as he became increasingly disillusioned by Protestant apathy and prejudice, he ceased even to seek them. Turning to education, he was unable through lack of support to open a school for which he had secured land. Rand was more successful in awakening Maritimers to the plight of the Micmacs and to the injustices they had been made to suffer. His principal achievements, however, were in philology and the study of folklore. To this day what most people know about Micmac traditions derives basically from Rand's investigation. The Capuchin historian Candide de Nant, who shared a pre-Vatican II horror of heretical interlopers, conceded that he 'sincerely loved the Micmacs, and did them some good.'[3]

Even within the major societies there continued to be a few mavericks who, like Rand, took an interest in the Indians as they were and not merely in their potential for Christianity and civilization. Probably the best-known scholar of any denomination was Emile Petitot, an Oblate who from the Mackenzie sent out not only comparative dictionaries of obvious use to the missions but also a stream of monographs related both to the ethnography and the natural history of the region. A.G. Morice, despite his eccentricities as a missionary, proved himself a worthy imitator in his scientific and historical writing. On the Protestant side the erudition of the Methodist John Maclean is evident from his large and well-selected collection of books on Indian subjects now in the library of Victoria University, although he has been criticized for relying more on reading than on field observations and thus attributing to the Bloods some traits properly associated with other tribes. Such curiosity about Indian culture was exceptional, but there was enough to add some spice to the missionary effort and to worry efficiency-minded administrators.[4]

Despite this persistent strain of individualism, the tendency was
towards a certain homogenization of missionary practice. In its pioneer
stages the Christian approach to the Indian inevitably involved a large
measure of improvisation. As missionaries applied experience gained in
other parts of the world or adopted procedures from the United States or
from their predecessors in Canada, however, there gradually emerged what
might be described as a classical pattern. One of its presuppositions, if not
indeed its primary one, was the necessity of settling Indians in permanent
locations where they could be subjected to sustained programs of acculturation. Since settlement began almost with first contact and proceeded at
different rates in various parts of the country, this pattern corresponded
with a stage of development rather than with a chronological period that
can be identified with precision. It was beginning to take shape at Sillery
and was already reaching maturity before the end of the seventeenth century in the reductions of New France. Even today, two centuries later,
there are missions in the far north and around James Bay where some
pioneer features are still evident. But in most parts of Canada the pattern
of the settled mission was thoroughly in place by the last decades of the
nineteenth century. Its triumph owed a great deal to the western treaties
and the laying-out of reserves that followed them, which not only resulted
in a great increase in the number of settled Indians but helped to determine the presuppositions of missionary and government policy in succeeding years.

In attempting to describe a 'classical' mission we might profitably begin
with the church building. This would vary considerably from region to
region and from denomination to denomination. On the prairies, where
building materials were scarce, it would usually be modest in size and plain
in construction. In coastal British Columbia, regardless of denomination, it
was likely to dominate the village. Protestants, including evangelical Anglicans, usually lavished little imagination on style and ornamentation.
Roman Catholics, by contrast, attached great importance from early times
to the adornment of the sanctuary. In 1721 Sébastien Rale wrote from his
Abenaki mission in the interior of Maine, 'I have built here a Church
which is commodious and well adorned. I thought it my duty to spare
nothing, either for its decoration or for the beauty of the vestments that are
used in our holy Ceremonies; altar-cloths, chasubles, copes, sacred vessels,
everything is suitable, and would be esteemed in the Churches in Europe.'
The purpose of this apparent extravagance was made clear by an Oblate of

the next century: 'Only after having seen the "Holy House of Prayer," with its decorations, its tableaus, its altar, its cross, and its images, did they begin to understand and to have a taste for the things of God.'[5] In the buildings of no denomination, prior to the twentieth century, would there have been any evidence that the Indians worshipped in them beyond the presence of hymn-books in syllabics, a few local touches in the construction, and perhaps a colour-scheme making some concessions to native taste.

Most descriptions of the worship that took place in these churches come from the early stages of the missions concerned, before the novelty wore off and the pattern came to be taken for granted. Later services cannot have been very different, although one may assume some erosion of the initial fervour. Nicolas Frémiot, Jesuit missionary at Thunder Bay in 1851, wrote home a long and eloquent account of the weekly routine there. Each day began with a bell at 5:30 calling to a series of prayers and chants. These were followed by an obligatory mass, and another at which many men and almost all the women remained. The afternoon was reserved for catechism for children and young people. In the evening the community reassembled for prayers and instruction, which were enlivened by choirs of small boys and girls. Saturday was given over mainly to confessions, although these took place on other days as well. On Sunday there were four services: two masses, vespers with the benediction of the Blessed Sacrament, and the public recitation of the rosary. The second mass had full musical accompaniment, and Frémiot noted with considerable pride the melodious use of Ojibwa in many of the chants. Thomas Woolsey more succinctly described a round of 'well-attended' Methodist services at Norway House that was almost as ambitious: 'Sabbath – 6 a.m., Cree, 11 a.m., English, with a class-meeting afterwards; 3 p.m., Cree, and a second class; the whole concluded by an evening prayer-meeting conducted exclusively by the Indians, under the supervision of their Missionary. There are 10 classes that meet during each week, and prayer-meetings on Tuesday and Wednesday.' These classes, it should be noted, were not instructional sessions but small gatherings, usually under mature Indian leaders, to discuss the spiritual progress of the members. Budd's account of his activities as an Anglican priest was similar, although with prayer services at his home in place of Methodist classes.[6]

These specifically ecclesiastical activities were supplemented by a network of subsidiary organizations: confraternities and sodalities among

Roman Catholics, young people's societies or YMCAs among Protestants, and temperance societies regardless of denomination. They differed from their white counterparts most frequently in having a greater impact beyond their membership. Some, composed of mature men, helped to enforce discipline within the community. At Wikwemikong a committee of five assisted the chief in keeping out whisky sellers, while the same group of watchmen kept order at church and ensured that women leaving mass were not subjected to annoying remarks by the men.[7] Protestant young-people's organizations often carried out evangelistic campaigns. Brass bands were ubiquitous and played at all significant community functions.

If the special event was no longer indispensable in reaching the Indians, it retained its importance as a means of breaking the unaccustomed routine of time and as an occasion for bringing fragmented tribes together. Roman Catholics were adept in this kind of showmanship, specializing in processions, choirs, salvoes of gunfire, and, naturally, brass bands. On the queen's birthday Catholic Indians staged elaborate floats on the Fraser before the governor and citizens at New Westminster, while the ceremonies on Corpus Christi Day at Wikwemikong on Manitoulin Island attracted visitors both white and Indian from as far as Arbre Croche, Michigan. Such spectacles took place with equal éclat where there were no curious onlookers to impress. Louis Lebret thus described ceremonies on the upper St Maurice to celebrate the arrival of a statue of Mary from Montreal: 'The "soldiers" formed a guard of Mary, while the children scattered flowers and greenery and the women prepared the float. After having blessed the statue, the procession took place when all the Indians had put on their festive clothes.' St Anne's moon of the Micmacs, although reduced in duration in later years, remained a great tribal reunion at which religion shared the spotlight with the transaction of business, the arrangement of marriages, and a general mood of celebration.[8] Protestants, less habituated to the Christian year and suspicious of holy days beyond the Christian sabbath, were in a poorer position to take advantage of Indian orientation to the seasons rather than to the week. Even they, however, could not ignore the appeal of the special occasion. Evangelical Anglicans, as faithfully as Roman Catholics, greeted visiting bishops with gunfire salutes. Methodists pitted revival meetings against native dances. Others had to make do with Christmas concerts, school commencements and prize-givings, YMCA conventions, and whatever else missionary ingenuity could devise.

Although there was a tendency for the rigid discipline of early missions to slacken with time, a well-established mission implied a tightly regulated community. At Wikwemikong G.A. Artus made night rounds to check on any who might be drunk and disorderly, as Claude Chauchetière had done in eighteenth-century Sault-Saint-Louis. For the most part, however, Roman Catholics depended on the penitential system of their church, which was to be exercised 'avec une grande douceur' but could still be formidable. Grave sins called for public penance, which sometimes meant kneeling before the church for hours or even days. When an entire community proved recalcitrant, it might be brought to heel by a threat to close its chapel. Although their orders were usually regarded within the church as relatively lenient in discipline, most nineteenth-century Jesuits and Oblates held back from the altar far more Indians than they admitted. Protestants, equally selective in admitting neophytes to communion, relied more in the case of serious breaches of morals on education, personal confrontation, and intervention by the police. Presbyterian missionaries in British Columbia made it their business to inform on local smugglers, gaining considerable ill will in the process.[9]

The missionary on an Indian reserve was a person of considerable importance, exercising functions far beyond those of spiritual oversight. In addition to assuming general responsibility for education and welfare he or she was likely to be called upon to administer first aid, dispense drugs, and even perform simple surgery. There might also be occasional calls to adjudicate local disputes. A missionary who spoke an Indian language was a natural person to represent Indian desires to the authorities and to interpret government policies to the Indians. No missionary, however, was content to be merely a go-between or general factotum without actively instigating change. Some missionaries promoted the economic progress of their communities, managing stores and establishing industries. A few, like Duncan, became virtual dictators. Such instances were exceptional, however, and were usually possible only in the initial period of adaptation to the European presence. The federal government was legally responsible for the administration of Indian communities, and by the 1880s the growth of the Indian department was transferring economic initiative into the hands of its agents. Yet the missionary, being locally accessible as the agent usually was not, was the person most constantly engaged in prodding the Indians to adopt more 'progressive' attitudes and in seeking out volunteers who would set examples for the rest.

All denominations sought to make room for Indian leadership within the mission church. Some of them offered openings as elders, church wardens, or class leaders, while Roman Catholics had their watchmen and *dogiques*. A major reason for the multiplication of organizations was simply the number of 'brass hats' they made available. Leadership roles in the church helped to replace opportunities for the attainment of status once accessible by other means. Participation in a successful evangelistic tour brought not a little social approval, while as late as the 1950s running a church choir or band was said to carry more prestige in British Columbia than holding office in a community-oriented organization.[10] This sense of privilege was enhanced by deliberate selectivity on the part of missionaries in admitting candidates to membership in confraternities or other organizations of the inner circle.

For an Indian to rise higher in the ecclesiastical hierarchy was more difficult. In an Anglican community there was a good chance that the local missionary would be Indian or part-Indian, for in 1916 the Missionary Society of the Canadian Church reported 75 native agents in its employ on Indian missions as against 92 white. Roman Catholics made a point of having priests in charge of every mission, and practically all priests were white. Other denominations employed Indians as professional missionaries, but sparingly and with decreasing frequency. The Presbyterians, who ran their Indian missions from Winnipeg, ordained a few Indians and country-born and employed a fair number as school teachers. The Methodists, once pacesetters in making use of native preachers, were reduced by the end of the nineteenth century to a few, mainly aging, clergy. Protestants found Indians useful in reaching their people, but preferred whites as mediators of civilization. Such at any rate was the reasoning of the Methodist mission secretary, Alexander Sutherland, and presumably of other executives.[11] Whatever the denomination, Indian congregations had no voice in the selection of their missionaries. Whatever the denomination, moreover, even Indians who attained positions of local leadership had virtually no access to the centres of power of the agencies that controlled the missions.

Most of the foregoing paragraphs apply with special force to communities in which the missions succeeded in securing the allegiance of the bulk of the people. This situation was by no means universal, even in the classical era. On many reserves, notably on the prairies, missions were able to maintain only a marginal existence that afforded them few opportunities to affect Indian behaviour. On many others they encountered stiff opposition, especially from older Indians who considered themselves custodians of tribal tradition. In British Columbia particularly, tension was endemic between 'progressives' who supported the programs of the missionaries and 'traditionalists' who opposed them or sought to restrict their application. Roman Catholics, with their hierarchical tradition, took special pains to forestall the jealousy of chiefs. These were ordinarily *ex officio* members of important committees and at Wikwemikong were guests of honour at the Epiphany feast of the three kings.[12] Even these precautions were not always effective. Alienation from a mission did not always, or even typically, express itself in the outright rejection of Christianity. When another denomination offered its services, as frequently happened in a highly competitive situation, the result might be the formation of a rival congregation.

As Warren Sommer has pointed out, missionary success in winning Indian support can sometimes be inferred from the location of the church building. Missionaries in British Columbia, hopeful of attracting Indians from their old ways, often selected sites on the outskirts of villages or even removed at some distance from them. In some cases the village eventually moved to the vicinity of the church; in others the church still stands in isolation, while not infrequently there are now two villages where once there was one. Elsewhere in Canada successful missions, as at Norway House and Providence, became the centres of new Indian settlements. Others, such as Lacombe's Saint-Paul-des-Cris, failed to catch on and were eventually abandoned. Schism occasionally led to the formation of new villages, of which the Salvation Army stronghold of Glen Vowell in the Skeena Valley is a striking example.[13]

To examine the anatomy of a local community of the classical period is to account for only part, and perhaps not the most important part, of the impact of Christian missions on the Indians. By the late nineteenth century, evangelism and pastoral oversight were supplemented and sometimes overshadowed by a network of auxiliary institutions that ultimately included schools, hospitals, and various agencies for social welfare. Some of these originated in response to local crises. Famine at Ile-à-la-Crosse led to the foundation of an orphanage, for example, while the appearance of child prostitution at Port Simpson was met by the establishment of a house of refuge.[14] The emergence of an institutional framework was, however, inherent in the nature of a program that was designed to meet material and cultural as well as specifically spiritual needs.

One result of this expansion of institutions was to introduce new types of personnel, such as doctors, nurses, and farm instructors, into an enterprise that had hitherto been dominated by the clergy. Teachers had always been present, of course, but now their numbers were multiplied. Women, first nuns and then representatives of Protestant women's organizations, became much more prominent. Many of these auxiliary workers were as dedicated to their task as any of the pioneers had been. Missionary doctors, in particular, often left behind almost legendary reputations. The redoubtable Kate Gillespie (later Mrs W.R. Motherwell), for many years in charge of a Presbyterian boarding school near File Hills, may well have been the most effective missionary of her denomination of either sex. A woman of forcible opinions and great practical sense, she was undoubtedly abler than many of the men who held more senior posts.[15] For others missionary work was only a means of earning a living, to be left when a more attractive opportunity offered itself. Auxiliary workers were also more likely than pastors in the field to meet Indians in such European settings as hospitals and schools, and therefore to judge them by their lack of conformity to the niceties of the Victorian code of behaviour. In many places, in consequence of this multiplication of institutions, Indians were confronted not merely by individual missionaries but by the imposing presence of a missionary complex.

Among auxiliary services Christian schools held undoubted pride of place. From the outset, education had been regarded as an indispensable adjunct to Indian missions. When the Davin Report of 1879 gave it national priority and opened new sources of funding to the churches, education took on added importance and came in the end to overshadow all other types of work. All denominations that had been seriously involved in Indian missions greatly expanded their educational programs during the 1880s and 1890s. The Presbyterians, who had relatively few commitments to pastoral missions, concentrated most of their resources on education. The pattern of Indian schooling established on the prairies soon became the norm for all of Canada, supplementing and often replacing the less formal arrangements that had been customary in the north. Wherever this pattern was adopted, it was the leading contributor to a general institutionalization of Indian missions that took place in this period.

Schools were of three main types. Day schools were precisely what their name implies. Most of them were located on reserves, although in a few cases Indian children were sent to schools in neighbouring white communities. Boarding schools, usually located on reserves, were founded on the initiative of churches or missionary agencies. Industrial schools, placed as a matter of policy in distant cities or towns, were directly sponsored by the federal government although confided for administration to the various churches. While boarding schools gave some practical training, industrial schools were intended also to prepare Indians for various trades. In fact, however, the distinctions were less clear than this brief summary would suggest. Most day schools and all boarding and industrial schools were run by the missions. Almost all schools received aid from the government, and few could have survived without it. The differences were chiefly in the amount of support. Originally the government assumed responsibility for all expenditures of industrial schools, although in 1892 it decided to support them like the others through per capita grants to the missions. In 1902 there were 221 day, 40 boarding, and 22 industrial schools. By denomination there were 100 Roman Catholic, 87 Anglican, 41 Methodist, 14 Presbyterian, and 41 undenominational schools. The department did not indicate how many schools of each type the various denominations maintained.[16]

Although there were always a few missionaries who would argue the contrary, the conventional wisdom of the classical period held that boarding and industrial schools were incomparably superior to day schools. The formal justification for boarding schools was that day schools could not adequately meet the need of the children of migratory Indians. Even where the Indians were relatively settled, however, it was believed that boarding schools made possible much greater control of attendance and behaviour. The industrial schools, with greater support from government and usually better physical plants, were the élite of the system. They did not always provide the training in skilled trades they promised, however, and the principals of some boarding schools claimed to offer better facilities for practical experience. For most purposes boarding schools and industrial schools can be regarded as similar in program.

Dr Andrew B. Baird, who was responsible for the general supervision of Presbyterian work among the Indians, gave an explanation of the industrial school that can serve for most boarding schools as well:

In the industrial school the children are withdrawn for long periods – and the longer the better – from the degrading surroundings of their pagan homes, and placed under the direct influence of all that is noblest and best in our Christian civilization. They are taught the elementary branches of an English education, and in addition the boys are trained in farm work, tilling the ground, and caring of cattle, and in some instances in the elements of carpentry and smithing, and the girls in knitting, sewing, baking, cooking, and general house-work, and all are taught to sing the psalms and hymns of the Church in English or Indian, sometimes in both, and to commit passages of Scripture to memory; while the day is begun and ended with reading the Word, and prayer round the common family altar.[17]

From this brief description it is evident that Indian education had a threefold aim, described by the Methodists as 'temporal, intellectual and spiritual improvement.' In the academic course nothing was expected beyond the three Rs, perhaps with a certain amount of bookkeeping. Indians were to be able to communicate and do business with others in a white-dominated society, but there was little thought of intellectual attainment for its own sake. More weight was assigned to practical training, with a nearly exclusive emphasis on agriculture that is betrayed by Baird's cautious claim that 'in some instances' there could be instruction 'in the elements' of other skills. E.F. Wilson's school at Sault Ste Marie maintained both a bookshop and a sash-and-door factory,[18] however, and Baird's statement may reflect a situation more prevalent in the west. The third element, character-building, was regarded as integral to the program and was seldom distinguished from religious instruction and nurture. Evangelism was a regular feature of school life, and accessions to church membership were duly noted.

In view of this concern not merely to impart instruction but to change work habits and personality patterns, the residential school was geared for a total impact on the child. It was to be 'something like a Christian home' and saw itself very much *in loco parentis*. Long lists of rules set the limits of acceptable behaviour, and corporate punishment was a regular feature of school life. The enforcement of European standards of cleanliness and tidiness also had high priority. Miss Foulkes, a teacher of the Colonial and Continental Church Society at Manitowaning, waxed eloquent on the drudgery of 'disentangling, or unweaving, or shearing of human hair which had been matted for years, and never felt a comb; or of scouring with soap and brush, where it is unbroken, skin which from infancy had been covered day and night with cloth rags or a tattered blanket, and withal tenderly treating those parts which had become ulcerated or sore.' Indian alumni recalled with no greater pleasure the regular delousing sessions to which they had been subjected. A rule against speaking Indian languages was part of the same effort to ensure a thorough transformation of character. Regarded with particular distaste today, it was hailed in its time as contributing to 'the spiritual and temporal welfare of these people' and even as 'having a marked effect on nearly the whole tribe.' It represented essentially a department policy, however, and some missionaries vainly sought permission to carry out instruction in Indian languages.[19]

Despite the intensity of the regime, results were not expected quickly. Securing children at the earliest possible age was considered vital, and children enrolled at seven were eventually required to remain until eighteen. By 1890 the Presbyterians were able to keep their industrial schools open for the whole year so that children would not have to return home, although it did not prove possible to enforce summer attendance. Joseph Hugonnard, principal of the Oblate-run industrial school at Qu'Appelle (now Lebret, Saskatchewan), expected graduates to regard themselves throughout their lives as members of the school community and encouraged them to celebrate betrothals and marriages within it.[20]

Then as now, missionary schooling came under frequent attack from those for whose benefit it was intended. Resistance to enrolment was widespread, and school burnings were more common than mere accident would explain. Arthur Barner, appointed by the Methodists in 1907 to revive their ailing industrial school at Red Deer, reported such hostility at Whitefish Lake that no one would undertake to drive him to the reserve. Yet this was Henry Steinhauer's old mission, and one of Steinhauer's sons was then in charge of it. Students expressed their dissatisfaction by periodically heading for home. At Wikwemikong runaways were discouraged by being incarcerated for a night in the local jail. Even E.F. Wilson, who was more understanding than most missionaries of difficulties experienced by Indians in a European setting, described with considerable gusto a dramatic chase after several escapees.[21]

The prestige of the schools can scarcely have failed to suffer from the shameless methods commonly used to fill them at the expense of those of rival denominations. One Presbyterian missionary, more candid than most, reported satisfactory enrolment at Portage la Prairie, but added:

Yet here the principal and his assistants find it necessary to take every opportunity of getting the Indians pledged to send their children to the school. The children are watched from the time they are babes in their mothers' arms. On every opportunity some reference is made by the representatives of the schools to the child attending school some day. Thus the parents get accustomed to the thought of the child going to school until on reaching school age the child is quite naturally committed to the care of the teacher.

Another missionary, while admitting that the indiscriminate distribution of clothing to adults had 'a tendency to pauperize,' justified its provision to school children as necessary 'not only for the comfort of the pupils but as a means in the hands of the teacher, when used discreetly, of increasing the attendance.' As these quotations indicate, missionaries themselves were aware of scandalous elements in the situation. A Presbyterian committee investigating the poor financial state of the Regina Industrial School concluded its report, 'That Principals of Schools should tramp the country, at great expense, competing with each other, and even bribing parents to secure children for their schools, is humiliating and demoralizing.'[22]

Even more troubling to Indian parents was their perception of what was happening to their children in missionary schools. Missionaries themselves complained of poor teachers, of a constant turnover of such teachers as could be secured, and consequently of a tendency to teach by rote. Health was an even more serious problem. Deaths were so frequent at the Anglican schools among the Blackfeet as to lead to public controversy, and similar conditions existed elsewhere. Missionaries rose to the defence of the schools, pointing to examples of low mortality and explaining embarrassing figures by citing high death rates among Indians generally and the reluctance of parents to allow healthy children away from home. Undoubtedly, however, most schools offered few amenities. Buildings were drafty and crowded, food scanty and often unappetizing. In some day schools the usual lunch was a single dry biscuit. Parents also objected to the amount of time that students were required to put into work around the mission, which they regarded as a form of exploitation. The school day was traditionally divided into equal portions for instruction and farm work, and Presbyterian women were only being realistic when they interpreted this as 'one half of each day in the school room, the other half working for the mission.'[23] Parents expressed further dissatisfaction when homecoming pupils offered wholesale condemnation of the way of life to which they were accustomed. The schools seemed to be agencies of alienation more than of education.

At the end of the process there arose a question to which no one seemed to have a ready answer: What was to become of students upon graduation? The system was based on the assumption that graduates would make use of their training to better themselves and ultimately the condition of their people, but this did not automatically happen. The usual complaint at the time was that graduates returned to their reserves and reverted to the style of life from which they had come; missionaries seldom commented on their possible unfitness for this life after schooling, although Indians certainly felt it. The executive of the Methodist Missionary Society warned the Indian department of 'a yawning chasm, without any bridge by which it may be crossed and into which even the most promising pupils must inevitably fall.' One attempted solution was to hire graduates out to whites as farm assistants or domestics. Another, more promising, was to set up farm colonies where progressive young Indians might encourage one another. Many good reports came from such a colony established by the government at File Hills, but it dealt with only a fraction of the problem.[24]

A system that has drawn so much negative criticism might be supposed to have been pieced together in a fit of absent-mindedness or inferred relentlessly from a set of abstract principles. Neither was in fact the case. On the contrary, most aspects had been worked out laboriously over many years and tested in experience. The main line of development led back at least as far as the manual-labour schools of the United States, which drew an enthusiastic response from Upper Canadian Indians who attended them. A number of features to which the most serious exception has been taken, such as insistence on the use of English, removal from parents, and the imposition of an ordered schedule, took shape as the result of experience in Upper Canada. They did so, as has already been noted, with the support of at least a considerable segment of the Indian community. Nor did the process of refinement take place without the exercise of considerable imagination. Missionaries drew on the latest methods of their times, such as the Pestalozzi, Lancaster, and Madras systems, and Barnley on one occasion requested for Moose copies of British and Foreign School Society books embodying the Glasgow training method.[25] Why did a system with such a distinguished pedigree not give greater satisfaction?

Many difficulties stemmed directly from inadequate funding by successive governments. In 1902 annual government grants to church boarding schools ranged from fifty to one hundred dollars per pupil. These sums were simply not sufficient in most cases to provide competitive salaries, decent accommodation, adequate nutrition, or even rudimentary health services. Principals had to resort to various expedients in order to balance their budgets. Wilson worked hard on a plan for feeding his pupils at the Shingwauk Home for four cents a day, although to his credit he never succeeded. The help of students around the school could not be spared, and a suggestion that the time devoted to manual labour sometimes reached two-thirds of the school day rather than the statutory one-half is entirely credible. The bales of clothing generously packed by eastern women helped to meet the needs of the schools as well as of the Indians. The system of per capita grants also lay behind frenzied attempts to boost enrolment. Principals contracted for as many pupils as possible rather than allowing them to be allotted to a rival institution and then had to work doubly hard to fulfil their quotas, while the effectiveness of local missionaries was increasingly judged by the number of pupils they sent forward.[26] Of course the missions could have declined to participate in Indian education on these terms, but they would have regarded the passing-up of such an opportunity as a betrayal of their obligation to seek disciples and would have been even more deeply stricken in conscience if they had allowed Indian children to pass without effort on their part into the hands of false teachers.

Although financial handicaps were almost enough in themselves to prevent mission schools from operating at a satisfactory level, there were also difficulties inherent in the missionary approach. The quality of education was not always valued as much as it might have been; after looking through a mass of correspondence relating to one school, a student remarked that the only criteria for a teaching post seemed to be piety and ability to play the piano. The collaboration of Indians in planning and support, so conspicuous in early Upper Canada, was as conspicuously absent later in the century. Admittedly the circumstances were different, but Indians had some reason to suspect a deliberate attempt to take their young people away from them. The most serious deficiency of all, perhaps, was a lack of clarity in determining the goal of Indian education. William Case had thought in terms of developing leaders, especially religious leaders, who would work among their people. The traditional Roman Catholic approach placed more emphasis on 'community-wide education.' The Indian school at Carlisle, Pennsylvania, which was widely admired in Canada, sought to prepare an élite for admission to the white community. Few Canadian planners succeeded in making a decisive choice among these incompatible aims, with the result that education was seldom designed to lead to any consistent outcome.[27]

Despite its well-recognized weaknesses, Indian education should not be judged solely on the basis of occasional horror stories. Most missionaries retained their faith in the method, seeing the desperate state into which many Indian bands had fallen and finding no ready alternative. Now and then they saw results that encouraged them to persevere. Neat Western-style homes and well-managed farms began to appear on some of the older reserves, and it was noted that more than half of the members of the Queen Charlotte council were Coqualeetsa graduates. The Indians themselves, despite their discontents, could not afford to ignore the benefits obtainable only from boarding and industrial schools. Institutions that succeeded in establishing a reputation for efficiency developed long waiting-lists, as is still true of those that remain. Even the formidable Miss Johnston, who was 'strong-hearted enough ... to keep these children in a home against their will,'[28] received thanks from a delegation of local chiefs for her persistence. Despite its shortcomings, the residential school evidently met a need.

By the end of the nineteenth century it was generally agreed that the overarching aim of missionary work was to prepare the Indians to assume the privileges and responsibilities of 'Christian citizenship.' The phrase, obviously a variant of the long familiar 'Christianity and civilization,' nevertheless carried a somewhat different resonance. Civilization was regarded as essentially a gift, and one deemed necessary to Indian survival. Citizenship, while conferring rights valued by white Canadians, also implied duties the Indians were expected to undertake. Civilization was a concept that could be applied universally, to Teutonic and Celtic tribesmen of the early Middle Ages as readily as to Indians of a later period, and one that, theoretically at least, left room for each people to take it up in its own distinctive way. Citizenship had a distinctively Canadian reference, carrying overtones of a demand for conformity to the mores of the majority. Missionary emphasis on it was consistent with the government's offer of enfranchisement, implying the same status as other Canadians, which Indians conspicuously did not rush to accept. It was also justified as necessary to the health of Canadian society. 'Our young and growing nation

cannot harbor within its borders solid masses of heathenism, such as
Indian reserves are, without suffering the contamination which must
come from the peculiar moral and social ideals entertained in these communities,' Andrew Baird wrote, anticipating language later often used of
Ruthenian and Chinese immigrants.[29]

Roman Catholic and Protestant missionaries, regarding Canada from
somewhat different perspectives, differed correspondingly in their concepts of Christian citizenship. Francophone Roman Catholics, conscious of
their minority status in both religion and language, sympathized with the
desire of Indian communities to maintain their distinctiveness as cultural
entities. This sentiment was most eloquently expressed, although with
more romanticism than realism, by Pierre Chazelle: 'Only the Catholic
Church, that wise and tender mother of all the inhabitants of the globe,
knows how to give to each people, as to each individual, what it needs for
this life and for the other. It can, while modifying the nature and customs
of the Indian, make him a fervent and happy Christian without his ceasing
to be a savage.'[30] Protestants, who in the era of the Riel agitation tended to
regard even the speaking of French as a serious aberration from the Canadian norm, were more likely to opt for outright assimilation. This was, for
many, the basic purpose of Indian education: 'Many graduates from industrial schools enter the general labour market ... all such are merged into
the body politic, and for them and their children the Indian problem is
forever solved.' Another Protestant report was even more explicit: 'The
only hope of the Indian race is that it should be finally merged in the life of
the country ... Our nation, if it is to be a nation at all, must be homogeneous.'[31] Such an attitude was natural enough, for Canadianism was
essentially a white, Anglo-Saxon, Protestant product.

There remained a good deal of common ground. Both Jesuits and
Oblates, while resisting any form of assimilation that would expose Indians to the influence of the Protestant majority, were equally committed to
the venerable program of civilization and to the inculcation of loyalty to
Canada. They may have placed relatively less emphasis on literacy, but
their desire to emulate Protestants led them on occasion to claim greater
effectiveness for their schools in imparting the skills required to compete in
Canadian society. Missionaries of all denominations would have agreed
that 'no robust Christianity can ever be developed in a people who live on
what comes to them in the guise of charity.'[32] Emphasis on self-reliance
and self-support, and therefore on industry, temperance, and thrift, often

identified as components of a 'Protestant work ethic,' were common coin of the entire missionary operation.

The purpose of the missions, of course, was to inculcate not merely citizenship but Christian citizenship. No matter how eagerly a recorder of missionary achievements might dwell on the transition from 'the tepee' to 'comfortable, clean houses' and from 'the wild hunter's life' to that of farmers and 'honest wage earners,' there was bound to be a climactic statement that 'instead of heathen worship Christian churches are dotting the reserves.'[33] It may not be fanciful, however, to detect a subtle shift in priorities, at least among Protestants, in the change of usage that reduced Christianity from a correlate with civilization to a mere modifier of citizenship. During this era there was taking shape a social gospel that insisted on the importance of the environment in determining the quality of life. This emphasis would eventually lead to a questioning of the stark contrast once drawn between Christianity and 'paganism' and thus to a more positive evaluation of Indian culture. Its immediate effect, however, was to intensify pressure on the Indians to abandon a way of life that was condemned not merely as un-Christian but as inefficient and unprogressive. To an extent that is seldom recognized, the assault on Indian culture bemoaned by social activists today was led by social activists of an earlier era.

An enterprise that sometimes came close to identifying Christianity with good citizenship called for close collaboration between church and state. In theory the government did not subsidize the work of the churches but merely paid them for services it would otherwise have had to provide itself. In practice the missions depended heavily on government money not only for schools but also for hospitals and medical workers, and they sometimes found ways of using educational grants to subsidize evangelistic work. Most of all, they looked to the government for the moral backing that gave their representatives an aura of official authority as they moved among the Indians. Calling for close co-operation, Bishop George Thornloe of Algoma expressed the opinion that 'the very fact of the civil power being behind would, in the main, suffice to make clerical supervision efficient.'[34] Sometimes the authority of the missionary was bolstered in more tangible ways. Duncan was not the only missionary to be a magistrate; Maclean was a school inspector, and John McDougall in his later years became Indian commissioner for the three westernmost provinces.

The government in turn derived some advantages beyond cheap education from its support of the churches. '... There has probably been no more potent factor in the elevation of the Indians than the religious instruction afforded them by the missionaries of the various churches,' the deputy superintendent-general of Indian Affairs reported in 1901, and the compliment was doubtless sincerely intended. The missionary could press for changes in Indian religious practice with which it would have been impolitic for a theoretically neutral state to interfere, and through his or her spiritual status was sometimes able to secure the co-operation of the Indian in government policies more effectively than would a secular agent have been able to do. Small wonder that an Indian has written, 'Sometimes it was difficult for my people to recognize whether they were talking to government representatives or church personnel because it was almost impossible to distinguish between the two.'[35]

However Indians might see the matter, co-operation was by no means without friction. Missionaries complained constantly of the poor quality of government agents and sometimes of the drunkenness and promiscuity of mounted policemen. Bishop John Hines of Saskatchewan characterized Indian agents as political appointees 'who neither care for the advancement of the Indians nor understand what is for their good,' while at Mistawasis the Presbyterians laid charges of misconduct against the government agent and the farm instructor that led to the dismissal of one and the removal of the other.[36] There was also, as one might expect, a good deal of grumbling about the inadequacy of educational grants.

Some problems were specific to particular groups. Roman Catholic missionaries had little easy rapport with the Indian Department, which they regarded as an essentially Protestant institution. Morice cited figures (apparently circa 1890) to show that while in the area now covered by the prairie provinces there were almost as many Roman Catholic as Protestant Indians, there were only three Catholic agents as against twenty-four Protestants. This disparity, he warned, might lead to the use of official influence to lure Catholic Indians into Protestant schools and hospitals and to import a Protestant bias to departmental regulations. Many Protestants, eager for progress towards assimilation, were soon disillusioned with the whole reserve system, which one official described as 'the very best scheme that could have been devised for the purpose of debauching, demoralizing and pauperizing the poor Indian.'[37] The government, on its side, did not find the missions easier partners. It was embarrassed by their ceaseless and often undignified competition and by their over-enthusiastic interference with customs that gave it comparatively little trouble when left alone. It was also not a little nettled by constant criticism from people whose work it was largely supporting.

Despite such griefs there was no thought on the part of the churches involved in Indian missions of breaking the relation. Only the Baptists, according to one of their prominent western ministers, declined to enter the field of Indian education because they could not conscientiously accept subsidies from the state. Before embarking seriously on the construction of boarding schools the Presbyterians appointed an unusually strong committee, of which Lieutenant-Governor Alexander Morris of Manitoba and the North-West Territories was eventually a member, to approach the government in search of grants. The churches urged, indeed, that the government should make still greater use of its authority to further their work, pressing the department to enforce school attendance upon Indian children and to make a Christian form of marriage compulsory. Although at first collaboration with the state was largely ad hoc and subsidiary to the specific concerns of the missions, there gradually emerged a consensus that the only hope for the Indian was 'a strong and vigorous policy, in which the Government and the Church shall be partners.'[38]

Partnership with the Indians was another matter. There was little thought of asking them what help they wanted from the missionaries or whether they wanted any help at all. Instead the missionaries came with a ready-made program into which the Indian was expected to fit. For this approach, so different from that expressed in earlier times in Indian support for manual-labour schools or in John Brant's journey to London to lay the claims of the Mohawks before the New England Company,[39] there was some practical warrant. The classical pattern took shape largely in response to the circumstances of the plains Indians, who needed help badly and had few Christian leaders to state a positive position to which the missions might have responded. The result, however, was that the Indians came to know the missionaries not as consultants but as truant officers, cajolers, and bringers of inducements.

This lack of consultation cannot be ascribed to any conscious desire on the part of the missionaries to keep the Indians down. On the contrary, they filled their reports with glowing accounts of young Indians who had become successful farmers and showed almost pathetic delight when a girl became a nurse or a nun or even a high-school student. Wilson expressed confidence that Indian boys could learn as quickly as whites and greeted with evident relish the assurance of Bishop Isaac Hellmuth of Huron that if his system had been followed forty years earlier, 'there would be many a man now from among them holding high official position in the country.' There may even have been on occasion too much pushing of bright students. A.N. McLaren of Birtle thought it 'a mistake to make a missionary or teacher of every Indian boy who acquires sufficient education' rather than cultivating leaders for their own people. On the other hand, low expectations may have been an inhibiting factor; one senses some defeatism in the suggestion 'that the Indian mind is not incapable of a fair degree of culture, and that with kind yet firm treatment, reasonable success may be obtained.' Expectations for Indian culture as such were even lower; hence the common assumption that the only answer to the Indian 'problem' was assimilation. In this pessimism the missionaries were only reflecting the social Darwinism fashionable in their time and even in considerably later times. Diamond Jenness, who had an unusually deep appreciation of Indian societies, brought down the same verdict: 'Culturally they have already contributed everything that was valuable for our own civilization, beyond what knowledge we may still glean from their histories concerning man's ceaseless struggle to control his environment.'[40]

Seeing the situation of the Indians as desperate and as unlikely to improve without outside intervention, the missionaries would have regarded as irresponsible any suggestion that they should wait upon Indian initiative or even upon Indian readiness to reciprocate. Not only was the future of the Indians at stake, but their condition constituted a 'dark spot on our beloved land' to 'be washed and made clean by the Gospel of Jesus Christ.' Thus convinced of both the rightness and the urgency of their program, the churches had few qualms about pressing it by all available means, including the coercive power of the state. This was a natural position for ultramontane Roman Catholics and establishment-oriented Anglicans. It was a strange one for denominations, such as the Methodist and Presbyterian, that customarily resisted the intervention of the state in religious matters. It did not, indeed, commend itself universally. John McDougall was a nonconformist on this as on some other issues, and a writer in the *Western Missionary* had to acknowledge that there were 'not a few good people in the Presbyterian and other Protestant churches who look with suspicion on the co-operation of church and state in this matter of Indian education.' The legal basis of the missionary argument was that since Indians were wards of the state and therefore minors in law, the government as legal guardian had the duty of providing for their spiritual as well as material needs. Its underlying presupposition, more often assumed than explicitly stated, was the equation of Christianity with morality and therefore of 'heathenism' with sin. On this assumption Indians who adhered to their traditional practices were in bondage to depraved superstitions, and it was the obligation as much of a Christian state as of the churches themselves to rescue them from it. Protestants found it difficult to avoid inconsistency, however, for one of their constant arguments was that 'so long as the Indian is treated as a ward and a minor, he never can be developed into a man and a citizen.'[41]

The upshot of these attitudes was a heavy dose of paternalism. Mission was conducted in the late nineteenth century for and to the Indians – 'our Indians,' as the title of a missionary booklet designated them – with less opportunity than in previous years for Indian Christian leaders to give significant direction to the enterprise. The activities regarded as most vital took place in schools that were often located so far from the reserves that Indians could neither interfere nor complain effectively. The objective was to create a controlled environment, for, as one missionary candidly stated of the children, 'it is necessary to have complete control of them to do permanent work.'[42] It would be unfair to judge such a remark, and many others like it, by today's standards. Most educators of the time would have expressed a similar philosophy with respect to white children, and the churches were only seeking to achieve a control over Indian behaviour that they had long sought to exercise in Canadian life as a whole. The Indian had less opportunity to resist, however, and could respond to missionary authoritarianism only by passive if by no means passionless acquiescence. Missionaries devoted much earnest effort to the service of the Indian, under the most difficult conditions and with inadequate support from either churches or governments. Their major mistake, understandable in the circumstances, was in relying too much on one-way communication.

CHAPTER NINE

The Onset of Doubt

By the end of the nineteenth century the missionary enterprise was well on the way to achieving its primary objectives. Out of one hundred thousand Indians counted by the federal government in 1899, more than seventy thousand were listed as having some denominational affiliation.[1] The Christian commitment or even understanding of some of these did not go very deep, but there were others whose fervour of belief and constancy of practice gladdened the hearts of the missionaries. Progress towards the adoption of the settled mode of life that seemed to most Canadians a necessary corollary of Christianity was admittedly slower, and missionary reports repeatedly warned that spectacular change could not be expected within a few generations. Nevertheless, the missionaries seemed to be in a strategic position to bring 'civilizing' influences to bear on the Indian. Their churches dominated many reserves, and a network of schools and other institutions made outreach possible to every part of Canada. They could scarcely doubt that time was on their side.

Indian missions enjoyed for the most part a good press, tempered somewhat by impatience for quicker results. Since the early years of the nineteenth century popular books such as Sara Tucker's *Rainbow in the North* and Peter Jones's *Life and Journals* had conveyed the impression of sweeping movements that must ultimately bring all the Indians to Christ. Various series of *Annales de la Propagation de la Foi* carried a similar message of costly but triumphant progress. Sunday-school publications later took up the same theme, and John McDougall's racy accounts of adventure on the plains found ready adolescent readers. Colourful missionaries such as James Evans, William Duncan, W.C. Bompas, and Albert

Lacombe became popular heroes. Occasionally a sceptical journalist echoed Sir Francis Bond Head's plea that a dying race should be allowed to follow its own way to oblivion, but on the whole the missionaries could count on broader support from government officials and the general public than ever before.

Despite this favourable image, missionary reports of the period betrayed more frustration than satisfaction. Year after year there were complaints of reversion to traditional practice and of hostility to the missionaries. Dependence on hand-outs was such a constant problem that in 1902 a Presbyterian missionary suggested that 'a little judicious leaving alone' might help. The usual summation was that although little change could be observed from year to year, a backward glance would show that significant progress had been made over a longer period. In discussing the moral condition of the Indians, however, Andrew B. Baird of the Presbyterians commented soberly in 1895, 'instead of gaining ground for the last twenty-five years, we have been losing.'[2] Disillusionment was compounded by a growing awareness of other enterprises in which the churches might invest their resources with the hope of greater returns. Openings overseas, especially in the Far East, were becoming yearly more alluring. Even more challenging were the religious needs of settlers pouring into the west, where population figures told their own story. Indians, in 1901 second only to people of British background in the present province of Saskatchewan, were by 1911 outdistanced by persons of German, Austro-Hungarian, Scandinavian, and French origin. The time was ripe for a reassessment of priorities.

As often happens, reassessment was hastened by a financial crisis. Most Anglican missions in western Canada were sponsored by the London-based Church Missionary Society. The stated policy of the society was to open a mission, bring it to the point of self-support, and then move on to a new field of operations. Implementation of this policy never proved feasible among impoverished Indians, however, and the society reluctantly continued to pay the bills. But this obligation seemed more logically to belong to Canadian Anglicans, and the formation of the general synod of the Church of England in Canada in 1893 prompted the CMS to suggest a gradual transfer of responsibility for Canadian missions. At this time Canadian Anglicans lacked a missionary organization capable of operating across the nation, but upon the formation of the Missionary Society of the Canadian Church (MSCC) in 1902 the CMS announced its intention of phasing out its Canadian operations within ten years.[3] This proposal, logical as it might seem to a committee in London, was greeted with consternation by MSCC officials. The Domestic and Foreign Missionary Society, hitherto the chief missionary arm of Canadian Anglicanism, had felt its resources strained by the demands of the diocese of Algoma and a small mission in Japan. The MSCC hoped to expand its base of support and thus its activities, but taking over a largely static operation was not a step calculated to arouse the enthusiasm of a church unaccustomed to large missionary commitments.

Among those who sought to resolve this unexpected problem was a person who would become the most trenchant critic from within of the churches' involvement in Indian missions. The Honourable Samuel Hume Blake, a prominent Toronto lawyer and former vice-chancellor of the Ontario Court of Chancery, was also a member of the executive and apportionments committees of the MSCC. An Anglican of strongly evangelical leanings, he was an active supporter of institutions ranging from Wycliffe College to the YWCA. He had a particular enthusiasm for foreign missions, serving on the Canadian committee of the undenominational but conservative China Inland Mission. His energy and intense commitment enabled him to devote apparently undivided attention to each of his causes, with the result that he tended to dominate all of them. He was also highly opinionated, denouncing both ritualism and modernism with a vehemence that few could match. Blake was always careful to back his opinions with facts; at meetings of the Wycliffe board, for example, he was said never to have accepted a financial statement until he had carefully checked the addition.[4] His approach, however, was that of a lawyer marshalling evidence for a case rather than that of a scholar dispassionately seeking the truth.

It did not take Blake long to reckon that the cost of maintaining the Indian work would absorb all of the anticipated revenues of the MSCC and thus seriously inhibit support for the foreign missions to which he was primarily committed. He already had some doubts about the effectiveness of Indian missions, for as a member of the seemingly innocuous maps committee of the MSCC he had made himself aware of the location of each mission, the amount of money spent on it, and the returns in baptisms and confirmations. In 1904, when he was named chairman of a committee to investigate Indian missions, he had an opportunity to apply his legal talents. With characteristic thoroughness he prepared questionnaires on methods and results and sent them to the responsible bishops. The replies, which consisted mainly of generalities, only fuelled his suspicions. He pressed his investigations and hinted broadly at scandal: teachers were of poor quality; schools turned boys into thieves and girls into prostitutes; the Indians were pauperized by paternalism; there was little outreach to pagans. Further ammunition was supplied by a report by Dr Peter H. Bryce in 1907 that exposed deplorable sanitary conditions and an appalling death rate in boarding schools, and Blake put it to full use. He was convinced that the bishops, for their own purposes, were making claims they could not justify. He dismissed Emmanuel College at Prince Albert, ostensibly a training school for native missionaries, as a device of Bishop John Hines to secure eastern money. He accused Bishop Cyprian Pinkham of Calgary, a particular *bête noire*, of making extravagant claims for his schools among the Blackfeet while carrying out 'no real old-time missionary work.'[5] In 1908 he vented his indignation in a pamphlet, *Don't You Hear the Red Man Calling?*

As Blake's anger mounted, he came to query many common missionary assumptions. At first he was chiefly concerned to persuade the government to assume a larger proportion of the financial load, although he also believed that Indian missions were giving a small return for a large investment and that better results could be obtained if missionaries were set free from administrative duties. The first report of his committee of investigation in 1904 accepted boarding schools as the best means of promoting civilization, but by October 1906 he was asking whether the church should not leave schooling altogether to the government, apart from sustaining specifically religious teaching in 'such schools as may be open to it.' Withdrawal from the costly field of education, he suggested, would allow the MSCC to confine its aid to the support of travelling missionaries who would spend their days 'among the bands of Indians as they wandered through their hunting grounds or assembled in their encampments when the hunting was over.' By the following year he was arguing, contrary to almost unanimous missionary opinion, that improved day schools would be healthier and potentially more effective than industrial or boarding schools.[6]

Blake's course inevitably brought him into collision with missionaries in the field and especially with their bishops. He saw himself as a knight in shining armour defending the MSCC against wasteful expenditure on projects that had proven to be ineffective. To those directly responsible for missionary work he was a bureaucrat more familiar with facts and figures than with Indians, a Torontonian ready to tell the west how to mind its business, and a Canadian lukewarm towards an enterprise into which English missionaries had put many years of sacrificial effort. Pinkham complained to him on one occasion, 'the members of our Indian Committee who reside in the East think they know more of this question than we who have been dealing with it ourselves,' and added bluntly, 'Don't give our case away.'

In some quarters, however, Blake was able to muster considerable support. Canon L. Norman Tucker, the executive secretary of the MSCC, was a consistent ally. F.H. Grisborne, the only other lay member of the Indian committee, was a frequent and sympathetic correspondent. In 1907 the MSCC adopted the secularization of Indian education as its policy. Meanwhile the beginning of negotiations that would lead to the formation of the United Church of Canada had raised the possibility of a joint approach to the government. Pinkham himself had proposed common action to Methodists and Presbyterians in 1902, and the Presbyterians responded favourably in 1905.[7] Blake took advantage of this ecumenical climate to enlist the support of Alexander Sutherland and R.P. MacKay, respectively the Methodist and Presbyterian mission secretaries. Like him, they were enthusiastic for the promotion of foreign missions, which were included in their portfolios, and discouraged by the drain of money into what seemed a relatively unproductive Indian operation. In the case of the Methodists, this accounted at the turn of the century for a third of their total missionary budget.[8] In the circumstances Blake had little difficulty in persuading the missionary secretaries to join forces in an attempt to persuade the government to assume a larger share of responsibility for Indian education.

With this backing, Blake sent off a barrage of letters to the minister of the Interior, Frank Oliver. The latter's replies, although infrequent, seemed sympathetic. Since Blake was usually careful to agree with Oliver's diagnosis of the situation, a reader easily gains the impression that the two were in perfect harmony. General endorsement of his proposals by a conference convened in England in 1908 by the New England Company and attended by several Canadian bishops strengthened Blake's hand further. He was in for a bitter disappointment. His ideas were good, Oliver wrote him late in 1908, but for the moment nothing could be done because the Roman Catholics would not go along. Oliver, who depended for the running of Indian schools on the co-operation of the missions, must have been aware that opposition was by no means limited to Roman Catholics. Most of the Anglican bishops were unreconciled, while neither Methodists nor Presbyterians were really anxious to dismantle their educational programs. Sutherland regarded Oliver's plan to revert to day schools as 'an altogether retrograde measure,' while MacKay had warned in 1906 that Presbyterians would regard the secularization of Indian schools as 'a national calamity.'[9]

Reading the minutes of a meeting of the MSCC executive in October 1910 leaves an impression much like that of watching a movie reel hastily run backwards. A series of resolutions, apparently pre-arranged, was moved by the leader of the western delegation, seconded by Pinkham, and for the most part passed with little debate. The executive authorized a special grant of ten thousand dollars in support of the residential schools. It rescinded resolutions of 1906 and 1907 that had been passed on Blake's insistence, abolished the special committees he had used so effectively, and named a new investigating committee of which he was not a member. Later that year, after a conference in November with officials at Ottawa, representatives of the churches signed a new memorandum of agreement with the government. Industrial schools would gradually be phased out. Residential schools would continue, reduced in number and held to higher standards but also eligible for higher grants. Grants would be proportioned to facilities and standards, and to this end existing schools were ranked in several grades. These arrangements would be effected through contracts with bishops and church officials. Significantly, nothing was said about any special emphasis on day schools, on which Oliver is said to have changed his mind as the result of a visit to the Mackenzie.[10] Perhaps the government's most significant step in response to requests from the churches was the appointment of a superintendent of Indian education. The person selected was Duncan Campbell Scott, a poet and the son of a Methodist minister. More sensitive than his predecessors to the values of Indian culture, he also approved of the work of the missionaries and listened carefully to their advice.

The storm that Blake whistled up was something of a tempest in a teapot, and Anglican writers have customarily dismissed it in a few words. Nevertheless, the episode marked an important turning-point in the history of Indian missions. It brought into the open a number of doubts about the efficacy of the missions that had often been expressed in private. It demonstrated a significant difference in attitude to government intervention between Protestants and Roman Catholics. And although Blake was

essentially a reactionary and a romantic, his criticisms of missionary institutionalism anticipated complaints that have been made with increasing
insistence in recent years. The resolution of the controversy, while far
from what Blake had proposed, contained provisions for improved accommodation and teaching and above all for the removal of the financial incubus that had always been his chief concern. Presumably it struck him as a
satisfactory 'out-of-court' settlement. By making it possible for missionary
agencies to continue their operations along familiar lines, on the other
hand, it enabled them to avoid serious grappling with their problems for
another half-century.

The memorandum of agreement represented, at last, something close to
the long-cherished missionary dream of close collaboration of church and
state for the christianization and civilization of the Indians. It was greeted
by a fresh spurt of optimism in missionary circles. In 1911 a conference of
Methodist workers among the Indians saw a new era dawning, and in
1919 the Presbyterians could still report that the prospects had never been
more encouraging.[11] In keeping with greater dependence on government
support, Presbyterians and Methodists transferred responsibility for Indian
missions from foreign- to home-mission departments. There was some
reason for optimism, for the agreement brought genuine and substantial
gains. There was a virtual end to horror stories about high mortality rates,[12]
about a single biscuit as lunch-time fare, and about draughty and unsafe
buildings. Teachers, if not always satisfactory, were at least better qualified. Here and there school nurses were appointed and TB preventoria
established. Nor did progress in co-operation end in 1910, for the Department of Indian Affairs gave evidence more than once of its readiness to
listen to missionary pleas. Meanwhile the churches were able to divert
considerable revenue to more exciting mission projects, not by reducing
their Indian work but by persuading the government to accept more
responsibility for its 'wards.'
    On the whole, however, continuity with the past was more conspicuous
than change. The goal of most missionaries was still a combination of
Christianity and civilization that was in practice usually identified with
the white man's way of life. The favoured method was still the paternalistically run residential school, and since revenue continued to depend on
per capita grants, some of the old recruiting techniques persisted. Field
reports retained their customary pessimism, often qualified by the familiar

assurance that over a long period there had been remarkable improvement or by the promise that the newest approach was bound to yield spectacular results. Anglicans had the special problem of continuing to work out some of the implications of the transfer of responsibility from the CMS to the MSCC, and complaints were still exchanged of inefficiency in the field or of a lack of sympathy from officials in Toronto.[13]

As the euphoria inspired by the 1910 agreement gave way to the realization that larger resources had not guaranteed greater success, missionaries looked increasingly to the law to achieve what persuasion apparently could not. Most missionaries had never been averse to compulsion, but as various obstacles to success were removed, the waywardness of the Indians themselves came to loom as the one that must finally be overcome. 'So long as education is not compulsory, the potlatch permitted, the Siwash doctors allowed to practice and the Indians not trained to make their living by some activity, the work of the church must remain comparatively ineffectual,' a Presbyterian missionary wrote from British Columbia in 1914. Compulsory education, the first objective, received official sanction in 1921. School enrolment immediately shot up, and reports became optimistic again.[14] When even this step failed to produce significant changes on the reserves, the churches pressed for the enforcement of laws against potlatch and the sun dance that had long remained dormant. Although the notorious potlatch case among the Kwagiutls in 1921 was initiated by a government agent, it was missionary interest that kept the issue alive for several decades thereafter.

Reading between the lines of Protestant reports, one senses a desire to disengage from activities that were proving costly, unproductive, and embarrassing. Well before the middle of the twentieth century many Indian missions had become essentially holding operations. In 1916 the Methodists reported that their missionaries were dying off and that younger men were showing little eagerness to replace them. In succeeding years their missions tended to be filled by new graduates already looking towards greener fields or by veterans for whom no 'better appointments' were available. Naturally such recruits were seldom diligent in the study of Indian languages. The Anglicans never completely recovered from the withdrawal of the CMS. In the deanery of Mackenzie River, where they had long competed unsuccessfully with Roman Catholics, only two Protestant missionaries were at work by 1930. The Depression, which depleted church revenues, was a further blow. A sense of duty forbade any thought

of abandoning Indian missions, but the churches seemed unable to muster
either the resources or the imagination to resolve a situation that was
admitted to be unsatisfactory. Suggestions that schools and hospitals
should become non-sectarian were received with increasing favour.[15]

Roman Catholics saw matters from a different perspective. They embraced the same general aim of christianizing and civilizing the native
peoples. They experienced, in greater or lesser degree, practically all of the
same frustrations. They had much less faith in government agencies, however, regarding them as foreign, Protestant, and secularly minded. When
problems arose, they preferred to settle them not through public agitation
or appeals to secular authority but through priestly admonition or the
application of church discipline. In 1921 they co-operated with Protestants
in a rare joint appeal to the government to institute compulsory education.[16] For the most part, however, their plea was essentially, 'Let us handle
our own Indians in our own way.' They were not averse to legislation in
restraint of native practice, but their chief concern was to hold the Indians
within a Catholic environment.

As late as the 1960s Roman Catholics maintained this essentially defensive posture in relation to the state. Their constant plea was that Catholic
patients should be treated in Catholic hospitals and that Catholic schools
should be examined by Catholic inspectors. They made a great deal of
parental rights and of freedom of Indian choice, meaning substantially the
right of Catholic Indians to deal so far as possible with Catholic institutions. They sought in every way to restrict the activities of the Indian
Department and to minimize the impact of governmental agencies on the
Catholic population. This suspicion did not imply dissatisfaction with
existing arrangements with the government. On the contrary, Roman
Catholics valued the control vested in them by the contract arrangement
and were alarmed by the apparent willingness of many Protestants to hand
over the administration of their hospitals and schools. 'The present system
of education approved by the Dominion Government and set up by the
Indian Affairs Department is satisfactory to us, and no change whatever is
either desired or will be accepted by us,' declared the Oblate Commission
on Indian Work in 1946.[17]

After the Second World War the example of independence movements
in formerly colonial areas, along with the popularity of the mosaic model
in an increasingly multicultural Canada, encouraged the search for a new

way of meeting Indian aspirations. The officially favoured path was 'integration,' which was advertised as significantly different from assimilation. The cultural contributions of the native peoples would now be recognized, but they would also be invited to take their place in the mainstream of Canadian life. The chief practical consequence of the new emphasis was the enrolment of Indian children in ethnically mixed classes. There, it was urged, they would learn to be at home in Canadian society without feeling the necessity of disowning their own cultural traits. By 1966, when the Hawthorn Report gave this program scholarly sanction, governments had already begun to put it into practice.[18]

Protestants generally welcomed this policy. It suited their general aim of bringing the Indians out of isolation and making them self-supporting, while avoiding the patronizing aspect of the earlier approach. It also promised some relief from the frustrations of a baffling enterprise. Among Roman Catholics, however, it caused considerable heart-searching. They could not reject out of hand an approach that promised to further their long-professed objective of preparing Indians for Canadian citizenship. On the other hand, they had reservations about integration that few Protestants shared. The Oblate Commission, warning that Indian children felt inferior in mixed schools and lost their incentive to learning, urged as a better way that bands should be directed towards maturity within the more secure environment of their own reserves. The Catholic Indian League, founded in 1954, saw integration as a threat to residential schools while arguing that Indians did not have to forsake their heritage in order to contribute their share to Canadian culture. While not condemned outright, integration was held on many grounds to be premature. These arguments reflected traditional objections to the exposure of Catholic Indians to Protestant and secular influence, but also a genuine concern for the integrity of native society to which Indians could readily relate. Even the Protestant Indians of Morley would later reject integration as another vehicle of white domination, despite the eagerness of their missionaries to urge it on them.[19]

While the policies of the traditional missions were thus marked mainly by continuity, the situation in which they operated was being altered beyond recognition. It would be difficult to illustrate the impact of change more graphically than by quoting a young Anglican missionary's simple description of a day's events in northern Quebec in 1962:

The pilot circled Chibougamau so that we could photograph it, flew down the Copper Valley, then up past Waconichie and on to Mistassini. We landed there on the calm lake and got out at the big Hudson's Bay dock. There was a great delegation of people to meet us and it was a pleasure to see old friends again. Mr. Russell was there with the X-ray survey. I had not seen him for two years and there was Bob McLeish who had come from Waswanipi as H.B.C. clerk. The mounties were there too, big men in their scarlet coats. There were three ornithologists from the United States, some young anthropologists from Montreal, Government men with the fisheries, Mr. Penny the administrator and a number of tourists.[20]

In such a crowded environment there was simply no place for many of the roles that had once given missionaries such importance in the Indian economy: for the peacemaking activities of a Lacombe or a McDougall, for the influence with traders that had made Morice a powerful local boss, still less for a theocracy such as William Duncan had once been able to institute. The traditional role of helper and advocate was increasingly usurped by anthropologists, who had the advantage of sympathizing with the desire of many Indians to remain as they were. The rise of local self-help organizations and the building of community halls likewise put an end to a missionary near-monopoly of social initiative, while the advent of the welfare state with its family allowances and old-age security made missionary boxes forever irrelevant.

Even the residential school, after pioneering days the chief bastion of missionary influence, began to lose its importance. Shortly after the Second World War there was a belated shift of interest to the reserve schools once advocated by Blake and now approved by many missionaries as consonant with the current concern for keeping the family together. Integrated schools followed, and by 1962 a government official could describe residential schools as 'essentially for orphans, children from broken homes, children of migrant parents, and for those children for whom there are no local day-school facilities.'[21] Government assumption of the control of Indian education in 1969, leaving to the churches the privilege of supervising student residences, was thus more a recognition of previous change than a radical departure. Today most Indian children attend federal reserve schools for the first six grades and then transfer to provincial systems. Especially among Protestants the passing of the residential schools was little mourned, but they had relied on them so heavily both as means of evangelism and as sources of missionary revenue that in many areas their disappearance deprived the enterprise of much of its visibility and coherence.

To portray the twentieth century as a period of unrelieved missionary decline would, however, be to paint a vastly over-simplified picture. A great deal of effective and often self-effacing work still went on, and a scholarly observer could describe northern missionaries as 'impressive persons evincing a commendable toughness of body and mind that no random sampling in the South could duplicate.'[22] Those who spent many years among native peoples often came to accept so many aspects of their way of life that they felt ill at ease when returned to white society. In the hinterland of James Bay and in many parts of the north, pioneer conditions continued into the twentieth century and missionaries continued to report many conversions. New methods also came into play. The use of radio became commonplace, and Gabriel Breynat, 'the flying bishop,' was one of a number of missionaries who found the airplane useful in reaching outlying settlements.

To a number of new entrants into the mission field, indeed, the late twentieth century has been the great period of Indian response to the gospel. As early as 1907 a series of Pentecostal revivals in Winnipeg drew many Crees from the north, some of whom returned to their people as ordained ministers. Around the end of the Second World War John Spillenaas began to cover the areas east and west of Hudson Bay from his plane *The Wings of the Gospel*, and by 1950 outriders of Pentecostalism were on their way down the Mackenzie. In more recent years a number of other agencies have entered the field. Most of them are conservative evangelical in orientation, Baptist or Mennonite by affiliation, and American in origin. Relying on faith, they expect daily miracles of it.[23] Here and there also, right up to the shores of the Arctic, Seventh Day Adventists and Jehovah's Witnesses proclaim their particular doctrines, Latter Day Saints remind Indians of their special place in the divine dispensation as descendants of the lost tribes of Israel, and emissaries of Baha'i offer their faith as a culmination of all religions including those indigenous to the native peoples.

These newer groups do not so much compete with established agencies as simply ignore their existence, reporting the first entry of the gospel into communities as familiar in the missionary story as Moosonee, Mistawasis, and Ile-à-la-Crosse. For the most part they offer a conventional message of salvation and an emotional experience reminiscent of the older Metho-

dism, along with evangelistic techniques familiar to any viewer of tele-
vision. They have the great advantage of not being encumbered with an
obsolete civilizing mission, and their lack of stringent educational requirements for ordination has enabled them to recruit native leaders freely and
to send them out after brief study at a Bible school to present the message
in their own way.[24] The Pentecostals, whose charismatic approach has
affinities with Indian concepts of communion with the spirits, have been
especially successful in winning native converts and in developing native
leadership. Confident in the truth of their message, however, few representatives of these groups seem to have sought to learn any lessons from
the experience of earlier missions that began with equal enthusiasm and
apparent success.

After centuries of exhortation by white mentors the Indians began in the
late 1960s to speak up vocally for themselves. They had their opportunity,
in part, because the federal government, wishing to leave no tile of the
Canadian mosaic unpolished, encouraged them to participate visibly in its
centennial celebration. Plans were laid for films portraying native experience, for tribal displays, and for a small pavilion at Expo '67. Although
Indian participants complained of manipulation by government officials,
the exhibit and the films opened the eyes of many Canadians to the existence of serious Indian grievances. Soon angry Indian authors began to
rewrite Canadian history with the roles of heroes and villains reversed.
Harold Cardinal's *The Unjust Society*, which appeared in 1969, was one
of the first and for this reason perhaps the most shocking.[25] At about the
same time there emerged several native leaders gifted with considerable
personal charisma: Cardinal himself, Kahn-tineta Horn, the Métis Duke
Redbird, and others. Political agitation ensued, and in 1969 the American
Indian Movement became active in Canada. White Canadians, accustomed to thinking of themselves as benefactors struggling at considerable
cost to help the Indians achieve a new and higher life, suddenly found
themselves portrayed as destroyers of a culture they had never taken pains
to appreciate.

The timing of the revival of Indian consciousness rightly suggests an
association with the civil-rights movements of the 1960s. Oppressed social
and ethnic groups were demanding recognition all over the world, and
Indians could scarcely fail to recognize parallels with their own situation in
injustices protested elsewhere. A common rhetoric pervaded all of these

movements, and devices such as marches and sit-ins that had been used effectively by blacks were readily borrowed by Indian militants. Like other forms of colonial protest, also, Indian resurgence was aided and perhaps even made possible by a Western crisis of conscience that followed two disastrous world wars and the explosion of the first atomic bombs. The resulting loss of face made claims for the superiority of the Western way of life seem less credible to Europeans and others alike. Especially when many whites turned to Eastern religions for inspiration, Indians began to wonder why they had accepted so uncritically the missionaries' low estimate of native religion.

Although in part a response to outside stimuli, the aggressive Indian self-consciousness of the last two decades has also drawn upon deep roots in the past. The Ojibwas of northwestern Ontario, the Blackfeet of Alberta, the Kwagiutls of British Columbia, and a substantial minority of the Six Nations never reconciled themselves to the destruction of their traditions, and even among other tribes the occasional emergence of prophetic movements testified to a latent unwillingness to accept the white man's values. This self-awareness, sometimes cherished almost as a guilty secret, received unexpected validation from the researches of anthropologists such as Franz Boas and from the enthusiasm of naturalists such as Ernest Thompson Seton and Taylor Statten. Indians acquired knowledge of legal and parliamentary procedures as they pressed land claims or resisted prosecutions for breaches of the potlatch law. They were stirred to more aggressive action by the emphasis on self-determination for peoples that followed the First World War and encouraged in 1927 by success, in co-operation with American Indians, in enforcing a provision of the Jay Treaty that assured Indians of free movement across the border. Indeed, the story throughout has been in large measure one of movements from the United States crossing a frontier never recognized by the Indians. The regime of John Collier as Commissioner of Indian Affairs under Roosevelt's New Deal, which resulted in the official recognition of Indian religions and in the encouragement of greater home rule on reserves, awakened new expectations in Canada. The current wave of protest may be said to have begun with a series of 'fish-ins' in the state of Washington in 1964.[26] In keeping with Canadian tradition, however, violent confrontations have been rare north of the border.

Awareness of this long-continued struggle to maintain a distinctive identity imparted to Indian protest an orientation different in several important respects from that of the American civil-rights movement or even of colonial movements in the Third World. Its aim could not be the achievement of an integrated society, for assimilation had been the white man's chief weapon in what Indians now came to term 'cultural genocide.' Nor could it be independence, however desirable this might seem, except in such a modified form as the recognition of a 'Dene nation' within Canada. Instead the main appeal has been for the preservation of Indianness itself, which calls for the reassertion or, if necessary, the recovery of native tradition. About 1970, when the Alberta Indian Education Centre sought to raise the consciousness of young Indians, its first step was to comb the province in search of elders whose knowledge of Indian history could generate 'the moral, spiritual, and political process which underpins the Indian struggle of today.' Since religion was an integral part of native culture, a return to spiritual roots was an important element in resurgence. Traditional practices are prominent in the programs of 'survival schools' such as Wandering Spirit. Knowledge of them has been fostered even among the Micmacs of the long-settled Maritimes by the articles of Noel Knockwood. They have been considered important enough to be the subject of a learned conference convened at Edmonton in 1977.[27] They are best known to most Canadians through the inspiration they have provided to native artists.

Christian missionary activity, as one of the most conspicuous expressions of the European presence, has provided critics with an obvious target. Missionaries have been accused of disrupting Indian social patterns in order to fulfil their own need for self-expression, of fragmenting Indian communities by introducing denominational rivalries and setting up sectarian organizations, and of adopting a condescending, paternalistic attitude that has led them to impose programs on the Indians without consultation. Residential schools have been exposed to scorn by disgruntled graduates for their authoritarian discipline and heavy-handed indoctrination into European moral and religious values, and not least for their constant insinuations of Indian inferiority. The most serious charge against the missionaries, however, has been that of complicity in the white man's takeover of the Indian patrimony. By their very presence, it is said, they prepared the way for land-grabs, validated the government's good faith in treaty-making, and provided spiritual justification for the European's sense of destiny.[28] Such criticisms have effectively discredited an enterprise that not long ago was almost universally applauded.

The alienation of many Indians from the traditional churches has been an inevitable result, although this alienation has been expressed in varied ways. Here and there one hears rumours of the presence of the peyote religion of the Native American Church, while as early as the 1920s the Longhouse religion of Handsome Lake was winning followers in the Roman Catholic reservations near Montreal. Disillusionment with conventional missions has doubtless also been a significant factor in the spread of Pentecostalism and other recent movements that allow more outlets for native initiative. In the absence of current syncretistic movements of widespread appeal, however, a simple return to traditional practice is for the disaffected the favoured alternative to conventional forms of Christianity. In 1972 a Roman Catholic commentator noted that those affected by the resurgence of native religious practice were 'precisely the same young persons who were taught so carefully the doctrines of Christianity.' The case of Norval Morrisseau is especially instructive. Greatly affected in his youth by the Roman Catholicism that had long been established on his reserve, he sought for some years to combine Christian with native motifs in his art but finally found it necessary to reject his Christian profession in order to develop his art more freely.[29] Oddly, but perhaps significantly, he has recently turned to Eckankar, a religion with Eastern overtones emphasizing soul-travel that he sees as compatible with native beliefs.

It would be unrealistic to accept criticisms made in the heat of long-repressed anger as the mature judgment on Christianity of the Indians of today. There has been a natural tendency, on the one hand, to exaggerate examples of missionary insensitivity and, on the other, to idealize the state of the Indian societies to which the missionaries came. The myth of the noble missionary seeking to reclaim degraded barbarians has been replaced, in many quarters, by the myth of the noble savage (a European creation, in the first place) spoiled by meddlesome missionaries. A close examination even of the recent literature of Indian protest, however, turns up a surprising number of exceptions to the general indictment. Missionaries are complimented for their genuine concern for the Indians, their dogged refusal to accept the general view that Indians were doomed to extinction, their recognition of the urgency of taking action to preserve Indian communities, and their willingness to resist pressures from white society. It is admitted, further, that the churches offer the most promising medium of moulding a more favourable public opinion among whites and that their resources and expertise can be of great service to the Indian cause. An Indian often critical of the churches offers what may be the fairest verdict: 'It is as difficult to live without the church as it has been to live with it.'[30]

Something of this ambiguity towards the missions has been reflected in Indian political action. Indians tended at one time to identify themselves largely in terms of religious affiliation and to maintain contact with one another largely through denominational channels. The first organizations upholding Indian rights, especially in British Columbia, tended to follow denominational lines. Liaison with missionary or religiously motivated white advisers was close, and native leaders found their readiest constituency in their own churches. As early as 1931, however, the Native Brotherhood of British Columbia represented Indian rather than missionary initiative and sought a broad non-denominational base.[31] The National Indian Council, founded in 1961 and disbanded in 1968 to form the National Indian Brotherhood, was formed without missionary assistance and against some missionary opposition. Especially since the incursion of the American Indian Movement, no native organization could survive the suspicion of being a missionary front. Yet several of the originators of the brotherhood had close church connections and would have identified their Christian faith as important in inspiring their activities.

Recent indictments of Indian missions, although inevitably coloured by emotion and more often informed by romantic reconstructions of the past than by sober historical research or even accurate memory, nevertheless contain much shrewd observation and correct analysis. Based on long-standing resentments that had to be brought out into the open if fruitful dialogue was to ensue, they have posed a challenge impossible for the churches to ignore. Missionaries and mission executives, already labouring under a sense of discouragement and beleaguerment, could not carry on without a profound reassessment of their aims and methods.

Although church leaders were taken aback by the sudden onslaught of criticism, they were not altogether unprepared to respond to it creatively. Their approach to the Indian was already changing, indeed, when Indians themselves began to bring their grievances into public view. Reappraisal began haltingly and without any coherent plan. In 1944 E.E.M. Joblin of the United Church urged 'working with, not for Indians,' and in 1947 a United Church delegation to a special parliamentary committee called for the abolition of wardship and for more self-government on reserves. By

1958 the Oblate Commission was prepared to recognize that there had
been an element of paternalism in missionary operations. The most
striking positive note during this period was a call from both Protestants
and Roman Catholics for greater encouragement of an Indian clergy,
along with recognition on both sides that traditional methods of training
were not working well. About 1946 the Anglicans set up a school for
Indian lay readers and catechists at Dauphin, Manitoba. Roman Catholics, while actively promoting native vocations during the 1950s, were
unable to agree on the advisability of a special seminary.[32] Indicative at
least of dissatisfaction with existing policies was a succession of special
committees of investigation sponsored by all major denominations. They
brought little immediate change, but their existence implied some recognition of a need for it.

By the 1960s a new attitude was more clearly beginning to emerge. In
1963 *Tel-Ind*, a newly founded Oblate information bulletin, reported several significant developments. One of them was the ordination in southern
Alberta of a Blood, the first treaty Indian ever to become a priest. In the
same year the Anglican diocese of Moosonee admitted lay delegates, thus
giving for the first time an official voice to Indians to remote communities.
By 1966 the United Church had several urban drop-in centres that were
actually staffed by Indians.[33] In 1967 the Anglican general synod declared
its penitence for wrongs done to the native peoples by adopting a 'Centennial Profile for Indians and Eskimos' and authorized an inquiry that would
lead in 1969 to the publication of Charles E. Hendry's searching study
Beyond Traplines. Thus the churches were already moving to new positions before they were under serious external pressure to do so.

This anticipation of criticism calls for some explanation in view of the
generally unimaginative posture of the churches during the earlier part of
the century. In previous years they had even lagged somewhat behind
their American counterparts in this respect, if one may judge on the basis
of papers delivered at a joint conference at Toronto in 1939 on the theme
'The North American Indian Today.' The speaker on American Protestantism believed that 'missions must be willing to accept as a starting point
some of the concepts that already exist in the Indian native religion,' while
his Roman Catholic counterpart made much of the advice of Pope Gregory
the Great 'to eradicate only what is specifically pagan and to leave everything useful undisturbed.' Canadians, for the most part, were still following the traditional line of Christianity and civilization, and even their

Catholic speaker showed little sign of having heard of Pope Gregory. Nor did attitudes change with breathtaking speed thereafter, for even in 1947 United Church moderator George Dorey could dismiss a desire for the recognition of native religion as 'something that has been conjured up.'[34]

Despite this reluctance to abandon long-held attitudes, the churches were in a better position than most white-controlled institutions to respond sensitively to Indian dissatisfaction. For one thing, they had a longer and closer association with the Indians than almost any others. They had always desired the welfare of the Indians, according to their lights, and on many occasions had taken their side against oppressive officials and traders. They had also given significant help towards the establishment of the first Indian organizations. Such associations as the Alberta-based Catholic Indian League in the 1950s, although organized on a confessional basis that Indians would later repudiate, at least provided opportunities for co-operation on a more or less equal footing. Having thus encouraged Indian initiative, the churches were predisposed to listen when Indians spoke up clearly. They also possessed, through their networks of missionaries, unrivalled opportunities for knowing what Indians were saying. Less than others, therefore, were they taken by surprise by the sudden outburst of Indian dissatisfaction in the 1960s.

Possibly of even greater importance was experience in intercultural contact gained by the churches through their missions abroad. Although paternalism was as much in evidence there as among the Indians, policy-makers could not fail to recognize that ultimate success depended on bringing into existence what in the middle of the nineteenth century CMS secretary Henry Venn had called 'self-governing, self-supporting, and self-propagating' churches.[35] This recognition gave rise at an early stage to the identification of two necessary processes: 'devolution,' whereby responsibility and authority are gradually transferred to indigenous leaders; and 'adaptation,' through which the message is made locally intelligible and converts are enabled to shape congenial forms of liturgical and theological expression. Protestants, fearful of any departure from scriptural norms of worship but relatively uncommitted to particular ecclesiastical structures, have taken the lead in measures of devolution. Almost from the beginning native workers constituted the bulk of their missionary force abroad, and in some thriving fields the number of Western missionaries eventually became quite small. Roman Catholics, bound to a mystique of clerical celibacy uncongenial to most non-Europeans but readier than

Protestants to recognize the legitimacy of variant forms of devotion, have placed more emphasis on adaptation. Despite papal condemnation of early Jesuit attempts to give Catholicism an Asian dress, there existed by the nineteenth century a considerable literature on the subject.

Although some attempt was always made to apply these principles in the Indian setting, their impact was delayed by the inclusion of Indian missions within predominantly white jurisdictions and by the assumption that Indians would eventually be assimilated into Canadian society. Even overseas, indeed, they were long paid lip-service more than they were actually applied. With the rise of anti-colonial sentiment after the Second World War, however, action could no longer be delayed. Christian nationals made their feelings known in no uncertain terms, and churches around the world moved towards a relation of co-operation as equals. Implications for Indian communities of Christians were only gradually and sometimes reluctantly recognized even then, but at least the Indian voices that began to be raised had a familiar ring.

Rethinking was encouraged by significant changes in the general social outlook of the churches. Earlier Christian thinking about society, as represented both by the Protestant social gospel and by several papal encyclicals, emphasized the improvement or uplift of the underprivileged. It called for a greater measure of justice and for the provision of greater opportunities for advancement, but also for a considerable amount of guidance from above and for careful regulation by ecclesiastical or secular authorities. Although many radical Christians moved beyond this position in the 1930s, its continuing influence in official circles encouraged the survival of paternalism. The post-war colonial revolt, represented to Canadians chiefly by the American civil-rights movement of the 1960s, created awareness of the desire of hitherto oppressed people to make choices for themselves. Thanks to articulate movements in Latin America, 'liberation' became the theological watchword of the 1970s. The cumulative effect of these developments was to divert the attention of the churches from the 'problems' of the Indians to their grievances.

The ecumenical movement likewise produced striking changes in the atmosphere in which missions were carried on. The Roman Catholics made generous provision at the Second Vatican Council for observers from other Christian bodies and put on record for the first time a positive evaluation of ecumenism. The siege mentality that had pervaded the church since the Counter-reformation was suddenly lifted, and Catholic sources began to quote the reports of anthropologists, sociologists, and even Protestant missionaries not as examples of what the enemy was saying but as the opinions of potential or actual collaborators.[36] Protestants, who had congratulated themselves on being more open-minded than Roman Catholics, found themselves in danger of being outstripped and hastened to reassess their own prejudices. Although the new spirit has penetrated rather slowly into isolated areas, the intense competitiveness that had characterized Indian missions was on the way out, at least among the more traditional agencies. Nor did the new openness affect only relations among churches. Many Protestants had for some time begun to call attention to the values inherent in other cultures and even other religions, and at the council Roman Catholics moved in the same direction.

As a result of these and other developments the churches were quick to respond to Indian expressions of dissatisfaction by giving their affairs high priority on their agenda. The Anglicans did a good deal of the pioneering, and their 1969 report *Beyond Traplines* was responsible for stimulating much later interest. In 1971 the Oblates convened a conference on native work that reflected diverse points of view but was able to urge the Canadian Catholic Conference to come out in favour of 'a native church permitting and encouraging it to develop in accordance with its local vitality as expressed in local customs, social structures and peculiar charisms.' In 1975 the Roman Catholic bishops of Canada directed their Labour Day message to the issue of northern development as affecting the native peoples, and native issues were prominent on the agenda of both the Anglican general synod and the United Church general council during the 1970s. In 1979 the Saskatchewan Conference of the United Church inaugurated a year of repentance for injustices to the native peoples.[37] At the official level, at least, the churches have made clear their desire to recognize and learn from past mistakes.

Within the last decade or so there has been a renewed attempt to apply the concept of devolution to Indian missions. The emphasis is no longer on finding clever young Indians who can be sent to white-dominated theological colleges but on equipping natural leaders to serve in their own or similar communities. In northern Ontario the Anglicans have been training 'trapper-priests' in summer sessions. Roman Catholics are preparing tried Indians to serve as catechists in their own communities.[38] In all denominations a fair number of congregations are under the supervision of Indian leaders, no longer as an expedient but as a deliberate means of indigenizing the church. In 1981 the United Church accepted a proposal from the Northern Elders' Council to form an all-Indian Keewatin Presbytery in northern Manitoba, and a similar one is being considered for Saskatchewan.

One hears from various parts of Canada of experiments in adaptation. Sweet grass, the sacred pipe, drums, and other traditional items are all in use in a Roman Catholic parish in Toronto that ministers to many Indians. Among the Anglican Nishgas of British Columbia traditional ceremonies and vestments have been incorporated into church as well as tribal feasts.[39] Such innovations depend largely on the initiative of interested individuals and may, when fostered by well-intentioned white leaders, contain an element of the folkloric. Usually welcomed by younger Indians, they are not always well received by elders who warn against the danger of syncretism. Nevertheless, they reflect a positive assessment of native culture that would have been unthinkable a few years ago.

Aware of a long record of pushing ready-made projects, the churches have attempted at last to work with and not merely for Indians. A token of good faith was an Anglican decision in 1973 to appoint a group of eight native consultants to advise the national staff. Co-operation has also been the aim of Operation Beaver of the Canadian Council of Churches, which sponsors work projects in Indian and Métis communities. In 1974 the Mennonites, from whose ranks Protestant residential schools had long drawn many of their teachers, appointed Menno Wiebe as their agent for 'Native Concerns.' His mandate was not to found Mennonite congregations but to work with Indians on projects that would stimulate their community life. Wiebe expressed the hope that the Mennonites' early experience of persecution might enable them to forge natural bonds with the Indians. Since 1980 the United Church has convened a series of consultations in various regions of Canada on training for native ministry. At these, rather surprisingly, the strongest condemnations of ecclesiastical paternalism have come from white rather than native delegates. Perhaps the most significant Indian contribution has been insistence on reaching decisions only after seeking consensus through consultation with home communities.[40]

A notable example of readiness to welcome native initiative has been support for summer gatherings known as Indian Ecumenical Conferences. The first such conference, designed to bring together Indians of all religious persuasions, was held in 1970 at the Crow Agency in Montana. The planning group included both Indians and friendly whites and both committed Christians and persons with some hostility to the church. Subsequent conferences, held at the Morley reserve in Alberta, have drawn large crowds each summer. Preachers of the major churches, evangelists from newer Christian groups, and medicine men in the native tradition all have their place.[41] The Anglican Church in particular has shown courage in subsidizing these gatherings, for they obviously involve some risk to historic allegiances. Other meetings have been designed specifically to give Indians the floor in discussion. In 1976 several churches combined to sponsor a 'Native Peoples, Church Persons Listening Conference' at Orillia, and in the following year the Canadian Council of Churches held a special meeting at Thunder Bay to hear and discuss Indian views on ecology and other matters of concern. Although first-hand reports suggest that whites still did a good deal of the talking, Indians expressed gratitude that the churches were willing to expose themselves to criticism.

As the churches began once again to listen closely to the Indians, they discovered that many of their concerns were political. They have taken up a number of these with gusto. In 1969, when the federal government's White Paper on Indian Policy proved generally unacceptable to Indians, both the Roman Catholic bishops and the Anglican primate wrote the prime minister to pledge co-operation with the Indians in their efforts to secure fair treatment and asked the government to provide money to aid Indian organizations in researching their case. In 1973, breaking with a long Oblate custom of avoiding political issues that did not directly affect the church's operations, René Fumoleau retold in *As Long as This Land Shall Last* the story of the northwest treaties as remembered by native informants. In 1974 some members of the Society of Friends, engaged in a cross-country tour and study of 'justice to the Canadian Indian,' made contact at Kenora with the Ojibwa Warrior Society at the time of a confrontation at Anisinabe Park there. Peter Newbery, employed as a physician on the Grassy Narrow reserve as a result of this meeting, interested himself in the pollution issue and arranged for a visit of representative Indians to Japan to study the effects of Minimata disease.[42] On other occasions the churches have pressed for the recognition of aboriginal rights and for the enshrinement of protection for the native peoples in the Canadian constitution.

The most controversial involvement of the churches has been in issues arising out of development projects affecting native communities and ways of life. In 1973 a group of clergy in southern Manitoba began to meet in response to a request for help from a community at South Indian Lake that was menaced by a proposed hydro development. Out of this developed an

Interchurch Task Force on Northern Flooding that held public hearings in September 1975. Meanwhile the churches had become concerned about the possible effects of proposed oil and gas pipelines in the far north, and in the same year 'Project North' was set up by the Anglican, Lutheran, Mennonite, Presbyterian, Roman Catholic, and United Churches. Its professed aim is not to formulate a policy of its own but to mobilize public support behind solutions determined by the native peoples themselves.[43] In 1976 it issued a call before the Berger inquiry for a moratorium on pipeline construction, and in more recent years it has extended its operations to oppose a power project in Labrador and the dumping of mine tailings in the fishing grounds of the Nishgas of northern British Columbia.

The religious alignment on a typical Indian reserve today bears little resemblance to what it would have been in 1900 or even in 1945. Along with the traditional Roman Catholic, Anglican, or United church there is now almost certain to be a Pentecostal tabernacle or Bible mission. In some places, especially where the missionary has been unpopular or there has been a rapid turnover of missionaries, the newer group will practically have taken over the clientele of the old. More likely, however, the local inhabitants will attend all services indifferently. Traditional Indian practices are likely to be a part of the religious mix, either on a regular basis or through the visits of prophets or persons with shamanic powers. Most of those who take part in them will also regard themselves as members of some Christian denomination. Exclusivism has never been the Indian way.

An even more conspicuous change from the old days is the virtual disappearance of the white-controlled authority-structure of the mission. Its local representative – whether Anglican, United, or Pentecostal – is more likely than not to be an Indian, and merely by this fact a considerable measure of indigenization will have taken place. The situation is still somewhat different in Roman Catholic communities, but even there the gradual death or retirement of an aging missionary force demands an increasing use of lay agents. Gone with the white missionary, almost certainly, is the residential school with its formidable sanctions vested in principal and staff. Gone too is the long-standing partnership in authority between missionary and government agent or Hudson's Bay factor. Even where the missionary in charge is white, he or she knows well now that success depends on winning the confidence and stimulating the initiative of the local people.

The traditional churches are increasingly on the defensive on the
reserves, and despite valiant individual efforts have had little success in
reaching the estimated third of the Indian population that now lives in
urban areas. The recent outburst of long-repressed Indian resentment
afflicted many missionaries with a paralysing sense of guilt that led them
virtually to abdicate responsibility for initiating significant change. Para-
doxically, however, the morale of those engaged in Indian work is higher
today than it has been for many years. If their expectations are more
modest, they have a new sense of direction and an unaccustomed assurance of being involved creatively with Indians. Most positively of all, they
have an exhilarating sense of being on the Indians' side rather than part of
an oppressive white establishment.

And yet one has a disquietening sense of having been through it all
before. Is the message brought by many evangelists to Indian communities
today, allegedly for the first time, so different from that which under
Methodist auspices spread like wildfire a century and a half ago? Did not
Cockran and Evans too have the exhilaration of defending Indian interests
against the exactions of an oppressive company? Does not the urging of
equality for Indian women before the law, plainly right by contemporary
white standards and in the long run by Indian, nevertheless recall earlier
attempts to reform Indian manners in line with the latest Western ideas?
May not efforts to advance uneducated native leaders, helpful as they may
be in the circumstances, have the effect in the long run of creating a class
of 'native preachers under white supervision' such as was envisaged by the
CMS? Such thoughts cannot be allowed to paralyse action in the different
circumstances of today, but well-wishers of the Indians might profitably
take heed of the subtle pressures that easily transform helpfulness into
control, leave faction as the end-product of revival, or (just to leave no one
out) dissipate dreams of cultural rebirth into reactionary fantasies.

The situation in sum is one of remarkable fluidity. What seems a
wholesale rejection of missionary leadership is tempered, in many cases, by
the retention of denominational allegiances that will not easily be broken.
Bonds newly forged through political alliance, while significant, are extremely fragile and depend as yet more on hope than on shared trust. One
cannot accept as firm evidence of continuing trends what may be over-
reactions on either side arising out of resentments or feelings of guilt.
Whatever may come out of the encounter between Christianity and the
Indians of Canada, one safe prediction is that it will not remain as it is.

CHAPTER TEN

The Flaming Banners

Not many years ago one of the chief difficulties confronting the author of a book on Indian-Christian encounter would have been to make sense to the average reader of the religious practices of the Indians and to explain the strange inability of some of them to recognize the superiority of Christianity. Today, at least among the student generation, it is the missionary who has become the puzzle. Once almost universally acclaimed as a self-sacrificing benefactor, he or she is now more commonly dismissed as an interfering busybody and in all probability a misfit at home who could find only among the colonized a captive audience on whom to impose a narrow set of beliefs and moral taboos. Since any billboard provides sufficient evidence that propagandist zeal has not diminished among us, the source of puzzlement must be sought in the particular convictions that have inspired the propagation of Christianity among peoples not raised to it.

Some of these convictions were integral to Christianity from the outset, distinguishing it already from other religions of the Roman Empire. Ethnic religions represented the traditions of particular peoples and, apart from the Judaism from which Christianity sprang, extended no welcome to outsiders. Popular cults appealed to particular clienteles and in many cases catered to particular needs. Even the imperial religion, while obligatory upon all subjects of Rome, limited its demands to the public aspects of life. Christianity, by contrast, offered a 'new nature' wherein there could be no distinction of 'Greek and Jew, circumcised and uncircumcised, barbarian, Scythian, slave, free man.' By the same token its assertion that God had bestowed on Jesus 'the name which is above every name' joined to this offer an exclusive claim upon the allegiance of all peoples.[1] There inevitably resulted a sense of compulsion to propagate the faith, which might become latent in periods of decline or stagnation but needed only some new impulse or opportunity to surface in the Christian consciousness.

Periods of renewed missionary initiative, when an endemic impulse became epidemic, were normally associated with movements of religious resurgence within Christendom. Typically the process began with individuals for whom the familiar message of Christianity took on renewed urgency as the result of a conversion experience or a sense of social crisis. If the impulse was strong enough and conditions favoured, a natural desire to share a new enthusiasm gave rise to the contagion of a popular movement. Only then, but then almost invariably, a conviction gradually took shape that a message that could arouse the careless or recapture the estranged within Christendom would have the same power among peoples who had never heard it. Two such movements were mainly responsible for directing Christian attention to the Indians of Canada. The late flowering of the Catholic Reformation in France created an atmosphere of intense devotion that inspired the heroic missions of the seventeenth century. A slower but more prolonged swell that began as pietism in Germany in the late seventeenth century, convulsed English-speaking countries with a series of evangelical revivals in the eighteenth century, and finally caught up Roman Catholics in the wake of revulsion against the French Revolution, made the nineteenth century throughout the world what K.S. Latourette called the 'great century' of Christian missions.[2] Similarly, evangelistic and charismatic movements of the twentieth century have been responsible for the rise of Pentecostal and other conservative Protestant missions.

The origin of the missions in the hothouse atmosphere of resurgent Christianity determined to a considerable extent the characteristics of those who volunteered to serve them, especially in periods of expansion. Typically owing their own fervour to revival, they were eager to share their faith and likely to assume that the methods and appeals that had spoken to their hearts would prove equally effective in other settings. For those seeking ways of expressing their commitment in action, indeed, missionary service came to be regarded in the circles that sponsored it as the ultimate expression of dedication to the cause of Christ. When Lacombe was designated for work among western Indians, the bishops and canons who took part in the ceremony kissed his feet in recognition of the superiority of his vocation.[3] Undoubtedly the prospect of serving in a cause that excelled all others attracted some misfits who could have hoped to excel in no other way. It also appealed to some people with outstanding qualities of leadership. Occasionally the two categories overlapped, for some who proved most effective as missionaries might have been difficult to fit into comfortable slots at home.

Association with movements of renewal also acted as a theological sieve in determining the selection of missionaries. Although representatives of practically every Christian school of thought eventually shared in missionary work, those of liberal and even middle-of-the-road inclinations were slow to respond and usually preferred to serve in countries such as India and China that had long traditions of literacy. In expansive periods, missions particularly attracted adherents of ardent versions of Christianity that linked salvation closely with the holding of specific beliefs or the profession of particular types of religious experience. Ultramontane Roman Catholicism and evangelical Protestantism, with their strong emphases on fidelity to pope and Bible respectively, dominated the missionary scene not only among the Indians of Canada but in many other parts of the world. People professing such theologies, while differing on many fundamental issues, agreed in seeing little value in any form of religion but their own.

Once in the field, missionaries continued to be influenced by the movements that had inspired their original sense of vocation. Most of them were sponsored by societies or orders that had come into being as a result of these movements, and were subject to their continuing direction. CMS and Wesleyan missionaries of the nineteenth century were required not only to send in annual reports but to keep daily journals for later scrutiny, while Roman Catholic missions were reported not only to the superiors of their orders but to the Congregation of the Propaganda at Rome. Even more significantly, perhaps, both missionaries and their directors found it necessary to maintain the interest of the constituencies on which their support ultimately depended. In the seventeenth century these consisted mainly of patrons such as the marquis de Gamache, who received credit in the 1630s as the major benefactor of the Jesuit missions.[4] By the nineteenth these had been replaced by a mass of more modest supporters who dropped mites into missionary boxes. Maintaining interest back home was the motive that inspired the writing of the Jesuit *Relations* and the sending of lengthy letters from the field to the *Annales de la Propagation de la Foi*, while the hope of culling inspirational tidbits for popular consumption was a major factor behind Protestant requirements of journal-keeping.

The existence of this international network of communication imparted a certain homogeneity to the missionary movement, at least within its Protestant and Roman Catholic segments. Missionaries in various countries had to adapt their methods to local conditions, sometimes radically, but there was enough of a common pattern that John West could know even before his departure for the Red River that one of his responsibilities was to found a school and could recruit his first students before reaching his destination. The same network provided a mass of information and opinion on which missionaries could draw. During the 1850s, for example, Abraham Cowley was able to apply on the shore of Lake Manitoba an experiment in itinerant ministry among the Telugus of south India with which he was familiar through regular reading of reports of CMS missionaries around the world.[5] It also brought into existence a community of mutual prayer and concern as nuns in French convents or women in British missionary societies read aloud accounts of the spiritual struggles of converts or prospective converts in many parts of the world. In these and other ways, missionaries were constantly reminded of the impulse that had sent them out in the first place and of the expectations of the less adventurous but often equally committed partners whom they had left at home.

In modern times the missionaries were not the only European travellers to find their way into other parts of the world. The first spectacular outward thrust of Christianity during this period followed the voyages of Columbus and Vasco da Gama and would scarcely have been conceivable apart from them. When European interest turned from military adventure to the import of luxury goods, missionary enthusiasm languished. When it shifted again to the export of such staples as cotton, which called for changes in the habits and attitudes of non-Europeans, the missionary movement entered its 'great century.' The contribution of Western imperialism to the possibility of missionary success can scarcely be exaggerated. Europe provided the physical requirements for Christian expansion: ships to transport missionaries overseas and armed forces to ensure their safety, as well as technological resources that made it possible for them to sustain their missions and to extend their operations into varied fields of material service, from medicine to sanitation. European wanderlust was also important in inspiring its missionary counterpart. The pioneer Baptist missionary William Carey traced the first stirring of his concern for the heathen to a reading of Captain James Cook's narrative of his last voyage,[6] while others from Marquette to Morice found it natural to combine the roles of missionary and explorer. On their side, the missions by their very existence furnished numerous pretexts for Western political or military intervention. These varied and close interconnections distinguish the modern period of Christian missions sharply from earlier times when missionaries lacked both the advantages and the drawbacks of association with a superior worldly power.

The dependence of modern Christian missions on Western imperialism has been so generally acknowledged that they are commonly regarded as no more than its spiritual arm. It is less often recognized that incompatible elements of agenda always made the association an uneasy one. At home the movements that inspired missionary involvement, while for the most part politically conservative, were uniformly reformist in terms of morals and of social conditions that might affect morals. Likewise, missionaries who spoke in terms of 'christianization and civilization' held up as their ideal European civilization not as it was but as they thought it ought to be. As a result, conflict with secular agencies was as common as co-operation. Missionaries agitated against whisky sellers and land-grabbers, while governments often regarded missionaries as trouble-makers. There was in fact a missionary imperialism, distinct from although often associated with Western imperialism, and to leave it out of account is to miss an important aspect of the story. As Benoît Lévesque has suggested, missionaries were on the look-out for pliable societies in which they could hope to set up anticipations of the New Jerusalem more readily than in jaded Europe.[7]

The connection between Christian and European expansion, while real and significant, was also subtle and nuanced. Its most powerful effect, perhaps, was to bolster the confidence of each party in the legitimacy of its enterprise. To the missionaries the evident superiority of Europe was a convincing demonstration of the superiority of Christianity, European success an assurance that their efforts too would ultimately be successful. To secular imperialists, conversely, the presence of Christian missionaries abroad was evidence that God had assigned to Europe a sacred task in which they too were participants. The practice of showing pictures of European scenes as a means of awakening Indian interest in Christianity, reported by missionaries of different denominations and periods, indicates how close the identification could become.[8] Missionaries rationalized it by attributing the 'higher' civilization of the West not to superior racial endowment but to the influence of Christianity. In 1632 Paul Le Jeune asserted that 'before the faith was received in Germany, Spain, or England, these nations were not more civilized' than the Indians he met at Quebec, tactfully omitting a reference to France. Two centuries later the native Methodist missionary to the Mississaugas, Peter Jones, visiting the site of a Druid temple, observed basins carved out of rock to catch the blood of human victims and commented, 'Surely God has done much for England.'[9] It was only natural that missionaries should regard European conquests as providential and that, especially in the nineteenth century, they should have recourse to the language of millennial prophecy to explain the opportunities they provided for missionary work.

The convergence of these influences forged a missionary mentality that blended self-sacrificing humanitarian concern with confident triumphalism. This combination had been prefigured as early as the sixth century, when the poet Venantius Fortunatus, attributing the triumph of Christianity in the Roman Empire at once to the cross of Christ and to the victorious legions of the emperor Constantine, composed the *Vexilla regis*: 'The flaming banners of our King / advance through his self-offering.'[10] His hymn became the marching song of the crusaders, who regarded themselves as at once soldiers of Christ and penitents expiating their sins. It was later intoned in Canadian forests, with Indians cast in a double role as beneficiaries of selfless service and targets of a quasi-military operation. Its noble but dangerous juxtaposition of metaphors of sacrifice and conquest was typical of the modern missionary movement. Although it seems unnatural to most people today, this combination of ideas had considerable plausibility in centuries when Europe was making unprecedented progress not only in technology but apparently also in morals and religious commitment.

Christian missionaries to the Indians of Canada carried with them, in an almost infinite variety of individual expressions, a mental set identical in its essentials with that of fellow workers in Burma or Sierra Leone. In it were combined, inseparably if sometimes incongruously, elements from the original gospel of Christianity, from the particular beliefs and practices of aggressive religious movements, and from the complex cultural tradition of Europe. The presuppositions that shaped it determined in large measure the missionaries' perceptions of the people they encountered, the objectives they sought, and the methods they adopted in pursuit of them.

On the one hand, missionaries were bound to take a high view of the spiritual potential of the Indians. In 1537 Pope Paul III affirmed optimistically in the bull *Sublimus Deus*: 'The Indians are truly men and are not only capable of understanding the Catholic faith but desire exceedingly to receive it,'[11] and apart from realistic doubts about unanimous Indian eagerness no missionary would have disagreed with him. To have doubted the ability of the Indians to become exemplary Christians would have been to negate the offer of salvation to all peoples inherent in the gospel they preached, and indeed to deny the possibility of their own success from the outset. In their homelands, moreover, the missionaries had witnessed or been privy to conversions so surprising that no class or race seemed beyond the possibility of redemption. Whatever others might think, therefore, they approached their task with high expectations.

On the other hand, the same mind-set predisposed the missionaries to a low estimate of the actual spiritual state of the Indians. According to the most charitable view, expressed by Chrestien Le Clercq in the seventeenth century, they lived virtually in a spiritual vacuum: 'The Gaspesians, if we except those who have received the faith of Jesus Christ with their baptism, have never really known any deity, since they have lived down to our day without temples, priests, and any indication of religion.' More commonly Indian ritual practices were recognized as religious but condemned as manifestations of demonic forces. John West could see around him at the Red River only 'a Heathen land, which Satan hath held bound, lo! not these 18 years or a century, but probably since the Creation of the world.'[12] This negative appraisal was what might have been expected in view of the conviction of the missionaries that only Christ could meet the needs of all peoples and that he had a corresponding claim on their allegiance. To people whose faith had been moulded in the crucible of resurgent Christianity, indeed, nothing short of complete commitment to Christ would have passed for better than irreligion or idolatry.

The near-identification of Christian with European values suggested the extension of these judgments to all aspects of native culture. To say that Indians were capable of Christian faith was to say in effect that they were capable of European civilization, a proposition which missionaries constantly defended in the face of an opinion widespread among both scholars and the general public that they were inherently incapable of it. To say that the Indians needed Christian faith was, by the same logic, to suggest that they needed to adopt a European manner of life and thus to pass a negative verdict on the whole of their traditional culture. Thomas Hurlburt, a Methodist who was said to have spoken Ojibwa like a native,

characterized unchristianized Indians as 'destitute of fellow-feeling ...
superstitious, imbecile in mind, and degraded in social habits.' A present-
day reader of missionary reports is likely to be struck most forcibly by the
almost complete lack of appreciation for Indian aesthetics they reveal.
Huron chants were described as 'howlings' and Longhouse ceremonies as
consisting of 'horrid and frightful postures,' while as late as 1918 an Anglican missionary reported with satisfaction that totem poles were being cut
up for firewood. Such judgments, which today seem uncharitable and insensitive, were made possible by the conviction that beyond the boundaries of Christendom only heathen darkness lurked and by unbounded
confidence in the ability of Christian civilization to overcome the darkness. Bishop George Mountain, reporting on cult objects brought back
from a trip to the Red River in 1844, described them as 'far from having
either beauty, costliness, or neatness of execution' and drew the obvious
conclusion, 'they are, however, tangible proofs of imposture, delusion, and
darkness.'[13]

Besides these considerations, which applied indifferently to all cultures
outside Christendom, there were others that pertained particularly to the
Indians. Non-literate societies were a puzzle to Europeans, whether
missionary-minded or sceptical, who regarded them as inferior and as
incapable of surviving contact with an advanced culture. Le Jeune, who
as a Jesuit was ready to attribute both natural religion and natural virtue
to non-Christians, ranked the culture of the North American Indians in
the lowest of Aristotle's stages of human society.[14] Later missionaries
would make the same point in terms of a scale of evolution. By the early
nineteenth century, largely through the interest of humanitarians, the
Indians were seen not merely as primitive and barbarous but as immi-
nently threatened by extinction. That well-wishers should be more concerned to preserve them than their culture was only natural, especially
since their culture was regarded as a major hindrance to their survival.

Missionaries to the Indians thus felt themselves impelled by a triple
compulsion. The very fact that the Indians were not Christians entitled
them to the blessings of the gospel and of European achievement. The
relative poverty of their culture, as Europeans saw it, made their need all
the greater. The crisis of survival with which European contact had confronted them gave a particular urgency to the task. Given such pressing
considerations, no missionary thought for a moment of waiting for an invitation or of asking whether Indians might appreciate a proffered remedy.
'They may not want you, but they need you,' was the motto prefaced to

Thomas Crosby's *Among the An-ko-me-nums*. John Semmens of Nelson House spelled out the message even more clearly: 'Physicians do not prescribe to suit the varying inclinations of fever-stricken and debilitated patients. They attack the disease, to the present discomfort of the sufferer, satisfied to wait for the favor of their subject until restored health proves the wisdom of the treatment.'[15]

In view of this diagnosis the program of christianization and civilization to which reference has been made repeatedly in these pages was not only logical but virtually inevitable, for its elements were seen as sides of a coin rather than as separate enterprises. Christianization that did not include civilization was, to all but a handful of romantics like Morice, simply inconceivable. Civilization without christianization, even the secular journalist Nicholas Flood Davin urged, would unleash 'desires, which, in the midst of enlightenment, constantly break out into the worst features of barbarism.' Missionaries might argue as to which should precede the other, as John McDougall and William Cockran did at considerable length and to their mutual enjoyment in the latter's living-room, but there was seldom a suggestion that one could ultimately stand without the other. To people who reasoned thus it made sense to regard a hat on an Indian's head as a reliable token of his growth in grace or to promote Handel oratorios in place of Bella Bella chants as a means of bringing about the same end.[16]

The first necessary step towards the implementation of this program was the establishment of effective communication with the Indians. Some Protestants, including George McDougall and most of the Anglicans at the Red River, were content to depend on interpreters throughout their ministries. Over the centuries, however, missionaries achieved an impressive output as grammarians, translators, and transcribers. With remarkable consistency their works reflected a concern for transmitting rather than receiving messages. Petitot, Morice, and Maclean often gave free rein to their scientific interests, but for the most part missionary publications consisted of Bibles, prayer books, and catechisms that were designed as instruments in their program of change. Their very considerable usefulness to linguists and ethnologists and later to Indians in search of lost fragments of their heritage were by-products of their primary functions. Since Indian cultures were passing away, missionaries intent on speeding the process saw little reason to study them for their own sakes.

Once elementary tools of communication had been devised, the next step was to persuade Indians of the truth of Christianity or of some particular brand of it. Since attempting to reach Indians one by one soon proved impractical and unproductive, missionaries were obliged to catch Indians at seasonal gatherings or to arrange special assemblies such as camp meetings or fortnightly missions. These occasions called for considerable improvisation, for missionaries had to be ready with on-the-spot answers to questions and to be alert for changes in audience mood that might call for intensified pressure. Success in this initial stage depended largely on natural – and perhaps supernatural – gifts, although in the course of time most missionaries assembled a stock-in-trade of arguments that were likely to prove effective. Even when successful, however, persuasion led to no permanent results unless it was followed by systematic instruction. This began with the beliefs, forms of worship, and moral and disciplinary requirements of the denomination concerned. In most situations it went on to the conveyance of skills of reading, writing, and arithmetic that would enable Indians to hold their own in a society dominated by Europeans. Not least, it sought to instil habits of mind that would impart a genuinely Christian and civilized character.

It soon became evident that the greatest obstacle to the institution of a systematic program of education was the Indian habit of moving about. Already in 1610 Marc Lescarbot expressed the opinion that efforts to christianize and civilize would always be of limited effect among tribes as migratory as the Micmacs. The same conviction became the basis of sustained efforts to reach sedentary tribes and to settle migratory ones, of which the reductions of the St Lawrence represented an early culmination and the missionary settlements so feared by the Hudson's Bay Company a later expression. This sense of a need for Indian stability was common to all missions and all periods. Only in a settled community could there be the regular round of worship which, in one form or another, all denominations regarded as essential. Only there could one have a mission school, with a bell calling the children to classes each morning. Stability was especially necessary to the civilizing program which the missions saw as integral to their task. Missionary reports contain frequent suggestions that Indian piety often held up better in the woods than on the reservation. Roman Catholics learned to mark feasts and days of abstinence on the trail, while Methodist boatmen rested on the sabbath in defiance of a powerful company. An experienced Anglican bishop went so far as to assert that among nomadic Indians 'religious work has been ninety-nine percent better in every possible way than in the more settled parts of Canada.'[17] So long as they maintained a migratory pattern, however, Indians would not acquire the skills or adopt the attitudes of the civilization of the West.

Despite its advantages, settlement did not prove to be a cure-all. Indians continued to slip away to the woods on occasion and returned with many lessons unlearned. Attendance at school was seldom regular, and almost any form of family employment was offered as a valid reason for absence. The alcohol problem did not abate. Missionaries soon decided that they must secure some measure of social control if their work was to be effective. Indirect rule through *dogiques* and captains, already instituted in the early seventeenth century at Sillery, continued to be favoured by Roman Catholics to the time of Durieu's watchmen and beyond. The periodic cabin inspections and the round of bells marking divisions of the work day at Grape Island, along with such devices as Duncan's black flag, served as Protestant equivalents. Gradually, in pursuit of the twin aims of christianization and civilization, the missionaries assumed the role of guardians. They found it difficult to replace what Le Jeune called 'the wicked liberty of the Savages' with the 'yoke of God'[18] but saw little prospect of success unless they could prevent the Indians from following their inclinations.

These considerations go far towards accounting for the two most distinctive features of Indian missions, their almost obsessive preoccupation with agriculture and their eventual concentration of effort on boarding schools. The choice of farming as an alternative to hunting and fishing was in many respects obvious. In a country as empty as Canada the land has always seemed a logical source of subsistence for a group constituting a problem, whether demobilized soldiers or unemployed factory workers. The choice must have seemed particularly obvious in the case of the Indians, who were already accustomed to outdoor living, especially where depletion of game made food supplies chronically unreliable. Indians unaccustomed to agriculture did not take readily to it, however, and some other trades might have been equally effective in encouraging the habits of regular industry that were regarded as an essential component of civilization. Missionaries persisted in encouraging agriculture because from their point of view it offered several distinct advantages. More than any other form of settlement, it tied its practitioners to the soil and thus promoted stability. It also made possible a large measure of self-sufficiency, minimizing occasions on which Indians would need to have dealings away from the mission. Individual land tenure, which many missionaries favoured, could be yet another incentive to stability as well as a hedge against the persistence of communal traditions. Above all, agriculture facilitated the creation of a controlled environment.

The point at which this program most consistently broke down was in its failure to overcome the inertia of Indian patterns of behaviour, which persisted even when the Indians themselves manifested a desire to break with the past. This failure showed up most frequently in a lack of progress on the part of children, who repeatedly unlearned at home the lessons in civilization they were taught at school. The best solution seemed to be to retain them for as long as possible within an environment where missionary influence would be undiluted. The residential school, with its combination of character formation, elementary education, and the inculcation of habits of industry, represented the missionary program of christianization and civilization in its most fully developed form. It ensured over a significant proportion of the lives of those entrusted to it a maximum of stability and control, while pointing to farm life as its natural outcome.

Despite the existence of many common elements of program the Christian mission to the Indians was far from monolithic. Each agency had an ethos that was not quite identical with that of any other. Each individual brought a set of convictions, talents, and sometimes idiosyncrasies that make generalization difficult and dangerous. No one, after all, could account for a Duncan, a Morice, or a Rand simply in terms of denominational background. Approaches were also affected by circumstances, for a program that proved effective in the farm belt of Upper Canada might make no sense in the far north.

Some differences in the dealings of Protestant denominations with the Indians could be predicted from a general knowledge of their characteristics in other settings. No one will be surprised to learn that Methodists showed more favour than Anglicans to displays of emotion, that Presbyterians were especially at home in the schoolroom, or that Baptists insisted on baptism by immersion of believers only. Other differences became apparent only in the field. Evangelical Anglicans, while allowing little deviation from the doctrinal norms of their church, were remarkably relaxed in their readiness to trust local congregations to the care of native leaders either clerical or lay. Methodists, while more readily accepting Indian preachers as colleagues and friends, suffered from a centralized polity that gradually stifled local initiative and discouraged native vocations. Moravians, while ruling their flock with a heavy hand, were unusually receptive to the adaptation of Indian customs for use in church. Perhaps the most significant distinction was between predestinarian Calvinists, who included Presbyterians, Baptists, and Anglicans of the CMS, and Arminians, such as Methodists, high-church Anglicans, and, in effect, Moravians, who acknowledged some place for the human will in the process of salvation. The former expected a definite profession of saving faith to precede participation in the fellowship and sacraments of the church. The latter, in this respect closer to Roman Catholics, placed more reliance on sacraments to effect growth into fullness of faith and thus tended to be less stringent in their requirements for admission. The most evident practical implication of this difference was that Arminians made more deliberate use of various means of grace, whereas Calvinists relied more on simple indoctrination.

Variations within the Roman Catholic Church were most evident in the days of New France. Jesuits were the intellectuals of the missions, careful and even cunning in their search for souls and increasingly suspect to governments of putting missionary before national objectives. Sulpicians were aristocrats, able to bring to the missions considerable resources both intellectual and financial, although handicapped by a certain aloofness from their charges. Récollets, apart from the outstanding Chrestien Le Clercq on the Gaspé coast, were on the whole willing amateurs, more at home operating out of French forts than organizing mission stations. Graduates of the Seminary of the Holy Spirit, on whom the Society for Foreign Missions relied almost entirely during the eighteenth century, were zealots who might have been more effective if they had not been caught up in the cross-fire of war. In the nineteenth century the Roman Catholic missionary approach was much more homogeneous, for both Jesuits and Oblates admired the pre-1773 Jesuit order and drew heavily on its experience. One is tempted to describe Jesuits and Oblates as representing respectively the classical and romantic wings of nineteenth-century missions. The former may have inclined more to proven methods, while the latter were certainly relentless in pressing towards the Ultima Thule of the Arctic. In aim and general methodology, however, the two were practically identical.

The difference that really counted, however, at least until the changes of the 1960s began to take effect, was that between Roman Catholics and Protestants of any description. While distinctions within each tradition were subtle and subject to dispute, there was a difference in atmosphere between a Protestant and a Roman Catholic mission that could not have been missed by the most casual visitor. A Protestant mission was open at

least to the more official aspects of Canadian life. If in the north, it was
likely to stand in close proximity to the local HBC post; if in the south, it
might seem almost an extension of the Indian Department. A Roman
Catholic mission was much more an entity to itself, representing either the
enclosed space of a self-contained settlement or the enclosed time of an
annual gathering. In a Protestant mission one could observe the makings of
a Christian congregation, in its Catholic counterpart those of a Christian
band or clan. In both the missionary was certain to be a person of some
authority, but priests and nuns were surrounded by a mystique of separate-
ness which the Protestant clergy did not share. This difference reflected
contrasting conceptions of vocation. Roman Catholics often came close to
identifying sanctity with suffering. 'It is the desire of suffering that has
made me come into these missions, I am going to be able to satisfy myself,'
wrote Louis Babel of the Saguenay, while Bishop Grandin had in his college days 'lovingly gazed' on the instruments of torture by means of which
early missionaries had won their crowns.[19] Protestants were more inclined
to think of hardships as obstacles to be overcome in the athletic spirit of
British Christianity. Bompas, fresh from England upon his appointment to
the north, startled the missionary at Fort Simpson by arriving most unsea-
sonably on Christmas morning.

The place of native elements in the two missions would have been
subtly but palpably different. On a Protestant mission there was likely to
be greater pressure to conform to European norms and more evidence of
the effects of such pressure. Roman Catholics might habitually use the
same rhetoric of Christianity and civilization, but acculturation was clearly
secondary to catechism. By contrast, Roman Catholics kept a closer check
on Indian behaviour and religious practice, whereas a Protestant mission
was likely to allow Indians more freedom of action and to place fewer
practical limits on their exercise of leadership. Indian initiative was more
conspicuous around a Protestant mission, one might fairly say, while the
ambience of a Catholic community was more recognizably Indian.

These obvious differences were manifestations of a basic theological
disagreement with regard to the manner in which one becomes a Christian. Catholics, operating with a scholastic theology of analogy, envisaged
conversion as the completion of nature by grace operating through the
sacraments. Regarding the Indians as essentially children, they sought to
nurture them towards sanctity by surrounding them with imagery rich in
dramatic and visual appeal. They showed considerable tolerance for native

ways, which they did not expect to be outgrown suddenly, but expected to retain complete control of the pedagogical process. Protestants, professing a theology that stressed a complete and preferably sudden change of heart, saw the Indians as essentially sinners to be wrenched out of heathen darkness into the light of the gospel. For this purpose they relied on the warnings and promises of Scripture, distrusting visual images and gestures whether associated with Roman Catholicism or with traditional Indian practice. Since they regarded conversion as a definite step rather than as a process, however, they had fewer qualms about making use of Indians who had given evidence of it as missionaries or catechists. Despite many similarities in program between Roman Catholics and Protestants, theologies of continuity and discontinuity produced results that were sometimes strikingly different.

The polarization of missionary forces that resulted from this divergence gave rise to a conflict that went much deeper than mere denominational competition, for each party was convinced that the other was leading the Indians to perdition. Roman Catholics, who could not accept the possibility that a heretic might have a genuine missionary vocation, attributed Protestant efforts to mere jealousy or self-seeking. Protestants, who did not doubt the zeal of Catholic priests but regarded their religion as a form of superstition, made little distinction between them and the shamans they sought to replace. During the nineteenth century bad feelings were exacerbated by an atmosphere of suspicion that clouded relations between Protestants and Roman Catholics everywhere. French priests carried with them perceptions derived from the situation in Europe, where a beleaguered church was under constant attack from anticlericals and secularists. In Canada they readily assimilated the Protestants who opposed them to the same camp, attributing their hostility to a mere dislike for the church or even for orthodox Christianity. English Protestants, alarmed by the rise of Anglo-Catholicism and by Pope Pius ix's restoration of an English hierarchy in 1850, saw all around them evidence of a vast international conspiracy that posed a deadly threat to British and Protestant liberties. The resulting atmosphere of mutual hostility, which did little to commend Christianity to the Indians as a religion of love, lifted only after the Second Vatican Council.

Approaches to the Indians varied not only from mission to mission but also over time in response to developments at the home base or to the changing circumstances of the Indians. The first missions of New France were launched on a wave of religious exaltation that especially affected sections of the aristocracy. France was beginning to recover from the turmoil of the Huguenot wars, and Catholic resurgence and the recovery of confidence in French *grandeur* seemed part of a single movement. Not sharing the English prejudice against miscegenation, the French saw in the mingling of settlers with the native population their best prospect for the establishment of a strong colony in North America. Royal policy favoured such a development, and missionaries of all orders eagerly complied. Since the Jesuits were for the most part well born, they envisaged this new society in hierarchical terms. If they had found in Indian society equivalents to the philosopher-kings of the Orient, they would have welcomed opportunities to collaborate with them. Foiled by Indian equalitarianism, they anticipated that Indians and low-born settlers would constitute a solid peasant base for the colony. Even so, they sought to cultivate an élite within the Indian community by handing out honorific offices.

The transfer of attention to segregated missionary settlements represented not so much a deliberate rejection of this optimistic program as a gradual adjustment to experience. Chronic disorder consequent on the liquor trade seemed to render impossible the formation of stable Christian communities in the Iroquois cantons. The demoralization of the Algonquins of Sillery upon their removal to Quebec in 1650 suggested that intimate contact with the French was equally disastrous. The reductions represented a tacit compromise whereby the missionaries agreed to accept the continuance of a largely native way of life in return for adherence to Catholic practice and to a Christian moral code. In time the Jesuits came to see this compromise as offering not merely a tolerable substitute for assimilation but some distinct advantages over it. Government officials fumed at first over this abandonment of official French policy, but in time even they came to recognize its inevitability.

As rivalry for the control of North America came to dominate official thinking, indeed, both French and British governments began to reason that the military importance of the Indians demanded that they should not lose the native skills that made them valuable in war. Secular authorities increasingly pressed on missionaries the importance of retaining the loyalty of the Indians among whom they worked, and apparent threats to the very survival of their religion placed the missionaries themselves in a position where they had to attach greater priority to the allegiance of the Indians than to their piety. Such missionaries as Gaulin and Le Loutre continued to press for the measure of acculturation that was implied by agricultural settlement, but out of necessity they devoted most of their attention to maintaining their position as tribal leaders. Ironically the missionaries became in many ways more important to both governments and Indians, but they were able to devote less attention to long-range efforts to combine Christianity and civilization than at any time before or since.

The renewal of attempts to institute a broader missionary program owed nothing to the British conquest or to the American Revolution, which merely confirmed the strategic importance of the missions in attaching the Indians to one side or another while discouraging any interference with native culture that might alienate them or render them less fit for military service. It came about, rather, because a wave of missionary and humanitarian enthusiasm in Europe and the United States coincided with a change of circumstances in British North America that transformed the Indians from military assets into economic liabilities. Emphasis now shifted from the extension of the kingdom of God into new territories to the eradication of attitudes and habits that were increasingly seen as obstacles to the progress of both colonists and Indians. In this situation the familiar remedy of christianization and civilization appealed to missionaries, philanthropists, and politicians alike. Its intended result was the eventual assimilation of the Indians into Canadian society, whether through outright absorption or, as a later and more sophisticated line of thought suggested, through integration into a complex mosaic of compatible ways of life. Oddly, what proved to be the most effective program of acculturation was motivated by concern for Indian souls much more than for Indian bodies.

By the 1840s the wheel was turning again. The critical situation of the Indians, of which the existence of the Aborigines Protection Society operated as a constant reminder, was an important factor in attracting missionary attention to them. It was, however, no longer so crucial as it had been even in the previous decade. In the early years of the nineteenth century most missionary operations had been small in scale, but increasing public support now encouraged more expansive thinking. The dream of carrying Christianity to 'the ends of the earth' had a particular appeal for the romantic imagination of the time, and in the minds of zealots remote and forbidding Rupert's Land qualified admirably for this designation.[20] From this period date the first large-scale enterprises among the Indians of Canada since the Jesuit missions of New France. The earliest were undertaken almost entirely on European initiative. Later, with the growth and consolidation of Canadian churches, they too began to take part. Canadian missions now formed a segment of an international movement in which the glory of France or the plight of the Ojibwas was secondary to considerations of general Christian strategy. The inseparability of Christianity and civilization was by no means forgotten, especially in more accessible areas where missionaries recognized the inevitability of future European settlement; Duncan's experiment at Metlakatla is sufficient by itself to prove the point. The extension of the faith was the chief motive, however, and in many parts of the north no other would have made much sense.

Missionary interest continued to increase during the later decades of the nineteenth century and into the twentieth, reaching a peak among Roman Catholics only after the Second World War. Long before this time, however, the centre of missionary attention had shifted elsewhere. In 1859 Henry Venn, even in commending the northwest missions for kindling a 'flame of missionary zeal,' suggested that the time had come 'to place these native converts upon a self-supporting system, so that all the energies of the Society may be concentrated upon the great centres of the human race.' The Indian field became something of a backwater, and Frits Pannekoek has suggested that the CMS reserved Canada for training-school alumni while sending university graduates to fields of higher priority in the Orient.[21] The effects of this eclipse may not all have been bad, for the Indians received dogged workers who may have been more effective than some of the virtuosi who made names for themselves in Asia and Africa. Some serious thinking about the aims and methods of Christian missions overseas was beginning to take place, however, and little attempt was made to apply it to Indian missions.

Even before the turn of the twentieth century, indeed, Indian missions were coming to be regarded as part of the internal operations of the Canadian churches, and by no means the most glamorous part. In the Presbyterian and Methodist churches the shift was symbolized by the transfer of work among Indians from foreign- to home-mission departments. Roman Catholics and Anglicans, continuing to secure most of their missionary candidates in Europe, were able to retain longer a sense of exciting service in faraway places. Even among them, however, as work among European settlers began to predominate in many dioceses, there were widespread complaints that Indian missions received only tag-ends of ecclesiastical attention. Emphasis on the cultivation of Christian citizenship was a natural consequence of this new perspective, and often it was far from clear whether the future of the Indians or the future of Canada was at the centre of concern. A sense that the great days of Indian missions were in the past was accentuated by a process of routinization that inevitably set in when the churches were unable to find satisfactory replacements for methods that seemed increasingly obsolete. Even more serious was the absence of a vision of an exciting future to which the missions might be leading.

Signs of a significant change of missionary attitude began to appear only with the loss of confidence in European capability that accompanied the breakdown of the colonial system. Although this sense of disillusionment is by no means universally felt, it has affected the churches traditionally involved in mission work among the Indians to the point where old slogans linking christianization and civilization have almost completely lost currency. The churches have come to recognize merit in non-European societies and at least a measure of validity in religions other than their own, notably including those of the Indians. Henceforth, it is clear, they must take into account not only the needs but the wishes of the Indians, and not only their future but their past. These changes signify the end of the missionary era that began with the voyages of Columbus and Vasco da Gama, and they have irreversibly altered the terms of Indian-Christian encounter. The Christian mission had been going on for fifteen hundred years before it began to receive ambiguous support from Western colonizers, however, and presumably it is capable of further transformations in the future.

Despite differences among denominations and periods, the missionary approach to the Indians exhibited remarkable consistency over the centuries. Many of its features have little appeal today for the mass of Canadians, who take for granted the right of the various peoples of the world to order their lives as they see fit, at least in such uncontroversial matters as religion. Given the goals of the missionaries and the assumptions about social dynamics which they shared with most other Europeans of their times, however, their methods were for the most part logical and even inevitable. The agricultural settlement and the residential school scarcely needed to be invented, we might fairly say, because circumstances conspired to suggest them. The motives that led missionaries to adopt such programs, while encouraging in them attitudes to native culture that are likely to strike us as arrogant and insensitive, also inspired them as they inspired few others to devote their lives to the welfare of the Indians, live in their camps, share their hardships, and stand up on occasion for their rights. Despite this basic consistency of purpose, however, the enterprise was marked by a number of ambiguities which the missionaries were not always able to resolve. Some of these were the result of circumstances over which they had no control. Others arose out of their own pursuit of objectives that sometimes proved incompatible in practice.

One of the most perplexing problems faced by the missionaries derived from their own ambivalence towards European society. On the one hand, their identification of European values as Christian made acculturation an inescapable part of their program. On the other, their perception of Europe as still corrupted by sin suggested a need to protect the Indians from the influence of undesirable whites. Protestants, on the whole, favoured at least some exposure to whites as the only possible models of Christian civilization. Roman Catholics, more frankly protective of the religion and morals of the Indians under their care, leaned to segregation. Neither found a satisfactory solution to the problem of bringing about the transition from native to European patterns. Premature or excessive contacts with whites proved demoralizing to Indians, while measures of apartheid merely postponed the issue. Failure to make a decisive choice for either option had the effect of creating a sort of missionary half-world that isolated its inhabitants both from Canadian society and from traditional ways. Over the centuries a considerable measure of acculturation took place, but the wardship that was originally designed as a temporary measure to ease the Indians over the period of transition became virtually a permanent state. Missionaries shared this dilemma with governments, which had no greater success in resolving it.[22]

Holding their religious and humanitarian efforts in tandem gave the missionaries difficulty from the outset. Their commitment to 'civilization' implied a disinterested concern for the material and cultural welfare of the Indians, whereas their desire to propagate Christianity made them in many ways highly interested parties. The missionaries would have admitted no inconsistency, for to their minds Christ was the greatest gift they had to offer and the one that alone could give meaning to secular progress. Any success in christianization, they therefore reasoned, would ultimately prove a boon to the Indians. In practice, religion and humanitarianism did not always blend smoothly. The imposition of Christian moral regulations, in particular, could prove disruptive to a closely integrated social fabric. The kindly Egerton R. Young bemoaned the havoc wrought by the dissolution of a polygamous marriage even while he felt himself obliged to enforce the rule that a childless first wife must take precedence over a later one with a large family. In other cases, such as that of the western treaties, missionaries found it natural to identify the interests of the Indians with those of the missions. An equally natural Indian response was to accuse the missionaries of coming not 'pure and simple, in the spirit of brotherhood,' but 'stealthily in the spirit of Christian brotherhood, a different concept.'[23]

Missionaries went among the Indians to help and to give, but how were they to do so without in effect buying favour? Never far out of sight in missionary reports is the figure of the 'tobacco Christian,' usually identified as the product of another mission. A few missionaries deliberately used the time-honoured device of giving or withholding rewards as a means of securing Indian support, but more typical was the perplexity of the missionary who desired only genuine converts but observed, like Sérafin Dumoulin, that 'avec rien on n'a fait rien.' The basic problem was not that missionaries were inherently unscrupulous but that it is in the nature of generosity to create a sense of obligation, a sense which among the Indians was very highly developed. The problem was compounded, however, by a readiness on the part of some missionaries to accept the legitimacy of some short-cuts in advancing a cause that seemed to them manifestly right. Indians might be pardoned for thinking sometimes that they were being bought, and outsiders did not hesitate to draw cynical conclusions. W. Sinclair of the Hudson's Bay Company wrote of the CMS mission at White Dog, 'as long as the flour & pemmican lasts, there will be no want of converts; when that's done, there will be an end of religion.'[24]

The availability of forms of power even more direct than material inducements further compromised missionary attempts to persuade Indians to their views. Although governments never sought to compel conversion, the existence of the authority of the state helped to give visibility and weight to the missionary presence. It is doubtful whether the missionaries could have established themselves without European protection; in any case they did not do so until a measure of it was available. If government support did not give them the power to compel adult Indians to their faith, it could be used to nip indigenous movements in the bud, to regulate community morals, and to bring children within the range of missionary influence. Such help was often of considerable immediate advantage to the missionaries, but they paid a price for it. It complicated their task of discriminating between specifically Christian goals and those of Europeans in general. It identified them, in Indian eyes, with a white authority-structure standing over them. It was a formidable obstacle to the effective devolution of authority. Much as missionaries might seek to persuade the Indians that the churches established among them were theirs, the realities of power suggested otherwise.

Disparities in resources and power, along with the superior confidence of the European, combined to bring missionaries and Indians together on unequal terms. This may have been the most serious of all sources of ambiguity, for it inhibited the cultivation of personal relations of genuine mutuality. Intent on changing the Indians' way of life and convinced that they knew what was best for them, missionaries found it difficult to listen to what Indians had to say and even, on occasion, to hear it. Superintendent T.G. Anderson recorded, apparently at the insistence of one of the Indian participants, a most revealing conversation on Manitoulin Island involving two missionaries and two Indians. F.A. O'Meara, an Anglican, and J.-B. Proulx, a Roman Catholic, were discussing the relative merits of British and French arms while paying no attention to the two Indians, despite the fact that Shinguacouse, or 'the Pine,' was the leading Anglican Ojibwa of the region. Let John Bell, the Indian narrator, continue the story:

In the meantime I observed to the Pine that it was a pitty they should be quarelling about religion [sic!] but, if there was 7 or 8 of different persuasions it would be still worse – the Pine said Yes! and speaking to the Gentlemen said, Stop! & a second time said I tell you to stop, it is my turn to speak, & said, this is the way the Black Coat acted at the Sault before I became a Christian, each one of six denominations wished to make me believe his was the best, I had an idea of joining the Roman Catholics but determined to go to Toronto and take the advice of the Governor.

By the time Shinguacouse had finished narrating his story of how the governor advised him to join the 'English religion,' the two missionaries had evidently returned to their argument. Only when the noise had subsided again was he able to ask a few pointed questions.[25]

At the root of this breakdown of communication was incompatibility between the control that the missionaries deemed necessary for the implementation of their program and the rapport with Indians that alone could evoke a spontaneously positive response. When Indians were offered for their free decision a program in which they could see the promise of individual and social renewal, as happened in the Iroquois cantons in the early days of Sault-Saint-Louis and again in Upper Canada during the Methodist revivals, they showed themselves capable of not merely co-operation but initiative. When the missionaries made residential education the focal point of their strategy, virtually abandoning the attempt to convince adult Indians of the advantages of Christian citizenship in favour of pre-empting their children for indoctrination into it, they invited the alienation of the people they were trying to serve. They became no longer collaborators with the Indians in an attempt to overcome adverse conditions but collaborators with government in an attempt to remake them regardless of their desires.

To point out ambiguities and even contradictions in the approach of Christian missionaries to the Indians is not to suggest that they might have adopted a radically different program with better results. The options available to them were limited both by circumstances and by the limits of imagination which they shared with other Europeans. The resources and power of which they were able to avail themselves were given factors in the situation. They accepted them as part of the workings of divine providence and would have considered themselves poor stewards if they had failed to take advantage of them. Methods for which they are roundly criticized today, such as incentives and punishments, strictly supervised education, and even agricultural settlement, were based on methods of dealing with groups resisting assimilation that were considered advanced in their times.[26] Some of the media they devised to convey their message, such as syllabics, adaptations of various systems of shorthand, and the game of 'Point to Point,' reflected imagination and initiative well beyond the ordinary. Their achievements and mistakes were those of Europeans of their times.

In reading through the reports of missionaries and their directors, nevertheless, one marvels that they so seldom paused to ask whether their methods were congruous with the goals they ultimately hoped to achieve. It was not long after the middle of the nineteenth century that Venn made the obvious point that missionaries should eventually make themselves unnecessary by nurturing into existence 'self-governing, self-supporting, and self-propagating' Christian communities. The institutions they set up, however admirable in other ways, were scarcely designed to bring about this result. They were, rather, ones which only the missionaries could run and which, in the end, only governments could pay for. In this lack of vision the missionaries were by no means alone. According to one analyst, British officials in India recognized for many years that they would eventually hand over power, presumably when Indians were ready to exercise it. The founders of the system had made no provision for preparing Indians to take over, however, and their successors continued to operate the machine on familiar lines until change came about not by readiness but by demand.[27] Missionaries to the Indians of Canada, despite the best of intentions, showed a similar inability to imagine the future.

CHAPTER ELEVEN

A Yes That Means No?

To think of encounter between Christianity and the Indians of Canada is almost inevitably to conjure up a picture of dominant missionaries gathering Indians around them, collecting them into villages, and forcing on them a strange religion and an alien culture. This picture captures an element of painful reality, but it is unfair not only to the missionaries but to the Indians: recognizing only the former as actors, it reduces the latter to the role of passive recipients. Since the Indians were under no direct compulsion to embrace Christianity, there could have been no native Christian communities unless they had voluntarily converted themselves. To round out the story, therefore, we need to consider how the Indians responded to Christianity, what they made of it, and how they used it to reshape their lives and societies.

In situations where the native culture was relatively intact and the white man was a tolerated visitor, the initial reaction was usually to reject Christianity out of hand. Le Caron, the first missionary to visit the Hurons, reported that they were interested in French knives and beads but almost totally indifferent to his message. Two centuries later, David Jones observed that the Indians of the Red River, seeing white men adopt their ways, took this as an acknowledgment of their superiority and regarded all things European with contempt.[1] As Christianity became better known, resistance to it often hardened. This might take the form of heightened shamanic activity, of countermovements, or even of threats of violence against the missionaries. Among the Ojibwas of northwestern Ontario and the Blackfeet of southern Alberta, rejection continued over decades of missionary occupation and defeated the strenuous efforts of both European and native promoters of Christianity.

Although Indian reasons for rejecting Christianity varied, a fairly standard repertoire of objections followed the missionaries as they penetrated new areas. Customary rites were more effective in ensuring success in the hunt. The examples set by most whites gave no reason for thinking Christianity superior to native traditions. Indians who accepted Christianity would be separated from traditionalist friends and relations in the afterlife. Worse still was the fate foreshadowed by a dream, often encountered in Upper Canada and reported from as far west as Edmonton, in which a Christian Indian was turned back from one heaven as a Christian and from another as an Indian. The most common objection in all parts of Canada, however, was simply that the Indians had no need of a new religion. 'Aota Chabaya,' the Micmacs told Biard; 'you can have your way and we will have ours; everyone values his own wares.' The argument was capable of many transmutations. Peter Jones heard it as the creation by the Great Spirit of two peoples, to each of whom he gave a religion. Brébeuf was told not only that there were two creations but that they were the work of different gods. The Delawares of Muncey, familiar with blacks from residence in the United States, raised the number to three.[2]

The case for ancestral traditions was never put more eloquently than by Ojaouanon, a warrior-chief of Walpole Island, in a long debate with the Jesuit superior Pierre Chazelle in 1844. The debate took place with all the formality required by Indian etiquette, and Chazelle, who entered fully into the spirit of the occasion, seems to have recorded the Indian speeches as faithfully as he could. The entire account is worth reading as a classic of Indian eloquence, but two paragraphs will at least give some idea of the traditionalists' point of view:

I, an Indian, know that the Great Spirit has given us all that we have: eyes to see, ears to hear, and a spirit to think of him and to understand the things he has created. I know that he is here, I know that he is elsewhere, that he is everywhere. I know that he sees us to the bottom of our hearts. I know that we ought to do his will. The Indian understands well these truths and many others; they are present to his spirit wherever he goes.

It is not in books, my brother, that I have learned what I know. The Great Spirit has taught my elder, and my elder has spoken to me of what the Great Spirit had told him. I am happy to have had these teachings. I keep them in my heart, and never will I renounce them.[3]

Other Indians came to a different conclusion, although the manner of their conversion to Christianity varied a great deal from place to place. Many Indians were practically swept into the church as the result of mass movements. Other decisions for Christianity were made, with greater deliberation and sometimes calculation, by tribal and band councils. At Deer Lake in northern Ontario, a crisis precipitated by the arrest of local leaders for the killing of a wendigo led the Crees there to call in a Methodist missionary. In some communities along the British Columbia coast bitter contests took place between Christian and 'pagan' parties, and deaths on either side were attributed to the spiritual manipulations of the other. Many Indians made up their minds as individuals, sometimes suddenly and sometimes after lengthy reflection; one Haida attributed his conversion to a New Testament that had been presented to him eighteen years earlier. Some conversions were preceded by intense internal conflict, which might be betrayed by failure in the hunt or even by violent behaviour. Others took place with apparent ease; the Babines were not the only Indians found saying their prayers when the missionaries arrived.[4]

While many conversions followed such conventional European patterns that one suspects careful missionary coaching, special interest attaches to ones that took place in distinctively Indian ways. Although the missionaries consistently warned the Indians to put no stock in their dreams, it was through dreams that many of them became Christian. A woman named Marguerite became a pious Roman Catholic after dreaming of the church at Chatham, Ontario. John Sunday owed his conversion to Methodism to a vision of 'two Beings standing in the air,' the nearer one of whom told him that he must address his prayer to the more distant. Peter Jones told of a woman who described to him a remarkable dream in which 'the heavens and the earth passed away with a great noise, and the Son of God made his appearance, and called her to himself.'[5]

One of the most elaborate of such accounts was related to Dominique du Ranquet by an old Ojibwa named Ataghewinini from the north shore of Lake Huron, who claimed never to have encountered a missionary when the events took place. At a time when he was very ill and apparently close to death, Ataghewinini suddenly saw a path opening to the sky. Following it for some time, he met two Frenchmen who advised him to go on. The spirit of God descended on him, and he looked down with dismay on a crowd of men and women disappearing into the shades. After further adventures he was advised by the doorkeeper of heaven to seek out 'the

Catholic prayer.' Upon his return to earth he narrated his experiences, which so horrified the elders of his band that he determined to put them out of his mind. One is not surprised to learn, however, that after further adventures that included the dream of a man later identified as Bishop Alexander Macdonell, two Frenchmen duly appeared to baptize him. Shamans, accustomed to traffic with the spirit world, were prone to similar experiences. Although they usually put up stubborn opposition at first, they often became on conversion extremely zealous Christians and eager proselytizers.[6]

By the end of the nineteenth century the great majority of the Indians of Canada were at least nominally Christian. Of approximately 100,000 Indians enumerated by the Department of Indian Affairs in 1899, all adhered to some Christian denomination except 15,000 listed as 'pagan' and another 14,000 designated 'religion unknown.' By the 1971 census the total had risen to 313,000, including Eskimos, while 'other religions' (including traditional beliefs and a few Christian groups such as the Moravians) and 'no religion' counted only 9,000 each. The proportion for 'other religions' was smaller than for Canadians of British origin, that for 'no religion' only half as large. Of those listed as Christians in 1971 Roman Catholics accounted for 174,000, or somewhat more than half. Anglicans were second with 69,000, a figure that included a large proportion of the Inuit. The United Church, inheriting Methodist and some Presbyterian work, had 32,000. There were 6,000 Pentecostals, representing a remarkable increase in recent years and one that has presumably continued. Baptists and Presbyterians each numbered 4,000. These figures correspond roughly with the time and effort expended by the various denominations.

The existence of a considerable Christian majority in all provinces and territories indicates that no substantial body of Indians was immune to the appeal of Christianity. More indicative of regional disparities are the figures for those who have resisted Christianity. In 1899 most of these were in areas of late or thin missionary penetration. British Columbia and the prairies accounted for a large proportion, while Christians were still a distinct minority in the Yukon. This pattern changed drastically over the years. Those reckoned to aboriginal religions almost disappeared from the Yukon and British Columbia. Alberta, the home of the originally recalcitrant Blackfeet, became almost unanimously Christian, while Saskatchewan continued to have a large although gradually decreasing number professing 'aboriginal beliefs.' In 1971 the most conspicuous body of Indians adhering to 'other religions,' in excess of 3,000 and still as numerous as in 1899, was in long-missionized Ontario. The great bulk of these hold-outs, adherents of the Good Message of Handsome Lake, were located within the highly industrialized Golden Horseshoe.[7] These substantial pockets of resistance can be accounted for more readily by the presence of countervailing forces than by variations in the appeal of Christianity. In southern Ontario the existence of a well-developed native religious organization blocked the expansion of Christianity. For Saskatchewan the explanation seems to be more complex. The Blackfeet of Alberta, after initial resistance to Christianity and white ways, made a deliberate accommodation to them. The Saulteaux and Crees of Saskatchewan, wounded less severely by the extermination of the buffalo, clung more persistently to remnants of the old way of life.

The rate of Christian growth was in many ways impressive. It was more rapid than in most other areas in which Christian missionaries were at work, so that Smithurst could assert that the CMS had achieved more with £12,000 in Rupert's Land than in any other field.[8] It involved in many cases not mere acceptance but active initiative on the Indian side. Sympathetic chiefs granted protection to many early missionaries and gained a hearing for many later ones. Zealous converts spread the message beyond the confines of the missions or attracted fellow tribesmen to them. Once Christian communities had been established, *dogiques*, elders, and class leaders were important in keeping them alive.

This acceptance and initiative were in the cause of a religion that presented unusual difficulties to people schooled in native traditions. Christianity demanded that its creed should be accepted as true and that all beliefs and practices incompatible with it should be renounced as false. It set up absolute standards of right and wrong that went beyond customary considerations of appropriate and inappropriate behaviour. It placed a premium on order, regularity, and discipline. None of these requirements can have been readily comprehensible, let alone easily complied with. In many cases, too, those who opted for the new way had to make up their minds in an atmosphere in which the motives of the missionaries were widely distrusted. Since people do not ordinarily embrace a new religion without compelling reasons, its acceptance calls for explanation more urgently than the measure of resistance it met.

Reasons adduced for accepting Christianity were as varied as the ways in which conversion took place. Some of them were remarkably down to

earth. William Case reported, in the broken English commonly attributed
to Indians at the time, the testimony of a Mississauga at Grape Island
named Pigeon: 'When I first came here from Kingston, I had but one small
kettle; my blanket was all torn; no sheet; no shoes, now I got all this, I owe
no man. I got little money too.' Archdeacon W.H. Collison attributed
many conversions among the Haidas to the inability of medicine men to
cure smallpox, the disease of the 'iron people.'[9] Leadership roles, with the
opportunities for prestige that attached to them, doubtless attracted a number. Chiefs could find advantages in Christianity as they sought to consoli-
date their power, and some of their favour to missionaries may have been
in hope of such a return.

Beyond such tangible motives was the possibility of harnessing new
sources of spiritual power through the rituals and ceremonies of Christianity or through the use of its sacred books. Even the fear inspired by a
strange religion contributed to its fascination. Indians were accustomed to
associating spiritual power with danger, and the greater the danger, the
greater the power was likely to be. Nor should we underestimate the fear
of hell and the hope of heaven that were so assiduously implanted by many
missionaries. The early Jesuits relied on the former to convince the
Hurons to spare their lives, while Pierre Duchaussois noted the latter as a
powerful inducement in the north.[10]

Among this welter of reasons a few constants stand out. One is that
while the European associations of Christianity were the most formidable
obstacle to its acceptance, they also constituted its chief attraction. In
many cases those who opted for it were, by the very act of conversion,
consciously opting also for the adoption of a European mode of life. Even
those who retained most of their native ways were in some measure
accepting the applicability to themselves of European standards. The basic
appeal of Europe was the access it provided to forms of wealth hitherto
unavailable. Joseph Chihwatenha, the model Huron convert, expressed this
pull of the cargo eloquently in his rhetorical question, If European hatchets
and knives, why not European beliefs? More was involved, however, than
the acquisition of the medicine of an apparently more powerful people.
Emerging out of regions that had not been known to exist, Europeans by
their very presence compelled Indians to try to make sense of a cosmos
broader than their mythology envisaged. Christianity was well equipped to
meet this need. Its dynamic view of history helped to make change comprehensible, while the permanence and uniformity of its documents made

traditional myths seem evanescent and unreliable. 'The Great Spirit has not given you any such *Book*, but he has given it to *us*,'[11] was an argument that Indians found difficult to answer.

A second common factor, closely related to the former, was the deep trouble into which most Indian societies had fallen. What would have been the eventual result of an encounter between Christianity and healthy native cultures we can only surmise, for evidence with regard to such contacts is at best fragmentary. Conversion to Christianity was essentially a phenomenon of the moon of wintertime, when ancestral spirits had ceased to perform their expected functions satisfactorily and angel choirs promised to fill a spiritual vacuum. George McDougall commented of the Ojibwas of Garden River: '... they are fast passing away. Nor are they ignorant of it. Many of them are now ripe for the Gospel.' The Mississaugas of the Credit were reported to have given up most of their traditional practices already when the Methodists approached them. At the lowest level, Christianity provided in such situations new centres of interest that helped to relieve a sense of ennui. More positively, it offered a means of reintegrating societies in which old standards had broken down. When the Ten Commandments were read to a group of Mississaugas, the assembly broke into tears. This reaction, almost incomprehensible to a generation still in revolt against Victorian taboos, made sense in the context of a society that had fallen into moral chaos. Even more effective could be the telling of the gospel story, with its assurance that God cares for everyone, to people whose worth was commonly denied. Where Christianity made such an appeal, it might aptly be described as a movement of revitalization. That many Indians sensed a need for such revitalization is suggested by frequent references to their readiness for the Christian message even before the arrival of missionaries.[12]

Although many reasons offered for conversion are likely to strike us as self-serving, we should be well advised to cultivate a healthy mistrust of our own cynicism about them. Indians were not in the habit of making the sharp distinctions between spiritual and material benefits that seem self-evident to Europeans. Success in hunting was not a reward for pleasing the spirits but something that inevitably followed when one lived in harmony with them and thereby maintained the equilibrium of nature. Neither was medicine a magical apparatus for compelling the spirits but rather a means of attaining a vision of the spirit world that would banish disharmonies making for disease. Similarly, a desire for Western-style houses or education could be equivalent to the recognition that Europeans possessed a spiritual power that enabled them to succeed. Sincere converts did not attempt to purchase success by adopting a religion acceptable to Europeans. Their expectation, rather, was that success would attend persons with the spiritual discernment necesssary for traffic with the eternal order. Since Christianity was the religion of Europeans, European success implied that there must be something of worth in Christianity. Duncan may have hit the nail on the head with his observation that Indians were convinced that whites possess 'some great secret about eternal things.'[13]

Inevitably one raises questions. How genuine was the Christianity to which these Indians were converted? Did they undergo a real change of heart, or was their Christian profession a veneer that barely and sometimes not altogether successfully concealed a view of nature and the spiritual order radically at variance with that of Christianity? Such questions are raised not only by the existence of nominal Christians, which even the most optimistic missionary would scarcely have denied, but also by the faith and practice of converts whose sincerity and devotion cannot be doubted. Even in the case of these, if one looks honestly at the record, one is nagged by a suspicion that what they embraced was so different from Christianity as the missionaries understood it as to be classified more properly as a mere imitation of its externals or, at best, as a blend neither quite Christian nor quite traditional.

Missionaries, understandably, inclined to a positive assessment of the results of their work. They wrote glowing reports of converts outstanding for piety, for preaching ability, for apostolic zeal, for perseverance under ridicule, and, in early days, for willingness to endure martyrdom. They boasted of communities where their message was accepted with eagerness, where frequent services were regularly attended, and where worship and instruction continued even in their absence. The Methodists of Upper Canada described the Mississaugas as 'a nation ... born to God in a day,' while Steinhauer applied the same phrase to the Crees at Whitefish Lake. Bishop Ridley of Caledonia asserted that he had never seen 'such a change as in the condition of the Indians of North-Western Canada when our Missions were first started and the condition of the Indians today.' Faraud wrote from the Mackenzie, 'I simply do not know how to make you understand the dispositions of these primitive Christians.'[14] Even disappointments could always be assuaged with the reflection that over the years much progress towards an understanding of Christianity had been made.

This positive assessment of Indian Christianity was based on more than evidence of the existence of genuine fervour. To begin with, an element of deliberate choice in the acceptance of Christianity was vouched for by the surrender of medicine bags and other paraphernalia of traditional religion, which at least in some areas was a normal concomitant of conversion. Many Indians were able to give a good account of their understanding of Christian doctrine, even though we may suspect some exaggeration in the assurance of one missionary that a Mohawk woman in his flock was so well instructed as to 'know all that is most difficult in the Mystery of the holy Trinity' and 'to distinguish the two natures in JESUS CHRIST.'[15] Most convincing of all were changes in individual and community mores, including the elimination of violence and alcoholism and the acquisition of habits of industry. All such changes were evidence that the acceptance of Christianity implied significant decisions about belief, religious practice, and manner of living.

From anthropologists one receives a different impression. They describe a remarkable continuity of traditional practice through at least the early years of missionary occupation and in some cases virtually until the present, dismissing the influence of Christianity not so much by explicitly minimizing it as by demonstrating the survival almost undiminished of practices apparently incompatible with it. From reading Jenness's *The Ojibwa Indians of Parry Island*, for example, one would scarcely guess that Methodist services, Sunday schools, and class meetings had been taking place regularly for three-quarters of a century in the community described.[16] David Merrill Smith traces belief in i^nko^{n}ze or supernatural power among the Chipewyans into the twentieth century, attributing its recent decline less to the influence of priests and medical practitioners than to the weakening of bonds with the bush.[17] Some missionaries have accounted for discrepancies in perception by suggesting that anthropologists listen too readily to wily Indians who know what they want to hear and willingly oblige them. While there is doubtless some truth in this contention, it raises a suspicion that missionaries have sometimes been similarly gulled.

Direct evidence of the continuity of traditional practice is not the only ground on which the thoroughness of conversion to Christianity may be questioned. Since apparent agreement may conceal fundamental differences of understanding, an Indian who sincerely accepted everything the missionaries said might also interpret what he heard in terms of presuppositions at odds with those of the missionaries. An Indian student called to my attention one such difference in viewpoint that was bound to colour all others. Christians regard themselves as inherently powerless, he said, and therefore pray to God to make power available through Jesus Christ. Indians, on the other hand, have traditionally expected contact with the spirit world to provide a direct accession of power that is theirs to control and use. Although the contrast may be exaggerated, it helps to illuminate differences in apprehension that could exist even when there was no outward disagreement. A priest, for example, might be regarded not merely as a dispenser of sacraments over which he had no proprietary right but as a shaman giving and withholding blessings at will. Petitot with his European assumptions was astonished to learn that his hearers accepted what he told them because they assumed that it had come to him directly in dreams.[18] On the same reasoning, Methodist conversion could be assimilated to the traditional vision, resulting not so much in a sense of dependence on God and affiliation with the church as in an assurance of personal validation.

These positive and negative assessments, although contradictory in many respects, rest on a common set of assumptions. Both take for granted the incompatibility of Christianity with native traditions and therefore measure the thoroughness of conversion by the extent to which one set of values and practices has replaced another. Missionaries have derived satisfaction from this replacement, while anthropologists for the most part have regretted it, but both have customarily applied the same set of criteria. On this scale, Indians who remain Indian in their basic attitudes can only be superficially Christian, whereas those must be reckoned the most authentic Christians who have gone furthest in rejecting their past. There is a measure of truth in this way of putting the matter. Authentic Christianity is incompatible with some beliefs and practices and must therefore always be in tension with the culture in which it is set. On the other hand, it can be argued that Christianity has not really taken root in a community until it has fused with its culture sufficiently to make possible its appropriation in distinctively indigenous ways. If this argument is valid, the success of Christian penetration can never be measured simply on a scale of displacement.

The criteria by which Indian Christianity has commonly been measured are by no means self-evident, although not many years ago they seemed so. As missiologists have tried to come to terms with varied expressions of Christianity in countries of differing traditions, they have been less inclined to identify Christianity with the European mould in which it has been cast for many centuries. It may be most helpful to begin not by trying to estimate the sincerity of conversion, which in many cases was unquestionable, or even its authenticity, the criteria of which are debatable, but simply by asking what conversion meant to Indians who embraced Christianity. What did they conceive themselves to be doing, accepting and renouncing, in becoming Christian? How did they understand the relation between their Christian profession and what they had always been? At least three possible models suggest themselves.

We might, in the first place, think of Indian Christians as not in rebellion against their traditional ways but rather as finding in Christianity opportunities to supplement them. Certain Christian beliefs or practices might offer exciting new possibilities of access to spiritual power or might fill gaps for which existing methods failed to provide satisfactorily. An interesting example of enrichment was the incorporation into the mythology of the *midewewin* or medicine lodge of the Ojibwas of substantial portions of the cosmology of the early chapters of Genesis, evidently without any sense of incongruity with native elements. The Têtes-de-Boule of the St Maurice, according to Jean Baribeau, filled a gap by looking to Christian priests for help in coping with death, while finding their services redundant in the case of hunting.[19] Such procedures created no difficulties in terms of traditional ways of thought. Indians commonly added songs, stories, and rituals to their repertoire when they perceived them as helpful sources of spiritual power, and there was no difference in principle if the song, story, or ritual happened to have a Christian origin. We need not rule out this simple process of addition even in cases where attachment to Christianity entailed the rejection of customary practices, for this could be interpreted in traditional terms as simply the addition of another taboo. This element of continuity in the adoption of new beliefs and practices is the basis on which many anthropologists regard Christian traits as largely superficial, adding to an existing stock of methods of contact with the spiritual realm without radically changing the nature of the contact.

In many cases, however, we have to recognize that Indians were deliberately breaking with elements of their past. 'All gone now' was the eloquent comment of a converted chief on his former dignities. The struggles of conscience experienced by some Indians testified to a change that went

well beyond the addition of a few items to the existing stock. That Indians
themselves were conscious of having burned many bridges was graphically
illustrated by the separation of the Hurons into Christian and traditional
fur brigades and by the segregation of the Nanaimo Indians along Christian or Pagan Street. Nor are these indications of discontinuity surprising.
In a recent study of Christian approaches to the Indians of the United
States, Henry Warner Bowden assigns marks to various missions in terms
of their willingness or ability to capitalize on similarities between Christianity and native belief and practice.[20] His reminder that rigidity has
placed unnecessary obstacles in the way of conversion is timely, but we
should also remember that apart from significant differences there would
have been little incentive to adopt a new religion. Christianity appealed to
many Indians because they perceived it as, at least in some respects, superior to their traditional beliefs and practices in answering questions, solving
problems, and meeting needs.

Still another possibility, although seldom raised directly, is suggested by
frequent hints in missionary records. Is it conceivable that for many and
perhaps even for most Indians the profession of Christianity was a subtle
but effective way of rejecting it? Such a possibility lurks behind Le Caron's
summary of Huron response: 'They will believe all you please, or, at least,
will not contradict you; and they will let you, too, believe what you will.'
It was later conveyed eloquently to Claude Dablon by another Huron:
'You must know that we have a "yes" that means "no."' Åke Hultkrantz
has suggested, even more explicitly, that plains Indians included Christian
elements in the sun dance in order to make it more acceptable to missionaries and secular authorities. Such an accommodation would correspond
with the tendency, often noted in Indian society, to refrain from humiliating others by contradicting them directly. The yes that means no will not
come close to accounting for all Indian conversions, but it places a question
mark after a fair number of them.

These possibilities, although in appearance mutually exclusive, were not
necessarily so to the Indian mind. Any group of people belonging to a
particular culture will inevitably interpret a message originating elsewhere
in terms of familiar concepts and assumptions, for no others will be available to them. If it does not somehow meet existing needs or answer questions already to some extent posed, they will have no way of responding to
it. Conversion to Christianity might therefore be at once a deliberate act of
accepting innovation and a process of supplementing a familiar store of

responses to the spirit world; indeed it is difficult to see how the two could have been separated without severe psychic and social dislocation. It might also happen, as Hultkrantz has suggested, that Indians would bring 'alternate configurations of belief' into play in different situations without reflecting on their possible incompatibility.[21] In all such cases the boundary between authentic Christianity and illegitimate sycretism must ultimately be determined by theological criteria rather than by measurements of the degree to which one set of norms has been replaced by another. And even the third possibility is not necessarily so incompatible with genuine adherence to Christianity as it appears, for one must still ask more precisely what Indians have intended by their yes and their no. Was it always Christianity itself to which their yes meant no, or could it sometimes have been the frame in which it was mounted?

A few comparisons with the Christianity of Europeans may help to place that of Indians in better perspective. Historical memory commonly involves a certain telescoping of time, so that European Christianity gives the impression of having always been there. Yet not only was the process of christianization slower than it appears in retrospect, but the problems were often astonishingly similar to those encountered among the Indians. As late as the fifth century the clergy of Rome were seeking vainly to suppress the Lupercalia, and St John's fire was on the way out only in the eighteenth. The desire to recover the supposed purity of primitive Christianity from the contamination resulting from successive contacts with new cultures precipitated the major crisis of the Protestant Reformation a millennium after the introduction of Christianity to northern Europe. If the Indians have had their own misapprehensions of Christianity, these have not necessarily been more serious than many that have persisted in European congregations over the centuries. Some aspects, such as the inseparability of love of God from love of neighbour, they may have understood more readily. A young Mississauga convert summed up a reaction not infrequently expressed: 'To us Indians it is very strange you have the Bible and missionary so many years and you so many rogues yet; the Indian have missionary only little while, and we all turn Christian.'[22] Time has shown that he did not speak the whole truth, but he spoke a portion of it worth keeping in mind.

A realistic evaluation of Indian Christianity must take account not only of what the Indians made of Christianity but of what it did for them. That it

did a great deal for many individuals, and often for whole communities, is
scarcely open to question. Nothing less can be inferred from Indian testimonies and from descriptions of vigorous community life, even when due
allowance has been made for the over-optimism of missionary reports.
Some of the benefits so appreciated were immediate and tangible: freedom
from disorder in seventeenth-century Iroquoia, opportunities for replacing
old leadership roles that were losing their significance, not least brighter
prospects of survival and even a measure of prosperity. Other benefits were
less easy to measure. Nature as traditionally conceived could be too mysterious and threatening, Christianity a release from nameless fears. There
was a sociability and a sense of happening about many missionary communities that made them refuges from isolation and boredom, to the great
annoyance of company officials when they drew Indians from fur-produc-
ing areas. The primary benefit for many was simply the assurance of being
accepted by a God of love, an assurance especially important in situations
where the Indian was widely regarded as an anomaly on the road to extinction. To evaluate the impact of Christianity without taking account of this
element of delight or even ecstasy is to miss the most impressive feature of
Indian Christianity.

Despite this record of achievement, one cannot follow the story of Indian
Christianity over the years without becoming aware of a growing gap
between expectation and fulfilment. The typical mission went through an
all-too-predictable cycle. The start was often difficult, marked by heroic
efforts to introduce new ways and then by a bitter struggle to root out
remnants of traditional practice. There would follow a period of flowering,
marked by contagious enthusiasm on the part of converts and optimistic
reports of social changes willingly accepted if not always effectively carried
through. All too soon the mission would enter a period of stability, during
which the slogans of success retained their currency but few further signs
of advance were reported. Enthusiasm would gradually fade, and reports
would take on a note of pessimism or at best of hope deferred. In some
areas, notably the southern prairies, the period of flowering failed to intervene and missions passed imperceptibly from the period of initial difficulty
into that of apparent decline. Few even of the most successful missions,
however, were immune to the process of decay. Lorette, Sault-Saint-Louis,
Fairfield, Netley Creek, and Metlakatla were all held up in their day as
models of what a mission should be, only to fall victim to disillusionment
and domestic strife. Extremes of optimism and pessimism were probably

least evident in areas remote from white settlement, where success was more gradual and apparently longer-lasting.

The first sign of something wrong was usually a loss of the momentum that characterized the initial stages of contact. Indians still went to church and practised the duties of Christianity faithfully, but they seemed uninterested in making further progress. The native Christian leaders that at first seemed to appear as if by magic were no longer forthcoming, and those that could be recruited often lacked the charismatic appeal of their predecessors. Commitment to community improvement also seemed to dissipate. Indians began to neglect their farms, and after a while missionaries noted with dismay that some of them were returning to their former nomadic habits. In his 1860 charge Bishop Anderson of Rupert's Land summed up an almost universal complaint: 'The word is heard with joy and received with readiness; but it is the development of the rich fruit which the minister looks for, and looks too often in vain.'[23] Although we cannot be certain that this plateau of achievement was as unsatisfactory to Indians as to their missionaries, time would show that Anderson had some reason for concern.

With the passing of the first enthusiasm for change there was almost invariably associated a loss of good feeling. Sometimes, as in Huronia and later in coastal British Columbia, this was a direct result of the introduction of Christianity and took the form of confrontation between Christians and 'pagans.' In time, as most band members became at least nominally Christian, faction of this sort usually resolved itself into a tug-of-war between predominantly young 'progressives' who supported the missionaries' pressure for change and 'traditionalists' who opposed it. The missionaries, who depended on the support of the progressives, favoured them for positions of leadership and consequently had to try to placate threatened chiefs and elders. Since old status-structures proved remarkably resilient, the result was often a division of loyalties that lasted over generations. In other cases the sources of faction were within the community itself, sometimes personal jealousies and sometimes family quarrels that might have antedated the establishment of the mission. Difficulties could be particularly acute when members of different bands or even tribes were mixed together in a single village and when, therefore, new patterns of status had to be worked out. Whatever their source, they contributed to a fragmentation of communal life from which a mission was fortunate indeed to be free.[24]

Resentment was often directed against the missionaries themselves. Although dissension was not always the result of the missionary presence, it inevitably involved the mission. All factions might court it, or else one faction might claim its support and thus alienate the others. The frequency with which missionary intervention in community affairs raised tempers to white heat suggests a widespread lack of trust. At Fairfield, for example, Moravian opposition to a sale of land by the band chiefs set off an agitation that caused ill feeling for many years. More common, however, was a chronic sullenness that denied the missionaries the willing co-operation to which they believed themselves entitled. The Jesuits of Wikwemikong complained that parishioners would not contribute voluntary labour to the building of their own church or even unload provisions for the missionaries without charge.[25] At one stage in the history of this station, relations became so strained that the missionaries complained of being treated like strangers. Dislike of the missionaries did not necessarily mean relaxation of Christian fervour. Although relations at Wikwemikong were unusually stormy (or their chronicler unusually frank), the inhabitants could always stage an impressive display on Corpus Christi Day.

Rivalries and resentments were complicated, and sometimes permanently institutionalized, by the existence of competing agencies eager to take advantage of them. Schism eventually resulted from the dispute at Fairfield when the Methodists secured a following among the disaffected. They were no more successful than the Moravians in maintaining harmony among their members, and a further splinter group turned to the Anglicans. The Methodists were particularly anxious to rescue the Indians from Roman Catholicism, taking advantage of strife between priests and people to establish congregations at both Oka and Caughnawaga. Baptists got their start among the Tuscaroras through a dispute over the status of an Anglican catechist there. When the Methodists introduced their national Epworth League program at Port Simpson in 1900, the well-established Christian Band of Workers previously organized by Crosby refused to co-operate and thus provided a magnificent opportunity for the newly arrived Salvation Army. Indeed, the record of sheep-stealing raids is almost endless. Edward F. Wilson, although employed by the CMS ostensibly to reach Indians destitute of the gospel, was able to establish a circuit of four missions only by invading as many former Methodist strongholds.[26]

Confrontation reached a peak of absurdity in the battle of the cakes on Manitoulin. Both Anglican and Roman Catholic missions customarily entertained the islanders on New Year's Day. In 1850 the Anglican cakes at Manitowaning were noticeably larger than their counterparts at Wikwemikong, with the result that for a few hours a mass defection of Roman Catholics was threatened. T.G. Anderson wrote of this island, as might have been written of many parts of Canada:

The Tribes in this part of the country are not in the least indisposed (while they remain heathen) to associate together amicably, so far as similarity of habits is concerned; but when they embrace Christianity, and attach themselves to different Churches, it appears necessary to have each denomination in separate villages.[27]

The ultimate expression of dissatisfaction was a return to traditional practices. Although the implications of occasionally resorting to these seemed less serious to most Indians than to the missionaries, persistence in them was both a challenge to the missionaries and an indication of failure to satisfy Indian aspirations. Although missionaries made fewer references to such practices than one might expect, they were discouraged to find that ancestral traditions had a way of reappearing in places where they were thought to have died out. In 1910 a Methodist commission was told that 'pagan' customs were more entrenched in Alberta than they had been thirty years before. Sorcery, which had been discountenanced in pre-contact Indian societies, flourished more than ever in some Christian communities.[28]

These specific problems were symptomatic of a more general malaise of which the most persistent manifestation was an apathy that choked initiative and dampened morale. From comparatively early years many missionaries referred to the necessity of coaxing Indians to church or even of rounding them up at service times. Chants that thrilled converts to Roman Catholicism left their children indifferent. Local leadership was seldom forthcoming, and those who sought to exercise it found themselves ridiculed or put down as presumptuous. A Methodist missionary complained in 1925 that Indians expected to be paid even for whitewashing their own houses. The same apathy was a factor in personal problems. People with little to occupy their minds spent their spare time gossiping about each other, criticizing the clergy and other resident officials, and quarrelling with their spouses. They also engaged in various forms of antisocial behaviour, from alcoholism to Saturday-night altercations to petty crime.[29] The situation was one that made for a lack of frankness between missionaries and people. The yes that marked the first flush of conversion had become, in many cases, the yes that means no.

In 1937 J.C. Heinrich, an American missionary in the Punjab, analysed in *The Psychology of a Suppressed People* various responses to missionary work in his field. The book is larded with somewhat amateurish psychological jargon, but many of the practical observations are acute. Heinrich noted three common types of reaction among those whom he designated 'suppressed people.' 'Direct reactions' take the form of overt expressions of resentment, usually directed against members of the peer group. 'Concealment reactions,' as their name implies, involve an inscrutability that masks true feelings. 'Indirect reactions' include clever devices for humiliating or frustrating those who cannot be directly opposed as well as various forms of rebellion against social convention. Lethargy and sterile imitations of white ways are common, but underlying all is a deep antipathy towards the missionary. On the other side the missionary is also subject to severe strains. Finding himself under constant scrutiny but seldom able to bring about radical change, he is likely to accept compensation in 'the subtle reinforcement of his own sense of esteem and self-importance.'[30] Although such phenomena as concealment and jealousy of over-achievers have been traced back to attitudes of long standing in North American Indian culture, it is not difficult to recognize in Heinrich's descriptions many parallels with the pathology so often evident in Canadian missions.

To name the problem is to recognize that it was not solely, or even primarily, the creation of the missions. The symptoms that have been described are, as Heinrich notes, those typical of a social class weighed down by poverty and humiliation. The poverty and helplessness of the Indians were brought about by a great variety of factors: depletion by fur traders, lumbermen, and settlers of the resources on which their economy had originally depended; the diseases and demoralizing influences that seemed to be inevitable concomitants of white contact; a government policy of paternalistic wardship against which the missionaries repeatedly protested, along with a propensity for penny-pinching that starved church schools of the funds necessary for efficient operation and drove them to cutthroat competition. All too often, moreover, missionary attempts to alleviate the conditions under which Indians lived were frustrated by the land-hunger of whites who claimed to be Christian.[31] To note the demoralization evident in many missions is not to suggest that the most enlightened attitudes on the part of the missionaries would necessarily have brought about more than a marginal improvement of conditions. To a great extent they were prisoners of a situation that inevitably moulded their own approach as well.

If the missionaries did not create the so-called Indian problem, however, they made their own contribution to it. In 1875 George Young, the Methodist superintendent of missions for Manitoba and the northwest, reported after a visit to Norway House:

I felt it my duty here and elsewhere to speak with plainness on the real mission of a missionary, informing the Indians that it was not to scatter presents, either food or clothing, so much as to teach them the way to the Saviour. The idea of some of them seems to be, that a missionary must be a sort of unweariable giver, and with such I am sure I must have made myself very unpopular.[32]

Although he cannot have endeared himself to his host Egerton R. Young, who was famed for his open-handedness, he was one of the first to identify dependence on the missionaries as a major source of difficulty. Dependency began in material things, whether with food from the missionary's larder or with the clothing boxes regularly sent by women's societies in England and eastern Canada to the west.[33] It extended to a multitude of services; missionaries dispensing government drugs and performing a host of other functions became, as Arthur Barner remarked, 'more like fathers than ordinary missionaries.' In some cases the missionary was expected to oversee almost every aspect of community life. The precedent was established during the French regime of encouraging residents of the mission to seek the advice or even the permission of the missionary for any activities beyond the usual, and it was still being followed in the far north in the nineteenth century.[34] Fine as the motives and great as the need may have been, the very fact that the missionary was on the spot and eager to help encouraged the creation of a clientele rather than a responsible membership. The missionary often became, in effect, the only adult member of an Indian community. Parishioners, who had turned to Christianity in the hope of receiving a new accession of power, found instead that power slipped more and more into missionary hands.

If the problems of Indians today are by no means all the fault of the missions, the fact remains that Indians looked to the churches for a sense of belonging as they did not look to the government or the trading companies. When they now lump all three together as elements of a single oppressive presence, they include the churches with a particular sense of disappointment and betrayal. On them as on no others they pinned hopes of reintegration that have not been fulfilled. And if the limitations of Indian churches are not different in kind from those readily visible in others, they have been aggravated by factors making for a peculiar sense of alienation. White Christians, no matter how remote they may feel from the decision-making processes of their churches, are at least able to anticipate that for the most part the churches will legitimate and undergird the folkways and values of their culture. Indians, by contrast, have experienced the church as an institution constantly denigrating their culture and seeking to displace its values. It is not surprising, therefore, that recent expressions of Indian discontent have borne with special severity upon the churches.

Estimates of the effects of Christian missions on Indian life are likely to depend, in the final analysis, on whether they are distinguished from the total impact of the European presence or included as an integral part of it. If reckoned as a distinct entity, they may well be seen as mitigating some of its harmful effects. If lumped in, they will almost certainly be condemned for their complicity in undermining the bases of Indian society. Since the missionaries were at once emissaries of Christ and associates of Caesar, there is no basis on which one can make an unambiguous judgment between these alternatives.

An important chapter in Canadian history and a major determinant in the formation of contemporary Indian society, the encounter between Christian missionaries and the native peoples is also an instructive example of a more general phenomenon: the dissemination of a message across a significant cultural barrier. Such transmission has taken place on many occasions, successfully at least in the sense that the message has been accepted and has given apparent satisfaction to those receiving it. Christianity had already leapt two formidable cultural barriers when it encountered the Indians of Canada. Buddhism spread from India as far as Japan; Islam moved out from a narrow base in Arabia to encompass vastly diverse peoples from Spain to Indonesia, and even a religion as ethnocentric as Judaism made a profound impression on the Khazars of eastern Russia. Secular movements such as Marxism have demonstrated the same capacity. Whatever may have been the obstacles in the way, missionaries to the Indians were not attempting an intrinsically impossible task.

For successful transmission to occur, however, certain conditions must be met. It will be helpful if the bearers of the message have a strong desire to transmit it, almost essential that they have confidence in its truth and value. Those on the other side must have a desire to receive it, arising out of either a sense of unfulfilled need or the anticipation of possible enrichment. If the senders of the message take the initiative, we will speak of a missionary thrust; if the receivers, of religious, cultural, or ideological borrowing. In almost every case, however, elements of both will be present. There will also need to be a certain fit between the message and the perceived needs of the receiving culture. There must be enough points of contact that the message will be intelligible to those who hear it, enough differences that it will imply significant criticisms of the existing order and thus appeal to the actually or potentially dissatisfied.

The process of transmission involves serious risks. On the one hand, the assimilative power of the host culture may lead to a reinterpretation of the message that renders it essentially different from what it had originally been. Leslie Dewart has argued that Christianity was thus distorted in the process of being adopted by Graeco-Roman society, Thomas Hoover that Buddhism suffered a similar fate in passing from India to China. On the other hand, the message may so overwhelm the host society that in effect it destroys it or renders it dysfunctional. Edward Gibbon suggested this possibility in *The Decline and Fall of the Roman Empire*. In the former case the message will lose its distinctiveness and thereby its power to effect the transformation that made it attractive in the first place. In the latter, those who accept the message will lose the ability to respond to it creatively or to use it as a basis of renewal and reconstruction. As a sociologist has written, 'Missions are natural social laboratories in which the most critical (and dangerous) variables are customarily manipulated.'[35] Even where the results have been apparently most favourable, there are always those who contend that the price paid on one side or the other was too high.

If the hazards are to be minimized, some safeguards for both the message and the receiving society will be necessary. The natural custodians of the message are those who carry it, who must be vigilant to ensure its authenticity and must retain some authority to give or withhold legitimation as variant versions arise. Messages crossing cultural boundaries, such as Christianity, Islam, and in more recent times Marxism, have customarily and appropriately been protected by canons of scripture and other repositories of authoritative teaching as well as by provisions for an orderly succession of authorized teachers. The natural guardians of a culture are its representative leaders, whether kings, chiefs, elders, or shamans. They are the persons best able to judge when the weight of a message endangers the integrity of the culture and to stand up for what they see as valid and even essential in it, and to do so effectively they must retain their position and status. Some risks must be taken, however, if genuine communication is to be established. There can never be a complete fit between a message and the culture to which it is offered, for differences of language and background will affect the ways in which the message is heard, and the motives of those who welcome it will never correspond precisely with the intentions of those who offer it. Accordingly there will need to be adaptation on one side or the other, and probably on both. The message will have to be tailored in order to be exportable, while the culture will have to bend in order to receive it. Flexibility, tact, and sometimes stubbornness will all be necessary.

In practice, cross-cultural transmission has been greatly facilitated by the emergence of bridge figures, persons able to operate as insiders with respect to both the message and the host culture. St Paul is the best-known Christian example, while Hui Neng had a similar importance in naturalizing Buddhism in China. Such persons, operating on both sides of the boundary, have an unusual ability to make their message speak to the circumstances of those to whom it is addressed. They are able to take particular advantage of common elements in order to obtain a ready hearing. They recognize more readily than most the necessity of adaptation on both sides. Most helpfully of all, they are able to discriminate with exceptional clarity between expendable elements and ones that cannot be compromised. Their availability has sometimes made the difference between a mechanical blend of ideas and a creative process of adaptation.

Several of the elements necessary for successful transmission were clearly present in the encounter between Christian propagandists and the Indians of Canada. There was a strong sense of compulsion to present the message, despite formidable logistic difficulties and the anticipation of severe hardships. Equally there was eagerness to accept the message, conspicuous at one time or another in almost every part of Canada. If inevitably there was not a perfect fit between message and culture, there were important ingredients of one. Indians, especially of hunting-gathering cultures, could readily assimilate Christian beliefs in a creator God, in his manifestation as spirit, in the importance of individual response, and through their shamanic rituals in the experience of some sort of death and resurrection as essential to communion with God. They could also find in Christianity some elements which their own traditions lacked, notably a dynamic view of history that helped them to cope with unexpected and disconcerting change.

There were also factors that seriously inhibited the successful transmission of Christianity. Some of these were inherent in the nature of the encounter; to borrow the terminology of Northrop Frye, it was not easy for missionaries who understood only descriptive language to establish rapport with Indians who spoke habitually in metaphors.[36] The most serious difficulties, however, arose from the circumstances of contact. The message was hemmed in by almost too many safeguards, for the missionaries occupied a position of strength in which they were seldom compelled to make more than slight concessions to Indian taste and were almost never challenged to discriminate between essential and expendable elements of traditional Christianity. By contrast, the culture was under relentless pressure from a technically superior and militarily more powerful society, so that chiefs and elders were thus seldom able to negotiate adjustments that would help it to accommodate the message. The most serious obstacle to the reception of Christianity by the Indians was simply this lack of reciprocity. The insensitivity of the missionaries to Indian culture and values would have done little harm and might in a measure have been overcome if they had been compelled more often like Chazelle to argue their points in fair debate.

Measured by the criteria that have been suggested, the transmission of the Christian message to the Indians of Canada has been at least partially successful. The missionaries were persuasive enough, the host culture receptive enough, and the correspondence between offer and response close enough to bring most Indians into a Christian church and to make Christianity, for many, the great passion of their lives. Where the process broke down was in its failure to enable the message to be received in a manner that would release creative energies. There have been no significant Indian contributions to theology or liturgy, even heterodox theology or unconventional liturgy, and until recently no development of an indigenous Christian art. There has been only a handful of leaders influential beyond their own constituencies and (until the 1983 assembly of the World Council of Churches at Vancouver) no community that has contributed significantly to the life of the world church. Instead, a lack of opportunities to defend Indian culture legitimately within the church has commonly given rise to silent resistance, and such creativity as has been stimulated by Christianity has often been put at the service of movements hostile to the missions. If the measure of success is that most Indians have become Christian, the measure of failure is that Christianity has not become Indian.

And yet there have been moments when something more seemed possible, when a genuine Indian Christianity seemed in process of being born. One such moment was the heyday of Sault-Saint-Louis, when enthusiastic residents combed the Iroquois cantons to inform all and sundry of the marvellous new life that awaited them if they would only opt for settlement in a Christian community. Another was the springtime of Methodist revival in Upper Canada, when the Welsh-Ojibwa Peter Jones manifested many of the qualities of the bridge figure so vital to cross-cultural encounter. Assiginack, if he had not been allowed to become estranged from his church, might have performed a similar function.[37] One thinks also of the elusive pre-missionary Christianity of British Columbia and of the continuing leadership of families such as the Iserhoffs among the Anglicans of northern Quebec. Such spontaneous movements were welcomed, but always the missionaries seemed to feel a compulsion to bring them under control and ultimately to conform them to the safe patterns of European Christianity. There was always an eagerness to give Christianity to the Indians, seldom a willingness to allow them to receive it.

Such movements were not all phenomena of a distant past. Not long before his death, Dr Selwyn Dewdney recounted to me the story of an unusual Christian community in northern Ontario.[38] Early in this century the Crees and Ojibwas of the Big Trout Lake area were profoundly affected by the evangelical Anglican preaching of William Dick, a Cree catechist from York Factory. By 1960, however, Big Trout was overwhelmed by outside influences that polluted the lake as well as local morals. A number of older men, spurred on by the zeal of catechist Jeremiah Mackay, decided that the only remedy was to establish a truly Christian settlement some sixty miles to the east. Kasabonika, when he visited it in 1965, struck Dewdney as an extraordinary place. Clearly visible from the air was a large rectangular enclosure with a puzzling extension in the form of a cross. The enclosure, it turned out, was modelled on the New Jerusalem as described in Revelation 21. Streets were laid out in crosses and diagonals to conform with the design of the Union Jack, a reminder of the community's Anglicanism, although none of the houses yet built was sited in relation to the pattern. Most impressive of all was a collection of two or three thousand sheets of paper constituting what Dewdney described as 'no less than a Cree-Ojibwa "Talmud" commentary, perhaps interspersed with sermons.' There was no inclination to incorporate elements of traditional religious practice, which was anathema to devout evangelicals, but here was certainly an indigenous form of Christianity.

If this analysis is correct, it suggests an interpretation of the encounter between Christianity and the Indians of Canada other than that ordinarily given. The effective transfer of a message requires that it be both offered and received. Paying most attention to the offer, we have commonly pictured the Indians as reluctant and recalcitrant. Much evidence suggests, rather, that most of them were eager for Christianity but that they were allowed to receive it only on terms destructive to their culture and humiliating to their pride. On this understanding, syncretistic movements can be interpreted not as rejections of Christianity but as attempts to appropriate it on terms consonant with native modes of thought and relevant to perceived needs. Resistance, in this interpretation, was less often to Christianity itself than to the cultural genocide that seemed inseparable from it. Acceptance pointed to possibilities that in other circumstances might have been capable of realization.

Postscript

Surveying the position of the churches among the Indians of Canada today, one could easily conclude that the story told in this volume belongs essentially to the past. It has now become clear, as it should always have been clear, that no set of beliefs or values can be imposed on the Indians. They will decide their own religious future, and their decisions will inevitably be affected by unhappy memories of missionary father-figures and regimented residential schools. Understandably, many Indians identify Christianity with oppression and look wistfully to older traditions which the missionaries consistently attempted to wrest from their grasp. Among Christian denominations only Pentecostalism and other forms of conservative Protestantism are currently expanding, and their approaches are so obviously imported from the United States that one wonders how long even they can avoid being caught by a backlash against all forms of alien incursion. The outlook for Christianity does not seem promising. Yet an analysis of encounter in the past may warn us against closing the books prematurely.

It needs to be remembered, in the first place, that Christianity is not a recent arrival but has been a factor in Indian life for almost four hundred years. Over many generations Indians have been making the sign of the cross, treasuring prayer books in their own tongues, singing hymns to Jesus, and performing various leadership functions within Christian communities. In an era of rebellion against oppressive structures these memories have for many the taste of dust and ashes. In Indian communities the churches are distinctly on trial, and suspicion of the intentions of white Canadians is deeply rooted. Yet recent experience has turned up considerable evidence of readiness to respond positively when once the terms of the encounter are changed, and in some cases it seems that Indians have been waiting impatiently for opportunities to negotiate new terms. Christianity has penetrated the Indian consciousness so deeply that in the long run it may prove as difficult to eradicate as the indigenous traditions that have so often prematurely been pronounced moribund.

On their side the churches are no longer saddled as in the past with the civilizing mission that did so much to inhibit reciprocity in their relations with Indians. Conservative evangelicals probably owe a good deal of their success to the fact that they do not have to answer for the irritations of the old regime. Since the 1960s the approach of the longer-established missionary agencies has also changed almost beyond recognition. Instead of imposing ready-made programs they now appear eager to listen to Indians, to encourage and appropriate the values inherent in their traditions, and to support them in their concerns without seeking to control them. Quite apart from their own attitudes, the fact that the churches are no longer in a position to use their connections to compel a hearing forces them to depend on Indian responses to their message as they have not had to do since pioneer days.

In view of the widespread evidence of current disenchantment with Christianity, these assets may seem meagre. The disheartened members of broken tribes who once turned eagerly to the missionaries as offering their only hope of personal and social revitalization have been replaced by aggressive and militant graduates of residential schools who are determined to find their own path without reliance on know-it-all white advisers. It may yet prove, however, that the emergence of angry Indians capable of articulating their criticisms of the missions is precisely the catalyst needed to make possible the fruitful encounter between Christianity and Indian culture that has somehow always failed to take place. The factor most seriously inhibiting the transmission of Christianity in the past, I have argued, was a disparity in power between the senders and receivers of the message. In setting the terms on which Christianity would be accommodated into native societies the missionaries had to concede almost nothing, the Indians almost everything. The result was, all too often, a mere imitation of European Christianity and in the long run sullen resentment. The reassertion of Indian pride and self-awareness, on this analysis, is a necessary condition of achieving the reciprocity without which the transmission of Christianity is bound to be sterile and insecure. Venn's dream of self-governing, self-supporting, and self-propagating churches has received at least partial fulfilment in many parts of the world during the twentieth century. It has done so not so much through the magnanimity of Western missionary authorities as through the insistence of indigenous leaders, and change has come about only after the venting of considerable indignation. It is conceivable that current Indian critiques will be seen some day to have represented a major breakthrough towards the shaping of an indigenous Christianity. It is inconceivable that such a breakthrough should come about without the intervention of articulate and sometimes abrasive native leaders.

In this situation much will depend on the ability of the churches to respond creatively. The bond attaching Indians to the churches are fragile, and perhaps in some cases irretrievably broken. There remains a reservoir of Christian spirituality among the Indians but no corresponding reservoir of trust. The churches are learning lessons, but they still have lessons to learn. The more conservative churches have had considerable success in establishing personal rapport with Indians, but they have yet to demonstrate a will to understand Indian culture or an appreciation of the significance of Indian movements. Churches of longer experience are more in tune with native aspirations, but they retain a vast confidence in the universal efficacy of favoured remedies that may contain the seeds of new and more subtle forms of paternalism. In the past the churches concentrated on pressing Indians to accept what they had to offer. Now they must learn how to let the Indians receive the offer in their own way, and they will be able to do so only as they also learn to receive from the Indians. If such mutuality can be established, the hostility to Christianity evident in many quarters today may yet prove to have been a no that means yes.

Abbreviations

COLLECTIONS

AA	Archives of the General Synod of the Anglican Church of Canada
AAM	Archives de l'archevêché de Montréal
AAQ	Archives de l'archevêché de Québec
AASB	Archives de l'archevêché de Saint-Boniface
AD	Archives Deschâtelets (Oblate), Ottawa
AO	Archives of Ontario
HBCA	Archives of the Hudson's Bay Company, Micro PAC
PAC	Public Archives of Canada
UCA	United Church Archives

SOURCES

APF	*Annales de la Propagation de la Foi* (Lyon, if not otherwise noted)
APP	*Acts and Proceedings of the General Assembly of the Presbyterian Church in Canada*
CMS	Church Missionary Society. Unless otherwise noted, references are to the microfilm series in PAC.
FMC	Minutes of the Foreign Mission Committee of the Synod of the Presbyterian Church of Canada (from 1875 of the Presbyterian Church in Canada), UCA
JR	Reuben Gold Thwaites *The Jesuit Relations and Allied Documents* 73 vols (Cleveland: Burrows Brothers Company 1896–1901)

MMS   *Annual Reports of the Missionary Society of the Methodist Church.*
In view of substantial continuity through several ecclesiastical unions
and divisions, the same designation is used for the *Annual Reports of
the Missionary Society of the Canada Conference of the Methodist
Episcopal Church*, founded in 1825, and those of its successors
whether designated 'Wesleyan' or 'Methodist,' UCA.

MN   Until 1845 'Missionary Notices' were included in the *Methodist
Magazine*; from 1846 *Missionary Notices of the Wesleyan Methodist
Church (MN/W)*; from 1 Nov 1847 *Wesleyan Missionary Notices,
Canadian (MN/WC)*; from 1874 *Missionary Notices of the Methodist
Church of Canada (MN/MC)*, UCA.

MSCC   *Official Minutes of the Missionary Society of the Canadian Church*,
AA

SR   *Studies in Religion / Sciences Religieuses*

WC   Wesleyan Methodist Church (Great Britain) Foreign Missions: America, The British Dominions in North America, Correspondence,
1791–1893. Files on microfilm in UCA.

WFMS   *Annual Reports of the Woman's Foreign Missionary Society of the
Presbyterian Church in Canada (Western Section)*, UCA

Notes

1 TRANSATLANTIC ENCOUNTER

1 *The Voyages of Jacques Cartier* trans and ed H.P. Biggar (Ottawa: King's Printer 1924) 24f; *Collection de manuscrits ... relatifs à la Nouvelle France* 1 (Quebec: A. Coté et Cie 1883) 30

2 Marc Lescarbot 'The Conversion of Savages' *JR* 1: 109, 161–3; 31: 195–7; Pierre Coton to Lorenzo Maggio, 13 Feb 1605, in Lucien Campeau, sj *La première mission d'Acadie (1602–1616)* Monumenta Historica Societatis Iesu 96 (Quebec: Les Presses de l'Université Laval 1967) 8f; Pierre Lamart to Claudio Aquaviva, general of the Society of Jesus, 23 Sept 1608, ibid 33–5

3 Such at any rate was Biencourt's story. Campeau (ibid 206f) dismisses it as a lame excuse.

4 *JR* 1: 135–7

5 William V. Bangert, sj *A History of the Society of Jesus* (St Louis: The Institute of Jesuit Sources 1972) 21, 200f

6 A standard edition in English is *The Spiritual Exercises of St. Ignatius* ed Louis J. Puhl, sj (Westminister, Md: Newman 1951).

7 C.J. Mersereau 'The First Missionary in Canada, Ennémond Massé' *Canadian Catholic Historical Association Report* 19 (1952) 13–17; *JR* 2: 247–75

8 *The Works of Samuel de Champlain* ed H.P. Biggar (Toronto: Champlain Society 1922–36) 4: 27–9, 31

9 Chrestien Le Clercq *First Establishment of the Faith in New France* trans John Gilmary Shea (New York: John G. Shea 1881) 1: 93; Gabriel Sagard *The Long Journey into the Country of the Hurons* ed George M. Wrong, trans H.H. Langton (Toronto: Champlain Society 1939)

10 Le Clercq *First Establishment* 1: 264, 200f, 226f, 158

11 *JR* 5: 107–11

12 John Corbett 'The World to Come: The Millenarian Tradition in Christianity: Its Original Transmission' *Canadian Society of Church History Papers* 1975, 64–103; John Foster *Beginning from Jerusalem* (London: United Society for Christian Lit-

erature 1959) chaps 1–4; J. Labourt *Le christianisme dans l'empire perse sous la dynastie sassanide (224–632)* (Paris: Librairie Victor Lecoffre 1904)

13 For a fuller discussion of ecclesiastical initiative in discovery, see H.H. Walsh *The Church in the French Era* (Toronto: Ryerson 1965) 14–16.

14 A.P. Newton *The European Nations in the West Indies* (London: A. and C. Black 1933) 18f

15 Tertullian, Apology 21; Max J. Kohler 'The Doctrine that "Christianity is Part of the Common Law"' *Publications of the American Jewish Historical Society* 31 (1928) 105–34

16 J.W. Allen *A History of Political Thought in the Sixteenth Century* (London: Methuen 1928) 273f, 286

17 *Collection de manuscrits* 1: 70

18 Standard authorities are: on the eastern Algonquians, Alfred G. Bailey *The Conflict of European and Eastern Algonkian Cultures, 1504–1700* 2nd edn (Toronto: University of Toronto Press 1969); on the Hurons, Bruce G. Trigger *The Children of Aataentsic: A History of the Huron People to 1650* (Montreal: McGill-Queen's University Press 1976); on the Micmacs, William D. Wallis and Ruth Sawtell Wallis *The Micmac Indians of Eastern Canada* (Minneapolis: University of Minnesota Press 1955).

19 Weston La Barre *The Ghost Dance: Origins of Religion* (New York: Dell 1972) 125; S.A. Holling 'Pre-Columbian Medicine among Indians in Ontario,' unpublished paper presented to the Mississauga South Historical Society, 17 Jan 1978, 3; Bailey *Conflict of European and Eastern Algonkian Cultures* xix–xxi, 84ff

20 James G.E. Smith *Leadership among the Southwestern Ojibwa* Publications in Ethnology 7 (Ottawa: National Museums of Canada 1973) 17; Diamond Jenness *The Ojibwa Indians of Parry Island: Their Social and Religious Life* National Museum of Canada bulletin 78, Anthropological Series 17 (Ottawa: King's Printer 1935) 94

21 Wallis and Wallis *Micmac Indians* 212–22; JR 1: 283; Chrestien Le Clercq *New Relation of Gaspesia* ed W.F. Ganong (Toronto: Champlain Society 1910) 226; J.W.E. Newbery 'Ethics for Environment: Native American Insights,' in *Ethics for Environment: Three Religious Ideologies* ed Dane Steffenson, Walter J. Herrscher, and Robert S. Cook (Green Bay, Wis: UWGB Ecumenical Center 1973) 58. The term 'sacred hoop' is originally from Black Elk.

22 Mircea Eliade *The Sacred and the Profane: The Nature of Religion* trans Willard R. Trask (New York: Harcourt, Brace, and World, Harvest Books 1959) 21f; Mircea Eliade *Shamanism: Archaic Techniques of Ecstasy* trans Willard R. Trask, Bollingen Series 7 (New York: Bollingen Foundation 1964) 5–8. The most illuminating exposition of the meanings implicit in Indian religious practice is probably still Hartley Burr Alexander *The World's Rim: Great Mysteries of the North American Indians* (Lincoln, Neb: University of Nebraska Press 1953).

23 Bailey *Conflict of European and Eastern Algonkian Cultures* 157f. Oddly, Gluskap became well known only with the publication of Silas T. Rand *Legends of the Micmacs* (New York: Longmans 1894). Almost every early missionary in Upper Canada had stories about Nanabozho.

24 There is a detailed description of an Ojibwa vision-quest in Jenness *Ojibwa Indians* 47ff.

25 Lewis H. Morgan *The League of the Iroquois* (Secaucus, NJ: Citadel 1962) 156

26 *Voyages of Jacques Cartier* 61f; for the first reference to an 'optimum' period of contact, J.W. Anderson 'Eastern Cree Indians' *Historical and Scientific Society of Manitoba Papers* 3, no 2 (1946) 31; Bailey *Conflict of European and Eastern Algonkian Cultures*: on liquor, 66–74; on disease, 75–8; on sexual mores, 99–115

27 *JR* 2: 201; Sagard *Long Journey* 140; *JR* 5: 191; 7: 21; 8: 185. In comparing French and Indian attitudes, here and elsewhere, I am greatly indebted to the works of Cornelius J. Jaenen, especially *Friend and Foe: Aspects of French-Amerindian Culture Contact in the Sixteenth and Seventeenth Centuries* (Toronto: McClelland and Stewart 1976).

28 *JR* 1: 287; 2: 75; Le Clercq *First Establishment* 1: 216; *JR* 8: 27

29 Åke Hultkrantz 'The Problem of Christian Influence on Northern Algonkian Eschatology' *SR* 9, no 2 (1980) 173n

30 'A wandering Aramean was my father' (Deut 26:5); Diamond Jenness 'Canadian Indian Religion,' in *Religion in Canadian Society* ed Stewart Crysdale and Les Wheatcroft (Toronto: Macmillan 1976) 14

31 John M. Cooper 'The Northern Algonquian Supreme Being' *Primitive Man* 6, nos 3, 4 (July-Oct 1933) 42, 51; Werner Müller 'North America,' in Walter Krickeberg et al *Pre-Columbian American Religions* (New York: Holt, Rinehart, and Winston 1969) 187; Job 1:6

32 Benjamin Lee Whorf *Language, Thought, and Reality* ed John B. Carroll (Cambridge, Mass: MIT Press 1964) 154; George F.G. Stanley 'The Indian Background of Canadian History' *Canadian Historical Association Report* 1952, 20; for a distinction between 'compact' and 'diffuse' time, Philip K. Bock in *The Native Peoples of Atlantic Canada: A History of Ethnic Interaction* ed Henry Franklin McGee, jr, Carleton Library 72 (Toronto: McClelland and Stewart 1974) 153; between 'nuclear' and 'peripheral' territories, Tom McFeat in ibid 167; *JR* 2: 19

2 'OVERTHROWING THE COUNTRY'

1 Candide de Nant *Pages glorieuses de l'épopée canadienne* (Montreal: Le Devoir 1927) 112; for a detailed examination of possible reasons for the exclusion of the Récollets, John M. Lenhart, ofm cap 'Who Kept the Franciscan Recollects out of Canada in 1632?' *Franciscan Studies* ns 5, no 3: 277–300

2 *JR* 7: 31; Bailey *Conflict of European and Eastern Algonkian Cultures* 56f; *JR* 12: 163

3 *JR* 39: 49; 32: 99; 17: 11; 19: 125, 133–5

4 *JR* 15: 67, 187–9; 17: 229–31; Trigger *Children of Aataentsic* 702

5 *JR* 21: 187ff; 23: 223; 31: 115–19; 34: 227

6 *JR* 30: 187

7 De Nant *Pages glorieuses* 292, 262

8 *JR* 33: 261; 34: 87–93, 27–33; De Nant *Pages glorieuses* 291

9 *Spiritual Exercises* 32f; Le Clercq *First Establishment* 1: 265; *JR* 9: 17, 103; 19: 53–5; 20: 139; 38: 65; Le Clercq *First Establishment* 1: 183, 235; *JR* 11: 53

10 *JR* 18: 239, paraphrasing Ps 72:8–10; *JR* 6: 115; 17: 113–15; 34: 167

11 *Spiritual Exercises* 60–3

12 *JR* 4: 209–15; 7: 31; 5: 91; Sagard *Long Journey* 73f; *JR* 2: 11–13; 7: 21–3; 20: 71–3; Victor Egon Hanzeli *Missionary Linguistics in New France* (The Hague and Paris: Mouton 1969) 19

13 *JR* 2: 41–3; 15: 113; 17: 93; 15: 171; 17: 95, 117–19

14 Sagard *Long Journey* 92; *JR* 2: 73; 38: 257; 8: 121; 2: 77 (Biard); Le Clercq *First Establishment* 1: 216 (Le Caron); *JR* 33: 225–7 (Ragueneau); 23: 151–3; 2: 53

15 *JR* 8: 147; 6: 179; 1: 287f; 11: 69, 71, 261; 9: 239; 7: 157–63; 10: 39–43

16 *JR* 5: 189; 8: 45; 23: 313; 29: 141; 17: 39; 14: 145; 18: 127; 11: 131. Jesuit use of pictures and other visual aids is discussed in François-Marc Gagnon *La conversion par l'image* (Montreal: Bellarmin 1975).

17 *JR* 13: 167; 14: 7–9, 41–3, 67–9; 11: 107; 13: 45, 81; 58: 219

18 Le Clercq *First Establishment* 1: 142; *JR* 11: 139–41; 17: 33; 23: 139; 35: 259; 33: 145–7

19 *JR* 13: 9; 16: 251; 24: 103; 9: 103; 14: 263; 21: 135–9, 293–301

20 *JR* 25: 273–7; 22: 125; 27: 67; 18: 101–9; 24: 127; 18: 139; 19: 137–9

21 *Collection de manuscrits* 1: 65; *JR* 36: 250n–251n; 65: 181–5; 28: 55. The role of the secret Company of the Holy Sacrament in promoting the missions is discussed in E.R. Adair 'The Beginnings of New France' *Canadian Historical Review* 25, no 3 (Sept 1944) 246–78.

22 *JR* 7: 273

23 *JR* 18: 151–3; Trigger *Children of Aataentsic* 671; Gagnon *La conversion par l'image* 42–6; *JR* 5: 107; 13: 173

24 *JR* 8: 49; 11: 187; 14: 267–9; 15: 117–19

25 Sagard *Long Journey* 183; *JR* 12: 253; Sagard *Long Journey* 175

26 *JR* 9: 195–7; 10: 37–49; 12: 237–9; 13: 111; 14: 103; Gagnon *La conversion par l'image* 37f; *JR* 19: 215, 91; 31: 123; 13: 211

27 *JR* 5: 177; 13: 123, 127; 16: 161–3; 18: 205; 23: 49; 13: 171

28 *JR* 23: 129; 39: 123; 15: 177; 13: 145; 19: 197–9; 20: 27–9; 35: 279; Le Clercq *First Establishment* 1: 221

29 *JR* 18: 87; 23: 143–9; 29: 65; 37: 39, 53–5; 18: 197

30 *JR* 2: 23, 229; 13: 135–41; 15: 79; 17: 109; Sagard *Long Journey* 75; *JR* 2: 183

31 Guy Laflèche has suggested that the missionaries succeeded basically by beating the shamans at their own game ('La chamanisme des Amerindiens et des missionnaires de la Nouvelle France' *SR* 9, no 2 [1980] 157f). It was logical, on Indian assumptions, to attach oneself to the strongest power.

32 Trigger *Children of Aataentsic* 565; *JR* 17: 49

33 *JR* 16: 111; 21: 181; 25: 111; 38: 45–9; 19: 123–7; Peter G. LeBlanc 'Indian-Missionary Contact in Huronia, 1615–1640' *Ontario History* 60, no 3 (Sept 1968) 139; *JR* 24: 211

34 'A fourth proof of the true faith of this people was their continual thought of death' (*JR* 37: 47). Since writing this paragraph, I have been interested to note that Jean

Baribeau makes this same point with regard to nineteenth-century missions among the Têtes-de-Boule of the upper St Maurice ('L'influence de l'évangélisation sur la conception de la vie et de la mort chez les Têtes-de-Boule au dix-neuvième siècle' SR 9, no 2 [1980] 137–60).

35 JR 19: 197–9; 25: 249; 26: 25
36 JR 22: 223; 16: 79, 83; 20: 143–5; 33: 35; 29: 201; 21: 159; 25: 163; 2: 227; 26: 263; 27: 21
37 JR 14: 201–3; Sagard Long Journey 193; Le Clercq First Establishment 1: 219; JR 3: 117; 5: 159; 6: 201; 8: 123; 10: 195; 12: 19–23; 28: 53; 33: 193
38 JR 34: 105, 217
39 JR 42: 135; 43: 291
40 JR 42: 113; Trigger Children of Aataentsic 750, 828

3 AFTER THE EARTHQUAKE

1 JR 37: 99; 35: 53, 55–7; 36: 53; 60: 119, 129; 61: 103; 62: 205, 215
2 JR 35: 131; 33: 267; 40: 213; 42: 221; 44: 237, 249, 251
3 JR 45: 119–21. In 1650 Druillettes was said to have spent four winters with the Indians (JR 36: 53).
4 JR 43: 135; 42: 215–17; 44: 95
5 This mission is studied in some depth in James S. Pritchard 'For the Glory of God: The Quinte Mission 1660–1680' Ontario History 65, no 3 (Sept 1973) 133–48.
6 So it appears from a list of early graduates in Camille de Rochemonteix Les Jésuites et la Nouvelle-France au XVIIIe siècle 1: 25n.
7 JR 44: 15; 58: 183–5; 54: 69–73; 59: 71; 61: 229–31; 64: 177; 52: 171; 51: 231; 56: 189; 53: 261
8 H.-R. Casgrain Les Sulpiciens et les prêtres des Missions Etrangères en Acadie (1676–1762) (Quebec: Pruneau & Kirouac 1897) 23lf; JR 52: 149; 55: 153; 37: 261; 61: 159
9 JR 52: 119–21; 53: 207–9 ('Point to Point' is discussed at length in Gagnon La conversion par l'image chap 4); 55: 139–47, 153; 53: 207
10 JR 41: 99–101; 59: 231
11 JR 53: 213–25, 275, 229–37, 279–83, 293–5; 55: 193; 58: 43; 60: 227–9; 63: 257
12 JR 58: 53; 64: 63; 56: 167; 52: 147; 56: 59–61; 42: 151; 43: 289–91; 48: 123; 54: 55; 61: 125; 57: 255, 99; 'Teach us to pray, so that we may never feel hunger' (JR 58: 275).
13 JR 38: 19–21; 57: 231; 58: 275; 57: 209
14 JR 49: 25
15 JR 48: 37, 39, 41–57, 71
16 JR 45: 159; 68: 97–9; 69: 99; Saint-Vallier, in Collection de manuscrits 1: 369
17 De La Richardie's accounts are noted in JR 69: 241–77.
18 Nicolas Denys The Description and Natural History of the Coasts of North America (Acadia) trans and ed W.F. Ganong (Toronto: Champlain Society 1908) 449 (cf Le Clercq New Relation of Gaspesia 430; JR 22: 241; 28: 31; 48: 63); Casgrain Les Sulpiciens et les prêtres 104; Richard V. Bannon 'Antoine Gaulin (1674–1770), An

Apostle of Early Acadia' *Canadian Catholic Historical Association Report* 19 (1952) 55.

19 *JR* 33: 33; 68: 295; 67: 41; 66: 173; 67: 45

20 *JR* 62: 129; 55: 37; 66: 159; 52: 139; 63: 257; 57: 145; 62: 105–7; 46: 105

21 'L'eau-de-vie dans la société indienne' *Canadian Historical Association Report* 1960, 22–32

22 'Par toutes les voyes les plus douces qu'il pourra à la cognoissance de Dieu, et lumière de la foy, et la Religion Catholique, apostolique et Romaine' (*Collection de manuscrits* 1: 158; see also 1: 175, 220, 224, 336). Rochemonteix *Les Jésuites ... au XVIIIe siècle* 1: 161f.

23 On Abenakis, see *Collection de manuscrits* 3: 194; a chronology of successive Huron moves appears in *JR* 70: 207–9.

24 *JR* 55: 33–5; 58: 75–7, 247–9; 61: 199

25 I follow the dating of William N. Fenton and Elisabeth Tooker 'Mohawk,' in *Handbook of North American Indians* vol 15 *Northeast* ed Bruce G. Trigger (Washington: Smithsonian Institution 1978) 473. Bishop J.-O. Plessis gave the date as 1759 in *Journal des visites pastorales de 1815 et 1816 par Monseigneur Joseph-Octave Plessis* ed Henri Têtu (Quebec: Imprimerie Franciscaine Missionnaire 1903) 6.

26 Louis Rousseau, pss *Saint-Sulpice et les missions catholiques* (Montreal: Editions Edouard Garand 1930) 105, 109; *JR* 59: 259; 62: 251; 60: 89; 54: 291; 52: 237–9; 62: 113–15; John Gilmary Shea *History of the Catholic Missions among the Indian Tribes of the United States, 1529–1854* (New York: Edward Dunigan & Brother 1855) 300, 303; *JR* 66: 157

27 'Une sorte de mission perpetuelle' (Rousseau *Saint-Sulpice* 184; also 107); *JR* 65: 273; 55: 227–9; 68: 273

28 *JR* 63: 217; Henri Béchard 'Kateri Tekakwitha' *Dictionary of Canadian Biography* (Toronto: University of Toronto Press 1966–) 1: 636. There are many biographies of Kateri Tekakwitha, all hagiographical in intent. All are based largely on contemporary accounts by Pierre Cholonec (*La Vie de Catherine Tegakoüita, première vierge iroquoise* 1696) and Claude Chauchetière (*Vie de la Bienheureuse Catherine Tegakoüita, dite à présent la saincte Iroquoise* 1696).

29 Le Clercq *First Establishment* 1: 33, 255f; Rousseau *Saint-Sulpice* 130

30 *JR* 41: 229; 60: 277

31 Rousseau *Saint-Sulpice* 105; Bannon 'Antoine Gaulin' 44–59. Bannon reduces the number of Gaulin's sites to two by suggesting that 'a small river called Sainte-Marie which is twenty leagues west of Canso' could be the same as that at Antigonish, where Gaulin is known to have had a chapel and settlement, if 'west' were taken to mean northwest (56). In Nova Scotia the declination of the compass is such that in days when travel was normally by sea Antigonish might conceivably have been described as north of Canso but scarcely as west. Besides, there is a river still known as St Mary's approximately twenty leagues west of Canso along the Atlantic coast.

32 *JR* 63: 71. Despite G.-M. Dumas's advocacy of Le Clercq's controverted authorship of *The First Establishment of New France* ('Chrestien Le Clercq' *Dictionary of Canadian Biography* 1: 440) I have difficulty associating this book with Le Clercq the keen observer of Micmac customs and manners.

33 JR 63: 181; Rousseau *Saint-Sulpice* 183; JR 67: 73; 62: 199; 66: 175
34 JR 63: 37; 'chants lugubres,' ibid 67–9; 60: 43; 69: 37, 43–5; 60: 293; 67: 39–41,
    77–9; Le Clercq *First Establishment* 1: 408
35 JR 55: 263–7; 61: 65
36 Thwaites has, however, obligingly included the Canadian notices in his collection.
37 This is evident from a catalogue of Jesuits in New France in 1745 (JR 69: 75–9).
38 Casgrain *Les Sulpiciens et les prêtres* 60f. Carheil wrote a long letter on the sub-
    ject to Governor Callières in 1702 (JR 65: 189–253, especially 191–3).
39 JR 58: 83; 66: 171–3. Lorette was reported to be still holding out in 1716 (*Collec-
    tion de manuscrits* 3: 24).
40 JR 69: 237. A long account of this complicated case, favourable to Tournois, is con-
    tained in Rochemonteix *Les Jésuites ... au XVIIIe siècle* 2: 30–50.
41 P. Margry *Mémoires et documents* (Paris: Maisonneuve 1874–88) 6: 644
42 *Collection de manuscrits* 2: 175, 179; 'de fomenter la guerre de ces Sauvages avec
    les Anglais,' ibid 3: 127
43 Fenton and Tooker 'Mohawk' 474; William Kellaway *The New England Company,
    1649–1776: Missionary Society to the American Indians* (Westport, Conn: Green-
    wood Press 1961) 163–7; John Wolfe Lydekker *The Faithful Mohawks* (Cambridge:
    Cambridge University Press 1938) 16 and passim
44 Rousseau *Saint-Sulpice* 162ff; JR 67: 39–41, 77–9; Lydekker *Faithful Mohawks* 48,
    68; Kellaway *New England Company* 259f; *Collection de manuscrits* 3: 5, 19;
    Archives coloniales (France): Canada, Correspondance générale, 1715, vols 35–9,
    quoted in Rochemonteix *Les Jésuites ... au XVIIIe siècle* 1: 25n
45 Lydekker *Faithful Mohawks* 12; JR 66: 193; E.J. Devine, sj *Historic Caughnawaga*
    (Montreal: Messenger Press 1922) 214; S. Dale Standen 'Politics, Patronage, and the
    Imperial Interest: Charles de Beauharnais's Disputes with Gilles Hocquart' *Cana-
    dian Historical Review* 60, no 1 (March 1979) 26
46 L.F.S. Upton *Micmacs and Colonists: Indian-White Relations in the Maritimes,
    1713–1867* (Vancouver: University of British Columbia Press 1979) 33; Henry J.
    Koren *Knaves or Knights? A History of the Spiritan Missionaries in Acadia and
    North America, 1732–1839* Duquesne Studies: Spiritan Series 4 (Pittsburgh:
    Duquesne University Press 1962) 2; Norman McL. Rogers 'Apostle to the Mic-
    macs' *Dalhousie Review* 6, no 2 (July 1926) 169
47 The Wallises regard Le Clercq's use of ideographs as unfortunate, while noting that
    Maillard took them over without due acknowledgment (*Micmac Indians* 23). Cas-
    grain credited to Thury the translation of the principal liturgical offices often attri-
    buted to Maillard (*Les Sulpiciens et les prêtres* 215f).
48 Rousseau *Saint-Sulpice* 158–60; Shea *History of the Catholic Missions* 157; F.J.
    Nelligan, sj 'Historical Notes Concerning the Jesuits in Upper Canada during the
    19th Century,' ts in Archives of Regis College, Toronto, 15–18; Koren *Knaves or
    Knights?* 112f
49 W.J. Eccles *Canada under Louis XIV, 1663–1701* (Toronto: McClelland and Stewart
    1964) 87
50 Hanzeli *Missionary Linguistics in New France* 81, 50. James Mooney's article
    'Missions,' in *Handbook of Indians of Canada* (Ottawa: King's Printer 1913), while

outdated in most respects, contains useful information on missionary scholarship. For this period, see pp 292, 294. Lydekker *Faithful Mohawks* 155f, 181f.

4 CHRISTIANITY AND CIVILIZATION

1   Gordon M. Day 'Western Abenaki,' in *Handbook of North American Indians* vol 15 *Northeast* 152
2   Raymond W. Albright *A History of the Protestant Episcopal Church* (New York: Macmillan 1964) 94; S. Gould *Inasmuch: Sketches of the Beginnings of the Church of England in Canada in Relation to the Indian and Eskimo Races* (Toronto 1917) 33f; H.-R. Casgrain *Les Sulpiciens et les prêtres* 443; Koren *Knaves or Knights?* 80–3
3   PAC, New England Company, micro 7920–1: 74, 126, 170; 7920–2: 194. For an analysis of the company's approach, see Judith Fingard 'The New England Company and the New Brunswick Indians, 1786–1826: A Comment on the Colonial Perversion of British Benevolence' *Acadiensis* 1, no 2 (spring 1972) 29–42.
4   Wallis and Wallis *Micmac Indians* 13; Casgrain *Les Sulpiciens et les prêtres* 188, 299f, 316, 366f, 399n; Rousseau *Saint-Sulpice* 133f
5   Barbara Graymont *The Iroquois in the American Revolution* (Syracuse: Syracuse University Press 1972) 33–9, 43–6, 56–62; Lydekker *Faithful Mohawks*, esp chaps 7, 8
6   For a detailed and readable account of the Moravian mission, see Elma E. Gray *Wilderness Christians* (Toronto: Macmillan 1956).
7   E.S. Turner *Roads to Ruin* (London: Michael Joseph 1950)
8   *London Missionary Society General Meeting Reports* 1799, 1802, 1803, 1805, 1811, 1812; Upton *Micmacs and Colonists* 158f; Judith Fingard 'English Humanitarianism and the Colonial Mind: Walter Bromley in Nova Scotia, 1813–1825' *Canadian Historical Review* 54 (1973) 123–51; *Proposal for Forming a Society for Promoting the Civilization and Improvement of the North American Indians, within the British Boundary* (London 1806), copy in PAC; *The Journal of Major John Norton, 1816* ed C.F. Klinck and J.J. Talman (Toronto: Champlain Society 1970) xliii; Robert Addison, quoted in Charles M. Johnston *The Valley of the Six Nations* (Toronto: University of Toronto Press 1964) 242; Richard E. Ruggle 'A House Divided against Itself: the denominational antagonisms of the Grand River Mission' *Canadian Society of Church History Papers* 1978, 1
9   Noted in a discourse by Nathan Bangs (*Christian Advocate* 19 Oct 1827). Jones described his early life until and including his conversion in *Life and Journals of Kah-ke-wa-quo-nā-by (Rev. Peter Jones) Wesleyan Missionary* (Toronto: Anson Green 1860) 1–14.
10 Alvin Torry *Autobiography of the Rev. Alvin Torry, First Missionary to the Six Nations and the Northwestern Tribes of British North America* ed William Hosmer (Auburn, NY: William J. Mores 1861) 109–19; Jones *Life and Journals* 24–32, 143f; *Methodist Magazine* 9 (Jan 1826) 39f; Wade C. Barclay *Early American Methodism, 1769–1844* (New York: Board of Missions and Church Extension of the Methodist Church 1950) 2: 123; *Christian Advocate* 6, no 13 (1831) 50. The

best summary account of the revival is William Case *Jubilee Sermon delivered at the request of and before the Wesleyan Canada Conference, assembled at London, C.W., 1853,* copy in UCA, 14–31. Its progress can also be followed in Case's regular reports successively to the *Methodist Magazine* and *Christian Advocate* of New York and the *Christian Guardian* of Toronto.

11 *IR* 48: 75–7. The information in this paragraph is largely derived from Donald B. Smith 'The Mississauga, Peter Jones and the White Man: The Algonkians' Adjustment to the European on the North Shore of Lake Ontario to 1860,' unpublished PhD thesis, University of Toronto 1975.

12 William Case, journal, ms in UCA, 10 Nov 1808; Barclay *Early American Methodism* 2: 123; Walter N. and Ruth M. Vernon 'Indian Missions of North America,' in *Encyclopedia of World Methodism* ed Nolan B. Harmon (Nashville: United Methodist Publishing House 1974) 1: 1210; John Carroll *Case and His Cotemporaries* (Toronto: Samuel Rose 1867–77) 2: 349; *Methodist Magazine* 6 (1823) 425f; Torry *Autobiography* 75

13 Kellaway *New England Company* 8; Torry *Autobiography* 63; Barclay *Early American Methodism* 2: 112; 'Christianity and civilization go hand in hand when Christianity is the *elder sister*' (italics in original) – James Evans to John Beecham, 29 Mar 1836, WC 128: 2; MMS 1827, 7. Some of the rules are reproduced in Elizabeth Graham *Medicine Man to Missionary: Missionaries as Agents of Change among the Indians of Southern Ontario, 1784–1867* (Toronto: Peter Martin Associates 1975) 46.

14 Jones *Life and Journals* 284ff; MMS 1829, 17, 6f

15 *APF* 9 (Nov 1826) 101f; 16 (Jan 1829) 338; Andrew J. Blackbird *History of the Ottawa and Chippewa Indians of Michigan* (Harbor Springs, Mich: Babcock and Darling 1897) 46f; J.B. Assiginack to T.G. Anderson, 22 Sept 1827, PAC, RG 10, 497: 277; Anderson to J. Givins, 4 Oct 1827, RG 10, 496: 283; Joanna E. Feest and Christian F. Feest 'Ottawa,' in *Handbook of North American Indians* vol 15 *Northeast* 780

16 John West *A Journal of a Mission to the Indians of the British Provinces of New Brunswick and Nova Scotia and the Mohawks on the Ouse* (London: B. Seeley and Sons 1827); PAC, New England Company 7920–2: 82; WC 94: 12

17 Copies of the first seven annual reports are available in the Baldwin Room of the Metropolitan Toronto Library. Most of this material is also reproduced in *The Stewart Missions* ed W.J.D. Waddilove (London: printed for J. Hatchard & Son etc 1838).

18 There are many reports of Flood's work in *The Stewart Missions* and in *Report and Correspondence of the Bishop of Quebec's Travelling Mission Fund, 1844* ed W.J.D. Waddilove (Hexham: printed by Edward Pruddah 1844). The SPG made a small contribution for books and supplies. Jamieson's ministry is described at some length in a sketch by his great-granddaughter Mrs. Elizabeth Duncan Lee, in two letters from Jamieson to Rev. R. Walpole Sealy Vidd of Bideford, Devon, England, in 1882, and in a letter to a Miss Gibb on 24 Nov 1882. Copies of these documents are in the possession of Wallaceburg District High School. Wilson described his work in *Missionary Work among the Ojibway Indians* (London: SPCK 1886).

19 John Ryerson *Hudson's Bay* (Toronto: G.R. Sanderson 1855) 6f; Carroll *Case and His Cotemporaries* 4: 221, 226; Joseph-Urbain Hanipaux to provincial at Paris, 18 Oct 1850, in Lorenzo Cadieux, sj *Lettres des nouvelles missions au Canada, 1843–1852* (Montreal: Les Editions Bellarmin / Paris: Maisonneuve et Lavoie 1973) 666; Louise Foulds *Universalism in Ontario* (Olinda, Ont: The Unitarian Universalist Church 1980) 14

20 Power to Jean-Philipp Roothan, general of the Society of Jesus, 12 Nov 1842; Roothan to Power, nd but received at the beginning of June 1843; both in Archives of the Archdiocese of Toronto

21 Graham *Medicine Man to Missionary* 38; Julien Paquin, sj 'Modern Jesuit Indian Missions in Ontario,' ts in Archives of Regis College, 41; *Report and Correspondence of the Bishop of Quebec's Travelling Mission Fund, 1844* 341; Paquin 'Modern Jesuit Indian Missions' 44; Chazelle to a father of the same company, 24 Jan 1845, in Cadieux *Lettres des nouvelles missions* 269; Joseph to Pierre Jennesseaux, 1 Apr 1849, ibid 563

22 There is a considerable literature on Baraga, almost entirely in Slovene.

23 Maitland to Lord Bathurst, 29 Nov 1821, Great Britain, Colonial Office 42/266, quoted in J.S. Milloy 'The Era of Civilization in British Policy for the Indians of Canada, 1830–1860,' unpublished D Phil thesis, Oxford University, 1978

24 Eugene Stock *The History of the Church Missionary Society: Its Environment, Its Men and Its Task* (London: CMS 1899) 1: 296, 373

25 Jones *Life and Journals* 38, 46; MMS 1826, 19

26 Jones *Life and Journals* 156f, 223, 272, 323; minutes of Executive Council re Indian Department, 20 Sept 1836, S.P. Jarvis Papers, Metropolitan Toronto Reference Library; John Strachan *A sermon, preached at York, Upper Canada, third of July, 1825, On the Death of the late Lord Bishop of Quebec* (Kingston: Macfarlane 1826); 'A Review of a Sermon Preached by the Honourable and Reverend John Strachan, D.D., at York, Upper Canada, third of July, 1825, on the Death of the Late Bishop of Quebec, by a Methodist Preacher' *Colonial Advocate* 11 May 1826, 17–28

27 Milloy 'Era of Civilization in British Policy' 85–96; AO, Strachan Papers, 27 Feb 1827; 'Report on the Affairs of the Indians in Canada' *Journal of the Legislative Assembly, Canada* 1844–1845, appendix EEE, section I, quoted in J.E. Hodgetts *Pioneer Public Service* (Toronto: University of Toronto Press 1955) 205; WC 100: 40; *Stewart Missions* 28

28 A.C. Osborne 'The Migration of Voyageurs from Drummond Island to Penetanguishene in 1828' *Ontario Historical Society Papers and Records* 3 (1907) 123–66; Jean-Baptiste Taguinini to Bishop Alexander Macdonell, 28 July 1832, Archives of the Archdiocese of Toronto, AC07–01; same to Bishop Rémi Gaulin, 7 Oct 1832, AC07–02; Henry Solomon to Macdonell, 19 Dec 1832, AC07–03

29 John Bell to Macdonell, 2 Oct 1832, ibid AC14; Jones *Life and Journals* 153n; Jones to Egerton Ryerson, 24 July 1832, *Wesleyan Methodist Magazine* 3rd ser 11 (1832) 232; Jones *Life and Journals* 226f, 276f; chiefs to Macdonell, 2 July 1833, Archives of the Archdiocese of Toronto, AC07–06

30 *Stewart Missions* 78; *Society for Converting and Civilizing the Indians: 6th Annual Report* 1838, 16–19; F.A. O'Meara 'Report of a Mission to the Ottahwahs

and Ojibwas, on Lake Huron' *Missions to the Heathen: India and America* 1 (London: SPG 1848) 15

31 Alder to Lord Glenelg, 22 May 1837, Great Britain, Colonial Office *Return to an Address of the House of Commons: Correspondence respecting the Indians in the British North American Provinces, ordered by the House of Commons to be printed, 17 June 1839* 78f; Alder 'Communication on the State of the Indians' ibid 90–8; Milloy 'Era of Civilization in British Policy' 201–30

32 For a contemporary account of the experiment, see 'The Manitoulin Letters of the Rev. Charles Crosbie Brough' transcribed by Randall M. Lewis *Ontario History* 48, no 2 (1966) 63–80; for a scholarly appraisal, see Ruth Bleasdale 'Manitowaning: An Experiment in Indian Settlement' *Ontario History* 66, no 3 (1974) 147–57.

33 There are many accounts of the origins of Manitoulin settlement, not always in complete agreement: 'Manitoulin Letters' 75; O'Meara 'Report of a Mission' 13; *Society for Converting and Civilizing the Indians. 5th Annual Report 1834–5,* 16f; Rémi Gaulin in APF 12 (1839) 425; Paquin 'Modern Jesuit Indian Missions' 60f; 'Extract from the Rawson Report, 1845,' in *Manitoulin: The Isle of the Ottawas* compiled by F.W. Major (Gore Bay, Ont: Recorder Press 1934) 22f.

34 Barclay *Early American Methodism* 2: 281, 158; MMS 1849–50, x

35 James Evans, diary, 11 July 1838–17 Nov 1838, ms in E.J. Pratt Library, Victoria University, 51f; O'Meara 'Report of a Mission' 16f. The story of two heavens occurs in Benjamin Slight *Indian Researches* (Montreal 1844) 87f and in Cadieux *Lettres des nouvelles missions* 818.

36 George F. Playter *A History of Methodism in Canada* (Toronto: Anson Green 1862) 258; Jones *Life and Journals* 252; MMS 1836, 19. A standard account of the Longhouse religion or 'Good Message' is Anthony F.C. Wallace *The Death and Rebirth of the Seneca* (New York: Vintage 1969).

37 MMS 1841–2, 12; 'Letters of the Rev. James Evans, Methodist missionary, written during his journey to a residence in the Lake Superior Region, 1838–39' ed Fred Landon *Ontario Historical Society Papers and Records* 28 (1932) 61; *Christian Advocate* 19 Oct 1827; Slight *Indian Researches* 78–80

38 WC 222: 3; *Missionary Work among the Ojibway Indians* 66

39 *Stewart Missions* 103. An account of Wawanosh's conversion to Methodism is in Margaret Ray 'An Indian Mission in Upper Canada' Committee of Archives of The United Church of Canada *The Bulletin* 7 (1954) 11f. His later adoption of Anglicanism is noted in Wilson *Missionary Work among the Ojibway Indians* 16. He is portrayed as an opportunist in James A. Clifton *A Place of Refuge for All Time: Migration of the American Potawatomi into Upper Canada, 1830 to 1850* Mercury Series, Ethnology Division paper no 26 (Ottawa: National Museums of Canada 1976) 94.

40 Smith 'The Mississauga, Peter Jones and the White Man' 215

41 Jones *Life and Journals* 81; Paul Kane *Wanderings of an Artist among the Indians of North America from Canada to Vancouver Island and Oregon through the Hudson's Bay Company's Territory and Back Again* (Toronto: Radisson Society 1925) 3, 7f, 16; *Stewart Missions* 53; Jones to Beecham, 16 Feb 1836, WC 128; Playter *History of Methodism* 345; Gray *Wilderness Christians* 97f; MMS 1845–6, x

42 Playter *History of Methodism* 248, 245, 265; *Society for Converting and Civilizing the Indians, 3rd Annual Report* 1833, 51; Enamikeise (Conrad Van Dusen) *The Indian Chief: An Account of the Labours, Losses, Sufferings, and Oppression of Ka-zig-ko-e-ne-ne (David Sawyer) a Chief of the Ojibbeway Indians in Canada West* (London: sold at 66, Paternoster Row 1867) 14; Jones *Life and Journals* 375; Ray 'Indian Mission in Upper Canada' 14

43 *Stewart Missions* 103; Peter Jacobs *Journal of the Reverend Peter Jacobs, Indian Wesleyan Missionary, from Rice Lake to the Hudson's Bay Territory, and return* (New York 1858) 4

44 I have discussed missionary competition in Upper Canada at greater length in 'Rendezvous at Manitowaning' *The Bulletin* 28 (1979) 22–34.

45 John Crane confessed, 'I have been a great sinner against God ever since I can remember. I have lived in the ways of my forefathers' (MMS 1825, 4).

46 Roman Catholic missionaries regarded their claim to represent the Indians' ancestral faith and the presence of many French-Canadians around Lake Huron as significant assets (Cadieux *Lettres des nouvelles missions* 167, 169).

47 Strachan 'Religious State of the Indians' 7 May 1838, item 166, in *The Arthur Papers* ed Charles R. Sanderson (Toronto: University of Toronto Press 1943) 1: 115; *Upper Canada Clergy Society, 2nd Annual Report* (London 1839) 23. Musquakie or William Yellowhead complained in 1845 that Methodist missionaries attempted to persuade Indians to ignore the powers of their chiefs (T.R. Millman 'Musquakie,' in *Dictionary of Canadian Biography* 10: 590). Shinguacouse is reputed to have been the son of an Indian woman and a British officer of Scottish birth, according to J.G. Kohl *Kitchi-Gami, Wanderings Round Lake Superior* (London: Chapman and Hall 1860) 374.

48 WC 134: 3 and passim; 160: 1; *Christian Guardian* 29 Mar 1837; John Carroll *Past and Present* (Toronto: Alfred Dredge 1860) 57; Smith 'The Mississauga, Peter Jones and the White Man' 279–88; Paquin 'Modern Jesuit Indian Missions' 213

49 *Christian Guardian* 25 Sept 1833, 182f

50 Van Dusen *Indian Chief* 204

51 John Leslie 'The Bagot Commission: Developing a Corporate Memory for the Indian Department' *Canadian Historical Association Historical Papers* 1982, 39; MMS 1841, 217; 1853–4, xv. That neither Indians nor whites were unanimous on the language issue is noted in J. Donald Wilson '"No Blanket to be Worn in School": The Education of Indian Children in Early Nineteenth Century Ontario' *Histoire sociale / Social History* 14 (Nov 1974) 303.

52 Milloy 'Era of Civilization in British Policy' 281

5 THE RACE TO THE NORTHERN SEA

1 An attitude that has persisted, according to Antonio R. Gualtieri 'Indigenization of Christianity among the Indians and Inuit of the Western Arctic' *Canadian Ethnic Studies* 12, no 1 (1980) 56

2 APF 20 (1848) 74; Samuel Hearne, quoted in Diamond Jenness *The Indians of Canada* 5th edn (Ottawa: Queen's Printer 1960) 385; W.A. Sloan 'The Native

Response to the Extension of the European Traders into the Athabasca and Mackenzie Basin, 1790–1814' *Canadian Historical Review* 60, no 3 (Sept 1979) 281–99

3 Regulations and Governor's orders for the men's behaviour, 26 Sept 1714, quoted in Harold Innis *The Fur Trade in Canada* (Toronto: University of Toronto Press 1956) 287; Åke Hultkrantz 'The problem of Christian influence on Northern Algonkian eschatology' *SR* 9, no 2 (1980) 170f

4 *Documents Relating to Northwest Missions, 1815–1827* ed Grace Lee Nute (Saint Paul: Minnesota Historical Society 1972) 5; John West *The Substance of a Journal during a Residence at the Red River Colony* (London: B. Seeley and Son 1824) 2. For the origin and early history of the mission, see A.N. Thompson 'The Expansion of the Church of England in Rupert's Land from 1820 to 1839, under the Hudson's Bay Company and the Church Missionary Society,' unpublished PhD thesis, Cambridge University 1962.

5 'De retirer de la barbarie et des désordres qui en sont la suite des nations sauvages répandues dans cette vaste contrée' (*Documents Relating to Northwest Missions* 48); CMS, A77.1: 1; A78.2: 288; 'It is generally considered that the sphere of our influence is not to extend beyond the boundaries of the Colony' – Jones to CMS committee, 10 Feb 1829 (CMS: C C.1/0.39, quoted in Thompson 'Expansion of the Church of England' 201); *Documents Relating to Northwest Missions* 272–4, 314; APF 4, no 23 (Jan 1831) 718

6 CMS, A78.2: 328; William Cockran, journal, 10 Oct 1831, CMS: C C.1/0.18 (3), quoted in Thompson 'Expansion of the Church of England' 220; Bellecourt to Cazeau, 29 Aug 1832, AAQ, dossier RR4: 54. The standard biography of Bellecourt is J.M. Reardon *George Anthony Belcourt, Pioneer Catholic Missionary of the Northwest, 1803–1874: His Life and Times* (Saint Paul, Minn: North Central Publishing Co. 1955). His projects are discussed by Lynne Champagne, an employee of the Historical Resources Branch of the Ministry of Tourism of the Province of Manitoba, in an unpublished paper 'Baie St. Paul: première mission catholique chez les Indiens de l'ouest' 1979. For an incisive analysis of early missions in Manitoba, see also John Badertscher 'Irony in Canadian History' *The Annual of the Society of Christian Ethics* (1982) 45–70. For the ban on extension without special consent, which neither Anglicans nor Roman Catholics received at this time, see minutes, Governor and Committee, Chief Factors and Chief Traders, Northern Department, Mar 1838, HBCA, D.6/24: 259.

7 Governor and Committee to D. Finlayson, 4 March 1840, HBCA, A.6/25: 115; *Wesleyan Methodist Magazine* 3, no 20 (1841) 64; *Christian Guardian* 5 May 1841, 110; HBCA, A.6/25: 167f; John Smithurst to secretaries, 4 Aug 1842, CMS, A78.3: 32f. I have discussed the entry during this period of various agencies, including also the Jesuits, in 'Indian missions as European enclaves' *SR* 7, no 3 (summer 1978) 263–75.

8 John Ryerson and Thomas Vaux to Adam Townley, 14 Oct 1831, WC 94: 12; James to Ephraim Evans, 15 Oct 1838, in 'Letters of the Rev. James Evans' 61; *Wesleyan Methodist Magazine* 3, no 20 (1841) 172; Donald Ross letter, Provincial Archives of British Columbia, AB 20, no 83; James to Ephraim Evans, 15 Oct 1838, in 'Letters of the Rev. James Evans' 65

9 A.-A. Taché, omi 'Notes sur l'établissement de la Mission de la Nativité à Athabaska' AASB; *The Rundle Journals, 1840–1848* intro and notes Gerald M. Hutchinson, ed Hugh A. Dempsey (Calgary: Historical Society of Alberta / Glenbow-Alberta Institute 1977) 116; *Wesleyan Methodist Magazine* 4, no 1 (1845) 414f; Gaston Carrière, omi 'Fondation et développement des missions catholiques dan la Terre de Rupert et les Territoires du Nord-Ouest (1845–1861)' *Revue de l'Université d'Ottawa* 41 (1971) 267f

10 Simpson to Alder, 10 June 1845, WC 207: 9; Simpson to Governor and Committee, 10 June 1845, WC 207: 12; Governor and Committee to Simpson and Councils, 3 Apr 1846, HBCA, D.5/17: 554; Mason to secretaries, 23 Dec 1853, WC 273: 6; *The Letters of Letitia Hargrave* ed Margaret Arnett MacLeod (Toronto: Champlain Society 1947) lix; Simpson to D. Ross, 7 July 1846, HBCA, D.4/68: 125d; Simpson to Evans, 11 June 1845, WC 207: 11; G.G. Findlay and W.W. Holdsworth *The History of the Wesleyan Methodist Missionary Society* 5 vols (London: Epworth 1921) 1: 185; MN/WC 1 (Nov 1854) 6. The morals charge, with the committee's finding of 'unseemly and improper' behaviour, is discussed fully in Gerald M. Hutchinson 'James Evans' Last Year' Committee on Archives of the United Church of Canada *The Bulletin* 26 (1977) 45 and passim.

11 'Relation du voyage de l'évêque de Montréal en Europe' AAM, Registre des Lettres 9: 401; Jean Leflon *Eugène de Mazenod, Bishop of Marseilles, Founder of the Oblates of Mary Immaculate, 1782–1861* trans Francis D. Flanagan, omi, 4 vols (New York: Fordham University Press 1961–70) esp 2: 87–100; W.F. Butler *The Great Lone Land: Narrative of Travel and Adventure in the North-West of America* (London: Sampson Low, Marston, Low, & Searle 1874) 261f

12 Gaston Carrière 'The Early Efforts of the Oblate Missionaries in Western Canada' *Prairie Forum* 4, no 1 (spring 1979) 4f; Bellecourt to Cazeau, 14 July 1848, AAQ, dossier RR4: 158; A.-A. Taché *Vingt annees de missions dans le nord-ouest de l'Amerique* (Montreal: Eusèbe Senécal 1866) passim; APF 36 (1864) 379ff; Carrière 'Mgr Provencher à la recherche d'un coadjuteur' *La Société Canadienne d'Histoire de l'Eglise Catholique Sessions d'Etude* 37 (1970) 71–93; Mazenod to Taché, 19 Jan 1851, from copy of lost original in Archives générales des Oblats

13 Taché *Vingt annees* 91ff, 112, 165; Pierre Duchaussois, omi *The Grey Nuns in the Far North* (Toronto: McClelland and Stewart 1919)

14 Stock *History of the CMS* 1: 244ff, 376, 481f; George J. Mountain *Journal of the Bishop of Montreal, during a visit to the Church Missionary Society's North-west America Mission* (London: Seeley, Burnside, and Seeley, etc 1845) 168; Mason to secretaries, 21 Nov 1845, WC 240: 18; 23 Dec 1853, WC 273: 6. The qualifications and performance of CMS missionaries are discussed, for the most part unfavourably, in Frits Pannekoek 'The Churches and the Social Structure of the Pre-1870 West,' unpublished PhD thesis, Queen's University 1973.

15 *Proceedings of the Church Missionary Society for Africa and The East* 1853–4, 164; 1855–6, 179; Hunter to Venn, 30 July 1850, CMS, A79

16 Address at CMS anniversary, 1857, in Stock *History of the CMS* 2: 323; Leon Hermant, omi *Thy Cross My Stay: The Life of the Servant of God Vital Joseph Grandin, Oblate of Mary Immaculate and First Bishop of St. Albert, Canada* (Toronto:

Mission Press 1948) 58f. Hunter's journal of his expedition appears in *Church Missionary Intelligencer* 10 (1859) 207–16, 228–40, 264–6, 280–5. There is also a full account in F.A. Peake 'The Achievements and Frustration of James Hunter' *Journal of the Canadian Church Historical Society* 19, no 3–4 (July–Dec 1977) 150, 160f.

17 Joseph-Etienne Champagne, omi *Les missions catholiques dans l'ouest canadien (1818–1875)* (Ottawa: Editions des Etudes Oblates / Editions de l'Université 1949) 176f; A.G. Morice, omi *History of the Catholic Church in Western Canada* (Toronto: Musson 1910) 1: 343; 2: 82f

18 APF 17 (1845) 239–43; Gaston Carrière *Histoire documentaire de la Congrégation des Missionnaires Oblats de Marie-Immaculée dans l'est du Canada* 9 vols (Ottawa: Editions de l'Université d'Ottawa 1957) 3: 181, 185, 191, 205, 212; James Scanlon *The Inlanders* (Cobalt, Ont: Highway Book Shop 1975) 3; Carrière *Explorateur pour le Christ: Louis Babel, o.m.i., 1826–1912* (Montreal: Rayonnement 1963) chap 6

19 Thompson 'Expansion of the Church of England' 48; Andrew Colvile to Simpson, 11 Mar 1824, in *Fur Trade and Empire: George Simpson's Journal* ed F. Merk (Cambridge, Mass: Harvard University Press 1931) 181. The attitude of the Hudson's Bay Compagny to the missions is evaluated, for the most part positively, in Carrière 'L'Honorable Companie de la Baie d'Hudson et les missions dans l'ouest canadien' *Revue de l'Université d'Ottawa* 36 (1966) 15–39, 232–57.

20 Bellecourt to Cazeau, 21 July 1840, AAQ, dossier RR4: 71f; Smithurst to secretaries, 29 Dec 1845, CMS, A78.4: 26; Carrière *Histoire documentaire* 3: 286; Mason to secretary, 20 Aug 1844, WC 199: 8; Eden Colvile to Simpson, 22 Dec 1851, HBCA, D.5/32: 398; Governor and Committee to Eden Colvile and the Council of the Northern Department, 9 Apr 1851, HBCA, D.7/1: 98; Cockran to secretaries, 3 Aug 1838, CMS, A78.2: 306; *Rundle Journals* 158

21 *Fur Trade and Empire* 108f; Governor and Committee to Simpson, 4 Mar 1844, HBCA, A.6/26: 192; Simpson to Roderick MacKenzie, 3 June 1845, HBCA, D.4/67: 78f; Simpson to Governor and Committee, 20 June 1856, HBCA, D.4/76a: 755; Registre des Lettres, Archevêché d'Ottawa 4–41, quoted in Carrière *Histoire documentaire* 3: 240

22 Simpson to Provencher, 27 June 1846, HBCA, D.4/68: 206f; *Acts and Proceedings of the 8th Synod of the Canada Presbyterian Church* 1868, liv; Eden Colvile to Simpson, 22 May 1851, HBCA, D.5/30: 730v; Reardon *George Anthony Belcourt* 80ff, 111; Simpson to Georges Deschambeault, 15 Aug 1859, AASB 1787

23 'All things considered, it is the best system that could well be devised' – Robert Brooking, 5 Dec 1854 (in Ryerson *Hudson's Bay* 165); Norma Jaye Goossen 'The Relationship between the Church Missionary Society and the Hudson's Bay Company in Rupert's Land, 1821 to 1860, with a case study of the Stanley Mission under the direction of the Rev. Robert Hunt,' unpublished MA thesis, University of Manitoba 1975

24 Egerton R. Young *The Apostle of the North: Reverend James Evans* (Toronto: Revell 1899) 151–4; Young *By Canoe and Dog Train among the Cree and Saulteaux Indians* (New York: Eaton and Mains 1890) 69; Laverlochère to the directors of the Society for the Propagation of the Faith, 1851, APF 24 (1852) 109f; *The*

Diary of the Reverend Henry Budd, 1870–1875 ed Katherine Pettipas (Winnipeg: Hignill Printing Limited 1974) xxxix and passim

25 For a graphic account of the difficulties of reaching the missions of the upper St Maurice, Carrière *Histoire documentaire* 9: 204–9; Duchaussois *Grey Nuns in the North* 155f; Egerton R. Young *On the Indian Trail* (New York: Revell 1897) 53–5. That there was no significant settlement at Norway House before the missionaries came is noted in Louise Taylor 'Norway House, a Fur Trade Legacy,' unpublished honours essay, Laurentian University 1975, 1.

26 Pierre Duchaussois *Mid Snow and Ice: The Apostles of the North-West* (London: Burns, Oates and Washbourne 1923) chap 4; MN/WC ns 18 (Feb 1873) 283f

27 Valentin Végreville to Sr M. Colombe Cox, 11 June 1859, Monastère de la Visitation, Sainte-Marie, Le Mans, France; Duchaussois *Grey Nuns in the North* 125

28 Thompson 'Expansion of the Church of England' 81; T.C.B. Boon 'The Use of Catechisms and Syllabics by the Early Missionaries of Rupert's Land' *The Bulletin* 13 (1960) 11; Bruce Peel *Rossville Mission Press: the invention of the Cree syllabic characters and the first printing in Rupert's Land* (Montreal: Osiris 1974); Smithurst to secretaries, 2 Aug 1841, CMS, A78.2: 557

29 Boon 'Use of Catechisms and Syllabics' 12–17; Provencher to Lartigue, 25 Oct 1834, in *Les Cloches de Saint-Boniface* 18 (1919) 356; Baraga to the Central Council of the Society for the Propagation of the Faith, 1 Sept 1849, APF 22 (1850) 244; Taché *Vingt années* 45f

30 Mason to secretaries, 3 Jan 1852, WC 265: 1; Hurlburt, 11 Dec 1855, MN/WC 1856, 133

31 APF 30 (1858) 47; Duchaussois *Mid Snow and Ice* 77f; *Letters of Letitia Hargrave* 107; *Diary of the Reverend Henry Budd* 12 and passim

32 *Proceedings of the CMS* 1850–1, ccxxxviii; Morice *History of the Catholic Church in Western Canada* 2: 117; 'What advantage or profit do the poor ignorant Indians obtain by exchanging their wooden Idol for a brass and silver one, and the noise of their drums, for a bell and beads? – Mason to secretaries, 2 Sept 1841, WC 175: 14; 'The Catholic Church has the secret of making heroes and, thank God, these heroes will not easily be supplanted by the men whom heresy makes' – Louis Veuillot, quoted in Hermant *Thy Cross My Stay* 75; S. Tucker *The Rainbow in the North: a short account of the first establishment of Christianity in Rupert's Land by the Church Missionary Society* (London: James Nisbet and Co. 1851) 154; Smithurst to secretaries, 2 Aug 1841, CMS, A78.2: 558; James Hunter, journal, 5 Sept 1844, A78.3: 610; Taché to de Mazenod, 4 Apr 1854, in Paul Benoît *Vie de Mgr Taché* (Montreal: Beauchemin 1904) 1: 274; Morice *History of the Catholic Church in Western Canada* 1: 315; Champagne *Les missions catholiques dans l'ouest canadien* 125; H. George, journal, 30 Sept 1856, CMS, A87, and E. Watkins to secretaries, 29 Dec 1859, CMS, A90, quoted in Katherine Ann Pettipas 'A History of the Work of the Reverend Henry Budd Conducted under the Auspices of the Church Missionary Society, 1840–1875,' unpublished MA thesis, University of Manitoba 1972, 124, 149, 84; Smithurst to secretaries, 2 Nov 1840, CMS, A78.2: 529

33 Carrière *Explorateur pour le Christ* 124; *Rundle Journals* 21–31; Smithurst, report
of Cumberland, Aug 1843, CMS, A78.3: 203; Grandin to his family, 14 June 1857,
APF 31 (1859) 148; Petitot to Henri Faraud, 22 June 1864, APF 37 (1865) 377–95;
'Report of the Deputation Appointed to Visit Manitoba' MN/WC 2, no 7 (Nov 1872)
268; Ryerson *Hudson's Bay* 6

34 *Among the An-ko-me-nums or Flathead Tribes of The Pacific Coast* (Toronto:
William Briggs 1907) 17f

35 Taché to Bourget, 22 May 1851, in Benoît *Vie de Mgr Taché* 1: 229; Hurlburt,
14 Dec 1854, MN/WC 6, no 3 (May 1855) 38; *Proceedings of the* CMS 1850–1,
ccxxix; John Maclean *Henry B. Steinhauer: His Work among the Cree Indians of
the Western Plains of Canada* (Toronto: Methodist Young People's Forward Movement for Missions, nd) 22; HBCA, D.5/12: 176d. Although Roman Catholics vigorously combatted shamanic practice, Petitot reckoned its similarity to Roman
Catholicism as a hedge against the success of Protestant propaganda ('Etude sur
les Montagnais' *Les Missions de la Congrégation des Missionnaires Oblats de
Marie Immaculée* 6 [1867] 508).

36 'Doux par caractère, confiants à ce qu'on leur dit, désireux de bien vivre' –
Faraud to a priest of the same congregation, 20 April 1851, APF 24 (1852) 225;
Gould *Inasmuch* 146

37 *Proceedings of the* CMS 1850–1, ccxl; 1852–3, 14; Thompson 'Expansion of the
Church of England' 132; CMS, A78.4: 187ff. Since one of the complaints of the
Indian schoolmasters was that Hunter made them chop wood for him, it is interesting to note that Budd recorded in his diary that he had set his schoolmaster to the
same task (*Diary of the Reverend Henry Budd* 11f).

38 *History of the Catholic Church in Western Canada* 2: 116; Ronald P. Zimmer,
omi 'Early Oblate Attempts for Indian and Métis Priests in Canada' *Etudes
Oblates* 32 (oct–déc 1973) 276–91; Hermant *Thy Cross My Stay* 136

39 *Grey Nuns in the North* 77

40 I have discussed these movements at greater length, and with fuller documenta-
tion, in 'Missionaries and messiahs in the northwest' SR 9, no 2 (1980) 125–
36.

41 The fullest contemporary account of this movement is by George Barnley in *Wesleyan Methodist Magazine* 4, no 1 (1845) 202f. A valuable, provocative, and well-
documented discussion is Norman James Williamson 'Abishabis the Cree' SR 9, no
2 (1980) 217–47. I am unable, however, to accept his contention that there was
only one prophet.

42 Robert Hunt, journal, 11 June 1859, CMS, A90. Prophetic movements in the
Mackenzie basin are discussed perceptively in Martha McCarthy 'The Missions
of the Oblates of Mary Immaculate to the Athapaskans 1846–1870: Theory,
Structure and Method,' unpublished PhD thesis, University of Manitoba 1981,
308–27.

43 Cooper 'Northern Algonquian Supreme Being' 82f

44 Henry Budd, journal, June 1851, CMS, A83, quoted in Pettipas 'History of the Work
of the Reverend Henry Budd' 99

6 · TAMING THE THUNDERBIRD

1 *Contact and Conflict: Indian-European Relations in British Columbia, 1774–1890* (Vancouver: University of British Columbia Press 1977) 3–5, 47

2 Christon I. Archer 'Cannibalism in the Early History of the Northwest Coast: Enduring Myths and Neglected Realities' *Canadian Historical Review* 61, no 4 (Dec 1980) 475; Stock *History of the* CMS 1: 245; CMS, A77.1: 2; Jonathan S. Green *Journal of a Tour on the North West Coast of America in the Year 1829 ...* (New York: C.F. Heartman 1915) 103; *Stewart Missions* 25

3 Various traveller's reports are cited in Leslie Spier *The Prophet Dance of the Northwest and Its Derivatives: The Source of the Ghost Dance* General Series on Anthropology 1 (Menasha, Wis: George Bank 1935) 30–9. Further evidence apparently unavailable to Spier is noted in Thompson 'Expansion of the Church of England' 126–30.

4 *John McLean's Notes on a Twenty-five Years' Service in the Hudson's Bay Territory* ed W.S. Wallace (Toronto: Champlain Society 1932) 159f; *Prophet Dance of the Northwest* 63f

5 *The Hargrave Correspondence, 1821–1843* ed G.P. de T. Glazebrook (Toronto: Champlain Society 1938) 31f; Tucker *Rainbow in the North* 73; Spier *Prophet Dance of the Northwest* 27n, 35, 5–13. Spier, apparently unaware of some CMS sources, assumed that Pelly never returned home and was consequently puzzled by McLean's reference to two preachers.

6 A.G. Morice *History of the Northern Interior of British Columbia* (Toronto: William Briggs 1904) 238–40; John R. Swanton *Haida Texts and Myths* Bureau of American Ethnology bulletin 29 (Washington: Smithsonian Institution 1909) 312–15; Crosby *Among the An-ko-me-nums* 18f; *Prophet Dance of the Northwest* 30, 46

7 Simpson to Pelly, 31 July 1845, HBCA, D.4/67: 217f

8 Demers to Provencher, 10 Nov 1841, *Rapport des Missions de Québec* 5 (1843) 55–71; Blanchet to the archbishop of Quebec, 28 Oct 1842, ibid 6 (1845) 13–26; AD, O.M.I. Oregon Records, dossier Nobili; John Bernard McGloin, sj 'John Nobili, sj, Founder of California's Santa Clara College: The New Caledonia Years, 1845–1848' *British Columbia Historical Quarterly* 17, no 3 (1953) 218; Blanchet to Abbé de la Porte, 3 Nov 1840, Archives de la Propagation de la Foi, Paris: F1939 (also AASB); Morice *History of the Catholic Church in Western Canada* 2: 290n

9 Demers to Signay, 20 Dec 1842, *Rapport des Missions de Québec* 6 (1845) 13–26; Morice *History of the Northern Interior of British Columbia* 227f; Demers to Blanchet, 1858, AD, O.M.I. Oregon Records 19; Tucker *Rainbow in the North* 70. I owe the suggestion that chiefs may have been influential to Alfred Eli, an Okanagan student in one of my classes.

10 Bolduc to Cazeau, 15 Feb 1844, APF 17 (1845) 467; Demers to Blanchet, 12 July 1853, AD, O.M.I. Oregon Records 18; Demers to Lempfrit, 26 May 1852, Provincial Archives of British Columbia, Holy Rosary 707, frame 4149; Demers to presidents of the Association for the Propagation of the Faith, 26 Nov 1857, Archives de la Propagation de la Foi, Paris: F202 (also Archives of the Archdiocese of Vancouver); Louis Lootens to L.J. D'herbomez, 20 Mar 1859, AD, O.M.I. Oregon Records

11 D'herbomez to Mazenod, 26 June 1860, APF 32 (1860) 297; illustrated in John
    Veillette and Gary White *Early Indian Village Churches: Wooden Frontier
    Architecture in British Columbia* (Vancouver: University of British Columbia
    Press 1977); E.M. Bunoz 'Methods of Apostolate: Bishop Durieu's System'
    Etudes Oblates 1, no 4 (oct–déc 1942) 199f; David Mulhall 'The Missionary
    Career of A.G. Morice, O.M.I.,' unpublished PhD thesis, McGill University 1978,
    155–7

12 Paul Durieu 'Lettres de Mgr Durieu au R.P. Le Jacq sur la direction des sauvages,'
    copy of ms in AD

13 Jacqueline Kennedy Gresco (now Gresko) 'Missionary Acculturation Programs in
    British Columbia' *Etudes Oblates* 32, no 3 (juillet–sept 1973) 147

14 Review of Fisher *Contact and Conflict,* in *Canadian Historical Review* 59, no 4
    (Dec 1978) 498. Most of the information in this and the preceding paragraph has
    been derived from Mulhall 'Missionary Career of A.G. Morice.'

15 Commission Oblate indienne et esquimaude, minutes of annual meeting, 10–11
    Nov 1958, carbon copy of transcribed notes in AD

16 Demers, 16 Jan 1856, *Rapport des Missions de Québec* 14 (1861) 130f

17 Annie D. Stephenson *One Hundred Years of Canadian Methodist Missions 1824–
    1924* (Toronto: Missionary Society of the Methodist Church / Young People's
    Forward Movement 1925) 1: 141

18 In this and the following paragraphs I follow for the most part the well-docu-
    mented account in Jean Usher *William Duncan of Metlakatla: A Victorian Mis-
    sionary in British Columbia* (Ottawa: National Museum of Man 1974).

19 F.A. Peake *The Anglican Church in British Columbia* (Vancouver: Mitchell Press
    1959) 64, 87f; J.W. Arctander *The Apostle of Alaska* 2nd edn (Westwood, NJ:
    Revell 1909) 193f

20 Usher *William Duncan* 65; journal, 6 Mar 1860, William Duncan Papers, 1853–
    1916, C2154, quoted in ibid 50

21 Speech at the anniversary of the British and Foreign Bible Society, 3 Apr 1861,
    cited in W. Knight *The Missionary Secretariat of Henry Venn, B.D.* (London: Long-
    mans Green 1888) 248

22 Peake *Anglican Church in British Columbia* 17, 66–9

23 Crosby *Among the An-ko-me-nums* 25f, 30; Thomas Crosby *David Sallosalton*
    (Toronto: Department of Missionary Literature of the Methodist Church, Canada,
    nd); Stephenson *One Hundred Years of Canadian Methodist Missions* 1: 190

24 Crosby *Up and Down the North Pacific Coast by Canoe and Mission Ship*
    (Toronto: Missionary Society of the Methodist Church / Young People's Forward
    Movement 1914) 17–22; Stephenson *One Hundred Years of Canadian Methodist
    Missions* 1: 170; Crosby *Up and Down the North Pacific Coast*: for Amos, 249–
    59; for Clah, 166–75; for Jack, 143f; for Jim, 137–40; William Pollard, 19 Mar
    1874, MN/WC ns 24 (Aug 1874) 384f

25 Introduction to Crosby *Among the An-ko-me-nums* 4; Usher *William Duncan* 96

26 Crosby *Up and Down the North Pacific Coast* 58; J.S. Hicks 'Thomas Crosby
    Jubilee' *Western Methodist Recorder* May 1912, 8

27 Crosby *Up and Down the North Pacific Coast* 362; R.G. Moyles *The Blood and*

Fire in Canada: A History of the Salvation Army in the Dominion 1882–1976 (Toronto: Peter Martin Associates 1977) 112–15

28 Andrew B. Baird *The Indians of Western Canada* (Toronto: Press of the *Canada Presbyterian* 1895) 25

29 In 1869 E. White, a Methodist missionary, expressed the view that 'the days of pagan customs' were 'nearly numbered' at Nanaimo (MN/WC 6 [1 Feb 1870] 83).

30 'North America,' in Krickeberg et al *Pre-Columbian American Religions* 212

31 There is a good selection of articles on the potlatch in *Indians of the North Pacific Coast* ed Tom McFeat, Carleton Library 25 (Toronto: McClelland and Stewart 1966) pt 3.

32 George Woodcock *Peoples of the Coast* (Edmonton: Hurtig 1977) 179

33 Crosby *Up and Down the North Pacific Coast* 315; WFMS 38 (1913–14) 67f

34 Forrest E. LaViolette *The Struggle for Survival: Indian Cultures and the Protestant Ethic in British Columbia* (Toronto: University of Toronto Press 1973) 48f; 52, 72f, 80–91

35 Carole Henderson Carpenter 'Secret, Precious Things: Repatriation of Potlatch Art' *artmagazine* 12, no 53–4 (May–June 1981) 64–70

36 Gould *Inasmuch* 153; clause 15 of the Terms of Union, quoted in Fisher *Contact and Conflict* 176–8; Robin Fisher 'An Exercise in Futility: The Joint Commission on Indian Land in British Columbia, 1870–1880' *Canadian Historical Association Historical Papers* 1975, 79–94

37 Fisher *Contact and Conflict* 170; minutes of conference, the Methodist Church, 1889, 22f; LaViolette *Struggle for Survival* 126; D.L.S. [De La Seine] *Fifty Years in Western Canada: being the abridged memoirs of Rev. A.G. Morice, o.m.i.* (Toronto: Ryerson 1930) 97; APP 32 (1905) appendix, 173; *Victoria Gazette* 13 Apr 1860, quoted in Peter A. Cumming and Neil H. Mickenberg *Native Rights in Canada* 2nd edn (Toronto: Indian-Eskimo Association in association with General Publishing Co. Ltd. 1972) 177

38 Letter from the Methodist Missionary Society to the superintendent-general of Indian Affairs respecting British Columbia Troubles, May 1889, UCA; Usher *William Duncan* 120; H.B. Hawthorn, C.S. Belshaw, and S.M. Jamieson *The Indians of British Columbia: A Study of Contemporary Social Adjustment* (Toronto: University of Toronto Press 1960) 53; Usher *William Duncan* 55

39 Robin Fisher 'Missions to the Indians of British Columbia,' in Veillette and White *Early Indian Village Churches* 9

7 RANGE TO RESERVATION

1 Alexander Ross *The Red River Settlement* (London: Smith, Elder 1856) 241–74

2 Arthur J. Ray *Indians in the Fur Trade* (Toronto: University of Toronto Press 1974) 36–8

3 Bellecourt to Signay, 11 July 1834, AASB 2186: Reg 27; AAQ, dossier RR 2: 14–15

4 Rowand to Simpson, 4 Jan 1841, HBCA, D.5/6, quoted in *Rundle Journals* xxiv; Harriott to Simpson, 7 Jan 1848, HBCA, in ibid 338

5 Thibault to his father, 18 July 1842, in *Les Cloches de Saint-Boniface* 27 (1928)
   71–2; *Rundle Journals* 263, xxxvii, 154, 73, 209, 258. Cf Thibault to Provencher, 6
   Jan 1846, *Rapport des Missions de Québec* 7 (1847) 60.
6 Maclean *Henry B. Steinhauer* 28–49; MN/WC 1857, 223
7 Katherine Hughes *Father Lacombe: The Black-Robe Voyageur* (New York: Moffat,
   Yard and Company 1914) 82, 105. Taché (*Vingt années* 34) states that he named
   Saint Albert but does not relate the naming to Lacombe.
8 For McDougall, J.E. Nix *Mission among the Buffalo* (Toronto: Ryerson 1960);
   John Maclean *Vanguards of Canada* (Toronto: Missionary Society of the Methodist
   Church / Young People's Forward Movement 1918) 204, 130; *Les Missions de la
   Congrégation des Missionnaires Oblats de Marie Immaculée* 7 (1868) 208
9 *Home and Foreign Record of the Canada Presbyterian Church* 8, no 4 (June 1864)
   250f; minutes of the synods of the Canada Presbyterian Church: 6th (1866) xlvi,
   8th (1868) liii, UCA
10 Report of James Hunter, 31 July 1853, in *Proceedings of the Church Missionary
   Society* 1853–4, 164; Grant MacEwan *Between the Red and the Rockies* (Toronto:
   University of Toronto Press 1952) 31; Philip Carrington *The Anglican Church in
   Canada* (Toronto: Collins 1963) 156–8
11 John McDougall *Saddle, Sled and Snowshoe: Pioneering on the Saskatchewan in
   the Sixties* (Toronto: William Briggs 1896) 65, 92
12 *Church Missionary Intelligencer* 9 (1858) 54. Illustrative of the uncertainty that
   still prevailed, however, was the citation of an expert opinion identifying the most
   fruitful area as lying between the Saskatchewan River and Lake Athabasca (ibid
   55). Presumably the open plains were regarded as too dry.
13 W.S. MacTavish *Missionary Pathfinders* (Toronto: Musson 1933) 86f; letter of 10
   Sept 1866, in *Home and Foreign Record of the Canada Presbyterian Church* Jan
   1867, 73; Champagne *Les missions catholiques dans l'ouest canadien* 140
14 Robert McGuinness 'Missionary Journey of Father De Smet' *Alberta Historical
   Review* 15, no 2 (spring 1967) 12–19; *Rundle Journals* xlv, 192; Stephenson *One
   Hundred Years of Canadian Methodist Missions* 1: 95f; Hughes *Father Lacombe*
   120
15 MN/WC ns 4 (1 Aug 1869) 58; Nix *Mission among the Buffalo* 52–4
16 I have described clerical attitudes during the Red River troubles in somewhat
   greater detail in *The Church and the Canadian Era* (Toronto: McGraw-Hill Ryerson 1972) 31f. The pro-Canadian sentiments of English-speaking mixed-bloods are
   emphasized in F. Pannekoek 'Some Comments on the Social Origins of the Riel
   Protest of 1869' *Historical and Scientific Society of Manitoba Transactions* series 3,
   nos 34, 35 (1977–8, 1978–9) 39–45
17 Maclean *Vanguards of Canada* 130f; MN/WC ns 8 (1 Aug 1870) 125–7; Nix *Mission
   among the Buffalo* 59; Stephenson *One Hundred Years of Canadian Methodist
   Missions* 1: 103; for Prince Albert, minutes of the 2nd General Assembly of the
   Canada Presbyterian Church 1871, xciv; for The Pas, *Diary of the Reverend Henry
   Budd* 65; Nix *Mission among the Buffalo* 64f
18 In 1873 George McDougall collaborated with Chief Factor W.J. Christie to organize
   a petition to this effect (Maclean *Vanguards of Canada* 133).

19 George McDougall wrote to Governor William McDougall, 'Let no surveyor or any other class of white men show themselves till this is done, or some of us will pay the penalty with our lives' (MN/WC ns 8 [1 Aug 1870] 126).

20 FMC, 5 Aug 1865, 2 Oct 1867, 6 Oct 1869; Baird *Indians of Western Canada* 14

21 *Opening the Great West: Experiences of a Missionary in 1875–76* intro J. Ernest Nix, occasional paper no 6 (Calgary: Glenbow-Alberta Institute 1970); MN/WC ns 14 (Feb 1872) 219; Nix, intro to McDougall *Opening the Great West* 10. On one occasion George McDougall was warned by the church against excessive involvement in business (L. Taylor to G. McDougall, 20 Feb 1869, Wesleyan Methodist Church in Canada, Missionary Society letter books, 67, UCA).

22 *These Mountains Are Our Sacred Places: The Story of the Stoney Indians* (Toronto and Sarasota: Samuel Stevens 1977) 23; Hughes *Father Lacombe* 231f; Report on the North-West, 10 March 1871, appendix A: C.O. 42/698, cited in George F.G. Stanley *The Birth of Western Canada* (Toronto: University of Toronto Press 1960) 177

23 Alexander Morris *The Treaties of Canada with the Indians of Manitoba and the North-West Territories* (Toronto: Belford, Clarke and Company 1880) 172f, 247, 179, 256

24 *Opening the Great West* 28; Morris *Treaties of Canada with the Indians* 215

25 Ibid, appendix, 323; Emile J. Legal, omi *Short Sketches of the History of the Catholic Churches and Missions in Central Alberta* (Winnipeg: Western Canada Publishing Company 1914) 48; FMC, 25 June 1874

26 *Ocean to Ocean* (Toronto: J. Campbell 1873) 46; *The Field and the Work: Sketches of Missionary Life in the Far North* (Toronto: Methodist Mission House 1884) 178–80; Mis-ta-wah-sis at Fort Carlton, 22 Aug 1876, in Morris *Treaties of Canada with the Indians* 213

27 Stock *History of the CMS* 2: 408f; Morice *History of the Catholic Church in Western Canada* 2: 100

28 Baird *Indians of Western Canada* 19; minutes, executive of FMC, 12 July 1877; Elizabeth A. Byers *Lucy Margaret Baker: A Memoir* (Toronto: Woman's Missionary Society, Western Division 1920); Priscilla Lee Reid 'Lucy Baker,' in *Called to Witness* ed W. Stanford Reid (Toronto: Presbyterian Publications 1975) 67–82; FMC, 3 Apr 1879

29 Frank Gilbert Roe *The North American Buffalo: A Critical History of the Species in the Wild State* (Toronto: University of Toronto Press 1951) 477, 477n, citing C.N. MacInnes *In the Shadow of the Rockies* (London 1930) 146; Stanley *Birth of Western Canada* 224n; 'Quand le dernier bison sera mort, on pourra alors tenter quelque chose du côté des prairies' – Thibault to Provencher, quoted in Benoît *Vie de Mgr Taché* 1: 109; J.E. Nix 'John Maclean's Mission to the Blood Indians, 1880–1889,' unpublished MA thesis, McGill University 1977, 46f

30 Nicholas Flood Davin *Report on Industrial Schools for Indians and Half-Breeds, Ottawa, 14th March, 1879, to the Right Honourable the Minister of the Interior* 13

31 Gaston Carrière 'Le Père Albert Lacombe, omi, et le Pacifique Canadien' *Revue de l'Université d'Ottawa* (1967) 522–4

32 J.E. Chamberlin *The Harrowing of Eden: White Attitudes toward North American Indians* (Toronto: Fitzhenry and Whiteside 1975) 173, citing parliamentary debates of 1886

33 Riel's religious views are studied in depth in Thomas Flanagan *Louis David Riel: Prophet of the New World* (Toronto: University of Toronto Press 1979). The standard account of the rebellion is Stanley *Birth of Western Canada* bk 2, on which I have drawn freely for the information in this and the previous paragraph.

34 Bernice Venini 'Father Constantine Scollen, Founder of the Calgary Mission' *Canadian Catholic Historical Association Report* 10 (1942–3) 85; Morice *History of the Catholic Church in Western Canada* 2: 176. Methodist and Anglican missionaries were also exerting influence on the Blackfeet (Nix, intro to McDougall *Opening the Great West* 8).

35 FMC, 18 June 1885; Hermant *Thy Cross My Stay* 104, 116f

36 Ian A.L. Getty 'The Church Missionary Society among the Blackfeet Indians of Southern Alberta, 1880–1895,' unpublished MA thesis, University of Calgary 1971; 33f: Nix 'John Maclean's Mission' 78, 132, 142f

37 McDougall *Saddle, Sled and Snowshoe* 76; Nix 'John Maclean's Mission' 206; 'The Indian is one of the many alien of blood and speech that are waiting to be absorbed into our national life' – Rev. Mr Heron in WFMS 38 (1913–14) 57.

38 Baird *Indians of Western Canada* 28. I have traced this story in greater detail in 'Presbyterian Women and the Indians' *Papers of the Canadian Society of Presbyterian History* 1978, 21–36.

39 Nix 'John Maclean's Mission' 77n, quoting Paul F. Sharp *Whoop-Up Country* 139; letter of R.L. Norman in *Christian Guardian* 29 July 1914, 24f (cf Jacqueline Judith Kennedy 'Qu'Appelle Industrial School: "White Rites" for the Indians of the Old North-West,' unpublished MA thesis, Carleton University 1970, 216ff).

40 Nix 'John Maclean's Mission' 182; Maurice H. Lewis 'The Anglican Church and Its Mission Schools Dispute' *Alberta Historical Review* 14, no 4 (autumn 1966) 7; Tims to C.C. Fenn, 6 Sept 1883, CMS, A111, quoted in Getty 'CMS among the Blackfeet' 84; APP 31 (1905) appendix, 172; FMC, 17 Sept 1884, 13 June 1889, and many meetings thereafter

41 APP 29 (1903) appendix, 114; MMS 1888, xxv; Getty 'CMS among the Blackfeet' 101; Hughes *Father Lacombe* 324; APP 31 (1905) appendix, 166; 34 (1908) appendix, 185f; WFMS 37 (1912–13) 50; 38 (1913–14) 53

42 Maclean *Henry B. Steinhauer* 41f; Taché to the directors of the Association for the Propagation of the Faith, 16 July 1888, Archives de la Propagation de la Foi, Paris, F1938, also AASB; WFMS 32 (1907–8) 37, 43; *Journal of the Proceedings of the Eighth Regular Meeting of the Provincial Synod of the Church of England in Rupert's Land* 1899, 82

43 A generally negative appraisal of Indian response to Christianity on the plains is Mitsuru Shimpo 'Native Religion in Sociocultural Change: The Cree and Saulteaux in Southern Saskatchewan, 1830–1900,' in *Religion in Canadian Culture* ed Stewart Crysdale and Les Wheatcroft (Toronto: Macmillan / Maclean-Hunter 1976) 128–40.

8 THE CLASSICAL PATTERN OF INDIAN MISSIONS

1 UCA

2 Peter Paul Osunhirine, letters to the American Board of Commissioners for Foreign Missions, on deposit at Houghton Library, Harvard University, copy at UCA;

Stewart Missions 123; Gordon M. Day 'Western Abenaki' *Handbook of North American Indians* vol 15 *Northeast* 152

3 George E. Levy *The Baptists of the Maritime Provinces, 1753–1946* (Saint John: Barnes and Hopkins Ltd. 1946) 67f; Upton *Micmacs and Colonists* 157–9; de Nant *Pages glorieuses* 301

4 Various aspects of missionary scholarship are surveyed in James Mooney 'Missions,' in *Handbook of Indians of Canada* (Ottawa: King's Printer 1913) 291–304. Wilberforce Eames ('Bible Translations,' in ibid 32f) has useful information on Moravian and Anglican scholarship but omits any reference to other denominations. Linguistic works by Oblates are surveyed in Gaston Carrière 'Contributions des missionnaires à la sauvegarde de la culture indienne' *Etudes Oblates* (juillet-sept 1972) 165–204.

5 *JR* 67: 87; Carrière *Histoire documentaire* 3: 328

6 Frémiot to M. Micard, supérieur du Séminaire de Saint-Dié, 2 Feb 1851, in Cadieux *Lettres des nouvelles missions* 712–15; *MN/WC* 1859, 169; *Diary of the Reverend Henry Budd* passim

7 Hanipaux to provincial, 25 Feb 1849, in Cadieux *Lettres des nouvelles missions* 562; Paquin 'Modern Jesuit Indian Missions' 156

8 Morice *History of the Catholic Church in Western Canada* 2: 327; Paquin 'Modern Jesuit Indian Missions' 154f; '"Les militaires" formaient une garde de Marie, tandis que les enfants déposaient des fleurs et de la verdure et que les femmes préparaient le bransard. Après avoir béni la statue, on fit la procession alors que tous les Indians avaient revêtu leurs habits de fête' (Carrière *Histoire documentaire* 9: 62); Wallis and Wallis *Micmac Indians* 183–90

9 Paquin 'Modern Jesuit Missions' 130 (cf Gray *Wilderness Christians* 51); *JR* 62: 183; Carrière *Histoire documentaire* 3: 194; 4: 67, 232; Durieu 'Lettres de Mgr Durieu au R.P. Le Jacq sur la direction des sauvages' 3; *APP* 26 (1900) appendix, 155

10 Hawthorn, Belshaw, and Jamieson *Indians of British Columbia* 428

11 Report of Committee re Work among Indians and Eskimo, *MSCC* 19 Oct 1916; 10; *Missionary Outlook* June 1904, 126n

12 Paquin 'Modern Jesuit Missions' 80

13 Warren Sommer 'Mission Church Architecture on the Industrial Frontier' in Veillette and White *Early Indian Village Churches* 13; Moyles *Blood and Fire in Canada* 114

14 Grandin to the directors, 3 Dec 1861, *APF* 35 (1863) 350; Crosby *Up and Down the North Pacific Coast* 85

15 L.L. Dobbin 'Mrs. Catherine Gillespie Motherwell, Pioneer Teacher and Missionary' *Saskatchewan History* 14, no 1 (winter 1961) 17–26

16 *Report of the Department of Indian Affairs* 1901–2, xxv

17 *Acts and Proceedings of the 9th Synod of the Canada Presbyterian Church* 1868, liii; *APP* 15 (1889) appendix, xvii

18 *MMS* 1884, xix; Wilson *Missionary Work among the Ojibway Indians* 242

19 *APP* 14 (1888) appendix, xiv; 'Appeal of the Ojibwa Indians of Lake Huron, 1852' microfilm in *PAC*, quoted in H.A. Siegmiller 'The Colonial and Continental Church Society in Eastern Canada,' unpublished *DD* thesis for General Synod Board of

Examiners, Anglican Church of Canada 1964, 416; WFMS 40 (1903–4) 60. Frederick Frost (in *Sketches of Indian Life* [Toronto: William Briggs 1904] 116) singled out teachers as most zealous in pressing Indian children to adopt European ways. In the United States, missionary schools usually taught in Indian languages, while government schools insisted upon English (Hazel W. Hertzberg *The Search for an American Indian Identity: Modern Pan-Indian Movements* [Syracuse: Syracuse University Press 1971] 15).

20 Woman's Missionary Society of the Presbyterian Church in Canada *The Story of Our Missions* (Toronto: WMS 1915) 289; APP 16 (1890) appendix, xxix; Kennedy 'Qu'Appelle Industrial School' 124, citing *Report of the Department of Indian Affairs* 1890, 124

21 Arthur Barner to Alexander Sutherland, 19 Dec 1908, UCA, Sutherland Papers, box 7; Paquin 'Modern Jesuit Indian Missions' 28; Wilson *Missionary Work among the Ojibway Indians* 166–70; on school burnings: Moose, report of the MSCC, 1915, 45; Ahousat and Alberni, APP 41 (1915) appendix, 50; Round Lake, APP 50 (1924) appendix, 26

22 APP 33 (1907) appendix, 165; WFMS 24 (1899–1900) 28; report of the Committee Investigating the Financial Condition of Regina Industrial School to the superintendent-general of Indian Affairs, 11 Mar 1904, UCA, Presbyterian Church in Canada, Foreign Mission Committee Western Section, Indian Work in Canada, Correspondence 1892–1910

23 Canada Department of Indian Affairs *Confidential Report of Indian Schools, addressed to Sir John A. Macdonald, Superintendent General of Indian Affairs, 26 August 1887*; WFMS 28 (1903–4) 47; New England Company *Conference on Indian Evangelisation in Canada (convened by the Company) Thursday, June 11, 1908* (London: printed by Spottiswoode & Co. Ltd., nd) 42; Lewis 'Anglican Church and Its Mission Schools Dispute' 7–13; *Story of Our Missions* 289; Thompson Ferrier *Our Indians and Their Training for Citizenship* (Toronto: Missionary Society of the Methodist Church / Young People's Forward Movement, ca 1912) 27; *Story of Our Missions* 293

24 Letter to the superintendent of Indian Affairs from the Executive Committee of the Missionary Society of the Methodist Church of Canada, 1905, 242, UCA, Miscellaneous Documents, MMS; *Report of the Department of Indian Affairs* 1895, xxiv; Kennedy 'Qu'Appelle Industrial School' 128–48

25 WC 215: 16

26 Wilson *Missionary Work among the Ojibway Indians* 163; George Manuel and Michael Posluns *The Fourth World: An Indian Reality* (Don Mills: Collier-Macmillan 1974) 64; WFMS 25 (1900–1) 48; 31 (1906–7) 61

27 WC 185: 1; Kennedy 'Qu'Appelle Industrial School' 56; Hertzberg *Search for an American Indian Identity* 16. In 1856 the Methodists noted as 'one of the primary objects' of industrial schools 'the raising up among Indians, on Indian Lands, of a class of industrious and intelligent people, who would prove a blessing to their race, and a credit to the government' (MMS 1855–6, xx). Roger Jackson, studying the Mount Elgin Industrial Institution in a graduate course, found that almost exclusive attention was paid to academic achievement.

28 Stephenson *One Hundred Years of Canadian Methodist Missions* 1: 192; APP 24 (1898) 202
29 Baird *Indians of Western Canada* 6
30 'Seule l'Eglise Catholique, cette sage et tendre mère de tous les habitants du globe, sait donner à chaque peuple, comme à chaque individu, ce qu'il lui faut pour cette vie et pour l'autre. Elle peut modifier la nature et les habitudes de l'Indien, le rendre chrétien fervent et heureux sans qu'il cesse d'être sauvage' – Chazelle to the members of the central council of the Association for the Propagation of the Faith, 17 Apr 1843 (Cadieux *Lettres des nouvelles missions* 290).
31 Ferrier *Our Indians and Their Training for Citizenship* 37; APP 16 (1890) appendix, xxvi
32 Edouard Lecompte, sj *Les missions modernes de la Compagnie de Jésus au Canada (1842–1924)* (Montreal: Imprimerie de Messager 1925) 40; APP 16 (1890) appendix, xxiii
33 *Story of Our Missions* 297
34 Thomas Crosby, in MN/MC 3, no 18 (Aug 1878) 311; New England Company *Conference on Indian Evangelisation in Canada* 36
35 *Report of the Department of Indian Affairs* 1900–1, xviii; Snow *These Mountains Are Our Sacred Places* 20
36 Hines to S.H. Blake, 1 Sept 1906, AA, S.H. Blake file, Nov 1905–Oct 1906; APP 24 (1898) appendix, 176
37 Morice *History of the Catholic Church in Western Canada* 2: 254; Ferrier *Our Indians and Their Training for Citizenship* 16
38 C.C. McLaurin *Pioneering in Western Canada: A Story of the Baptists* (Calgary 1939) 24; FMC, 18 Apr, 20 Sept 1883; MMS 1889, lii; WFMS 33 (1908–9) 51; Thomas Neville, in MMS 1905, lxxiv
39 New England Company, micro 7920–2: 75, 82
40 Wilson *Missionary Work among the Ojibway Indians* 161f; APP 16 (1890) appendix, xxvii; 4 (1878) appendix, lxxii; Jenness *Indians of Canada* 264
41 WFMS 26 (1901–2) 40; *Western Missionary* Aug 1891, 87; Baird *Indians of Western Canada* 5f; Executive Committee, MMS, ca 18 Jan 1905, UCA, Miscellaneous Documents, MMS, 243
42 WFMS 33 (1908–9) 53f

9 THE ONSET OF DOUBT

1 *Report of the Department of Indian Affairs* 1899, 429
2 APP 28 (1902) 180f; Baird *Indians of Western Canada* 29
3 The process of disengagement is described in some detail in report of the general secretary, MSCC, to the Board of Management, Brantford, 21 Sept 1922, 10–12, AA.
4 Reginald Stackhouse 'Sam Blake: A man for then and now' *Insight* (bulletin of Wycliffe College 1978) 2f; Sidney Gould, in *Jubilee Volume of Wycliffe College* (Toronto: Wycliffe College 1927) 68
5 S.H. Blake to the Rev. Canon Pollard, 26 Nov 1904, AA, S.H. Blake file; Blake to the Hon. Frank Oliver, 18 April 1908, Blake file; Report of Indian Committee,

MSCC 11 Oct 1906, 6, AA; *Report on the Indian Schools of Manitoba and North-West Territories* (Ottawa: King's Printer 1907); Blake to T.R. O'Meara, 26 Aug 1908, Wycliffe College Archives, O'Meara Papers, General Correspondence, 1907–09

6 'Report of Special Committee on Indian Missions' *The New Era* Nov 1904, 359; report of Indian Committee, official minutes, MSCC, 11 Oct 1906; Blake to Oliver, 6 Feb 1906, Blake file; Blake to Oliver, 5 Nov 1907, UCA, Sutherland Papers, box 10, 1906–10

7 Cyprian Pinkham to Blake, 6 Feb 1906, Blake file; MSCC 24–5 Oct 1907, 10f; A. Sutherland to James Woodsworth, 27 Nov 1902, UCA, A. Sutherland letter box, 1902–3; J.C. Herdman to R.P. MacKay, 30 Jan 1903, UCA, Presbyterian Church in Canada, Foreign Mission Committee, Western Section, Indian Work in Canada, Correspondence, 1892–1910; minutes of the Indian Mission Committee of Manitoba and the Northwest, 4 Nov 1905, in preceding file

8 The proportion remained fairly constant, according to MMS, from 1897 to 1902.

9 New England Company *Conference on Indian Education in Canada, Convened by the Company, April 15, 1908* (London: printed by Spottiswoode & Co., nd) 27; Oliver to Blake, 18 July 1908, Sutherland Papers; Sutherland to Blake, 5 Mar 1908, Sutherland Papers; memorandum on Indian Mission Schools, Apr 1906, signed by MacKay, Blake file

10 Report of the Executive Committee, MSCC 13 Oct 1910, 8f; report of superintendent of Indian Education, *Sessional Paper* 28 (1911) 294f; *Indian Boarding Schools: Report of Conference and Memorandum of Proposed Agreement between the Department of Indian Affairs and the Churches Engaged in Educational Work among the Indians, 21 November 1910* (Toronto: Methodist Mission Rooms, nd); René Fumoleau, omi *As Long as This Land Shall Last* (Toronto: McClelland and Stewart, nd) 143

11 MMS 1911, 11; APP 45 (1919) appendix, 8

12 By 1923 the mortality rate was reported as only 2 per cent; a significant improvement (*Report of the General Secretary, MSCC, to the Board of Management, Calgary, 20 September 1923* 23).

13 *Report of the General Secretary, MSCC, to the Board of Management, Toronto, 9 September 1918* 63; J. Lofthouse, in *Report of the MSCC* 1913, 42

14 APP 40 (1914) appendix, 49; 48 (1922) appendix, 44; *For He Shall Reign* (special issue of MMS commemorating the 99th year of missions, 1923) 30. The report of the Department of Indian Affairs for 1923 notes only that a policy had for some time been in effect to fill all vacancies in residential schools.

15 MMS 1916, vi; *Special Joint Committee of the Senate and the House of Commons appointed to continue and complete the examination and consideration of the Indian Act, Minutes of Proceedings and Evidence No. 28, Thursday May 29, 1947* 1498, 1500; Commission oblate des oeuvres indiennes, minutes of annual meeting, 1946, 4, AD

16 MSCC 29 Sept 1921, 27f

17 Commission oblate des oeuvres indiennes, minutes of annual meeting, 1951, 3f; Catholic Indian League of Canada, minutes and proceedings, Alberta Division, 1954–65, 14, 121; Commission oblate, minutes of annual meeting, 1946 (all in AD)

18 H.B. Hawthorn *A Survey of the Contemporary Indians of Canada: A Report on Economic, Political, and Educational Needs* 2 vols (Ottawa: Indian Affairs Branch 1966–7)

19 Commission oblate, minutes, 1956, 7f; 1954, 5; Catholic Indian League, minutes and proceedings, Alberta Division, 1954–65, 9, 33; Snow *These Mountains Are Our Sacred Places* 115f

20 Scanlon *Inlanders* 26

21 T.C.B. Boon *The Anglican Church from the Bay to the Rockies* (Toronto: Ryerson 1962) 425; Catholic Indian League, minutes and proceedings, Alberta Division, 1954–65, 88

22 Antonio R. Gualtieri, in an unpublished manuscript in my possession

23 Gloria Kulbeck *What God Hath Wrought* (Toronto: Pentecostal Assemblies of Canada 1958) 141f, 192f, 188. Reliable information about many of these missions is not readily available. I am grateful to have been sent the anniversary issue (Dec 1978) of the *Northern Light Gospel Missions Newsletter*, Red Lake, Ontario, written by Mary Horst; 'A Brief History of Northern Canada Evangelical Mission, 1946–1973' in mimeograph; a brochure entitled 'Continental Mission Inc.: History'; and some information about Northern Youth Programs Inc., Dryden, Ontario.

24 On Pentecostal Bible schools, Erna A. Peters *The Contribution to Education by The Pentecostal Assemblies of Canada* (Homewood, Man 1971) chap 5

25 Manuel and Posluns *Fourth World* 171ff; *The Unjust Society* (Edmonton: Hurtig 1969)

26 Enos T. Montour *The Feathered U.E.L.'s* (Toronto: United Church of Canada 1973) 106f; Vine Deloria, jr, and William C. Sturtevant *The World of the American Indian* (Washington: National Geographical Society 1974) 336, 380; Chamberlin *Harrowing of Eden* 94ff

27 Howard Adams *Prison of Grass: Canada from the Native Point of View* (Toronto: New Press 1975) 29; Joseph E. Couture 'Native Training and Political Change: Future Directions,' mimeographed article, 7, 9; The Wandering Spirit Survival School, mimeographed prospectus; Kahnawake Survival School, prospectus published under the authority and general editorship of the Caughnawaga Combined School Committee, Mar 1979; Upton *Micmacs and Colonists* 177; Earle H. Waugh and K. Dad Prithipaul *Native Religious Traditions* (Waterloo, Ont: Wilfrid Laurier University Press for Canadian Corporation for Studies in Religion 1979)

28 Wilfred Pelletier *Two Articles* (np: Neewin Publishing Co., nd) 25; Cardinal *Unjust Society* 87, 102, 23, 61; Jane Willis *Geneish: An Indian Girlhood* (Toronto: New Press 1973) passim; Manuel and Posluns *Fourth World* 60; Adams *Prison of Grass* 29

29 Sister Margaret Denis, sos 'The Religious Education of the Indian and Metis People,' report submitted to the National Office of Religious Education of the Canadian Catholic Conference, Jan 1972, 22, AD; Norval Morrisseau in Lister Sinclair and Jack Pollock *The Art of Norval Morrisseau* (Toronto: Methuen 1979) 42, 47

30 Manuel and Posluns *Fourth World* 263. I owe this summary of Indian opinion to the research of Megan S. Mills, a student in one of my classes.

31 LaViolette *Struggle for Survival* 145

32 Papers of Eastern National Conference of Fellowship of Indian Workers, 20–2 Oct 1944, UCA; *Special Joint Committee of the Senate and the House of Commons ... 1947* 1496, 1510; Commission oblate, extracts from minutes of annual meeting, 1958, 14, AD; Carrington *Anglican Church in Canada* 293; Commission oblate, 'Recrutement et formation des vocations indigènes,' supplement 7 to minutes of annual meeting, 1955, AD

33 *Tel-Ind* 2, no 3: 3; Scanlon *Inlanders* 76; Stewart Crysdale *Churches Where the Action Is!* (Toronto: United Church of Canada 1966) 130, 134

34 *The North American Indian Today* ed C.T. Loram and T.F. McIlwraith (Toronto: University of Toronto Press 1943) 105, 82; *Special Joint Committee of the Senate and the House of Commons ... 1947* 1509

35 'The Dangers of Station Mission Work,' quoted in Knight *Missionary Secretariat of Henry Venn, B.D.* 309

36 A clear indication of this ecumenical attitude in Oblate records is Henri Légaré, omi 'A Study of the Oblate Indian-Eskimo Council,' a brief presented to the annual meeting of the General Assembly of the Oblate Indian-Eskimo Commission, Ottawa, 20–1 Nov 1969, 30.

37 Recommendations of the Canadian Oblate Conference to the Canadian Catholic Conference of Bishops, Mar 1971, in mimeographed report 'The Religious Situation of the Canadian Native People'; *Northern Development: At What Cost?* (Ottawa: Canadian Catholic Conference 1975); *Record of Proceedings of the 55th Annual Meeting of Saskatchewan Conference of the United Church of Canada* 1979, B121–3

38 *The Globe and Mail* 2 June 1972; 'Rapport sur l'effort missionnaire de l'église canadienne auprès des Indiens et des Esquimaux du Canada' ed Henri Goudreault, omi, Sept 1972, 41f, AD; *Highlights from Home Missions* (Toronto: Catholic Church Extension Society of Canada, nd)

39 Hugh and Karmel McCullum *This Land Is Not For Sale* (Toronto: Anglican Book Centre 1975) 186

40 *Journal of Proceedings, 26th General Synod of the Anglican Church of Canada* 1973, M52; Menno Wiebe 'Indian Talk-Back – Churches Back-Track' *Occasional Bulletin for Missionary Research* Apr 1978, 44; *This Is Your Church: A Guide to the Beliefs, Policies and Positions of the United Church of Canada* comp Steven Chambers (Toronto: United Church *Observer* 1982) 92f; 'Summary of reports submitted by Gladys Pavo and Ryk Allen re the Consultation on Training for Indian Ministry,' mimeograph at United Church House, Toronto

41 Snow *These Mountains Are Our Sacred Places* 144

42 George Hutchison *Grassy Narrows* (Toronto: Van Nostrand Reinhold 1973) 106, 113–31

43 Interchurch Task Force on Northern Flooding 'Report of the Panel of Public Enquiry into Northern Hydro Development,' mimeographed report, ii, UCA; H. McCullum and G. Russell Hatton 'Project North' *Canadian Dimension* 13, no 5 (1979) 44f

10 THE FLAMING BANNERS

1 Col 3:1; Phil 2:9
2 General title of vols 4–6 of *A History of the Expansion of Christianity* (New York: Harper 1941–4)
3 Hughes *Father Lacombe* 14
4 *JR* 8: 227; 21: 111
5 *Proceedings of the* CMS 1852–3, 175f
6 John Foster *World Church* (London: SCM 1945) 102
7 'Les communautés religieuses françaises au Québec: une émigration utopique? (1837–1875),' in Bernard Denault and Benoît Lévesque *Eléments pour une sociologie des communautés religieuses de Québec* (Montreal: Les Presses de l'Université de Montréal / Sherbrooke: Université de Sherbrooke 1975) 121–92
8 Pierre Milet showed pictures of France (*JR* 53: 269f), Jean de Lamberville of Paris (*JR* 62: 57), John Smithurst of London (CMS, A78.4: 198).
9 *JR* 5: 33; Jones *Life and Journals* 398
10 My translation, as in *The Hymn Book* (Toronto: Anglican Church of Canada / United Church of Canada 1971) no 445
11 Quoted in Chamberlin *Harrowing of Eden* 114
12 *New Relation of Gaspesia* 143; CMS, A77: 12
13 Jean Usher 'Apostles and Aborigines, The Social Theory of the Church Missionary Society' *Histoire sociale / Social History* 7 (Apr 1971) 32f; *Christian Guardian* (15 Mar 1843) 82; *JR* 20: 27; A.J. Clark, introduction and notes 'Earliest Missionary Letters of Rev. John Douse, written from the Salt Springs Mission on the Grand River in 1834–1836' *Ontario Historical Society Papers and Records* 28 (1932) 45; *Report of the General Secretary, MSCC, to the Board of Management, Toronto, September 9, 1918* 66, AA; *The Journal of the Bishop of Montreal, during a visit to the Church Missionary Society's North-west America Mission* (London: Seeley, Burnside, Seeley, etc 1845) 153f
14 *JR* 7: 7
15 P 9; *The Field and the Work* (Toronto: Methodist Mission Rooms 1884) 157
16 'Report on Industrial Schools for Indians and Half-Breeds' 14; McDougall *Saddle, Sled and Snowshoe* 143f; Peter Jones to Beecham, 16 Feb 1836, WC 128; J. Bernard Gilpin in *The Native Peoples of Atlantic Canada* ed H.F. McGee (Toronto: McClelland and Stewart 1974) 103; Stephenson *One Hundred Years of Canadian Methodist Missions* 1: 206f
17 'La conversion des sauvages' *JR* 1: 85; New England Company *Conference on Indian Education in Canada* 14
18 *JR* 5: 77
19 'C'est le déir de la souffrance qui m'a fait venir dans ces missions, je vais pouvoir me satisfaire' – Carrière *Explorateur pour le Christ* 69; Hermant *Thy Cross My Stay* 7
20 Stock *History of the* CMS 1: 284f
21 *Proceedings of the* CMS 1858–9; 'The Churches and the Social Structure of the Pre-1870 West,' unpublished PhD thesis, Queen's University 1973

22 'Report of the Special Committee to Investigate Indian Affairs in Canada' *Sessional Papers, Canada* 1858, pt 3, quoted in J.E. Hodgetts *Pioneer Public Service* (Toronto: University of Toronto Press 1955) 210

23 MN/WC ns 18 (Feb 1873) 283f; Cardinal *Unjust Society* 83

24 Dumoulin to J.-O. Plessis, 5 June 1821, in *Documents Relating to Northwest Missions* 310f; Sinclair to Sir George Simpson, 20 July 1851, HBCA, D.5631: 110

25 Relation of John Bell in T.G. Anderson's handwriting, nd, Toronto Reference Library, T.G. Anderson Papers, folder C-34

26 Peter Burroughs 'Tackling Army Desertion in British North America' *Canadian Historical Review* 61, no 1 (Mar 1980) 29–68; Thomas H. Wilson 'An Historical Study of the Relation of the Anglican Church of Canada to Kingston Penitentiary, 1835–1913,' unpublished PhD thesis, University of Ottawa 1978, xxv–xliii; Rainer Baehre 'Paupers and Poor Relief in Upper Canada' *Canadian Historical Association Historical Papers* 1981, 70f

27 Quoted in Knight *Missionary Secretariat of Henry Venn, B.D.* 307, 309

11 A YES THAT MEANS NO?

1 Le Clercq *First Establishment* 1: 210, 220; CMS, A77: 71

2 JR 53: 259; 13: 123, 127; chap 4, n 37; Kane *Wanderings of an Artist* 276f; McGuinness 'Missionary Journey of Father De Smet' 16; JR 3; 123 (cf Le Clercq *First Establishment* 1: 217; JR 42: 151; James Evans, diary, 11 July 1838–17 Nov 1838, ms in E.J. Pratt Library, Victoria University, 51f); Jones *Life and Journals* 118f; JR 11: 9; Gray *Wilderness Christians* 208.

3 Chazelle to a father of the same company, 24 Jan 1845, in Cadieux *Lettres des nouvelles missions* 255 (my translation)

4 Playter *History of Methodism in Canada* 361f; MN/WC ns 10 (1852) 170f; MN/MC 3: 16 (Feb 1878) 274; Stephenson *One Hundred Years of Canadian Methodist Missions* 1: 26; Crosby *Up and Down the North Pacific Coast* 142, 252 (cf JR 55: 193; 58: 43); Peake *The Anglican Church in British Columbia* 89f; Faraud to de Mazenod, 8 Dec 1856, APF 31 (1859) 289; JR 18: 87; 23: 155–9; MN/WC 1859, 272; MN/MC 3: 16 (Feb 1878) 276; Morice *History of the Catholic Church in Western Canada* 2: 243.

5 Chazelle 'Les Deux Sauvagesses du Haut-Canada,' in Cadieux *Lettres des nouvelles missions* 301; MN/MC 3, no 6 (Mar 1876) 98; *Life and Journals* 23

6 Du Ranquet to a father of the same company, 26 July 1847, in Cadieux *Lettres des nouvelles missions* 378–85; JR 61: 175; WC 127: 5; Pettipas 'History of the Work of the Reverend Henry Budd' 7

7 *Report of the Department of Indian Affairs* 1899, 429; Census of Canada 1971, bulletin 1.4–7

8 CMS, A78.3: 150

9 MMS 8 (1833) 6; CMS, A89: 55

10 JR 15: 115–19; Duchaussois *Grey Nuns in the North* 206

11 JR 17: 49; Case *Jubilee Sermon* UCA 20 (italics in original)

12 Nix *Mission among the Buffalo* 18; Smith 'The Mississauga, Peter Jones and the White Man' 125; Jones *Life and Journals* 90f; APF 37: 380; WC 135: 2; McDougall

Saddle, Sled and Snowshoe 119. The term 'revitalization' derives from Anthony F.C. Wallace 'Revitalization Movements' *American Anthropologist* ns 58, no 2 (Apr 1956) 264–81.

13   Usher *William Duncan* 46 (cf Wilson *Missionary Work among the Ojibway Indians* 203).

14   *MMS* 2 (1826) 15; *MN/WC* ns 11 (May 1871) 168; New England Company *Conference on Indian Evangelisation* 27. 'Je ne saurais ne vous point faire connaître les dispositions de ces chrétiens primitifs' *APF* 31 [1859] 283].

15   Peter Jones to Egerton Ryerson, 24 July 1832, *Wesleyan Methodist Magazine* 3rd ser 1 (1832) 232; *IR* 52: 133

16   I have heard an account from an older member of the United Church at Parry Island that gave no inkling of Jenness's findings.

17   *I^NKO^NZE, Magico-Religious Beliefs of Contact-Traditional Chipewans* [sic] *Trading at Fort Resolution, N.W.T., Canada* National Museum of Man, Mercury Series, Ethnology Division paper no 6 (Ottawa: Queen's Printer 1973) 20

18   Petitot to Faraud, 22 June 1862, *APF* 37 (1865) 382

19   Selwyn Dewdney *The Sacred Scrolls of the Southern Ojibway* (Toronto: University of Toronto Press 1975) 30; 'L'influence de l'evangélisation sur la conception de la vie et de la mort chez les Têtes-de-Boule au dix-neuvieme siècle' *SR* 9, no 2 (1980) 215

20   Playter *History of Methodism in Canada* 225; *American Indians and Christian Missions* (Chicago: University of Chicago Press 1981)

21   Le Clercq *First Establishment* 1: 221; *IR* 55: 297 (for the sake of euphony I have changed Thwaites's 'which' to 'that'); Hultkrantz *Belief and Worship in Native North America* ed Christopher Vecsey (Syracuse: Syracuse University Press 1981) 233, 23

22   P.A.B. Llewellyn 'The Roman Church during the Laurentian Schism: Priests and Senators' *Church History* 45, no 4 (Dec 1976) 424f; *MN/WC* 4 (1 Aug 1855) 52

23   *IR* 22: 207; *MMS* 19 (1843–4) vii; 23 (1847–8) xx; *Church Missionary Intelligencer* 11 (June 1860) 135

24   Roy F. Berkhofer, jr, devotes chap 7 of *Salvation and the Savage* (New York: Atheneum 1972) to an analysis of various patterns of faction.

25   Gray *Wilderness Christians* 277, 289; Paquin 'Modern Jesuit Missions' 329 (cf *IR* 67: 253–5); Nix 'John Maclean's Mission' 182.

26   Gray *Wilderness Christians* 291ff, 311f; Amand Parent *The Life of Amand Parent* (Toronto: William Briggs 1887) 101–235; Olivier Maurault *Nos Messieurs* (Montreal: Editions du Zodiaque 1937) 220–60; Graham *Medicine Man to Missionary* 46; Stephenson *One Hundred Years of Canadian Methodist Missions* 1: 214; Wilson *Missionary Work among the Ojibway Indians* 45

27   Paquin 'Modern Jesuit Indian Missions' 130; *Journals of the Legislative Assembly of the Province of Canada* 1847, appendix T, no 24, IV and query 1

28   *Report of the Alberta Province Indian Commission* appointed by the General Board of Missions, Methodist Church, 1910, 7f, UCA; Hawthorn, Belshaw, and Jamieson *Indians of British Columbia* 39; Wallis and Wallis *Micmac Indians* 301; Jenness *Ojibwa Indians* 87

29 *JR* 62: 171f; Kohler to superior, 21 Dec 1850, in Cadieux *Lettres des nouvelles missions* 690, 810f; *Minutes of the 9th Synod of the Canada Presbyterian Church 1869*, xvi; Carrière *Histoire documentaire* 9: 256; James P. Mulvihill, omi *The Dilemma for Our Indian People*, reprint of seven articles on Indian Affairs written especially for *Oblate News* (no publishing details) 24; *MMS* 1925, 24; Asen Balikei 'Bad Friends,' chap 7 in *Perspectives on the North American Indians* ed Mark Nagler Carleton Library 60 (Toronto: McClelland and Stewart 1972)

30 (London: George Allen & Unwin 1937) 77 and passim

31 WC 163: 3

32 *MN/MC* 3, no 3 (2 Apr 1875) 25

33 These boxes are frequently mentioned in the minutes of WFMS. The Women's Auxiliary of the MSCC ultimately accepted responsibility for clothing all girls in Anglican residential schools and all boys up to the age of twelve (Carrington *Anglican Church in Canada* 258).

34 *MMS* 1924, 43; *JR* 66: 257; 67: 93; Jean Tissot, 30 Jan 1855, *Rapport des Missions de Québec* 12 (1857) 34

35 Leslie Dewart *The Future of Belief* (New York: Herder & Herder 1976); Thomas Hoover *Zen Culture* (New York: Random House, Vintage Books 1978) 33; David R. Heise 'Prefatory Findings in the Sociology of Missions' *Journal for the Scientific Study of Religion* 6, no 1 (Apr 1967) 49

36 Northrop Frye *The Great Code* (Toronto: Academic 1982) 13

37 At one time the Roman Catholics greatly regretted their inability to offer him full-time employment (Rémi Gaulin to Alexander Macdonell, 25 Sept 1838, *APF* 12 [1839] 430f).

38 He later wrote it up in notes attached to a letter to me dated 15 June 1979.

Picture Credits

Glenbow-Alberta Institute: Methodist service conducted by Henry B. Steinhauer NA 626-2; McDougall orphanage, photo by A.B. Thom NA1677-1; Blackfoot Indians, photo by A.R. Cross NA2307-59

Royal Ontario Museum: Jean-Baptiste Assiginack

PAC: Peter Jones C4840; Salvation Army band C14099; passion play at Kamloops PA48471; Cree class at Lac la Ronge, National Film Board collection, photo by Bud Glunz, original negative 11, 317; Spogan Garry, photo by Corps of Royal Engineers C78966

Acadia University Archives: Silas T. Rand

AD: Ovide Charlebois; procession at Betsiamites; Cree syllabics adapted by Adrien G. Morice; Oblate writing from the Mackenzie Valley; Micmac ideographs; shorthand adapted by Jean-Marie Le Jeune

AA: Blackfoot Home sponsored by CMS P8211-25

Potlatch on Songhees reserve, courtesy Special Collections Division, University of British Columbia Library

Painting of Kateri Tekakwitha, photo by and by courtesy of Jean Désy and John Porter

UCA: Cree syllabics of James Evans

Index

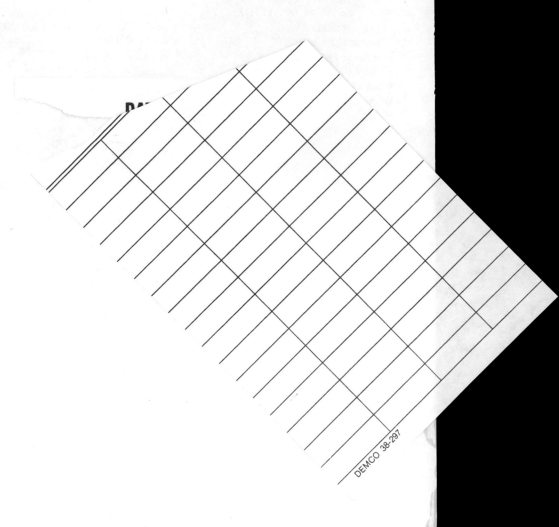